THOMAS KYD

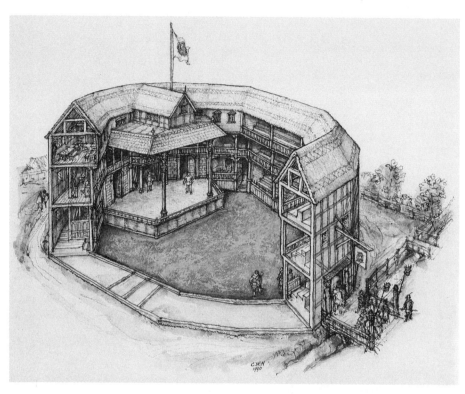

Frontispiece Sketch by C. Walter Hodges of an architectural reconstruction of the Rose Theatre, based on the 1989 excavations of the Bankside site by the Museum of London. Permission by the Hodges Estate.

Thomas Kyd

A DRAMATIST RESTORED

BRIAN VICKERS

PRINCETON UNIVERSITY PRESS
PRINCETON & OXFORD

Copyright © 2024 by Princeton University Press

Princeton University Press is committed to the protection of copyright and the intellectual property our authors entrust to us. Copyright promotes the progress and integrity of knowledge. Thank you for supporting free speech and the global exchange of ideas by purchasing an authorized edition of this book. If you wish to reproduce or distribute any part of it in any form, please obtain permission.

Requests for permission to reproduce material from this work should be sent to permissions@press.princeton.edu

Published by Princeton University Press
41 William Street, Princeton, New Jersey 08540
99 Banbury Road, Oxford OX2 6JX

press.princeton.edu

All Rights Reserved

ISBN 9780691211602
ISBN (e-book) 9780691267067

British Library Cataloging-in-Publication Data is available

Editorial: Ben Tate & Josh Drake
Production Editorial: Jaden Young
Jacket/Cover Design: Katie Osborne
Production: Danielle Amatucci
Publicity: William Pagdatoon & Charlotte Coyne

Jacket credit: This illustration, from the 1615 edition of *The Spanish Tragedy*, shows two episodes: Hieronimo discovering the corpse of his son Horatio, stabbed to death and ignominiously hung up on a garden trellis; and (an invented scene) Bel-imperia being threatened by one of the murderers. Pictorial Press Ltd / Alamy Stock Photo

This book has been composed in Arno

Printed in the United States of America

10 9 8 7 6 5 4 3 2 1

CONTENTS

List of Abbreviations   vii

Preface   ix

1	An Interrupted Life	1
2	*The Spanish Tragedy*	48
3	*Soliman and Perseda*	88
4	*Cornelia*	124
5	*King Leir*	147
6	*Fair Em*	195
7	*Arden of Faversham*	225
8	Denying Kyd	279
9	Kyd's Restored Canon	310
10	Kyd's Critical Reception	325

Index   355

LIST OF ABBREVIATIONS

BEPD A Bibliography of the English Printed Drama to the Restoration
STC Short Title Catalogue

Kyd's Works

AF Arden of Faversham
CORN. Cornelia
FE Fair Em
HP The Householder's Philosophy
KL King Leir
LP Letters to Puckering
SP Soliman and Perseda
SP. T. The Spanish Tragedy
VPJ Verses of Praise and Joy

PREFACE

THIS BOOK has two main goals, the first being to provide an accurate and accessible account of Kyd's accepted works. They include the play by which he is best known, *The Spanish Tragedy* (written ca.1585, published 1592), and two other plays: *Soliman and Perseda* (written ca.1588, published 1592), and *Cornelia*, translated from Garnier's *Cornélie* and published posthumously in 1594, although perhaps written earlier.[1] Kyd also published a collection of poems in English and Latin, *Verses of Praise and Joy* (1584; STC 7605),[2] celebrating Queen Elizabeth's escape from the Babington plot, followed by a prose work, *The Householder's Philosophie* (1586; STC 23702.5), translated from Tasso's *Il padre di famiglia*. That is a small enough canon for a dramatist described by one of his contemporaries as 'industrious Kyd'. In the opening chapter I give an unavoidably brief account of Kyd's life (so few documents having survived), describe his intellectual world, and comment on his early success as a dramatist. Evidence suggests that he worked for both the Queen's Men (for whom he probably wrote *King Leir*) and Lord Strange's Men, for whom he and Nashe wrote the *harey vi* play that Shakespeare subsequently adapted into *1 Henry VI*. I also introduce the three non-dramatic works mentioned above. In addition, I discuss the two Letters that Kyd wrote to Lord Keeper Puckering in 1593, having been erroneously imprisoned, and tortured, for involvement in a xenophobic libel.

My second goal is to justify my attribution to him sole authorship of three plays published anonymously: *King Leir* (written ca.1589,

---

1. All details of plays' performance dates are taken from Martin Wiggins, *British Drama 1533–1642: A Catalogue*, 10 vols (Oxford, 2012–).

2. I occasionally give a reference to the relevant entry in the *Short-Title Catalogue* (STC) when a work might not easily be located there.

published 1605), *Arden of Faversham* (written ca.1590, published 1592), and *Fair Em* (written ca.1590, published ca.1593). My reason for attributing these three plays is rather unusual. Normally, attributions are based on small-scale resemblances between the text of an anonymously published play and one or more plays of known authorship. Such resemblances can be of parallel phrases occurring in two plays by the same author and nowhere else in the drama of the period. Other stylistic resemblances can include distinctive uses of blank verse or rhyme. But my attributions to Kyd were based on large-scale resemblances, as I had noted when I first announced my discoveries.[3] I noticed that all three plays include plot elements that are found in *The Spanish Tragedy* and *Soliman and Perseda*, namely murderous intrigues, the use of comedy in tragedy, and the presence of vengeful women.

For the first plot element, in *The Spanish Tragedy* there are three intrigues. Lorenzo hires accomplices to kill Horatio, so that his friend Balthazar may woo Horatio's beloved, Bel-imperia. Secondly, in a subplot, set in the Portuguese court, the evil Villuppo gives false information to the Viceroy that his son has been killed in battle by Alexandro, who is arrested and condemned to death. But a true report arrives confirming that the son is still alive, so Alexandro is freed, and the evil courtier executed. Thirdly, in the main plot Hieronimo, the father of Horatio, joins with Bel-imperia to revenge Horatio's murder. Hieronimo writes a play to be acted at the Spanish court on the story of Soliman and Perseda, in which all his enemies take part and are killed. Kyd returned to that story for his tragedy *Soliman and Perseda*, which uses one main intrigue. Erastus, having killed a man in a quarrel, flees from Rhodes to Constantinople, where the emperor Soliman accepts him as a friend. Perseda, Erastus's beloved, follows him to the Turkish court, where Soliman falls in love with her. Brusor, the emperor's bashaw, advises him to have Erastus killed, and they use Brusor's wife Lucina as a decoy to keep Perseda occupied. In the final scene Perseda disguises herself in a man's

---

3. See Brian Vickers, 'Thomas Kyd, Secret Sharer', *Times Literary Supplement*, 18 April 2008, pp. 13–15.

armour to fight with Soliman. He kills her, but before dying she has her revenge on him with a poisoned kiss.

In both tragedies Kyd introduces comic scenes in a tragic context. In *The Spanish Tragedy* Pedringano, one of the plotters hired by Lorenzo to kill Horatio, is brought to trial. Lorenzo has assured him that he will send his Page with a pardon to be handed to the hangman on the scaffold. But the Page tells us that the box he is carrying is empty. Believing himself protected by the pardon, Pedringano insults the hangman outrageously in a very amusing manner, where the reader or theatregoer has difficulty stifling their laughter—until his hanging is simulated onstage. In *Soliman and Perseda* the braggart soldier Basilisco is a comic figure throughout, especially when Perseda asks him to kill Lucina, the woman who betrayed her husband. He takes a dagger, 'feels upon the point of it', and objects: 'The point will mar her skin'.

In both tragedies Kyd introduces vengeful women. It was a common belief in Renaissance society that women were too tender-hearted to carry out a murder. But in *The Spanish Tragedy* Kyd shows Bel-imperia determined to have revenge on the man who killed Horatio. Having been given the role of Perseda in Hieronimo's play-within-the-play, Bel-imperia succeeds in stabbing Balthazar before killing herself. In *Soliman and Perseda* the heroine, frustrated by Basilisco's cowardice, says 'What, darest thou not? Give me the dagger then!', before stabbing Lucina, after which, like Bel-imperia, she kills the man who had her lover murdered.

All three of the plays I ascribe to Kyd have intrigue plots. In *King Leir* Kyd follows the traditional story of the king dividing his kingdom between his three daughters but adds Leir's plot to make the division dependent on his daughters' choice of husbands. Since Gonorill and Ragan already have royal suitors, Leir reveals to his courtiers his plan to force Cordella to marry the King of Ireland, although she 'vows | No liking to a monarch, unless love allows'. Unfortunately for his 'sudden stratagem', the corrupt courtier Skalliger tells Gonorill and Ragan, who easily manipulate the ceremony and have Cordella banished. The main intrigue in the play is the evil daughters' plot to have their father murdered. First Gonorill decides to 'intercept the Messenger' who travels between the two sisters and corrupt him (just as Lorenzo corrupted

Pedringano) 'With sweet persuasions, and with sound rewards', to murder Leir and his attendant, the good courtier Perillus. Ragan makes the same approach and the '*Messenger, or Murderer*', as a stage direction describes him, accepts both bribes and promises to complete the contract. Within his intrigue plots Kyd is free to vary the importance of the protagonists' roles. Here he shifts attention from the contract-giver to the hireling assassin who will carry out the hit. He turns the Messenger into both a sinister and a comic figure, giving him more asides and soliloquies than any other character in his plays. In effect the Messenger provides a running commentary on his situation, full of black humour, enjoying his power to frighten his two victims, who we see through his eyes. He extracts more money from them, postponing their execution, until they manage to frighten him with fear of eternal damnation. Then, unpunished, he leaves them, befitting the decorum of the play as it turns into a tragicomedy.

If Kyd innovated with the hireling assassin in *King Leir*, he did so again with another recurrent feature of his plots, the role of vengeful woman. In his two tragedies both Bel-imperia and Perseda acted that role with moral legitimacy, avenging the murder of their beloved partners on the men who had ordered their execution. (In Renaissance revenge plays both Christian morality and efficient legal systems are in abeyance.) But Gonorill and Ragan have no moral legitimacy in planning to murder Leir. Kyd had picked up this motive from a brief reference in William Warner's treatment of the Lear story in his poem *Albion's England* (1586), to a plot element that, with his interest in vengeful women, may have attracted Kyd to this story in the first place: 'Gonorill . . . not only did attempt | Her father's death, but openly did hold him in contempt'. In his play she first orders Leir's murder, bribing the assassin. Ragan does the same, but Kyd gives her a far more violent nature. Not having seen or heard from the assassin she hired, she widens her anger to take in the whole male sex:

> A shame on these white-livered slaves, say I,
> That with fair words so soon are overcome.
> O God, that I had been but made a man,

Or that my strength were equal with my will![4]
These foolish men are nothing but mere pity
And melt as butter doth against the sun.
Why should they have preeminence over us
Since we are creatures of more brave resolve?

As throughout his playwriting career, Kyd put himself into the minds of his creations, imagining by what principles they motivate their actions.

He did this nowhere more successfully than with Alice Arden, who unites both roles of intriguer and vengeful woman. Her first speech when alone in scene 1, having just been informed that her husband will soon be going to London on business, is to wish his death so that she can enjoy her lover:

Ere noon he means to take horse and away!
Sweet news is this! Oh, that some airy spirit
Would in the shape and likeness of a horse
Gallop with Arden 'cross the ocean
And throw him from his back into the waves!
Sweet Mosby is the man that hath my heart;
And he usurps it, having nought but this:
That I am tied to him by marriage.
Love is a god and marriage is but words,
And therefore Mosby's title is the best.

There Kyd economically makes it clear that, like Gonorill and Ragan, in planning to murder her husband Alice has no moral legitimacy. Several times within the play Kyd makes her utter that death wish, right up to the murder that finally takes place in scene 14, line 229, when she echoes Perseda's command to Basilisco ('Give me the dagger then!') but in a much more gruesome context:

---

4. Cf. Beatrice's (misplaced) anger at Claudio for having rejected Hero: 'O that I were a man! . . . O God, that I were a man! I would eat his heart in the marketplace . . . O that I were a man for his sake! Or that I had any friend would be a man for my sake! But manhood is melted into cur'sies . . .'. *Much Ado about Nothing*, 4.1.303–19.

ALICE *[To Arden]*
What, groans thou? *[To Mosby]* Nay, then, give me the weapon.
[To Arden] Take this for hind'ring Mosby's love and mine.
    [Alice stabs Arden and he dies.]

In other Kyd plays the intriguer has at the most one or two associates. In *Arden* Kyd follows his source, Holinshed's 1587 *Chronicles*, but enlarges the cast of characters. Apart from Arden and his friend Franklin almost everyone else in the play is an accomplice of the two main plotters, Alice and Mosby. In *Leir* Kyd experimented with the role of the assassin, turning him into an entertainer; in *Arden* he turns all the would-be murderers into blunderers. The two professional assassins, Black Will and Shakebag, are also sources of laughter. They have a succession of failures, starting with a scene where Arden has been walking a turn in St Paul's, a common rendezvous for business deals. But the churchyard was also lined with booksellers' stalls, and just as Will is preparing to 'run [Arden] through' with his sword, a printer's apprentice shuts up shop: '*Then he lets he down his window, and it breaks Black Will's head*', leading to this comic dialogue:

WILL: Zounds, draw, Shakebag, draw! I am almost killed.
PRENTICE: We'll tame you, I warrant.
WILL: Zounds, I am tame enough already.

Will's self-deflating reply shows the comic nature of his role, as the audience laughs both with and at him. Their subsequent failures include losing their prey in the fog, with Shakebag falling into a ditch, coming to blows over their respective abilities as a 'cutter', and losing a sword-fight with Arden and Franklin. As the failures stack up, we may think they will never succeed, until the gruesome murder shocks us.

Kyd innovates further with the role of intriguer. In *The Spanish Tragedy* Lorenzo acts as the ruthless Machiavellian, hiring killers whom he intends to get rid of as soon as their contract is fulfilled. As he contemptuously puts it:

They that for coin their souls endangered,
To save my life, for coin shall venture theirs;

And better it is that base companions die,
Than by their life to hazard our good haps.
Nor shall they live, for me to fear their faith:
I'll trust myself, myself shall be my friend;
For die they shall, slaves are ordained to no other end.

In *Arden of Faversham*, as I observed, Alice and Mosby are the main plotters and we often see them together, discussing their plans and hopes of success. But Kyd shows Mosby alone, in a chilling soliloquy in which he reveals that, once Arden is dead, he intends to get rid of all his accomplices—Greene, Michael, the Painter:

Then, Arden, perish thou by that decree,
For Greene doth ear the land and weed thee up
To make my harvest nothing but pure corn.
And for his pains I'll heave him up awhile
And, after, smother him to have his wax;
Such bees as Greene must never live to sting.
Then is there Michael and the painter too,
Chief actors to Arden's overthrow . . .
     I'll cast a bone
To make these curs pluck out each other's throat;
And then am I sole ruler of mine own.

The ruthlessness, and the contempt for his accomplices ('curs') are in the exact mould of Lorenzo's contempt for his 'base companions' and 'slaves'. But Mosby goes beyond Lorenzo, for his extinction list extends to Alice, the woman he has feigned to love and sworn to marry: 'I will cleanly rid my hands of her'. Knowing his plans for her may make theatregoers and readers feel sorry for Alice, whose desire to have a happier life will be extinguished by the man who has power over her. Yet at the same time we cannot approve her ruthlessness, especially the brutal way she stabs her dying husband. To create such a complex character is an achievement for which Kyd deserves long-withheld recognition.

The third of my newly attributed plays is the comedy *Fair Em*, which survives in a much-abbreviated and damaged text, about half the length of a usual Elizabethan play. It contains neither vengeful women nor comedy in tragedy, but it includes intrigue in both plots. In the 'public' plot, involving historical figures (William the Conqueror, the Marquis of Lubeck) disguise is used for deceiving identity. In the 'private' plot Em (short for 'Emma') is wooed by three men, two of whom she doesn't like. To deter one of them she pretends to be blind, to deter the other she pretends to be deaf. She finally gets the man she loves, who intuits that she has only been feigning disability. The two plots are cleverly interwoven, and Kyd pokes fun at the two unwanted lovers, who utter identical formulaic speeches, as Perseda and Lucina do when they are separated from their lovers.

I have summarized that part of my attribution case based on major plot parallels between these three plays and Kyd's acknowledged work so that readers and theatregoers familiar with Elizabethan drama can get accustomed to this unusual feature. I provide detailed treatment of these plot structures both for the accepted canon (*The Spanish Tragedy* and *Soliman and Perseda* in chapters 2 and 3) and the newly attributed plays (*King Leir*, *Fair Em*, and *Arden of Faversham* in chapters 5, 6, and 7). I also compare similarities of plot structure between the accepted and the newly attributed plays.

For the new ascriptions I supplement those discussions with the small-scale approaches that usually form the basis of attributions. The most frequently used method in reading-based attribution is the identification of phrases that occur in both the anonymously published play and in a dramatist's acknowledged works. This method was used with great success by a series of scholars between 1903 and 1948 to identify Kyd's authorship of *Arden of Faversham*, citing hundreds of matches with his three plays and his prose work. Scholars with rival candidates used to reject such evidence as 'subjective' and 'biased', even though their evidence was there for all to see. Since 2017 that is no longer possible, thanks to Pervez Rizvi's publication of a corpus of all 527 plays published between 1552 and 1657 which he had programmed to identify every phrasal repetition in every play.[5] When the words are contiguous, linguists describe such repetitions as 'n-grams', where n is any number between one and ten. Rizvi discovered that the most effective lengths for attribution purposes are three words (trigram) and four words (tetragram). When the phrase is interrupted by other words, that is known as a collocation, which Rizvi limits to a maximum of ten words intervening. N-gram and collocation matches are acceptable evidence when a phrase occurs in the target play and in other works by the same author, but the strongest evidence is provided when the match is unique, occurring only in two plays. Users of this database will find full explanations of the principles on which Rizvi has selected the most significant n-grams and collocations from the millions that occur in his database. He also records several experiments that he has made, one of which, '*Arden of Faversham* and the Extended Kyd Canon', accepts my ascription of it to Kyd, along with *King Leir* and *Fair Em*.

The other main attribution method involves measuring features of dramatists' verse styles.

The pioneer study of prosody was P. W. Timberlake's dissertation on the incidence in Elizabethan drama of feminine endings,[6] that is, when a ten-syllable line receives an extra syllable, as in 'To be, or not to be, that is the ques`tion'. This feature had been successfully studied by Victorian scholars to identify the work of Fletcher and Massinger,[7] but Timberlake supplied reliable statistics and established a sound historical basis. He showed that the 'University Wits' (Peele, Greene, Lodge, Marlowe) used a regular iambic line with a low incidence of feminine endings, ranging from 0.5 percent to 3 (a statistic that removes any possibility of Marlowe as co-author of the *Henry VI* plays). His crucial finding for this study is that Kyd was the first dramatist to use feminine endings

---

5. Pervez Rizvi, 'Shakespeare's Text. A Collection of Resources for Students of the Original Texts of Shakespeare's Plays', https://www.shakespearestext.com/can/.

6. P. W. Timberlake, *The Feminine Ending in English Blank Verse. A Study of its Use by Early Writers in the Measure and its Development in the Drama up to the Year 1595* (Menasha, WI, 1931).

7. See Brian Vickers, *Shakespeare, Co-Author. A Historical Study of Five Collaborative Plays* (Oxford, 2002), pp. 47–53.

frequently, soon followed by Shakespeare. Timberlake's figures for the two authors were: *Soliman and Perseda* (1588) 10.2 percent; *King Leir* (1589) 10.8; *Arden of Faversham* (1590) 6.2; *Fair Em* (1590) 6.5; *Cornelia* (1594) 9.5; *2 Henry VI* (1591) 10.4; *3 Henry VI* (1591) 10.7. The advent in the 1930s of the Russian school of metrics, which abandoned the classical quantitative system for one based on stress, either 'Strong' or 'Weak' (the regular iambic pentameter alternates the two: W S W S W S W S W S) allowed scholars to count the stress pattern for every line and establish percentages. In 1969 the Estonian scholar Ants Oras produced a study limited to pause patterns within the pentameter line, based on punctuation.[8] His results for *The Spanish Tragedy* and *King Leir* are very similar. A much more comprehensive study was provided by Marina Tarlinskaja,[9] a pupil of the distinguished Russian prosodist M. L. Gavrilov. Her analysis of 'Kyd's versification' (pp. 87–116) endorses my attribution of *King Leir* and *Fair Em* to the Kyd canon. She originally gave the whole of *Arden of Faversham* to Kyd but seems to have been influenced by an unreliable stylometric study by Arthur Kinney (see chapter 8) that attributes scenes 4–8 to Shakespeare. Other prosodic features that she independently analyses ascribe these scenes to Kyd.

When large-scale approaches, such as my studies of Kyd's three main plot structures, are endorsed by those on a small scale, instanced by phrase matches and prosodic measurements, an attribution can be regarded as successful.

My research also identified Kyd's part authorship of two history plays, *1 Henry VI* and *Edward III*, to which Shakespeare also contributed. For the first, I identify its origin in the play that Henslowe recorded as 'harey the vi', performed with great success by Lord Strange's Men at the Rose theatre on 3 March 1592 and on numerous subsequent occasions that season.[10] I agree with earlier scholars that Nashe wrote

8. Ants Oras, *Pause Patterns in Elizabethan and Jacobean Drama. An Experiment in Prosody* (Gainesville, FL, 1960).

9. Marina Tarlinskaja, *Shakespeare and the Versification of English Drama, 1561–1642* (Farnham and Burlington, VT, 2014).

10. R. A. Foakes and R. T. Rickert (eds), *Henslowe's Diary* (Cambridge, 1961), pp. 16ff.

Act 1, but I attribute the remainder of the original text to Kyd.[11] I based the ascription partly on the many phrases that it shares with Kyd's other plays, and partly on resemblances in characterization and situation. When Strange's Men disbanded in 1593 their playbooks were divided between the Admiral's Men and the Lord Chamberlain's Men, Shakespeare's company. At some point in the mid-1590s Shakespeare added three scenes to the play: 2.4, giving a fictional account of the origin of the dispute between the York and Lancaster, 4.2 and 4.5, showing Talbot, the play's hero and Strange's ancestor, fighting the French. In *1 Henry VI* Shakespeare added to (and improved) an existing play by Kyd, but on *Edward III* they were co-authors. Shakespeare dramatized the love plot, in which the king is infatuated with the Countess of Salisbury, while Kyd dealt with the political and war scenes.[12] I base my attribution partly on some theatrical elements shared with Kyd's other plays, together with many resemblances with his phraseology. Tarlinskaja's prosodic analyses endorsed my ascription of both plays, although she observed some smaller differences. These may well be due to the difference of genres ('history play'), the use of Holinshed and Hall as source, and the 'givens' of historical events, all of which could have constrained Kyd's imagination.

Another project growing out of my research on Kyd is a new edition of all his works, including those that I newly attribute to him. Boydell and Brewer are publishing a two-volume *Collected Works of Thomas Kyd*, of which the first volume has been published. It contains *Verses of Praise and Joy*, edited by Daniel Starza Smith; my edition of *The Spanish Tragedy* (in a five-act version); *The Householder's Philosophy*, edited by Domenico Lovascio; *Soliman and Perseda*, edited by Matthew Dimmock; and *King Leir*, edited by Eugene Giddens. Volume Two will contain *Arden of Faversham*, edited by Darren Freebury-Jones (Associate Editor); *Cornelia*, edited by Lucy Rayfield and Adam Horsley; *Fair Em*, edited by me; and *Letters to Puckering*, edited by Rebekah Owens. The late David Bevington

11. Brian Vickers, 'Incomplete Shakespeare: Or, Denying Co-authorship in *1 Henry VI*', *Shakespeare Quarterly*, 58 (2007): 310–52.

12. Brian Vickers, 'The Two Authors of *Edward III*', *Shakespeare Survey*, 67 (2014): 69–84, and 'Kyd, *Edward III*, and "The Shock of the New"', *ANQ* (2019).

delivered annotated text editions of *1 Henry VI* and *Edward III* just before his death, to which I have added introductions and authorship commentaries. All my quotations come from these freshly edited texts. When the edition is complete, future readers and scholars will be able for the first time to appreciate the unity of Kyd's oeuvre.

Since serious literary scholarship began in the late nineteenth centuries, Kyd has had many admirers and some detractors. I deal with both in chapter 8, discussing *Arden of Faversham*. Although definitively ascribed to Kyd in studies by English, German, French, and Danish scholars between 1903 and 1948, it has been the object of 'disintegration' by MacDonald Jackson since his Oxford B. Litt. thesis of 1963 and in multiple publications since. Jackson began by claiming for Shakespeare scene 8, the second quarrel between Mosby and Alice, but in recent years he has expanded his claim to scenes 4 to 9. Jackson finds in those scenes abundant marks of Shakespeare's vivid imagination, poetic sensibility, and verbal artistry, all qualities that he denies to Kyd elsewhere in the play, while finding fault with *The Spanish Tragedy* and *Soliman and Perseda*. Praising Shakespeare, he denigrates Kyd for making an 'obvious connection . . . in a rather perfunctory fashion. His lines are worn poetic currency'. Kyd's imagery is 'characteristically confused', he uses words 'mechanically'. A passage in *Soliman and Perseda* is 'an assembly of nouns preceded by the most obvious of epithets . . . The passage is a tissue of inert expressions and other men's inventions'. To these incidental dismissals Jackson adds sweeping negative judgments. Of a passage in *Arden* he declares that 'the language [has] a vividness and concreteness never on display in Kyd's plays'. Elsewhere Jackson states that 'there is nothing in Kyd comparable to the verse of the Quarrel scene'. There is considerable irony in Jackson praising passages from *Arden* as being 'Shakespearian' when they were in fact written by Kyd. Jackson's bias towards Shakespeare co-exists with a very limited knowledge of Kyd.

Jackson makes these subjective personal judgments when comparing parallel passages from *Arden* with other Kyd plays or with Shakespeare. This is quite contrary to the ethos of modern attribution studies, where such evidence is used to show significant similarities between an anonymous play and one of known authorship. To compare their 'poetic quality' is irrelevant. Jackson violates modern attribution methods by continuing to use Caroline Spurgeon's discredited method of deducing biographical facts about an author from the classes of imagery that he uses. Jackson violates another cardinal principle of attribution studies by ignoring chronology. It is obvious that, if play B contains phrases similar or identical with play A, and if A was performed or published before B, then a scholar must at least consider the possibility of influence or imitation. But Jackson cites many matches between *Arden* and Shakespeare plays written anything between two and eight years after it was performed, and at one point acknowledges that fact without drawing the inescapable conclusion. He has never considered the possibility that Kyd was a major influence on Shakespeare.[13] Regrettably, his negative judgments, repeated many times over the last fifty years, have probably given Kyd a low reputation among scholars and students, deterring them from looking further. Jackson's claim of Shakespeare's part authorship of *Arden* has gained more readers since Gary Taylor included the play in the *New Oxford Shakespeare* (2016). This decision was catastrophic for attribution studies and for Shakespearian textual criticism.

When I first worked on these attributions I expected to meet with scepticism, since scholars were unlikely to instantly accept authorship identifications four hundred years after the event. They would naturally ask why these facts weren't discovered before. But I hadn't expected to receive hostility and rejection before my findings were properly set out. It is unfortunate that recently authorship attribution has become a hotly contested discipline, divided by partisan groupings. In the media much kudos attaches to a new attribution, or de-attribution, especially when the text is by Shakespeare. When the *New Oxford Shakespeare* was published, Taylor gave newspaper interviews in which he seemed to revel in having whittled down Shakespeare's canon, announcing that 'in the new edition 17 of 44 plays are identified as collaborative, "a little more

---

13. See now Darren Freebury-Jones, *Shakespeare's Tutor. The Influence of Thomas Kyd* (Manchester, 2022).

than 38%, close to two-fifths".[14] In this climate editors can become possessive and regard rivals with hostility. I regret that Taylor has gone on record dismissing my arguments for extending the Kyd canon before he has seen them. He told a reporter in 2018 that 'the Vickers edition is based on his own massively inflated definition of what Kyd wrote'.[15] In the *New Oxford Shakespeare Authorship Companion* Taylor and Loughnane reported that four of its contributors, who naturally accepted Jackson's attribution of *Arden*, 'all demonstrate that Kyd could not have written any significant part of the play'[16]—when none of them actually discussed that topic. Jackson himself began an essay disputing Pervez Rizvi's endorsement of my extended Kyd canon by saying that in 2008 I had made 'a startling announcement—that the small dramatic canon of the Elizabethan playwright could be expanded', and ended it by warning that 'the projected *Collected Works of Thomas Kyd* is at severe risk of including several works in which Kyd had no hand'.[17] We shall see how other scholars judge.

In preparing this book I have received valuable help of several kinds. I thank the editors of our new Kyd edition, who accepted the need to include both the accepted and the newly attributed works: the late David Bevington (University of Chicago), Domenico Lovascio (University of Genoa), Matthew Dimmock (University of Sussex), Eugene Giddens (Anglia Ruskin University), Daniel Starza Smith (King's College, London), Lucy Rayfield and Adam Horsley (both University of Exeter), Rebekah Owens (independent scholar), and Darren Freebury-Jones (Shakespeare Birthplace Centre), who has not only been a most efficient Associate Editor but has also read all of my manuscript in draft and made many helpful suggestions. I am alone responsible for any errors.

14. See Dalya Alberge, 'Christopher Marlowe Credited as One of Shakespeare's Co-writers', *Observer*, 23 Oct 2016.

15. *The Guardian*, 2 April 2018.

16. Gary Taylor and Gabriel Egan (eds), *The New Oxford Shakespeare Authorship Companion* (Oxford, 2017), p. 490.

17. MacDonald Jackson, 'The Use of N-grams to Determine the Dramatic Canon of Thomas Kyd', *Medieval and Renaissance Drama*, 60 (2021): 126–54 (126, 143).

Most scholars of early modern drama are able to cite a succession of predecessors, both editors and critics, who established texts and contributed historical scholarship illuminating relevant theatrical and literary contexts. When I began work on this book I only had two predecessors, probably due to Kyd's canon being so small: Arthur Freeman's biography, *Thomas Kyd, Facts and Problems* (Oxford, 1967), and Lukas Erne, *Beyond The Spanish Tragedy: A Study of the Works of Thomas Kyd* (Manchester, 2001). Freeman described his 'first concern' as 'factual, with matters of date, authorship, source and stage history' (p. vii.). In the first two chapters he brings together for the first time the meagre records of Kyd's life, with important discussions of the French Church libel and Kyd's imprisonment. He devotes two chapters to *The Spanish Tragedy*, one to *Soliman and Perseda*, and one to Kyd's minor works. Although his approach is avowedly factual, it is wide-ranging and includes many perceptive discussions of the dramatic structure and style of Kyd's two tragedies. Lukas Erne also focusses on *The Spanish Tragedy*, devoting four chapters to its origins, its 'framing of revenge', and to 'additions, adaptations, modern stage history'. He devotes two chapters to *Soliman and Perseda*, with a valuable account of its dramaturgy, one to *Cornelia*, and one to Kyd's other works. Erne's most original contribution is his account of *The First Part of Hieronimo* (1605), in which he detects two textual layers, one serious the other parodic. Erne identifies the former as a version of the Don Horatio story, which he sees as the surviving parts of the play listed in Henslowe's Diary as 'the comodey of doneoracio', performed several times in the spring of 1592 as a prequel to the events of *The Spanish Tragedy*, forming a two-part play. The parodic level, he argues, is a burlesque of *Don Horatio* performed by the Children of the Chapel. Although it is extremely difficult to distinguish one textual layer from the other, I find Erne's thesis convincing and worthy of further study.

Those were the two Kyd scholars established when I began work on Kyd, and their books are essential reading; a third has since joined them. In 2016 I was asked to act as external examiner for the doctoral thesis of Darren Freebury-Jones at Cardiff University, 'Kyd and Shakespeare: Authorship, Influence, and Collaboration'. I found it to be an unusually mature work, based on wide reading in primary and secondary literature, giving an extremely thorough examination of every text. Setting out to test my argument for Kyd's extended canon, Freebury-Jones had mastered the methods of authorship attribution and produced several new approaches, including Kyd's use of prefixes and suffixes as stylistic markers. He also used Rizvi's database more thoroughly than I had, showing a generational difference in the ease with which he used statistical arguments. In the intervening six years he has published many important scholarly articles, culminating in his book *Shakespeare's Tutor: The Influence of Thomas Kyd*, which marks a great advance on his thesis. It is pleasing to note the arrival of an independent scholar who will take Kyd studies further.

I would also like to thank two scholars who have helped me and all students of early modern drama by publishing electronic databases, each containing over 500 plays. The first is Martin Mueller (Emeritus, Northwestern University), with his pioneering collection *Shakespeare His Contemporaries*, subsequently absorbed into *Early Print*, a long-term project that aims 'to transform the early English print record, 1473 to the early 1700s, into a linguistically annotated and deeply searchable text corpus'. The second scholar to undertake such a massive task has been Pervez Rizvi (independent scholar) who in 2016 published a corpus of English drama comprising 527 plays, described above. The texts are modernized and lemmatized (that is, the lemma 'hope' includes all forms of that word), necessary procedures for high-speed electronic searches. Rizvi wrote programs allowing users to download the results of fully automated searches of every significant verbal repetition in this corpus. All language users repeat favourite phrases, and early modern dramatists did so frequently; if we can identify a dramatist by their repetition of unique phrases, this provides the most useful tool for identifying the authorship of an anonymously published play, or to differentiate the contributors to a co-authored play. The publication of Rizvi's corpus is the most important contribution to authorship attribution study and is already transforming that discipline. Rizvi, a professional mathematician, has also written a series of important critiques of recent quantified methods which have been very helpful in revealing the errors in recent attempts to deny Kyd's authorship of *Arden of Faversham*. As I show in chapter 9, both scholars tested my thesis of an expanded Kyd canon and independently endorsed it.

I am especially grateful to my publisher at Princeton University Press, Ben Tate, who encouraged my project over many meetings in Waterstone's Gower Street café; his assistant, Josh Drake; Jaden Young for editorial help; and my eagle-eyed copyeditor, Jane Simmonds.

Finally, I would like to thank the co-worker who has been associated with my Kyd research from its beginning in 2007, Valerie Hall. At that time she was working at the Institute of English Studies at London University, of which I am a Senior Research Fellow, and when the research grant expired she continued working for me in a private capacity. Having previously been an assistant editor at the *Times Educational Supplement*, she brought excellent keyboard and copyediting skills to the Kyd project. At the beginning I laboriously compiled handwritten lists of phrasal matches between the accepted Kyd plays and the newly attributed ones, which she edited and typed up. When I gradually learned how to use electronic resources, she converted the lists to a standard tabular format. As my research expanded, I started writing up my findings by longhand and drafting commentaries on them. Over the years the number of tables and essays expanded exponentially, but throughout the whole period she has maintained her organization skills and clarity. I have been lost sometimes, she never. I gratefully dedicate this book to her.

Brian Vickers
13 September 2023

THOMAS KYD

1

An Interrupted Life

THOMAS KYD'S LIFE, like that of so many other Elizabethan dramatists (apart from Shakespeare and Jonson), has left little trace in the official records. We have the briefest notices of his baptism, schooling, and burial. The only extended life records in his own hand are the two letters he wrote to Sir John Puckering in 1593, after his disastrous imprisonment in connection with the Dutch Church libel. None of the plays that Kyd wrote for the public theatre was published under his name—a not unusual occurrence in this period, since the play books belonged to the theatre companies, who were more concerned to advertise themselves than their authors. This introductory chapter begins by summarizing what is known about Kyd's life, from direct and indirect sources.

Where their parentage is known, most of the authors writing for the new medium of public theatre came from established middle-class professions. Marlowe's father was a shoemaker who subsequently became a parish clerk. Shakespeare's father was a glover, who also traded in commodities and served as Alderman and Mayor. Peele was the son of James Peele, clerk of Christ's Hospital, where Peele was educated. Lyly's father was a diocesan official at Canterbury; Munday's was a London draper. Jonson was the posthumous son of a minister of religion of Scottish descent; his stepfather has been identified as Robert Brett, a successful bricklayer who became Master of the Tylers' and Bricklayers' Company. Lodge's father, Sir Thomas Lodge, was Lord Mayor of London; Marston's father was a lawyer.

On 6 November 1558 the parish register of St Mary Woolnoth recorded the baptism of 'Thomas, son of Francis Kidd, Citizen and Writer of the Courte Letter of London'.[1] Kyd's father, Francis, rose to be Warden of the Company of Scriveners in 1580, the official body supervising 'a profitable and ancient trade'. Scriveners, officially known as 'Writers of the Court Letter', enjoyed 'a monopoly on engrossing charters, contracts, testaments, and official documents', functioning 'not only as notaries and copyists, but also as money lenders'. The need for verbal accuracy in their profession made them insist, in a mandate dating back to 1497, that

> any scrivener's apprentice who had not a 'perfect congruity of grammar, which is the thing most necessary and expedient to every person exercising the science and faculty of this mystery', was to study at a grammar school until 'he be erudite in the books of genders, declensions, preterites and supines, equivix, and sinonimes'.[2]

Francis Kyd had evidently had a grammar-school education and ensured that his son had the same good start in life. Thomas must have received his first education at home, for when he entered the nearby Merchant Taylors' School on 26 October 1565, just before his seventh birthday, he was expected 'to know "the catechysm in English or Latyn" and be able to "read perfectly and write competently"'.

In his *Survey of London* (1598; 1603), John Stow recorded that in Suffolk Lane (which today has the postcode EC1), 'turning up towards Candlewick Streete, is one notable Grammar schoole, founded in the yeare 1561 by the master, wardens, and assistants of the Marchant Taylors in the parish of Saint Lawrence Poultney. Richard Hilles sometime master of that companie, having before given 500 pound towards the

---

1. Biographical details in this paragraph are mostly taken from the essential biographical resource, Arthur Freeman, *Thomas Kyd. Facts and Problems* (Oxford, 1967).

2. A jumble of grammatical terms. According to *OED*, a preterit is 'the simple past tense of a verb'; a supine is a 'Latin verbal noun with the same stem as the passive participle, used only in the accusative and ablative cases esp. to denote purpose'. The word equivix is not in *OED*: perhaps an error for 'Equiuokes . . . such things as have one selfe name, and yet be divers in substance or definition' (T. Blundeville, *Art of Logike* (1599).

AN INTERRUPTED LIFE 3

purchase of an house, called the Mannor of the Rose . . ?.[3] Merchant Taylors' at once became the largest grammar school in England, with 250 pupils (St Paul's had 150), and one of the best.[4] The first person to hold the post of High Master, for which the Statutes specified 'a man in body whole, sober, discreete, honest, vertuous, and learned, in good and cleare Latin literature, and also in Greeke',[5] was Richard Mulcaster, who occupied it from 1561 to 1581, and subsequently became High Master of St Paul's School. Mulcaster was a distinguished humanist, whose published and unpublished Latin poetry survives, and who wrote two important educational treatises: *Positions, wherein those primitive circumstances be examined, necessarie for the training up of children* (1581), and *The first part of the Elementarie which entreateth of right writing of our English tung* (1582).

The curriculum of Merchant Taylors', as T.W. Baldwin showed in his magnificent study of the Elizabethan grammar schools,[6] was based on that of St Paul's, as laid down by Cardinal Wolsey in 1528, which in turn followed the scheme outlined by Erasmus in *De Ratione Studii* (1512). It envisaged six to eight years' intensive study of Latin grammar, as codified in the official 'King's grammar' of John Lily, reading a graded sequence of Latin authors (Cato, Terence, Virgil, Cicero's Letters, Sallust, Caesar, Horace's *Epistles*, Ovid's *Metamorphoses* and *Fasti*), and regularly composing Latin prose and verse, incorporating the figures of rhetoric. Those sceptics who have doubted Shakespeare's ability to read Latin, or even write plays, because 'he only had a grammar-school education', betray both snobbery and ignorance, for this was one of the most formidable educational systems ever devised. It had, of course, a very narrow scope, by modern standards, being essentially concerned with learning to read and write Latin, with a small amount of Greek added

---

3. C.L. Kingsford (ed.), *A Survey of London by John Stow*, 2 vols (Oxford, 1908), I.237.

4. See F.W.M. Draper, *Four Centuries of Merchant Taylors' School 1561–1961* (London, 1962), Richard De Molen, *Richard Mulcaster and Educational Reform in the Renaissance* (Nieuwkoop, 1991), and Jacqueline Cousin-Desjobert, *La théorie et la pratique d'un éducateur élisabethain: Richard Mulcaster ca.1531–1611* (Paris, 2003), revised as *Richard Mulcaster ca.1531–1611. Un éducateur de la Renaissance anglaise* (Paris, 2013).

5. Draper, *Four Centuries*, p. 241.

6. T.W. Baldwin, *William Shakespere's Small Latine and Lesse Greeke*, 2 vols (Urbana, IL, 1944; 1966), I.118–33, 395–404, 418–23.

4   CHAPTER 1

in the upper forms of the biggest schools. The Merchant Taylors' Statutes enjoined the masters to teach 'not only good literature but also good manners'.[7] A curriculum based on 'good literature' excluded history, geography, modern languages, mathematics, and the sciences. Although limited to Latin, the drilling in grammar, rhetoric, and classical prosody was so intense that it could hardly be matched in any modern university. Admittedly, classics students today read more authors, but they seldom achieve the intense familiarity that the Elizabethan grammar schoolboy had with his more limited knowledge of selections from Virgil's *Eclogues* and *Aeneid*, Ovid's *Metamorphoses*, and Cicero's letters, speeches, and philosophical works (*De Officiis, Tusculanae disputationes*).[8] Nor do modern students learn to write, speak, and even act in Latin. What is now a dead language was then still living.

Like all Renaissance grammar schools and gymnasia, the Merchant Taylors' curriculum laid great emphasis on Latin composition. In 1607 the school instituted 'probation days' three times a year, on which each of the six forms should be tested, the regulations giving what Baldwin describes as the best account 'as to exactly what in the way of compositional excellence was at this period expected of a learned grammarian'.[9] (These tests probably embodied existing teaching methods, for schools are notoriously conservative, and to introduce these graded stages of composition *ab ovo* would have necessitated a massive change in the curriculum.) In the upper school, the Fourth form boys aged ten or eleven were expected to write 'two, three, or more periods of some theme or sentence in Latine, and make two, or more verses upon the same'. The Fifth form, in the 'forenoone' examination, were expected to 'make a longer theme, or treatise in prose than the former forme did', and to write an unspecified number of 'verses upon the same theme or sentence'. Moreover, the regulations specified that in the afternoon the Fifth

---

7. Draper, 1962, p. 242.

8. On the limited curriculum of the Elizabethan grammar schools, see Robert Bolgar, 'Classical Reading in Renaissance Schools', *The Durham Research Review*, 2 (1955): 18–26.

9. Baldwin, *Small Latine*, 1.395. He reprints (pp. 395–8) these regulations from H. B. Wilson, *The History of Merchant Taylors' School: From its Foundation to the Present Time* (London, 1814), pp. 163–7.

form 'shall make some *parodiae*, or imitacons of Latine verses', and 'also make some *parodiae*, or imitations of Greeke verses'. By the time they reached the Sixth form, boys were expected to have mastered the major classical verse forms. The regulations for the forenoone examination specified that 'the schoolemaister having opened, on the sodayne, some part of Tully' (that is, one of Cicero's prose works), and dictated 'one period, word by word', the pupils 'shall turn it into Latin hexameters and pentameters, or sapphicks'. In the afternoon the master would dictate a passage from 'the Greeke Testament, Esop's Fables, in Greeke, or some other very easie Greeke author', and the pupils were expected to 'turne it into Greeke hexameters and pentameters, or sapphicks'. In 1611 William Haine (or Hayne), who had become Headmaster of Merchant Taylors' in 1599, recalled the texts he had used for Latin–English translations in his career, including the Ramist rhetoric of Talaeus, excerpts from Cicero's epistles, speeches, and philosophical works (Book I of *De Officiis, Tusculan Questions*), two plays by Terence, Virgil's *Eclogues, Georgics, Aeneid* (the first six books), and Horace's *Odes*, Book I.[10] The Elizabethan grammar schools deserve our respect for imprinting on their pupils the basic literary processes of analysis and composition. An inventory of the Merchant Taylors' library in 1599 includes several folio-sized Latin dictionaries and reference works, 'all rent' (Baldwin, l. 421), worn and torn by generations of pupils learning Latin.

In addition to a thorough acquisition of Latin, Kyd may have owed to Merchant Taylors' School his first exposure to drama. The headmaster William Mulcaster had been educated at Eton under Nicholas Udall, who had used Terence's plays as the basis for his pioneering florilegium, *Floures for Latine Spekynge* (1534). Anticipating Shakespeare's feat in *The Comedy of Errors*, Udall had combined two Latin comedies (Plautus' *Miles Gloriosus* and Terence's *Eunuchus*) for his *Ralph Roister Doister*, the first English classical comedy (probably written between 1545 and

---

10. Cf. Draper, *Four Centuries*, pp. 38–43 and Baldwin, *Small Latine*, 1.400–401, who cites Haine, *Certaine epistles of Tully verbally translated* (London, 1611). As the *Short Title Catalogue* indicates (no. 5304), Haine used Book 1 of the selection edited by Sturmius (Johannes Sturm).

6 CHAPTER 1

1552; published in 1567).[11] Mulcaster emulated Udall by encouraging drama at Merchant Taylors', alongside music and games. The benefits of acting in Latin drama had been celebrated by humanist pedagogues throughout sixteenth-century Europe, but few schools can have brought their performances to such a high level as to be invited to act at court. Mulcaster had contributed to Queen Elizabeth's royal entry into the City of London on 14 January 1559, being rewarded by the City 'for makyng of the boke conteynynge and declaryng the historyes set furth in and by the Cyties pageauntes'.[12] As a result of this honour, royal invitations for his troupe were issued at least eight times between 1572 and 1583. The Merchant Taylors' boys performed before the Queen on Shrove Tuesday 1573, in an unnamed play (on this and all other occasions the Office of the Revels providing 'Gloves for Munkesters boyes ii dozen'). During Candlemas 1574 the accounts list the

> Necessaries Incident for One Playe [*Timoclia at the sege of Thebes*, by Alexander] showen at Hampton Coorte before her Majestie by Mr Munkesters Children And One Maske (of Ladies with lightes being vi vertues) likewyse prepared and brought thither in Redynesse but not showen for the Tediusnesse of the playe that nighte.[13]

Although that performance did not please, later that year Mulcaster's troupe played *Percius and Anthomiris* on Shrove Tuesday 'at Nighte', and were invited back on subsequent feast days. The outlays recorded show that these performances attempted to create appropriate theatrical effects. Although unperformed, the masque of 'Six Vertues' still needed the provision of eight 'Bandes and Ruffes for children all spangled', at 25s. 8d., and eight pounds of 'Wyer to strayne cross the hall and to hang the braunches

---

11. Udall may also have been responsible for both *A new enterlude calld Thersytes* (1537), and the morality *Respublica* (ca.1554): cf. William Tydeman (ed.), *Four Tudor Comedies* (Harmondsworth, 1984), pp. 21–6. Martin Mueller has convincingly ascribed to him *Jacob and Esau*.

12. Draper, *Four Centuries*, p. 29.

13. Albert Feuillerat (ed.), *Documents Relating to the Office of the Revels in the Time of Queen Elizabeth* (Louvain, 1908), pp. 206, 208–11. Cf. also E.K. Chambers, *The Elizabethan Stage*, 4 vols (Oxford, 1923), 2.75–6; 4.88, 90–91, 99; Draper, *Four Centuries*, Appendix II, 'Mulcaster's Plays', pp. 252–3; and Wiggins, *British Drama*, 2.106–7, 109–10.

with the lightes', at 28s. Mulcaster's final performance, in 1583, was also his most spectacular, on a story taken from Ariosto's *Orlando Furioso*:

> A historie of *Ariodante and Geneuora* shewed before her majestie on Shrove tuesdaie at night enacted by mr Mulcaster's children, ffor which was newe prepared and Imployed, one Citty, one battlement of Canvas, viii Ells of sarcenet,[14] and ii dozen of gloves. The whole furniture for the reste was of the store of this office, whereof sondrey garments for fytting of the children were altered and translated.[15]

As anyone will know who has been involved in directing or performing in school plays, the preparation can stretch over several months, absorbing much energy within and outside school hours. Mulcaster's company also performed in the school hall in 1572–3 with an admission charge of one penny, 'the earliest record of a boy company playing before paying spectators'.[16]

The judge Sir James Whitlocke recalled his training under Mulcaster in the early 1580s:

> I was brought up at school under mr. Mulcaster, in the famous school of the Merchant taylors in London, whear I continued untill I was well instructed in the Hebrew, Greek, and Latin tongs. His care was also to encreas my skill in musique, in whiche I was brought up by dayly exercise in it, as in singing and playing upon instruments, and yeerly he presented sum playes to the court, in whiche his scholars wear only actors, and I on among them, and by that meanes taughte them good behaviour and audacitye [boldness, self-confidence].[17]

Another distinguished product of Mulcaster's enlightened humanist education was Edmund Spenser, who attended Merchant Taylors'

---

14. The ell was 'A measure of length varying in different countries. The English ell = 45 in.' (*OED*); sarcenet: 'A very fine and soft silk material made both plain and twilled, in various colours, now used chiefly as a lining material and in dressmaking' (*OED*).

15. Feuillerat, *Office of the Revels*, p. 350.

16. Michael Shapiro, *Children of the Revels: The Boy Companies of Shakespeare's Time and their Plays* (New York, 1977), p. 14.

17. Baldwin, *Small Latine*, 1.420–21.

between about 1561 and 1569. In the December eclogue of *The Shepheardes Calendar*, under the *persona* of Colin Clout, Spenser paid an affectionate tribute to his old teacher, recalling his carefree youth:

> And for I was in thilke same looser years
> (Whether the Muse so wrought me from my birth,
> Or I tomuch beleeued my shepherd peeres)
> Somedele ybent to song and musicks mirth
> A good olde shephearde, *Wrenock* was his name,
> Made me by arte more cunning in the same.   (37–42)

'E. K.', whoever he was, added this gloss to the word 'Musicke': 'Poetry as Terence sayth, *Qui artem tractant musicam*, speaking of Poetes'.[18] Other notable products of Mulcaster's school included Lancelot Andrewes, who was three years older than Kyd when he entered the school in 1565, leaving in 1571; Matthew Gwinne, a future Latin poet and playwright (1570–74); and Thomas Lodge, who was there for a year in 1571 before going up to Oxford. Kyd had one of the best schoolings available in England, and it is appropriate that he may have received his first experience of drama at a school on Suffolk Lane, near Thames Street, just across the river from the South Bank theatres.

There are no records of Kyd attending Oxford or Cambridge, so he presumably returned to his parental home, and may have followed his father's profession for a while. His plays use several legal terms,[19] and his 'handwriting, as it survives in two letters of 1593–4 to Sir John Puckering, is remarkably clear and formal',[20] perhaps that of a professional scrivener. His good handwriting, grammar-school education, and perhaps his knowledge of Latin, led Kyd to follow the path of many Renaissance humanists by taking up service with a noble lord in the post of secretary, responsible for correspondence, scribal-literary tasks, and perhaps some tutoring. A parallel example of this career choice would be Samuel Daniel

---

18. Edmund Spenser, *The Shorter Poems*, ed. Richard A. McCabe (London, 1999), pp. 149–50, 153, 573. The Terence quotation, '[competition for the palm] is open to all who practise poetry', is from the Prologue to *Phormio*, 18.

19. See F.S. Boas (ed.), *The Works of Thomas Kyd* (Oxford, 1901), pp. xvii–xviii.

20. Freeman, *Thomas Kyd*, p. 12.

(1562/3–1619), Kyd's contemporary, an Oxford graduate who served Sir Edward Dymocke from 1585 to 1591–2, when he entered the service of the Pembroke family at Wilton.[21] There he tutored the young William Herbert and joined the circle of writers around Mary Herbert, Countess of Pembroke, Sir Philip Sidney's sister. Daniel had ample time for his own writing at Wilton, which he described as 'my best Schoole', publishing in 1592 both *Delia*, with a dedication to the countess, and *The Complaint of Rosamond*. In that year Herbert published her translation of Robert Garnier's *Marc Antonie*, influencing Daniel to produce *The Tragedy of Cleopatra* (1594), based on the models of Garnier and Jodelle. In the winter of 1593, having lost the patronage of 'my Lord, whom I have served almost theis vi. yeares now', Kyd translated Garnier's *Cornélie*, entered in the Stationers' Register on 26 January 1594 as '*Cornelia, Thomas Kydd beinge the author*'.[22] Kyd dedicated his translation to Lady Bridget Fitzwalter, the Countess of Sussex, apologizing for its faults, acknowledging her 'honourable favours past', and announcing that his next project would be a translation of Garnier's *Porcie*.[23] That work never appeared, for Kyd died in August 1594, and this was his last attempt to seek a patron under whom he could pursue his writing career. But his plan to translate another of Garnier's plays should not be seen as a sign that he was turning his back on the public theatre to devote himself to closet drama (although in fact, Garnier's plays had been acted).

Non-dramatic works

The documentation of Kyd's existence is so fragmentary that the biographer has soon finished his work. But rather more evidence exists of his career as a writer, starting with two works that preceded his career as a dramatist.

---

21. This account of Daniel's early career draws on Joan Rees, *Samuel Daniel. A Critical and Biographical Study* (Liverpool, 1964), pp. 9–13, 43–50.

22. W.W. Greg, *A Bibliography of the English Printed Drama to the Restoration (BEPD)*, 4 vols (London, 1970), 1.195 (no. 116).

23. Boas, *Works of Thomas Kyd*, p. 102.

Verses of Prayse and Joye (1586)

The first work by Kyd published during his lifetime was a small pamphlet containing English and Latin poems, *Verses of Prayse and Joye*, written by 'T. K.' (*STC* 7605). In his 1901 edition F. S. Boas relegated Kyd's *Verses* to an Appendix (pp. 339–42), describing them, rather unkindly, as 'a specimen of his non-dramatic hack work' (p. xxv). Whatever their literary value,[24] they represent Kyd's spontaneous response to a national crisis, and in other circumstances might have attracted a powerful patron.

The year 1586 was notable for the failure of a Catholic conspiracy laid by Anthony Babington to assassinate Queen Elizabeth and free Mary Stuart from imprisonment. Subsequently, the conspirators hoped, the forces of Philip II and the Catholic league in France would invade Britain and restore Catholicism. But from the outset the conspiracy had been infiltrated by Walsingham's double agents, and the plotters were brought to justice and executed on 20 and 21 September, with varying degrees of cruelty. One of the plotters was the young Chidiock Tychborne (born ca.1558), a known Catholic who had twice been interrogated by the authorities on suspicion of 'popish practices'. On the scaffold Tychborne made a long speech in which he acknowledged his fault, 'and moved great pity among the multitude towards him', as William Camden noted in his *Annales, or, The historie of the most renowned and victorious Princess Elizabeth*.[25] Tychborne also left behind a now famous poem, 'Tychbornes Elegie, written with his owne hand in the Tower before his

---

24. Lukas Erne briefly noted that Kyd 'may have written a poem [*sic*] on the subject of Queen Elizabeth's escape . . . Commonly referred to as the "Hendecasyllabon", it is included in a collection of five short poems entitled *Verses of Prayse and Joye . . .*' (*Beyond* The Spanish Tragedy. *A Study of the Works of Thomas Kyd* (Manchester, 2001, p. 220). Regrettably, Erne echoed Boas's dismissive evaluation: 'the poetry is devoid of all intrinsic interest, a mechanical line-for-line answer to [Tychborne's poem], and any educated person would have been able to compose it' (ibid.).

25. Quoted by Penry Williams in his article on 'Babington, Anthony (1561–1586)', in *The Oxford Dictionary of National Biography*, online edition, article odnb/967.

execution', which begins 'My prime of youth is but a frost of cares'.[26] The poem had a considerable circulation in manuscript, as May and Ringler record, especially among Catholic sympathizers, and appears in several modern anthologies.[27]

Modern readers may well admire the modest, sincere pathos of these three stanzas, but Elizabethans could not overlook that their author had been a Catholic conspirator intent on assassinating the Queen, and several contemporary publications expressed the general indignation at the plot, and relief over its failure.[28] In 1586 the London stationer John Wolfe published a small black-letter pamphlet entitled *Verses of Prayse and Joye, Written upon her Majesties Preservation. Whereunto is annexed Tychbornes lamentation Written in the Towre with his owne hand, and an aunswere to the same* [by] *T.K.* This contains six poems by Kyd, four in English (here designated A–D), two in Latin:

(A) 'Verses of Praise, and Joy, Written upon her Majestie, after the apprehension and execution of Babington, Tychborne, Salisburie, and the rest'; 20 lines, unrhymed iambic pentameter, by Kyd.

A reprint of Tychborne's 'Elegie'; 3 stanzas of 6 lines, rhyming *ababcc*.

(B) 'Hendecasyllabon T.K. in Cygneam Cantionem *Chidiochi Tychborne*'; in English (despite the Latin title), using the same stanza and rhyme scheme.

'In nefariam Babingtoni cæterorumque coniurationem Hexasticon'; 6 lines,

Latin elegiacs by Kyd.

---

26. Text from Boas, *Works of Thomas Kyd*, p. 340.

27. Steven W. May and William A. Ringler, Jr., *Elizabethan Poetry. A Bibliography and First-line Index of English Verse, 1559–1603*, 3 vols (London and New York, 2004), 2.1055–6, lists some 40 copies. The poem was reprinted in vol. 3 of Holinshed's *Chronicles* (STC 13569, London, 1587), sig. 7M4v, and in John Mundy, *Songs and psalms composed into 3. 4. and 5. parts* (STC 18284; London, 1594), sig. D1. For a modern edition see Richard S.M. Hirsch, 'The Works of Chidiock Tichborne', *English Literary Renaissance*, 16 (1986): 303–18.

28. See Williams, 'Babington, Anthony (1561–1586)', in *The Oxford Dictionary of National Biography*. He does not mention *Verses of Prayse and Joye*.

(C) 'The Same in English'; 12 lines of '8 and 6' syllables (ballad metre), rhyming *abcb defe ghih*.

'Ad Serenissimam Reginam Elizabetham, Apostrophe'; 6 lines, Latin elegiacs, by Kyd.

(D) 'The Same in English'; 12 lines of '8 and 6' syllables, rhyming *abca defe ghih*.

Boas rightly observed that 'the Latin elegiacs mingled with the English verses' show a facility of composition in both tongues also found in *The Spanish Tragedy*. (A study of Kyd's Latin verse is much needed.)

The 62 lines of English verse alternate praise of the Queen with vituperation of the conspirators, most pungently in the point-by-point refutation of Tychborne's *Elegie*. As Daniel Starza Smith observes:

> the elegy is printed on the verso of a page, with Kyd's line-by-line riposte on the facing recto. The effect is both parodic and dialogic, as Kyd's speaker overturns Tychborne's statements one by one and collectively, mimicking his form by inverting or otherwise rephrasing each claim in order to undermine it.[29]

The young conspirator lamented his impending death in a series of paradoxes. The loyal respondent replies in kind, taking up the metaphors and 'over-going' them, as an Elizabethan might put it.

Tychborne's *Elegie*

My prime of youth is but a frost of cares,
　　My feast of joy is but a dish of pain:
My crop of corn is but a field of tares,
　　And all my good is but vain hope of gain.
The day is past, and yet I saw no sun,   5
　　And now I live, and now my life is done.

---

29. Daniel Starza Smith (ed.), *Verses of Praise and Joy*, in Brian Vickers (ed.), *The Collected Works of Thomas Kyd*, vol. 2 (forthcoming). I also cite Smith's modernized text of the two poems.

My tale was heard, and yet it was not told,
    My fruit is fallen, and yet my leaves are green:
My youth is spent, and yet I am not old,
    I saw the world, and yet I was not seen.
My thread is cut, and yet it is not spun,   10
    And now I live, and now my life is done.

I sought my death, and found it in my womb,
    I looked for life, and saw it was a shade:
I trod the earth, and knew it was my tomb,
    And now I die, and now I was but made.   15
My glass is full, and now my glass is run,
    And now I live, and now my life is done.

Kyd's reply

Thy prime of youth is frozen with thy faults,
    Thy feast of joy is finished with thy fall:
Thy crop of corn is tares availing naughts,
    Thy good God knows, thy hope, thy hap and all.
Short were thy days, and shadowed was thy sun   5
    T'obscure thy light unluckily begun.

Time trieth truth, and truth hath treason tripped,
    Thy faith bare fruit as thou had'st faithless been:
Thy ill-spent youth thine after-years hath nipped,
    And God that saw thee hath preserved our Queen.   10
Her thread still holds, thine perished though unspun,
    And she shall live when traitors' lives are done.

Thou sought'st thy death, and found it in desert,
    Thou looked'st for life, yet lewdly forced it fade:
Thou trod'st the earth, and now on earth thou art   15
    As men may wish thou never had'st been made.
Thy glory and thy glass are timeless run,
    And this, O Tychborne, hath thy treason done.

Although unconvinced of its authenticity, Boas pointed out several parallels between Kyd's response and his plays.[30] In line 4 the wordplay, 'thy **hope,** thy **hap** and all' recalls 'the **hopeless** father of a **hapless** son' (*Sp. T.* 5.4.85) and '**hopeless** to hide them in a **hapless** tomb' (*Corn.* 1.1.214). Line 7, '**Time tr**ieth **truth,** and **truth** hath **tr**eason **tr**ipped', is echoed: '**Time** is the author both of **truth** and right, | And **time** will bring this **tr**eachery to light' (*Sp. T.* 2.4.126–7). I add that in line 9, the metaphor of promising growth being prematurely blocked: 'Thy ill-spent youth thine after-years hath **nipped**' was one that Kyd used again in *King Leir* and *Arden of Faversham.* The loyal citizen left no doubt concerning his disgust with the plotters and his happiness at the Queen's escape.

Kyd's Intellectual Milieu

We have seen that Kyd received a good classical education at Merchant Taylors'. For many pupils that training would have been absorbed into their working lives, leaving no visible traces. Kyd was an exception, having chosen a career as a writer, beginning with *Verses of Praise and Joy.* We know nothing about Kyd's life after leaving school, and it seems likely that he worked in his father's scriptorium. One indirect witness to his activities in these years was recorded by Dekker in his pamphlet, *A Knights Conjuring* (1607). Dekker envisaged a scene in the Elysian fields, where a laurel grove shelters famous dead poets, one group including 'old *Chaucer,* reverend for prioritie', and '*Grave Spenser*'.

> In another companie sat learned *Watson,* industrious *Kyd,* ingenious *Atchlow,* and (tho hee had bene a Player, molded out of their pennes) yet because he had bene their *Lover,* and a Register to the Muses, Inimitable *Bentley*: these were likewise carowsing to one another at the holy well, some of them singing Pæans to *Apollo,* som of them *Hymnes* to the rest of the Goddes . . . [31]

---

30. Boas, *Works of Thomas Kyd,* pp. xxv–xxvi.

31. Thomas Dekker, *A Knight's Conjuring Done in earnest: Discouered in Iest.* (London, 1607; STC 6508), sig. K8ᵛ–L1ʳ.

For T.W. Baldwin the implication of Dekker's grouping was that 'Kyd had written plays before 1585, probably for the Queen's Men'[32]. The epithet 'industrious' suggests that Kyd's output was considerably greater than *The Spanish Tragedy*. The actor John Bentley died in 1585, and the scene Dekker describes must be dated around 1583, when the Queen's Men were formed. Modern historians of that company, commenting on Dekker's pamphlet, observed that 'only Kyd is known to have written for the common stage among this group, and he is not known to have written for the Queen's Men. But "known" is a rare quality when it comes to the authors of plays in the 1580s, even the titles of which have disappeared, with few exceptions.'[33] However, one play they confidently place in the Queen's Men repertory is *The True Chronicle History of King Leir*, which was performed in 1594 at the Rose, when the Queen's Men and Sussex's Men were playing together.[34] McMillin and MacLean define the Queen's Men repertory as 'largely based on the English History play, which they were the first professional company to undertake extensively'. They judge *Leir* to be 'a typical Queen's Men play in its concern with narrative completeness, piety, and truth'. Their remarks on its use of rhyme notice one element that contributes to the identification of Kyd's authorship, as we will see in chapter 5.

Dekker records that Kyd's other associates were two poets. Thomas Atchelow (or Achelley) published a narrative poem, *Violenta and Didaco* (1576), translated from Spanish, and some fragments of his verse survive in the miscellanies. The other poet was much better known: Thomas Watson, 'perhaps the foremost Latin poet of his day', as Arthur Freeman described him.[35] In addition to his eminence as a neo-Latin poet, Watson was the leading English Petrarchan poet of the second generation, best known for his *Hekatompathia, or passionate centurie of*

32. T. W. Baldwin, *On the Literary Genetics of Shakspere's Plays 1592–1594* (Urban, Ill., 1959), p. 178. See also Erne, *Beyond* The Spanish Tragedy, pp. 1–2, 163.

33. See Scott McMillin and Sally-Beth MacLean, *The Queen's Men and their Plays* (Cambridge, 1998), p. 29.

34. Ibid., pp. 33, 52, 87, 88, 94, 100–101, 107–8, 133–4, 137, 146–7, 166–7.

35. See Freeman, *Thomas Kyd*, pp. 13–21 for the fullest biographical account of Dekker's witness.

love (1582), a collection of a hundred eighteen-line 'Sonnets', including many translated from Petrarch and his continental imitators. We know that Kyd and Watson were friends, for each referred to the other's poetry.[36] The method in which they did this derived from the grammar-school practice of *parodia* (specified in the statutes of Merchant Taylors') used in the sense now more familiar from Renaissance music, 'a composition that employs reworked material from another piece or passage, with serious intent' (*OED*). Kyd included several such 'parodies' in *The Spanish Tragedy*, to the puzzlement of some editors. F. S. Boas, having dismissively described the classical attainments displayed in Kyd's works as 'the fruit of a clever schoolboy's reading, reinforced by later private study, rather than of a methodical university training', granted him 'a certain faculty of classical composition', as seen in the Latin verses in *The Spanish Tragedy*, albeit these having been 'constructed mainly out of familiar verse-tags'.[37] These condescending remarks betray Boas's ignorance of Elizabethan grammar-school training, fully documented for the first time in 1944 by T. W. Baldwin. Josef Schick, having had the classical German Gymnasium education, which made such a great contribution to the study of English and other literatures before the First World War, was more attuned to the classical tradition. In Act 1 of *The Spanish Tragedy*, when the Portuguese Viceroy '*Falles to the ground*', devastated by the (false) news of his son's loss in battle, he switches from English to Latin:

> Heere let me lye; now am I at the lowest.
>   *Qui iacet in terra, non habet unde cadat.*
> *In me consumpsit vires fortuna nocendo,*
>   *Nil superest ut iam possit obesse magis.*   (1.3.14–17)

Schick observed that the Quarto printers had failed to notice that the flanking pentameter lines should be typographically distinguished from

---

36. See Brian Vickers, 'Authorship Candidates for *Arden of Faversham*: Kyd, Shakespeare, Thomas Watson', *Studies in Philology*, 118 (2021): 308–41, and 'Thomas Watson, Thomas Kyd, and Embedded Poetry', *Studies in Philology*, 120 (2023): 557–601.

37. F. S. Boas (ed.), *Works of Thomas Kyd*, pp. xvii–xix.

the hexameter in the middle.[38] As for the origins of these lines, Boas speculated that this was 'probably another case of adaptation' (p. 396). It was left to W.P. Mustard to identify them: the first line comes from the *Liber Parabolarum* (2.19) by Alan of Lille, a collection of proverb-like statements with scriptural and classical echoes, written in elegiac couplets. This *sententia* expresses a common topos in the *consolatio* tradition, familiar to English readers from Bunyan's *Pilgrim's Progress*: 'He that is down need fear no fall'.[39] The Viceroy's second line is adapted from Seneca's *Agamemnon*, a speech by Cassandra foreseeing her inevitable destruction, and expressing a comparable sense of terminal disaster: 'For my part I do not try to placate the gods with any prayer: even if they should want to be brutal, they have no means of doing harm. *Fortune has used up all her resources!*'.[40] The third line is Kyd's own composition, summing up the two borrowed verses: 'There is nothing left that can harm me more'. This is exactly the technique of *parodia* or serious imitation that Kyd had learned at Merchant Taylors' School, one method of making the transition from *imitatio* to *aemulatio* that was fundamental to Renaissance literary creativity.[41]

Another instance of Kyd's creative use of *parodia* is Hieronimo's fourteen-line Latin dirge for his murdered son, as he and Isabella pick up Horatio's corpse and prepare to

> bear him in from out this cursed place.
> I'll say his dirge, singing fits not this case:
> O aliquis mihi quas pulchrum ver educet herbas
> [*Hieronimo sets his breast unto his sword*]

---

38. Josef Schick (ed.), *Herausgegeben von J. Schick. I. Kritischer Text und Apparat, Thomas Kyd's Spanish Tragedy* (Berlin, 1901), p. 127.

39. W.P. Mustard, 'Notes on Thomas Kyd's Works', *Philological Quarterly*, 5 (1926): 85–6. The *Parabolarum Alani cum commento* were printed four times in London between 1505 and 1525 (*STC* 252–254.7) and were doubtless pillaged for other such compilations.

40. *Agamemnon*, 696–9; ed. and tr. John G. Fitch, *Seneca IX Tragedies*, vol. 2, Loeb Classical Library (Cambridge, MA, and London, 2004), p. 183; my italics.

41. See, e.g., Brian Vickers (ed.), *English Renaissance Literary Criticism* (Oxford, 1999), pp. 22–39, and Gian Biagio Conte, *The Rhetoric of Imitation. Genre and Poetic Memory in Virgil and Other Latin Poets*, ed. And with a foreword by Charles Segal (Ithaca, NY, and London, 1986).

Misceat, et nostro detur medicina dolori;
Aut, si qui faciunt animis oblivia succos
Praebeat, (2.5. 65–70)

[If only somebody would mix a brew for me | From certain herbs
that the fair springtime nourishes, | And physic be provided
for what pains me; or | If they'd show me what extracts work
forgetfulness | In souls;][42]

This formal appeal to gather up whatever herbs that can heal their pain
begins with six lines of Kyd's own Latin verse, after which he inserts two
lines that condense four from Tibullus:[43]

Ipse bibam quicquid meditatur saga veneni,
Quicquid et irarum Circeia naenia nectit.

[I'd drink whatever drug | The sorceress concocts, whatever
madnesses The spell of Circe weaves..]

Other grammar-school graduates would have recognized the significance of this matching passage from Latin poetry, containing a similar
description of a man mixing herbs to alleviate distress. Kyd alludes to
Tibullus II. iv, a poem in which the frustrated poet complains at his
heartless mistress, who excludes him but admits rich suitors: 'Whatever
potions Circe or Medea have, | Whatever Thessaly's soil yields in
drugs . . . if my Nemesis will calmly look at me, | Let her combine a

---

42. I am grateful to Dr. Nick Moschovakis for allowing me to quote both his Latin text and
his verse translation (into iambic hexameters) from his essay, 'Stolen Elegy', *Times Literary
Supplement*, 12 January 2024. Dr. Moschovakis identified Kyd's source as the first fourteen
lines of 'Orion', a pastoral elegy on his dead wife by the pastor Johannes Fabricius Montanus
(1527–66). First printed in his *Poemata* (Zurich, 1556), the poem achieved wider circulation in
an anthology edited by Aegidius Periander, *Hortus Amorum* (Frankfurt-am-Main, 1567), copies
of which exist in the British Library, the Cambridge University Library, and the Bodleian. It
is regrettable that Moschovakis should accuse Kyd of having 'stolen' or 'pilfered' this passage.
In the Renaissance such borrowings were regarded as instances of *imitatio*, often, as I have
described it, being 'embedded' in the poet's new poem.

43. This was first pointed out by Schick, *Spanish Tragedy* (London, 1898), p. 130.

AN INTERRUPTED LIFE 19

thousand drugs! I'll drink'.[44] From Latin love poetry Kyd switches to epic for Hieronimo's conclusion:

> Emoriar tecum. Sic, sic iuvat ire sub umbras,
> Attamen absistam properato cedere letho,
> Ne mortem vindicta tuam tam nulla sequatur.   (78–80)

[I'll die with you. It suits me thus to go below, | Thus, to the shades—but I won't rush to yield to death, | Lest your death should be followed, then, by no revenge'.]

At this point the stage direction indicates the sword Hieronimo has been holding at his breast: '*Here he throws it from him and bears the body away*'. Line 78 of Hieronimo's speech is a deliberate 'parody' of the concluding lines of Dido's last words before committing suicide:[45]

> dixit et os impressa toro, 'moriemur inultae
> sed moriamur', ait. 'sic, sic iuvat ire sub umbras.
> hauriat hunc oculis ignem crudelis ab alto
> Dardanus et nostrae secum ferat omina
>   mortis'.   (*Aeneid*, 4.659–62)

[She spoke, and burying her face in the couch, 'I shall die unavenged,' she cries, 'but let me die! *Thus, thus I go gladly into the dark!* Let the cruel Dardan's eyes drink in this fire from the deep, and carry with him the omen of my death!']](46)

---

44. Tibullus, *Elegies*, II. iv. 55–60, tr. A.M. Juster, with an introduction by Robert Maltby (Oxford, 2012), pp. 76–7. Kyd may not have been aware that, as Maltby notes, 'Thessaly was the traditional home of witches and their potions. The relevance of witches' brews in this context is their use as love potions' (p. 119). In line 58 (not translated) Tibullus also referred to *hippomanes*, a well-known aphrodisiac.

45. Marlowe also cited this passage for the heroine's last words in *Dido, Queen of Carthage* (1588): 'Live false Aeneas, truest Dido dyes, | Sic sic iuvat ire sub umbras' [*Stabs herself and throws herself into the flames.*]

46. Virgil, *Eclogues, Georgics, Aeneid I–VI*, tr. H.R. Fairclough, rev. G.P. Goold (Cambridge, MA, and London, 1999), pp. 466–7.

But whereas Dido stabs herself with her sword, unable to wreak revenge on Aeneas, Hieronimo throws his away, resolving to stay alive to revenge Horatio's murder, as the final lines of his own composition underline. The significance of this counterpointing allusion would not be lost on those in Kyd's audience who had also had a grammar-school education.

From the Latin poems in *Verses of Praise and Joy* to Hieronimo's dirge, Kyd deserves to be taken seriously as a neo-Latin poet in a scholarly culture that understood and appreciated such skills.

The other major use of *parodia* in *The Spanish Tragedy* is a testimony to his friendship with Thomas Watson. I have shown elsewhere that Kyd quotes or alludes to many passages from Watson's *Teares of Fancie* and *Hekatompathia*.[47] In the first scene of Act 2, Lorenzo attempts to console Balthazar, whose courtship has been refused by Bel-imperia, by quoting from Watson's 'Passion' (Sonnet) XLVII, in which the Author complains at the stubbornness with which his lady refuses his courtship, worse than that of brute beasts:

> In time the Bull is brought to weare the yoake;
> In time all haggred Haukes will stoope the Lures;
> In time small wedge will cleave the sturdiest Oake;
> In time the Marble wears with weakest shewres:
> > More fierce is my sweete *love*, more hard withall,
> > Then Beast, or Bird, than Tree or Stony wal.[48]

That summation of the terms used is an instance of the rhetorical figure *synathroismus*, dubbed by Puttenham 'the collectour or recapitulatour'.[49] Watson gives only this clue to his source: 'The two first lines are an imitation of *Seraphino, Sonnetto* 103'. This is true but, whether intentionally or not, also deceptive. As I have shown elsewhere, Watson's source was

---

47. See Vickers, 'Embedded Poetry'.

48. *Hekatompathia* 47. 1–6 (author's italics). I cite Dana Sutton's valuable online edition of Watson's *Works*, revised 2022, http://www.philological.bham.ac.uk/watson/. Instead of 'Sonnet', Watson preferred 'Passion'.

49. George Puttenham, *The Arte of English Poesie*, ed. Gladys Willcock and Alice Walker (Cambridge, 1936, 1970), pp. 236–7.

in fact Ovid's *Ars Amatoriae*, Book 1. 467–78,[50] a sequence in which the experienced and cynical poet is advising a beginner that he should keep on sending his mistress love letters:

> If she does not receive your message and sends it back unread, hope that one day she will read, and hold to your purpose. In time refractory oxen come to the plough, in time horses are taught to bear the pliant reins . . . What is harder than rock, what softer than water? Yet soft water hollows out hard rock. Only persevere; you will overcome Penelope herself; late, as you see, did Pergamus [Troy] fall, yet fall it did.[51]

Ovid's erotic poetry was not included in the curriculum of the Elizabethan grammar school, but it is hard to imagine that a mature Latin scholar of Watson's stature would not know this poem. Perhaps he kept silent intentionally, to give knowledgeable readers the pleasure of recognition, a tactic certainly deployed by other writers using *parodia*.

Kyd's imitation is more direct in both vocabulary and syntax, appropriately so for a deferential speech in a play:

> My Lord, though Bel-imperia seem thus coy,
> Let reason hold you in your wonted joy.
> In time the savage Bull sustains the yoke,
> In time all haggard Hawks will stoop to lure,
> In time small wedges cleave the hardest Oak,
> In time the flint is piercèd with softest shower,
> And she in time will fall from her disdain
> And rue the sufferance of your friendly pain.   (2.1.1–8)

---

50. See Brian Vickers, 'Thomas Watson, Thomas Kyd, and the re-use of Ovid', *Notes and Queries*, 267 (2022): 88–9. Watson's life-long interest in Ovid can be gauged by his head-note to the opening poem in *Hekatompathia* alluding to 'a peece of worke, whiche he wrote long since, *De Remedio Amoris*'. (This could either have been a translation or a poem of his own.)

51. Ovid, *The Art of Love and Other Poems*, tr. J. H. Mozley, rev. G. P. Goold (Cambridge, MA, and London, 1979), pp. 44–5.

This is Ovid's upbeat conclusion, as we have seen,[52] extended as the experienced lover assures the neophyte that writing letters will bring success: 'Suppose she has read, but will not write back: compel her not; only see that she is ever reading your flatteries. She who has consented to read will consent to answer what she has read; that will come by its own stages and degrees.'[53] Ovid's message is full of hope and encouragement, but Balthazar has given in to despair, and Kyd makes him quote the closing couplet of Watson's stanza verbatim to reject such easy promises:

> No, she is wilder and more hard withal,
> Than beast, or bird, or tree, or stony wall.

On the surface this *parodia* is a straightforward tribute by one poet to another, with Kyd's expectation that readers will recognize Watson's text and appreciate its suitability to the dramatic situation at this point. A closer reading suggests that, in addition, Kyd had recognized the Ovidian 'invention' behind Watson's poem and alluded to it by his choice of English equivalents. Watson refers to 'the Bull', simply, while Kyd adds the epithet 'savage'. Ovid has '*difficiles . . . iuvenci*', troublesome or obstinate. Kyd may have exaggerated the danger, but it suggests that he was aware that Ovid's bull had some troublesome attributes. Where Watson has water dripping on 'the Marble', Kyd has the more accurate 'flint' (the Latin has '*saxo*'). Stronger evidence of Kyd's knowledge of the original Ovidian context is provided by the rest of Balthazar's speech, in which he rounds on himself for blaming Bel-imperia and laments his failures as a suitor:

> But wherefore blot I Bel-imperia's name?
> It is my fault, not she that merits blame.
> My feature is not to content her sight,
> My words are rude and work her no delight.
> The lines I send her are but harsh and ill,
> Such as do drop from Pan and Marsyas' quill.   (2.1.11–16)

---

52. Although the invocation of Greek and Roman epic, alluding to the constancy of Penelope and the fall of Troy, might mischievously undermine that assurance.

53. Ovid, *Art of Love*, 1. 479–82; tr. Mozley, p. 47.

That closing couplet shows Kyd's familiarity with Ovid's recommendation to woo by writing love letters, with an additional finesse. Just as Ovid undercut his experienced lover's confident assurance of success by alluding to the *Odyssey* and the *Iliad*, accounts of human actions stretching across many years, so Kyd shows Balthazar's lack of self-confidence with that painful allusion to Pan and Marsyas. As Philip Edwards observed, they had both 'foolishly challenged Apollo to contests in flute-playing'.[54] (Apollo skinned Marsyas alive.) Edwards correctly noted that '*quill* is a reed and not a pen', but Kyd was able to pun on both senses.

The Housholders Philosophie

Kyd's second publication was in a very different genre. On 6 February 1588 the Stationers' Register recorded an entry for 'the Philosophicall Discourse of the householder', a translation of Torquato Tasso's dialogue *Il Padre di Famiglia* (1583). When published later that year, by Thomas Hacket, whose shop was near the Kyd family house on Lombard Street,[55] the work was entitled *The Housholders Philosophie. Wherein is perfectly and profitably described, the true Oeconomia and forme of Housekeeping . . . First written in Italian by that Excellent Orator and Poet Signior Torquato Tasso, and now translated by T.K.* (London, 1588; *STC* 23702.5)—the same signature Kyd had used for the *Verses of Prayse and Joye*.[56] Tasso's dialogue, one of many that he wrote in the final period of his life, when imprisoned in the hospital of Sant'Anna in Ferrara following a nervous breakdown, took its origin in a trip he made to Turin in 1578. It is both 'a charming portrait of Renaissance country life,

---

54. Philip Edwards (ed.), *The Spanish Tragedy* (London, 1959), p. 30. A different version of the story tells of a similar musical contest between Apollo and Pan: see Ovid, *Metamorphoses*, 11.150–193.

55. Freeman, *Thomas Kyd*, p. 4.

56. A second issue in the same year (*STC* 23703) added a spurious 'dairie book for all good huswives'. All quotations from *The Housholders Philosophie* are from the modernized edition by Domenico Lovascio in Vickers (ed.), *The Collected Works of Thomas Kyd*, vol. 1, pp. 241–331. The text is through-numbered; references are to line numbers.

and a treatise on the family',[57] taking that term in its widest sense, akin to the Greek *oikos*, 'at once house and household, building and family, land and chattels, slaves and domestic animals, hearth and ancestral grave'.[58] The Index refers, inter alia, to 'Beauty forced by painting insupportable in a woman'; 'Body wedded to the soul;' 'Colour of wine, and what it ought to be'; 'Chastisement towards servants, what'; 'Difference betwixt exchange and usury'; 'Mothers ought to give their own children suck'; 'Shamefastness not improper to a married man'; 'Usury, how pernicious a thing it is'; 'Women married rather young than old'. Tasso's own ideas are mediated through classical texts, including Aristotle's *Nicomachean Ethics, Politics, Physics, Metaphysics*, and the pseudo-Aristotelian *Economics*, with additional touches from Terence, Virgil, and Cicero among the Romans, Dante and Petrarch among the moderns. It was perhaps Tasso's free mingling of classical philosophy and literature, together with his discussion of the family's internal structure and place within society, that attracted Kyd to translating this dialogue.

But Kyd was not a passive translator. Domenico Lovascio has calculated that 'the number of Kyd's amplifications and additions is roughly five times that of his omissions or condensations, none of which appear sizeable' (p. 247). The amplifications are mostly on a small scale, involving what Lovascio calls 'synonymic amplification', where 'Kyd takes a single word, phrase, or even clause in Tasso's text and turns into two roughly synonymous words, phrases, or clauses' (p. 247). As anyone familiar with sixteenth-century prose will know, such doubling was common in a period when writers were beginning to use English for serious topics. In addition, Lovascio notes, 'as this practice was frequent in the writing of English legal documents as a means to avoid misunderstandings, it might reflect the fact that Kyd may have learned the trade of his father, who was a scribe, and therefore daily engaged in transcribing legal

57. *Tasso's Dialogues*, tr. with introduction and notes by Carnes Lord and Dain A. Tafton (Berkeley, Los Angeles, London, 1982), p. 43. 'The Father of the Family' occupies pp. 44–149 in a facing page translation.

58. John Jones, *On Aristotle and Greek Tragedy* (London, 1962), pp. 83–4. See also M.I. Finley, *The World of Odysseus* (London, 1967, p. 66) and Brian Vickers, *Towards Greek Tragedy* (London, 1973), pp. 109–11.

documents and contracts' (p. 248). The largest addition to Tasso's *Il padre di Famiglia* is a 'vehement and protracted attack on the evils of usury' (p. 249). In 1901 Boas drew attention to Kyd's

> impassioned . . . indictment, for which Tasso gives little more than the hint, of the evils of usury . . . Not content with reproducing Dante's condemnation of it quoted by Tasso, he adds marginal references to Scripture, and inserts in the text an argument on the subject from Aristotle. It is noteworthy that in the Induction to *The Spanish Tragedie* usurers are placed in 'the deepest hell', where they are 'choakt with melting golde' (1.1.67), and Kyd's detestation of their practices may well have been the fruit of bitter personal experience.[59]

Tasso accepted that 'the real exchange of money might be in some sort reduced unto natural industry, wherewith usury can never be acquainted' (1,372). It has 'not only been condemned by Aristotle but also utterly inhibited by both the new and the old law' (1,379–80).[60] Kyd added this blistering denunciation of usury:

> being an artificial gain, a corrupter of a commonwealth, a disobeyer of the laws of God, a rebel and resister of all human orders, injurious to many, the spoil of those that most uphold it, only profitable to itself, more infectious than the pestilence and consorted with so many perilous evils as are hard or never to be cured. (1374–88)

At this point Kyd reproduces the passage from Dante denouncing usury cited by Tasso but follows it with further additional material that, as Lovascio discovered,[61] he took from Cristoforo Landino's commentary on Dante (1481). Although there is no other evidence of Kyd's interest in Dante, his knowledge of Landino may derive from his interest in Renaissance humanism, or from a Latin or Italian treatise on usury. Lovascio gives a well-informed account of the dissemination of Landino's commentary and makes the not unlikely suggestion that Kyd's invective

59. Boas, *Works of Thomas Kyd*, p. lxiv.

60. *Tasso's Dialogues*, tr. Lord and Tafton, p. 143.

61. See Domenico Lovascio, 'Thomas Kyd's *The Householder's Philosophy* and Cristoforo Landino's *Comento sopra la Comedia di Dante*', Ben Jonson Journal, 27 (2020): 84–104.

against usury was 'connected with his father's profession'.[62] I mentioned earlier that scriveners also functioned as moneylenders, who supplied an essential service to the Elizabethan economy. In 1571 Parliament legalized the payment of interest up to 10 percent, but some lenders demanded 12 percent, and several contemporary writers condemned the practice, including Thomas Lodge in his *Alarum against Usurers* (1583) and Philip Stubbes in his *Anatomie of Abuses* (1583). Lovascio poses the questions 'Had Francis Kyd ever been suspected of usury? Did Kyd himself suffer from such accusations?'[63] Neither can be answered at present, but one avenue not yet explored in this connection is Kyd's dedication of *The Householder's Philosophy* to 'Master Thomas Reade':

> Worth more than this, digested thus in haste,
> Yet truly set according to the sense,
> Plain and unpolished for making waste
> Of that which Tasso's pen so highly graced,
> This work I dedicate to your defence.
> > Let others carp, 'tis your discretion
> > That must relieve mine imperfection.

The key phrase is 'I dedicate to your defence', which might mean 'I dedicate my work to the defence of you' (if, for instance, Reade was a scrivener who had been unjustly accused of usury or some other offence). However, it could also mean 'I dedicate my work to you in the expectation that you will defend it'.

The Householder's Philosophy has links with Kyd's later works. That dedication used a 'modesty topos' apologizing for the 'plain and unpolished' style in which he tried to render 'that which Tasso's pen so highly graced'. Kyd used that topos again in dedicating *Cornelia* to the Countess of Sussex, excusing this 'so rough, unpolished a work' for the 'grace that excellent Garnier hath lost by my default'. These rather more than

---

62. Ibid., p. 86.

63. Lovascio provides a useful bibliography of 'the current scholarly debate on usury in Early Modern England', ibid., p. 101 n. 10.

conventional modesty formulae recur in the Epilogue to *Arden of Faversham*, spoken by Franklin:

> Gentlemen, we hope you'll pardon this naked tragedy
> Wherein no filèd points are foisted in
> To make it gracious to the ear or eye;
> For simple truth is gracious enough
> And needs no other points of glozing stuff.

There are many striking verbal parallels between the translations and Kyd's plays, as Boas first noted. Where Garnier wrote a rather banal instance of *chronographia*—

> Apres l'Hyver glacé le beau Printemps fleuronne,
> L'Esté chaud vient après, après l'Esté Autonne.

In *Cornelia* Kyd expanded it with a more enthusiastic welcome to autumn:

> When icy winter's past, then comes the spring
> Whom summer's pride, with sultry heat, pursues;
> To whom mild autumn doth earth's treasure bring,
> The sweetest season that the wise can choose.[64]

In *The Householder's Philosophy* Kyd had translated Tasso's discussion of the comparative merits of the four seasons, which followed the tradition of biblical commentaries on Exodus by arguing that 'no time may be compared to Autumn'.[65] Having listed 'the inconveniences and discommodities of the winter and summer, whereof the spring and autumn are not to be touched' (313–15), Tasso played off these two seasons against each other, finding 'the spring so far inferior to autumn as hope is to effects, and flowers to fruits, whereof autumn most aboundeth of all other seasons . . . Therefore, I conclude that autumn is the most noble

---

64. See *Cornelia*, ed. Lucy Rayfield and Adam Horsley, 2.1.132–5, in Vickers (ed.), *The Collected Works of Thomas Kyd*, vol. 2.

65. 'And the Lord spoke unto Moses and Aaron in the land of Egypt, saying This month shall be unto you the beginning of months: it shall be the first month of the year to you' (Exod. 12:1–2). See also *Tasso's Dialogues*, tr. Lord and Tafton, p. 29 n. 16.

and best season of the year' (319–31). This reminiscence of his Italian translation accounts for Kyd's otherwise ungrounded expansion of Garnier.

The Danish scholar Paul Rubow pointed out in 1948 a striking match between *The Householder's Philosophy* and *The Spanish Tragedy*.[66] In the former the Father of the family argues that a good husband ought to be continent before marriage, so as not 'to offend the league of matrimony . . . for, if he himself do not first **violate** the bands by so **defiling of the marriage bed**, he shall doubtless much confirm [support] the woman's **chastity**' (*HP* 539–44). In the play Arden, suspecting that his wife has been conducting an adulterous relationship, swears that any

> injurious ribald that attempts
> To **violate** my dear wife's **chastity**
> (For dear I hold her love, as dear as heaven)
> Shall on **the bed** which he thinks **to defile**
> See his dissevered joints and sinews torn   (*AF* 1.1.36–40)

Lovascio commented that 'the closeness between the two passages . . . seems all the more significant given that in *The Householder's Philosophy* Kyd is actually expanding Tasso's text by introducing the phrase "by so defiling of the marriage bed", possibly in order to make the accusation against adulterous husbands sharper than it is in the source text' (*HP*, p. 255)

Rubow noted another significant match: 'Thou **but a member**, but to whet the knife' (*AF* 3.162), with 'be housekeeping wholly or **but a member,** part, or Minister thereof' (*HP* 1193–4). Using anti-plagiarism software, I discovered many matches with Kyd's extended canon. The phrase '**the princely lion**' (*HP* 578) recurs two years later in *King Leir* (7.60). While Kyd, like other dramatists, often used this epithet, Lovascio has pointed out that, in choosing the adjective 'princely', Kyd was making a deliberate addition to Tasso's text.[67] Many of Kyd's favourite phrases were already part of his lexicon in the Tasso translation, such as

---

66. Paul Rubow, *Shakespeare Og Hans Samtidige* (Copenhagen, 1948), pp. 115–16.
67. Lovascio, *HP*, p. 254.

the sentence 'it **giveth** us **to understand that** married women are not forbidden . . .' (*HP* 643–4). Kyd repeated this syntactic construction in *King Leir*: 'there **shall be given to understand that** my father hath detracted her' (12.89–90) and in *Fair Em*: 'It **is given** us **to understand that** your daughter is suddenly become both blind and deaf' (11.22–3). As Lovascio observed, 'in this case, the similarity is more impressive in light of the fact that the same syntactic construction is used each and every time to talk about people in the family ('married women', 'my father', 'your daughter') (*HP*, p. 245) I have found more links with Kyd's other works, as can be seen from my website.[68] The formative status of *The Householder's Philosophy* in Kyd's idiolect will become clear when readers are able to study his whole oeuvre.

An Emerging Playwright

With his fluent ability to compose Latin verse, shown in the *Verses of Praise and Joy* and *The Spanish Tragedy*, Kyd had established himself as a learned dramatist, able to impress an educated public. But all his subsequent plays were written not for the erudite but for the general public that thronged the London theatres. Boas, in his dismissive account of Kyd's classical learning, correctly observed the paucity of references to Latin authors in the succeeding plays. In *Soliman and Perseda* Latin is used by the uneducated Piston, who distorts Cicero's *O tempora, O mores*, into *O extempore, o flores!*, earning Basilisco's Holofernes-like correction: 'O harsh uneducate, illiterate peasant! Thou abusest the phrase of the Latin' (1.3.12–14). Basilisco himself is no better, uttering the exclamation *O coelum, O terra, O maria Neptune!* (4.2.58), although Boas describes this as being quoted 'intentionally in inaccurate form.'[69] None of the newly attributed plays use Latin.

Kyd's decision to dedicate himself to the native English drama was justified by his rapid production of four sole-authored plays: *Soliman*

---

68. See https://brianvickers.uk/work-in-progress.

69. Boas, *Works of Thomas Kyd*, p. xviii. Boas also identifies a few phrases translated from the Latin.

and Perseda (1588), *King Leir* (1589), *Arden of Faversham* (1590), and *Fair Em* (1590). In addition, he wrote two co-authored plays: *1 Henry VI* (1592), with Nashe, and *Edward III* (1593), with Shakespeare.[70] His *Cornelia*, translated from Garnier's *Cornélie*, was published posthumously in 1594, but had perhaps been begun earlier, since he echoed passages from it in *The Spanish Tragedy*.

This sudden burst of success drew the attention of two dramatists already established in the London theatre world who were not given to welcoming newcomers. As far as we know, Kyd had no university education, and it was his misfortune to fall foul of the two most vociferous of the 'University Wits', anxious to defend their status against interlopers, first Greene in 1587, then Nashe. (I shall discuss Greene's attack on *Fair Em* in chapter 6.) In 1589 Kyd received a second attack from the copious and caustic pen of Thomas Nashe. We may take their joint displeasure as proving that Kyd was beginning to make an impact in the London theatre. Greene criticized the author of *Fair Em* for two trivial solecisms, a common attitude among those dramatists who cherished a sense of scholarly superiority over their fellows.[71] Nashe went much further, attempting a comprehensive put-down in his Preface to Greene's romance, *Menaphon. Camillas alarum to slumbering Euphues, in his melancholie Cell at Silexedra* (entered S.R. 23 August 1589). In an address to a learned audience—'Epistle to the Gentlemen students of both Universities'—Nashe commended some writers and condemned others, inveighing against 'a few of our triviall translators'. I label the points that seemingly refer to Kyd.

> It is a common practise now a dayes amongst a sort of shifting companions, that runne through every Arte and thrive by none, to leave *(A)* the trade of *Noverint*, whereto they were borne, and busie themselves with the indevours of Art, that could scarcelie Latinize their

---

70. These attributions will be justified in volume 2 of *The Collected Works*.

71. Compare Jonson's disapproving comments on Shakespeare's errors: 'His wit was in his own power; would the rule of it had been so too. Many times he fell into those things, could not escape laughter: as when he said in the person of Caesar, one speaking to him, "Caesar, thou dost me wrong"; he replied, "Caesar did never wrong, but with just cause"; and such like: which were ridiculous'. *Timber: or discoveries made upon men and matter*, in Brian Vickers (ed.), *English Renaissance Literary Criticism* (Oxford, 1999), pp. 561–2.

necke-verse if they should have neede; yet *(B)* English *Seneca* read by Candle-light yeeldes many good sentences, as *Bloud is a begger,* and so forth; and if you intreate him faire in a frostie morning, hee will affoord you *(C)* whole Hamlets, I should say handfulls of Tragicall speaches. But O griefe! *Tempus edax rerum,* whats that will last alwayes? The Sea exhaled by droppes will in continuance bee drie, and *Seneca,* let blood line by line and page by page, at length must needes die to our Stage; which makes his famisht followers to imitate *(D)* the Kid in *Aesop,* who, enamoured with the Foxes newfangles, forsooke all hopes of life to leape into a new occupation; and these men, renouncing all possibilities of credite or estimation, to intermeddle with *(E)* Italian Translations: Wherein how poorely they have plodded, (as those that are neither prouenzall [provincial] men, nor are able to distinguish of Articles,) let all indifferent Gentlemen that have travelled in that tongue discerne by their two-pennie Pamphlets. And no marvell though their home borne mediocritie bee such in this matter; for what can be hoped of *(F)* those that thrust *Elisium* into hell, and have not learned, so long as they have lived in the Spheres, the just measure of the Horizon without an hexameter? Sufficeth them *(G)* to bodge up a blanke verse with ifs and ands, and otherwhile for recreation after their Candle-stuffe, having starched their beardes most curiously [carefully] to make a Peripateticall path into the inner parts of the Citie, and *(H)* spend two or three howers in turning ouer French *Dowdie,* where they attract more infection in one minute, then they can do eloquence all daies of their life, by conversing with any Authors of like argument.[72]

Nashe's diatribe, so dense with sarcastic wit, has often been discussed, and although McKerrow and Edwards disagreed, the balance of scholarly opinion is that several details in this passage identify the anonymous writer as Kyd.[73] I summarize the modern consensus:

---

72. R.B. McKerrow (ed.), *The Works of Thomas Nashe,* 5 vols (Oxford, 1904–10), rev. F.P. Wilson (Oxford, 1958), 3:315–16.

73. See V. Østerberg, 'Nashe's "Kid in Aesop"', *Review of English Studies,* 18 (1942): 385–94; Freeman, *Thomas Kyd,* pp. 39–48; Erne, *Beyond* The Spanish Tragedy, pp. 51–3, 57–9, 81–2, 146–50; and Harold Jenkins (ed.), *Hamlet* (London, 1982), pp. 82–5.

(A) 'Noverint' or 'noverint-maker' were cant terms for scrivener (from the formal commencement of documents, "Noverint universi per praesentes", i.e. "Know all men by these present") ... distinctly derisive in the Elizabethan era' (Freeman, p. 2), and referring to the profession of Kyd's father.

(B) 'English *Seneca* ... yeeldes many good sentences' refers to *The Spanish Tragedy*, which begins with a prologue featuring the Ghost of Andrea and Revenge, obviously recalling the Ghost of Tantalus and Fury in the prologue to Seneca's *Thyestes*. Moreover, 'the opening lines of the third act follow Seneca's *Agamemnon* (ll.57–73) so closely that Kyd could expect part of his audience to recognize the debt to Seneca', while others would notice the Senecan allusions in Hieronimo's *Vindicta mihi* soliloquy (Erne, p. 81). Nashe's sneer that Kyd was dependent on English translations was grossly inaccurate, since he could write Latin verse.

(C) The phrase 'whole Hamlets' refers to a Senecan-style tragedy, and might identify Kyd as the author of the play *Hamlet*, which Philip Henslowe recorded as having been performed at the Newington Butts theatre on 9 June 1594, and to which Thomas Lodge referred two years later in *Wit's Miserie*, writing of 'ye ghost which cried so miserally, at ye Theator like an oister wife, *Hamlet, revenge*' (Østerberg, pp. 392–3; Erne, pp. 149–53). As for the phrase 'Bloud is a beggar', presumably from the lost *Hamlet* play, Østerberg (pp. 343–4) pointed out that *The True Tragedie of Richard the Third*, a Queen's Men play, which 'has many indisputable links with Kyd', includes the collocation 'blood is a threatner'.[74]

(D) Nashe's allusion to 'the Kid in *Aesop*' is an intentional pun on Kyd's name, but it confuses Aesop with an episode in the May eclogue of Spenser's *Shepheardes Calendar*,[75] which Nashe in fact echoes.

---

74. See *The True Tragedy of Richard the Third 1594*, ed. W.W. Greg (Oxford, 1929; Malone Society Reprints), 900–901: 'for blood is a threatner and will have revenge'.

75. See Spenser, *The Shorter Poems*, pp. 77–81. In this episode (*Maye*, 170–305) a buck-kid, left alone at home, is visited by a fox, in the guise of a peddler. Just like Shakespeare's Autolycus, the fox feigns injury to attract the kid's attention, dazzles him with some trinkets, gains entry to the house, and devours him.

Spenser describes the peddler's mirror as 'a glass ... Wherein, while Kiddy unawares did look, | He was so enamoured with the newell [novelty] | That ...'; Nashe refers to the Kid being 'enamoured with the Foxes new fangles' (Østerberg, pp. 389–901; Freeman, pp. 44–5). Kyd often quotes Aesop, but so did many other writers.

(E) The reference to 'Italian translations' alludes to the English tract, *The Housholders Philosophie* (entered in the Stationers' Register on 6 February 1588), 'translated by T.K.' from Tasso, and incontestably by Kyd.

(F) Nashe's jibe about 'those, that thrust *Elisium* into hell' mocks a passage in the opening scene of *The Spanish Tragedy* where Andrea records how, in the underworld, he had 'trod the middle path, | Which brought me to the fair Elysian green' (1.1.72–3). Lukas Erne's careful scrutiny of this passage has shown that Kyd did not confuse Virgil's account of Aeneas' descent to the underworld (*Aeneid* 6.540–56), as Nashe alleged. Kyd consciously differed from his classical model by adding to the Virgilan alternatives of Tartarus or Elysium a third path. Kyd hints at a kind of Christian purgatory from which Andrea's soul (like the Ghost of Hamlet's father) has returned to earth to supervise the revenge it has been promised. Erne also showed that Kyd may have been inspired by a thematically related passage in Garnier's *Cornélie*, of which his translation appeared in 1594 (Erne, pp. 51–5).

(G) Nashe's jeer at one who can 'bodge up a blanke verse with ifs and ands' refers to a line in *The Spanish Tragedy*, Lorenzo's exclamation 'What, villain, ifs and ands?' (2.1.77), a scene which was parodied in Jonson's *Poetaster* years later (Freeman, pp. 45–6).

(H) Finally, Nashe's mockery of those who 'spend two or three howers in turning over French *Dowdie*' uses a scatological term ('dudie' or 'doudy', meaning excrement), possibly alluding to Kyd's translation of Garnier's *Cornélie*, which, as Josef Schick suggested,[76] he may have begun (or completed) some years before its 1594 publication, perhaps in 1588–9. Or it might just be a coarse jest.

---

76. Schick, *Spanish Tragedy*, pp. xiii–xv.

Nashe described his outburst as having been written in a 'declamatorie vaine', suggesting that it was not to be taken entirely seriously, the *declamatio* being a rhetorical genre connected with mock praise and mock blame. He also tried to cover his traces by directing his remarks against 'a sort of shifting companions', where 'sort' means 'group'; but Nashe elsewhere used the plural when a single author was meant (Freeman, pp. 40–41; Erne, p. 150). Arthur Freeman was reluctant to postulate 'a presumptive socio-artistic split in the [fifteen-] eighties between the self-educated artisans of the drama like Kyd and Shakespeare and the college men like Nashe, Marlowe, and Greene' (p. 47), but that is surely one element both in Nashe's jibes against Kyd and in Greene's attack on Shakespeare in 1592. As G. K. Hunter put it, 'the attacks on these two dramatists in the pamphlets of 1589–92 tell us very clearly that they were regarded, by some of the inner group at least, as unqualified interlopers, incapable of genuine scholarship, pilfering employment from better men, and acquiring reputations for work they could only have stolen from the university-trained writers around them'.[77] Despite his professional hostility to a less well-educated dramatist, Nashe was in fact quite correct in drawing attention to a few errors in Kyd's Italian translation.[78] To sum up, Nashe's long and exuberant piece of mockery establishes that *The Spanish Tragedy* was known in the London theatre long before Henslowe's single record of it being performed, and it seems to suggest that Kyd may have been the author of an earlier *Hamlet*.[79] At all events it records Nashe's not altogether welcoming reaction to the fact that a new grammar-school product had appeared on the London theatrical scene, one who represented a sufficiently great challenge to the university-educated writers as to be worth a sarcastic page or two designed to put him in his place. However, it is unlikely that anyone outside Nashe's circle recognized the object of the attack. Apart from

77. G. K. Hunter, *English Drama 1586–1642. The Age of Shakespeare* (Oxford, 1997), p. 69. See also pp. 22–34, 85–6 for a perceptive analysis of the University Wits' status anxieties.

78. See Boas, *Works of Thomas Kyd*, pp. 446–57, and Lovascio, pp. 252–3.

79. The case for Kyd's authorship of a lost *Hamlet* has recently been urged by Lukas Erne (pp. 146–56). I am sympathetic to this argument but share Freeman's view (pp. 174–5) that the evidence does not offer sufficient substance for further discussion.

mockery, Nashe made no serious criticisms, and his satire had no effect on Kyd's growing status as a dramatist. Indeed, within two or three years Nashe happily joined Kyd in writing the play that Henslowe called '*harey the vi*', a great success at the Rose theatre in the season of summer 1592.

As we have seen, there is some evidence that Kyd was associated with the Queen's Men in the mid-1580s, and while no definite record exists of any plays written for them, the internal evidence for his authorship of *King Leir* is very strong. The crucial step, as far as we can tell, was that in about 1587 (calculating back from the 'vi yeares' service that he counted in 1593),[80] Kyd transferred his allegiance to Lord Strange's Men, the company in the service of Ferdinando, fifth Earl of Derby. Earlier companies connected with the Derby family had been a mixture of actors and tumblers, but their Elizabethan formation was a formidable group of actors, many of whom were to have long and influential careers.[81] Their leading actor was Edward Alleyn, who retained his status as a member of the company patronized by Charles Howard, Lord Admiral, in a flexible amalgamation between the two companies which lasted from 1589–90 until 1594. In that year several troupes collapsed during the plague that devastated London. The other members of Strange's Men mentioned in a Privy Council document of May 1593 included William Kemp, Thomas Pope, John Heminges, Augustine Phillips, and George Brian.[82] They enjoyed a 'remarkable success . . . in the winter of 1591–2, during which they were called upon to give six performances at Court . . . as against one each allotted to the Queen's, Sussex's, and Hertford's men'. Modern theatre historians agree about their eminence: one writes that the company reached 'the pinnacle of their national reputation in 1591–3' (Thomson, p. 41); another, that 'Lord Strange's Men had been formed and [were] working at a high level

---

80. See his Letters to Puckering, discussed below.

81. My account of Strange's Men is largely based on Chambers, *Elizabethan Stage*, 2:118–27, and Andrew Gurr, *The Shakespearian Playing Companies* (Oxford, 1996), pp. 259–77. See also Carol Chillington Rutter (ed.), *Documents of the Rose Playhouse*, rev. edn. (Manchester, 1999); Peter Thomson, *Shakespeare's Professional Career* (Cambridge, 1992), pp. 23–51.

82. In 1594–5 Kemp was one of the recently constituted Chamberlain's Men, as were Heminges, Pope, and Phillips: see Chambers, *Elizabethan Stage*, 2.326, 321, 333, 334.

for several months before moving into the Rose', at which time 'they were London's most prestigious company' (Rutter, p. 50); a third, that by 1591 they 'had climbed to the peak of esteem' (Gurr, pp. 258–9). That Kyd should have worked in turn for the two leading London theatre companies shows the high standing he enjoyed among his peers.

The first play that Kyd wrote for Strange's Men was *Fair Em*, which, as the undated Quarto (ca.1593) declares, 'was sundrie times publiquely cited in the honourable citie of London, by the right honourable the Lord Strange his servants'. Despite that claim, no record of its London performances has survived, and it exists in a much-abbreviated version, preserving about half of the original play (see chapter 6). Fortunately, Kyd's high standing in Lord Strange's Men can be confirmed from the records kept by Philip Henslowe of their season in the spring and early summer of 1592.[83] Between 19 February and 23 June, when an outbreak of plague closed the London theatres, they played six days a week for a period of eighteen weeks, apart from Good Friday and two other days, giving a total of 105 performances. When the theatres briefly re-opened, from 29 December to the end of January 1593, Henslowe recorded twenty-nine further performances. During their first season at the Rose, Strange's Men performed twenty-three different plays, and added three more to their repertoire in the shorter second season. Inevitably, many of those have perished, including such evidently popular plays as *Sir John Mandeville*, and *Henry of Cornwall*, which remained in their repertoire until the end. The plays of known authorship displayed the leading dramatists appearing side-by-side. Their opening performance was of Greene's *Friar Bacon and Friar Bungay*, which was performed seven times. Next came 'Muly Molloco', probably Peele's *The Battle of Alcazar*, which was played fourteen times. The third piece was Greene's *Orlando Furioso*, which had only one outing. Marlowe's *The Jew of Malta* was performed thirteen times, while the company gave a single performance of 'the gyves', Marlowe's play on the Duke of Guise, *The Massacre at Paris*.

---

83. See R.A. Foakes and R. T. Rickert (ed.), *Henslowe's Diary* (Cambridge, 1961, 2000), pp. 16–20; Rutter, *Rose Playhouse*, pp. 49–51, 57–60, 66–9; and Chambers, *Elizabethan Stage*, 2:121.

The co-authored play by Lodge and Greene, *A Looking Glass for London*, was performed four times, and a play of (as yet) unknown authorship, *A Knack to Know a Knave*, was played seven times.

Theatre historians document the activities of companies, their repertoire, and the venues at which they performed, but seldom consider the authors who provided the plays. An invisible demarcation line runs through contemporary scholarship, setting theatre historians on one side, literary historians on the other. Neither group has paid much attention to authorship attribution studies, an oversight which has perpetuated the occlusion of Kyd from the recognition he deserves as the leading playwright of Lord Strange's Men. Kyd's most famous play, 'Jeronymo', or *The Spanish Tragedy*, was given sixteen times in their seasons at the Rose in 1593–4. It was often accompanied, either on the day preceding or following, by the piece which Henslowe variously named 'spanes comedye donne oracioe', 'the comodey of doneoracio', 'doneoracio', and 'the comodey of Jeronymo', given seven times. This play must have been by Kyd, it being inconceivable that any other dramatist would have been allowed to write a comedy for Strange's Men on (presumably) the pre-history of Horatio before the events depicted in *The Spanish Tragedy*. Two respected scholars have argued (not altogether convincingly, I think) that parts of Kyd's 'comodey' survive in a short burlesque play, *The First Part of Ieronimo* (1605).[84] The third play which came mostly from Kyd's pen, I shall argue elsewhere, was *harey the vi*, performed on 3, 7, 11, and 28 March; 5, 13, and 21 April; 4, 7, 14, 19, and 25 May; 12 and 19 June. On 16 March Henslowe noted simply receipts for *harey*, which could refer to another play in Strange's repertory, *harey of cornwell*. In the short winter season *harey the vi* was performed on 16 and 31 January 1593, in all a total of sixteen outings, with average receipts over £2. The biggest earners of this season, earning over £3, were that play and *The Spanish Tragedy*. In fact, of the 134 recorded performances by Strange's Men, thirty-nine, or more than a quarter, were of plays

---

84. Andrew S. Cairncross (ed.), *[The Spanish Comedy, or] The First Part of Hieronimo and The Spanish Tragedy [or Hieronimo is Mad Again]* (London, 1967); Erne, *Beyond* The Spanish Tragedy, pp. 14–46.

wholly or partly by Kyd. If we add to this point his authorship of *Fair Em*, Kyd emerges as the foremost dramatist of Lord Strange's Men. Henslowe also recorded two performances of Kyd's *King Leir* at the Rose theatre (the Queen's Men and Sussex's Men acting together) on 6 and 8 April 1594, five months before Kyd's death, in August. There were also two performances of *Hamlet* (if that was Kyd's) on 8 and 9 June.[85]

Another relevant detail which theatre historians have missed concerning Kyd the playwright, is the fact that he alone of the four known dramatists whose work was performed by Strange's Men served his patron in another capacity. From about 1588 to 1593 he was employed by Strange, probably as a secretary responsible for correspondence in both English and Latin, and for preparing official legal documents. Kyd's loyalty to his patron can be seen from the prominence that he and his co-author Nashe, gave in *harey vi* to the character of Talbot, a distinguished ancestor of Strange, who appears only in this play among the surviving corpus of Elizabethan drama. (Nashe's authorship of Act 1 of *1 Henry VI* has been firmly settled.[86]) Nashe had just as much reason to praise Lord Strange as Kyd, for in the summer of 1592 Strange became Nashe's patron. In *Pierce Penilesse* (entered in the Stationers' Register on 8 August 1592), Nashe celebrated those 'patrons and Benefactors' whose 'exceeding bountie and liberalitie' provide writers with material support, singling out 'thou, most courteous Amyntas'.[87] McKerrow recorded that, long ago, 'Malone identified the Amintas of the present passage with Ferdinando Stanley . . . who is alluded to under the same pastoral name in Spenser's *Colin Clout*, 1595', an identification with which F. P. Wilson concurred.[88] It is no coincidence that Kyd and Nashe should have elevated Talbot to such eminence, and added a complete list of all the titles which Lord Strange's ancestor had earned, including the obscure 'Lord Strange of Blackmere' (4.7.65).

85. Foakes and Rickert (ed.), *Henslowe's Diary*, p. 21; Rutter, *Rose Playhouse*, pp 80–81.

86. See Vickers, 'Incomplete Shakespeare', 311–52, esp. 328–39, 343–5.

87. McKerrow (ed.), *Works of Thomas Nashe*, 1:243.

88. Ibid., 4:151, and F. P. Wilson's *Supplement* to *Works of Thomas Nashe*, 5:15–16. Wilson convincingly argued that Nashe also dedicated *The Choice of Valentines* to Lord Strange (5:141 n. 1).

The fact that Nashe and Kyd were now co-authors and colleagues, both in Strange's employ, casts a curious light retrospectively on Nashe's satiric attack on Kyd three years earlier. Was a reconciliation necessary, or did Kyd accept it as normal in that context?

Letters to Puckering (1593)

The fact that Kyd had been in the service of a noble lord from about 1588 to 1593 only emerged in 1899, when F. S. Boas published a letter that Kyd wrote in June 1593 to Lord Keeper Puckering.[89] This letter also gave the first inkling that Kyd had been associated with Marlowe by an accident of employment that gave rise to a tragic series of events. In April 1593 an outbreak of xenophobia in London resulted in offensive libels attacking foreigners being circulated, and on 5 May a provocative verse ultimatum calling for their expulsion was posted on the walls of Austin Friars, the Dutch church in Broad Street. Only the opening four lines of this poem had been known until 1973, when Arthur Freeman discovered a manuscript containing all 54 lines.[90] This 'Libell' expressed xenophobic sentiments still current in these islands (such as: foreigners damage British jobs by undercutting our merchants' prices, working for lower wages, living 'twenty in one house', marrying our women), and threatened that

> Weele cut your throates, in your temples praying
> Not paris massacre so much blood did spill
> As we will doe just vengeance on you all . . .   (39–41)

That bloodthirsty allusion to the massacre of French Protestants on St Bartholomew's Day 1572 could also be seen as a reference to Marlowe's play *The Massacre at Paris*, which Lord Strange's Men had performed at

---

89. See Boas, 'New Light on Marlowe and Kyd', *The Fortnightly Review*, 65: 386 (Feb. 1899): 212–25, and 'The Arrest of Thomas Kyd', *The Fortnightly Review*, 66: 393 (Sept. 1899): 519–22, and his edition of *The Works of Thomas Kyd*, pp. ix, cviii–cx. The second letter was published by Ford K. Brown in the *Times Literary Supplement*, 2 June 1921 (Freeman, *Thomas Kyd*, p. 30).

90. Arthur Freeman, 'Marlowe, Kyd and the Dutch Church Libel', *English Literary Renaissance*, 3 (1973): 44–52.

the Rose, on 30 (26) January 1593.[91] The last few lines of the 'Libell' could also be seen as a reference to Marlowe, for the poet inveighs against those in authority who tolerate the foreigners 'for lucres sake':

> For which our swords are whett, to shed their blood
> And for a truth let it be understoode
> Flye, Flye, and never returne.   (52–4)

The poem ends with a declaration of authorship, '*per* Tamberlaine'. The Privy Council can be forgiven for seeing this as another reference to Marlowe and his most famous play, and thus a declaration of authorship. Matthew Dimmock has convincingly ascribed the authorship of this libel to Thomas Deloney.[92] In 1588 Deloney published three single-sheet ballads on the Armada, which predicted that the Spaniards will 'cut our throats, | as we lye in our beds. | Our childrens brains, to dash upon the ground'; another warned that they intend to 'deflower | our virgins in our sight: | And in the cradle cruelly | the tender babe to smite'. As Dimmock noted, in June 1595 Deloney 'and two other members of the Weavers' Company were identified as authors of a printed letter to the Ministers and Elders of the French and Dutch churches, complaining at the conduct of immigrant weavers and merchants', who 'flaunt their freedoms "even to the very cutting of our throats"'. The Ministers complained to the authorities 'and had Deloney and his accomplices imprisoned in Newgate jail'.

Arthur Freeman justifiably takes this poem to be the 'probable first cause of Marlowe's implication in the libel affair',[93] but the first victim was Kyd. At their next meeting the Privy Council 'instructed their officers "to make search and aprehend everie person so to be suspected" of writing these libels, giving them authoritie "to make like search in anie the chambers, studies, chestes, or other like places for al manner of

---

91. Foakes and Rickert (ed.), *Henslowe's Diary*, p. 20.

92. Matthew Dimmock, 'Tamburlaine's curse. An answer to a great Marlowe mystery', *Times Literary Supplement*, 19 Nov 2010, pp. 16–17. He concludes his essay: 'The riots never came, and Christopher Marlowe was [Deloney's] only victim'.—No, the real victim was Kyd. Oddly enough, Mark Bradbeer, unaware of Dimmock's essay, subsequently ascribed the poem to Marlowe: see 'Authorship of the 1593 Dutch Church Libel Poem', *Notes and Queries* 65 (2018): 502–4.

93. Freeman, 'Marlowe, Kyd and the Dutch Church Libel', p. 51.

writings or papers."[94] As Freeman suggests, the Council's officers, knowing that Marlowe and Kyd were associated, probably set out to arrest Marlowe, but he was staying at Thomas Walsingham's house in Scadbury, Kent.[95] Instead, on about 11–12 May 1593 they seized Kyd, having found in his possession a manuscript which, they believed, contained certain '"vile hereticall Conceiptes denying the deity of Jhesus Criste our Saviour found emongst the papers of Thomas Kydd prisoner'"; to which another hand has added, presumably on a later occasion, 'which he affirmethe that he had from Marlowe'.[96]

Modern scholarship has shown that the 'papers' in Kyd's possession were a three-page excerpt from an early sixteenth-century Theistic treatise, quoted and refuted in John Proctor's *The Fal of the Late Arrian* (1549). The authorities failed to recognize that the pages had been copied from a printed book over 40 years old and were certainly not 'atheistic'.[97] However, the Privy Council had given its officers licence to seize any suspects and 'put them to the torture in Bridewel, and by th'extremitie thereof . . . draw them to discover their knowledge concerning the said libells'. The Bridewell torture was indeed extreme, for some of those who suffered it were literally broken and had to be carried away on a stretcher.[98] On 18 May the Privy council issued a warrant for

94. Ibid., p. 45.

95. See Charles Nicholl, *The Reckoning. The Murder of Christopher Marlowe*, rev. edn. (London, 2002), pp. 53–4, 400–401. Nicholl believes that both the Dutch Libel and the excerpt from the anti-Arianist tract were intentional incriminations of Marlowe by government authorities. Park Honan, however, in *Christopher Marlowe Poet and Spy* (Oxford, 2005), rejects such 'conspiracy theories' (p. 245), citing Marlowe's love of confrontation and uttering shocking opinions (p. 248). As he well observes, 'Anyone wishing to accuse [Marlowe] of atheism would not have needed to suborn the searchers of Kyd's papers . . .' (p. 338).

96. Boas printed a facsimile of the first letter, with a transcription misreading Kyd's 'vi yeeres' as 'ii'. I quote from Freeman, *Thomas Kyd* (1967, pp. 181–3), expanding contractions.

97. See W.D. Briggs, 'On a Document concerning Christopher Marlowe', *Studies in Philology*, 20 (1923): 153–9, and G.T. Buckley, 'Who was the late Arrian?', *Modern Language Notes*, 49 (1934): 500–503.

98. In 'Thomas Kyd and the letters to Pickering', *Notes and Queries* 251 (2006): 458–61, Rebekah Owens found a contradiction between accounts of the torture's severity and Kyd's ability to write a legible hand in his letters to Puckering. However, if the authorities wanted

one of their officers 'to repair to the house of Mr. T. Walsingham, in Kent' and to bring Marlowe before them. Marlowe was examined but released on 20 May, with instructions 'to give his daily attendance on his Lordships, until he shall be licensed to the contrary'. But within little more than a week, on the evening of 30 May, following a day's drinking in a Deptford tavern, Marlowe was stabbed to death in a quarrel.

At some point following Marlowe's death Kyd wrote two letters to Sir John Puckering, Lord Keeper of the great seal, principal officer of the Privy Council.[99] Kyd complained about the 'pains' and 'undeserved tortures' he had undergone and denied that he had ever been guilty of that 'deadly thing' atheism, in thought or word. His explanation in his first letter of how these excerpts came to be in his possession is poignant in the extreme:

> When I was first suspected for that Libel that concerned the state, amongst those waste and idle papers (which I cared not for) and which unasked I did deliver up, were found some fragments of a disputation touching that opinion, affirmed by Marlowe to be his, and shuffled with some of mine (unknown to me) by some occasion of our writing in one chamber two years since.

That Kyd should have voluntarily yielded up the documents which incriminated him, and which were among the jumble of papers resulting from his having shared a room with Marlowe, shows his possession of a clear conscience, but it is a dreadful irony that it should have resulted in unjust and life-destroying torture. Although Marlowe scholars have not thanked him for doing so, it is understandable that Kyd should have wished to distance himself from that 'irreligious' scoffer. Marlowe's atheism was notorious, condemned by several contemporaries, The significance of Kyd's reactions to our understanding of his mind and temper is that he partially defines himself in opposition to Marlowe. 'That I should love or be familiar friend, with one so irreligious, were [would

---

documentary evidence in the prisoner's own handwriting, they might well have instructed their officers to hurt Kyd in other parts of his body.

99. The letters are quoted from the modernized text edited by Rebekah Owens and Daniel Starza Smith to appear in Vickers (ed.), *The Collected Works of Thomas Kyd*, vol. 2.

have been] very rare', Kyd avows, citing a maxim from Cicero's *On Friendship*—that '"they are worthy of friendship who have within their own souls the reason for their being loved", which neither was in him, for person, qualities, or honesty, besides he was intemperate and of a cruel heart, the very contrary to which, my greatest enemies will say by me'. In addition to Marlowe's scandalous utterances, Kyd and others disliked 'his other rashness in attempting sudden privy injuries to men', the brawls that he got into. Sometimes

> they did overslip [overlook], though often reprehend him for it. And for which, God is my witness, as well by my Lord's commandment as in hatred of his life and thoughts I left and did refrain his company.

Kyd was most of all disturbed by Marlowe's 'monstrous opinions' concerning religion, some of which he recorded in the second, unsigned letter.[100] These included Marlowe's custom 'to jest at the divine scriptures, gibe at prayers, and strive in argument to frustrate and confute what has been spoken or written by prophets and such holy men'. Kyd placed first the most shocking of these jests: 'He would report St John to be Our Saviour Christ's Alexis—I cover it with reverence and trembling—that is, that Christ did love him with an extraordinary love'. In Virgil's Second *Eclogue* Alexis is the object of the shepherd Corydon's unrequited love. Claims that Christ was a homosexual were commonplace in heretical thought, but Kyd's shock testifies how repugnant they were to orthodox Christians at that time. The second of Marlowe's gibes that Kyd records throws light on his own writing plans: 'That for me to write a poem of St Paul's conversion as I was determined he said would be as if I should go write a book of fast and loose, esteeming Paul a juggler'.[101] That Kyd was planning to write a poem on the conversion

---

100. Robert D. Parsons, in 'Thomas Kyd's Letters', *Notes and Queries*, 225 (1980): 140–41, doubts the authenticity of the unsigned letter on palaeographical grounds, but Lukas Erne records 'the judgment of Malcolm Parkes, former professor of palaeography at the University of Oxford . . . that the consistency of a series of scribal habits and practices in the two letters strongly suggests that they were written by the same hand': Erne, *Beyond* The Spanish Tragedy, p. 216 n.13.

101. 'Fast and loose' was an old cheating game, 'in which people bet on whether the end of a coiled rope is fastened or not' (David Crystal and Ben Crystal, *Shakespeare's Words. A Glossary*

of St Paul opens a new perspective on him as a devout Christian poet, and confirms the sincerity of his affirmation in the first letter that 'Of my religion and life I have already given some instance to the late commissioners and of my reverend meaning to the state'.

For Kyd the disastrous consequence of this accusation, apart from the shattering effects of the torture, was that he had been dismissed from the service of 'my Lord, whom I have served almost these 6 years now, in credit until now, and now am utterly undone'. Kyd's account of how he came to know Marlowe is revealing of the nature of Kyd's life in the service of this noble lord:

> My first acquaintance with this Marlowe, rose upon his bearing name to serve my Lord although his Lordship never knew his service, but in writing for his players, for never could my Lord endure his name, or sight, when he had heard of his conditions, nor would indeed the form of divine prayer used daily in his Lordship's house, have quadred[102] with such reprobates.

It is indeed unlikely that Marlowe's 'conditions'—in Elizabethan English, 'personal qualities, ways, morals'—would have endeared him to a household in which communal prayers were observed. This tragic episode, which destroyed Kyd's life, may at least shed some light on his employment. The fact that Kyd's patron supported a company of players, for whom Marlowe produced at least one play, narrows down the candidates to three: Ferdinando Stanley, Lord Strange, who became Earl of Derby in September 1593; Henry Radcliffe, fourth Earl of Sussex; and Henry Herbert, second earl of Pembroke. Freeman opted for Sussex while Erne argued for Pembroke.[103] I have always thought that Lord Strange was the more likely candidate, a conclusion that Marlowe scholars have long

---

and *Language Companion* (London, 2002). Shakespeare refers to it three times. The word 'juggler' had purely negative connotations, 'conjurer, trickster, fraud'.

102. As Rebekah Owen notes, 'the rare verb "quader" is unique to Kyd'. *OED* gives two senses: (v.1) 'To square (a number)' and (v. 2), used intransitively, 'To conform; to agree or be in harmony *with*'. Kyd uses it in *The Householder's Philosophy* in connection with 'the quadering and making even of the entries with the expenses' (995), so 'suited'.

103. See Freeman, *Thomas Kyd*, pp. 32–7; Erne, *Beyond* The Spanish Tragedy, pp. 227–9.

AN INTERRUPTED LIFE 45

accepted. Of recent biographers, David Riggs concludes that 'Thomas Kyd entered Strange's service in 1587–88, around the time that his employer decided to patronize a newly formed company of adult actors', which soon 'became the premier acting company in London'.[104] With Alleyn as its leader, for whom Marlowe had written the role of Tamburlaine, it was natural that Marlowe also 'attached himself to Strange's Men, and in this way crossed the outer threshold of Ferdinando Stanley's personal retinue. The playwright Thomas Kyd had a proper place, perhaps the office of secretary, in Strange's household'.[105] Earlier arguments that Marlowe worked for Strange were confirmed by R.B. Wernham's discovery in 1976 of documents implicating Marlowe in the forging of Dutch coins in Flushing in the winter of 1591–2. Betrayed by the informer Richard Baines, 'Christofer Marly, by his profession a scholar', was brought before the authorities in January 1592. The Governor reported to Burghley that 'the scholer [Marlowe] sais himself to be very wel known both to the Earle of Northumberland and my Lord Strang[e]'.[106] A recent study of Lord Strange's Men has confirmed that Kyd was employed by Strange.[107]

We do not know when Kyd entered Strange's service, nor on what occasion. If a date of 1587 for *The Spanish Tragedy* is correct, that would have antedated his appointment. Perhaps that play drew him to Strange's notice, or perhaps it was his loyal *Verses of Prayse and Joye* (1587), celebrating the Queen's escape from the Babington plot. Marlowe wrote *The Jew of Malta* for Strange's Men 'by 1592', according to one authority,[108]

104. David Riggs, *The World of Christopher Marlowe* (London, 2004), pp. 259–61. See also Nicholl, *The Reckoning*, pp. 268–9.

105. Riggs, *World of Christopher Marlowe*, p. 261.

106. See E. B. Wernham, 'Christopher Marlowe at Flushing in 1592', *English Historical Review* 91 (1976): 344–5; Riggs, *World of Christopher Marlowe*, pp. 273–9; Nicholl, *The Reckoning*, pp. 278–85, and Honan, *Christopher Marlowe Poet and Spy*, p. 243.

107. See Lawrence Manley and Sally-Beth MacLean, *Lord Strange's Men and their Plays* (New Haven, CT, London, 2014), pp. 162, 399 n. Although a valuable study of the company in its theatrical context, both in London and on its frequent tours, Manley's attempts to associate Shakespeare with Strange's Men, and even to ascribe sole authorship of 1 *Henry VI* to him, fly in the face of well-attested scholarship: see my review in *Modern Philology* 113 (2015): E81–E86.

108. Alfred Harbage, *Annals of English Drama 975–1700*, rev. S. Schoenbaum (London, 1964), p. 52. Wiggins in *British Drama* dates it 1589 (2.465–70).

46 CHAPTER 1

and *The Massacre at Paris* by January 1593. The play that Marlowe was writing when they shared a room in 1591, then, may have been *The Jew of Malta*, which shows many signs of Kyd's influence.[109] As for the location of this room, Kyd, being in the service of Lord Strange, most probably lived in the Derby family's London residence. We know that in October 1552 Edward, Earl of Derby, paid £117. 6s. 8d. for some ground in Cannon Row, near the Thames (where Westminster Bridge now stands), to build a new house. In 1570 he spent a further £321 7s. 10d. for two additional buildings in the garden side, and in 1603 Earl William extended the house further.[110] These large sums of money suggest that Derby House was large enough to accommodate two dramatists sharing a room.[111]

Having been dismissed from his position in the summer of 1593, by a patron anxious not to offend the authorities, in January 1594 Kyd dedicated his translation/adaptation of *Cornélie* to the Countess of Sussex, probably in the hope of finding a future employer.[112] In his dedication Kyd described himself as 'having no leisure . . . but such as evermore is travailed with the afflictions of the mind, than which the world affords no greater misery', one of the bleakest personal statements in any Elizabethan dedication, from a writer cut adrift in the world through no fault of his own. A tragic note breaks into Kyd's conventional appeal for indulgence to the work's deficiencies: 'what grace that excellent Garnier hath lost by my default, I shall beseech your Honour to repair, with the regard of those so bitter times, and privy broken passions that I endured in the writing it'. Kyd imagines the Countess 'passing . . . a winter's week [reading] desolate Cornelia', and promises her with 'my next summer's better travail, with the tragedy of Portia', that is, Garnier's *Porcie*. But the parish register of St Mary Colchurch soon carried the entry: 'Thomas

---

109. See Thomas Merriam, 'Possible light on a Kyd canon', *Notes and Queries* 240 (1995): 340–41; Honan, *Christopher Marlowe Poet and Spy*, pp. 250–53.

110. B. Coward, *The Stanleys, Lords Stanley and the Earls of Derby, 1385–1672. The Origins, Wealth and Power of a Landowning Family* (Manchester, 1983), pp. 25, 27, 30, 57. See also Robert Lemon (ed.), *Calendar of State Papers 1547–1580* (London, 1856), p. 404.

111. I owe this information to Lawrence Manley.

112. Erne, *Beyond* The Spanish Tragedy, pp. 211, 229.

Kydd the sonne of ffrauncis Kydd was buryed the 15 day of August 1594.'[113] He had evidently returned to live with his parents, who on 30 December formally renounced the administration of their son's estate. As Freeman explained, they were 'simply attempting to escape their dead son's creditors' (ibid.). Kyd was 36 when he died, possibly from ill health following his torture in Bridewell a year previously.

In his career as a dramatist, spanning the years 1587–94, Kyd wrote five sole-authored plays and co-authored two others—one with Nashe, the other with Shakespeare. He translated a treatise by Tasso from the Italian, a play by Garnier from the French, and published verses in English and Latin. That may well have been typical output for a professional dramatist and translator who liked to keep busy. Shakespeare maintained a similar productivity, but in a career extending three times as long from 1591 to 1612. He wrote thirty-eight plays, both sole- and co-authored, two long narrative poems, a collection of sonnets, and some lyrics. It is tantalizing to think what Kyd might have produced, had he enjoyed Shakespeare's longevity and secure working conditions.

113. Freeman, *Thomas Kyd*, p. 38.

2

The Spanish Tragedy

THE FIRST OF Kyd's plays to be published was his undisputed master-piece, *The Spanish Tragedy*. Most scholars date it to a period before the Spanish Armada, variously 1583–4, 1583–7, 1585–7, and 1587.[1] Had it been written after 1588, they argue, it could hardly *not* have mentioned this famous victory in a drama that represents a war between Spain and Portugal, especially since Hieronimo presents a masque portraying three *English* warriors who allegedly defeated the Portuguese and Spanish forces (1.5.23–32). In terms of verse style, the play is an outlier in its sparing use of feminine endings, a prosodic resource in which Kyd was an innovator. In *Soliman and Perseda* (1588) he used this extra syllable at a rate of 10.8 percent, a figure only matched by Shakespeare in *2 Henry VI* (1592), with 10.4 percent.

The text became the object of a dispute between two London sta-tioners, Edward White and Abell Jeffes, in the spring of 1592. Jeffes had apparently published an (unregistered) edition of *The Spanish Tragedy* and had been caught printing *Arden of Faversham*, which had been legitimately entered to Edward White on 3 April 1592, for which Jeffes was 'committed to ward', remaining in prison until December. White seems to have retaliated by acquiring an authentic text which

---

1. See T.W. Baldwin, 'On the Chronology of Thomas Kyd's Plays', *Modern Language Notes*, 40 (1925): 343–9, revised in Baldwin, *On the Literary Genetics of Shakspere's Plays 1592–1594* (Urbana, IL, 1959), pp. 177–99; Schick (ed.), *Spanish Tragedy* (London, 1898, pp. xxi–xxv; Boas, *Works of Thomas Kyd*, pp. xxviii–xxxi; Freeman, *Thomas Kyd*, p. 77; Erne, *Beyond* The Spanish Tragedy, pp. 55–9; Wiggins, *British Drama*, 2.369–75.

he duly published. The title page of the only surviving copy, now in the British Library, reads:

The Spanish Tragedie, Containing the lamentable end of Don Horatio, and Bel-imperia: with the pitifull death of olde Hieronimo. Newly corrected and amended of such grosse faults as passed in the first impression. At London. Printed by Edward Allde, for Edward White.

The tit-for-tat nature of this dispute is shown by the fact that, on 6 October, while still in prison, 'Abell Jeffes Entred for his copie . . . a booke whiche is called the Spanishe tragedie of Don Horatio and Bellimpera'. On 18 December the Court of the Stationers' Company fined both men for publishing a title entered by the other and confiscated all copies of their editions. W.W. Greg summarized the ironic outcome of this dispute:

In the case of *The Spanish Tragedy* Jeffes's original edition, legitimate but defective, wholly perished, whereas White's superior but piratical edition has survived in a single copy. In that of *Arden of Faversham*, on the contrary, it is White's original edition, containing a sound text, that has survived in three copies, and Jeffes's piracy, perhaps a mere reprint, that has perished.[2]

In fact, Jeffes's original edition may not have 'wholly perished' but survived—at least in part—until the twentieth century. In 1909, the American drama scholar George P. Baker[3] published an essay strangely overlooked by Greg and all subsequent editors of *The Spanish Tragedy*, together with Kyd scholars. In it he recorded that some years previously he had bought at auction a copy of *The Spanish Tragedy*:

When it came to me, I found it was printed almost half in Roman type and in black letter. As an inexperienced bibliophile I felt sure that some unscrupulous bookseller had foisted on the public a pieced

2. W.W. Greg (ed.), *The Spanish Tragedy (1592)* (Oxford, 1949; Malone Society Reprints), pp. ix–x.

3. George Pierce Baker (1866–1935) published *The Development of Shakespeare as a Dramatist* (New York, 1907), and from 1905 onwards conducted a postgraduate course in playwriting at Harvard, called 'English 47': one of his students was Eugene O'Neill.

copy. As at the time there was no bibliography complete enough to clear up the matter, I returned the book.[4]

Later, having access to 'the work of Greg and others', Baker learned that none of the surviving editions is in black letter, and he could only ruefully speculate how this chimera, this 'composite copy of *The Spanish Tragedy*', might have been created. Since the surviving copy of White's edition is in Roman type, that printed by Jeffes must have been in black letter. Baker did not mention whether he collated this copy, but since it would be extremely unlikely that the division of the printed sheets would be identical in two independent editions, it was probably patched together with either a lacuna or an overlap between the two. The motives which led early modern printers to choose one type font or the other are not altogether clear, but the three surviving copies of White's piratical edition of *Arden of Faversham* are black letter, as are those of its second Quarto (1599); not until the third Quarto (1633) was it set in Roman type.

The title page of White's edition of *The Spanish Tragedy* names neither the author nor the theatre company (or companies) which had performed the play, and which, under different circumstances, might have claimed ownership. The fact that Jeffes and White seem to have had access to two different copies of the play may suggest that at least two companies had played it. Its first known performance—presumably a revival—was at the newly refurbished Rose Theatre, by Lord Strange's Men. Their backer, Philip Henslowe, noted in his ledger the receipt of 38 shillings for a performance of 'Joronymo' on 20 March.[5] Together with a related play, 'the comedy of Jeronymo', apparently a prequel, as we would call it (which may have shown the earlier love affair between Bel-imperia and Don Andrea), it was performed sixteen times between 20 March 1592 and 22 January 1593. The Quarto was reissued in 1594, with Jeffes and White sharing the printing and publishing, having settled their dispute.

4. George Pierce Baker, 'Some Bibliographic Puzzles in Elizabethan Quartos', *Bibliographical Society of America, Papers*, 4 (1909): 9–20, at p. 9.

5. Foakes and Rickert (ed.), *Henslowe's Diary*, p. 17.

Kyd's authorship only came to light when Thomas Heywood, in a vigorous defence of the theatre in his *Apology for Actors* (London, 1612), diligently collected evidence of the high standing of drama in earlier times, citing the fact that some Roman emperors sponsored plays. (However, this is an ambivalent testimony, since Nero included condemned criminals in the cast, who were really killed on stage.) For his latest witness Heywood called on an English play, which had just gone into its sixth edition:

> Therefor M. *Kid*, in the *Spanish* Tragedy, upon occasion presenting itselfe, thus writes.

> Why Nero thought it no disparagement,
> And Kings and Emperours have tane delight,
> To make experience of their wits in playes.[6]   (4.1.87–9)

(In a 1656 catalogue, discovered in modern times, the bookseller Edward Archer attributed *The Spanish Tragedy* to one 'Tho. Kyte'.) The tenuous status that Kyd's work held for posterity is shown by the fact that Heywood's authorship identification disappeared from view until 1767, when Richard Farmer retrieved it for his *Essay on the Learning of Shakespeare.*[7]

My discussion of the play will examine several fundamental characteristics of Kyd's dramaturgy, which I shall revert to in the chapters discussing both the canonical plays and those I newly ascribe to him: the use of intrigue plots, the introduction of comedy into tragedy, and the depiction of vengeful women. The natural place to begin would be with his treatment of sources, but since no source is known for *The Spanish Tragedy* (apart from the Soliman and Perseda story), I shall first discuss his construction of intrigue plots.

---

6. Thomas Heywood, *An Apology for Actors* (London, 1612), sig. E3^v–E4^r.

7. See Rebekah Owens, 'Thomas Hawkins's attribution of the authorship of *The Spanish Tragedy*', *Notes and Queries*, 252 (2007): 74–5, and D. N. Smith (ed.), *Eighteenth Century Essays on Shakespeare* (Glasgow, 1903), pp. 210, 343.

52 CHAPTER 2

Kyd's excellence in plotting has long been recognized. The great German scholar, Gregor Sarrazin, comparing Kyd's dramaturgy with that of his contemporaries, observed that *The Spanish Tragedy* is better constructed than any play of Greene's (with the possible exception of *James IV*), and surpasses most of Marlowe's tragedies in this respect'.

> In Kyd especially we find a greater unity of plot, a stronger focus of interest upon fewer characters. More than any of his contemporaries, Kyd's tragedies may be called tragedies of intrigue. In this respect they recall Italian Renaissance tragedy. Shakespeare's *Hamlet* and *Othello* have a similar character.[8]

In 1919 G. Gregory Smith paid tribute to

> the advance which Kyd's plays show in construction, in the manipulation of plot, and in effective situation. Kyd is the first to discover the bearing of episode and of the 'movement' of the story on characterization, and the first to give the audience and reader the hint of the development of character which follows from this interaction. In other words, he is the first English dramatist who writes dramatically.[9]

Intermittently, later commentators have noted Kyd's development of intrigue as a driving plot element. The young T.S. Eliot granted Kyd's debts to the Senecan tradition, but found in *The Spanish Tragedy* 'another element' which, he speculated, 'may have relations among the Italian progeny of Seneca', containing 'nothing classical or pseudo-classical' in it:

> 'Plot' in the sense in which we find plot in *The Spanish Tragedy* does not exist for Seneca. He took a story perfectly well known to everybody, and interested his auditors entirely by his embellishments of description and narrative and by smartness and pungency of dialogue; suspense and surprise attached solely to verbal effects. *The*

---

8. Gregor Sarrazin, *Thomas Kyd und sein Kreis. Eine Litterarhistorische Untersuchung* (Berlin, 1892), p. 66. Unless otherwise noted, translations from the German are mine.

9. G.G. Smith, 'Marlowe and Kyd. Chronicle Histories', in A.W. Ward and A.R. Waller (eds), *The Drama to 1642, Part 1* (Cambridge, 1910), p. 163.

Spanish Tragedy, like the series of Hamlet plays, including Shakespeare's, has an affinity to our contemporary detective drama.[10]

That concluding analogy may seem condescending, but a leading classical scholar once described the plot of *Oedipus Tyrannos* as that of 'a detective novel'. Certainly, both plays are masterpieces of 'suspense and surprise'.

The intermittent progress of Kyd scholarship, which has yet to achieve the critical mass needed to establish a continuous tradition, has meant that earlier insights have seldom been followed up. When, in 1954, Madeleine Doran published *Endeavors of Art*, her outstanding synthesis of Renaissance theories of drama and the English vernacular response to a European tradition, she was in effect starting over again in describing Kyd's relation to his predecessors. Doran divided Elizabethan tragedy into 'three main types, according to theme and pattern: *De casibus* tragedy, or the fall of the mighty, with ambition as a chief motivating force; Italianate intrigue tragedy, with love or jealousy usually the central passion; and domestic tragedy, or the tragedy of crime in the lives of ordinary citizens'.[11] The first type derives from the traditional medieval conception of tragedy, and is represented in Tudor England primarily by the collection of stories from English history in *The Mirror for Magistrates*, although elements of it appear both in the chronicle plays based on the reign of an English King and in the struggles for political power that animate so many tragedies based on British and Roman history. Seneca's tragedies included plots based on tyranny, and others on 'revenge incited by jealousy', which became the main subject matter of 'the second great class of English renaissance tragedy, the Italianate tragedies of intrigue centered about crimes of passion' (p. 128). In this long-lived line of revenge play 'the central themes are love and jealous hatred, as they are in Seneca's *Medea, Agamemnon, Phaedra*, and the two

---

10. T.S. Eliot, '*Hamlet*' (*Athenaeum*, 26 September 1919) in *Selected Essays*, 3rd edn. (London, 1951), p. 142.

11. Madeleine Doran, *Endeavors of Art. A Study of Form in Elizabethan Drama* (Madison, WI, 1954), p. 115.

Hercules plays' (p. 130). By making this filiation Madeleine Doran was not 'treating "revenge" as a class of tragedy, but as a motive' which frequently operates in 'the Italianate tragedy of intrigue', a genre initiated by *The Spanish Tragedy*. Doran described Kyd's masterpiece as 'a lively play of intrigue, psychologically motivated, in which there is a love affair (as well as the motive of ambition) and in which revenge within revenge cleverly managed furnishes exciting action' (ibid.). As she demonstrated, the type of story on which these plays were based are found in 'the Italian *novelle* . . . turned out in great quantities in the Renaissance, well known in the original language as in French and English translations and offering a vast collection of stories featuring illicit love and its consequences' (pp. 131–8). These *novelle* also gave rise to native Italian tragedies, some of which were known in England.

While sketching in the antecedents for the centrality of intrigue in Kyd's plays, both tragic and romantic (*King Leir*, *Fair Em*), my aim is not to relate Kyd to previous drama, valuable though that topic may be. Rather, I want to try and establish a simple grammar of intrigue plots, to alert readers to the norms and conventions of this genre. The following reflections are unsystematic, intended as a repertoire or fund of narrative sequences which can structure plot sequences large and small. Further, each of them may appear more than once.

One person comes to feel that he or she lacks some thing, quality, or relationship that another person enjoys. The lack can be perceived as political (a crown; high office), social (status), material (riches), or erotic (a desirable man or woman). The person feeling this lack decides to remedy it by attacking the person/s who enjoy it. We may call him (or her) the "harmer".

The attack may be open, visible to all, as in Tamburlaine's desire for conquest and empire; but it is more often concealed, using intrigue and subterfuge.

The audience in the theatre, like the reader, is usually made aware of the intrigue. Sometimes a dramatist will present two or more characters preparing a plot, but more often the main plotter confides his intentions to the audience in a soliloquy. In *Julius Caesar*, for instance, we see Brutus taking part in a plot to kill the tyrant (2.1.10–227), apparently acting as an autonomous agent. But Cassius previously informed us that he has manipulated Brutus, and we have seen him doing so (1.3.308–22).

Some harmers work alone, as Claudius seems to have done in poisoning Hamlet's father. Others have accomplices: so Claudius involves Laertes in a double attempt to poison young Hamlet, by sword and cup. In this instance Laertes is fully informed of the subterfuge and agrees to join it. In other cases, the accomplice is given partial or misleading knowledge as to the reasons for the attack. Macbeth is shown labouring to convince the hired assassins that they owe it to their self-respect to kill Macduff (3.1.73–139).

In delegating the violent act to an accomplice, harmers gain a helper but lose their own autonomy. The harmer is then always at the mercy of the accomplice, who can simply renege on the contract, or else disclose the intrigue and the identity of the harmer to those s/he intends to harm, sometimes for a larger, or additional fee. Laertes fulfils Claudius's subterfuge but is outfenced and given a deadly blow by Hamlet. In remorse, before he dies, Laertes reveals Claudius's plot. As Machiavelli, the supreme authority on *ragione di stato* advised, 'Men should either be caressed or crushed; because they can avenge slight injuries, but not those that are very severe. Hence, any injury done to a man must be such that there is no need to fear his revenge'.[12]

As a result of the harmer's contract, the accomplice also becomes vulnerable. Anyone who is willing to hire them for a harmful action (murder in tragedies, slander in comedies) would be equally ready to destroy them once the contract is carried out. If they have foresight, accomplices can try to protect themselves by providing, or threatening to provide, incriminating evidence to the authorities.

---

12. Machiavelli, *The Prince*, ed. Quentin Skinner and Russell Price (Cambridge, 1988), p. 9. As L. Arthur Burd noted in his great edition, *Il Principe* (Oxford, 1891, 1968): this is 'A maxim which Machiavelli is never tired of repeating', citing numerous examples (pp. 188–9).

By initiating a violent course of action, the harmer opens himself to a set of unknowable consequences. Brutus and his fellow plotters destroy Julius Caesar, but despite Cassius's warnings they fail to realize the danger posed by Mark Antony, who kills them in turn. The law of unexpected consequences plays a major role in revenge plays.

All co-operative enterprises, good or evil, depend on an element of trust between the participants, which means that individuals must subordinate their own desires to help achieve the collective goal. Conspirators, or groups of harmers, must also be able to count on their fellows being well-intentioned, helping each other to achieve the intended harm.

In all intrigue one side of the action (that visible to the reader or theatregoer) is transparent, the other—that visible to the targeted person(s)—must be opaque. Plotters must feign harmless intentions while intending the opposite. In comedy the deception, which sometimes involves disguise, is usually for a purpose leading to social concord: choosing the right partners in marriage and protecting them from the wrong ones, or exposing socially destructive behaviour (a jealous husband in *The Merry Wives of Windsor*, an overbearing servant in *Twelfth Night*). In tragic intrigues not only the initial targets but society at large is damaged. Once put into action, malicious pretence is not easily controlled.

These general remarks are intended to outline some of the recurring features of intrigue plots. Kyd uses all these patterns of behaviour in both his tragedies and comedies, following conventions but also turning them to new purposes.

If we apply this simple model to *The Spanish Tragedy*, we can appreciate the care with which Kyd constructed the plot. The initial situation draws on harms committed before the play's action, during a battle between their respective armies over Portugal's refusal to pay tribute to Spain. In this battle a Spanish Knight, Don Andrea, was killed by the Portuguese Don Balthazar assisted by his halberdiers, against all the laws of chivalric combat. Balthazar was then defeated by Andrea's friend Horatio, son of

Hieronimo (the Spanish Knight Marshal), and brought back to Spain in captivity. We hear of Andrea's defeat three times.

(1) In the opening scene his ghost appears, attended by the allegorical figure of Revenge, to whom he briefly recounts his death (1.1.15–26) and subsequent journey to Hades, where Queen Proserpine gave him permission to return to earth, to watch over his revenge.

(2) In the second scene the Spanish King hears a report of the battle in which Andrea was killed and Balthazar captured (1.2.63–81), He then adjudicates a dispute between Horatio and Lorenzo, nephew to the Spanish king, as to who should receive the ransom and the spoils of battle. Balthazar is treated more like a guest than a captive, and Lorenzo, being of the same aristocratic class, becomes his associate (1.2.132–190).

(3) In the play's fourth scene Bel-imperia, daughter of the Duke of Castile, learns from Horatio how her beloved Andrea—who had 'In secret . . . possessed her' (1.1.10–11)—was killed (1.4.9–26). Horatio then reports how he captured Balthazar, gave Andrea's corpse a proper funeral (27–41), and took from the corpse the scarf Bel-imperia had given Andrea as a favour. Bel-imperia allows Horatio to keep it as a mark of gratitude and friendship (42–59). But, as the old adage has it, 'A gift always looks for a return', and she sees a use for Horatio.

From this point on two intrigue plots develop. Left alone, Bel-imperia reveals a sudden change of focus:

Yet what avails to wail Andrea's death,
From whence Horatio proves my second love?   (1.4.60–61)

This surprising change is brought about by Bel-imperia's desire to 're-venge the death of my beloved', an unexpected motivation for a female character in Elizabethan drama. However, she initially plans no violent action against Balthazar, only intending to use Horatio as a means of blocking the Portuguese prince's love for her:

I'll love Horatio, my Andrea's friend,
The more to spite the Prince that wrought his end.   (1.4.65–8)

It may seem rather ineffective for Bel-imperia to use her 'just disdain' to punish Balthazar for his 'murderous cowardice' in killing Andrea (69–75), but as a woman, according to Renaissance concepts of womanhood, she can hardly take any other action. However, her ostentatious favouring of Horatio (who is low born) in Balthazar's presence has an outcome that she certainly did not intend, for it generates the second intrigue plot.

Lorenzo, having taken on the role of helping Balthazar satisfy his desire for Bel-imperia, coolly takes stock of the situation and what needs to be done:

Some cause there is that lets you not be loved:
First that must needs be known and then removed.
What if my sister love some other knight?   (2.1.31–3)

Lorenzo emerges as the full-blown Machiavel, the first in Elizabethan drama.[13] He has a complete knowledge of the syntax of intrigue, with the appropriate vocabulary: 'I have already found a stratagem' (2.1.35), he says, and resolves to find the truth 'By force or fair means' (39). He co-opts Balthazar as an accomplice, demanding complete acquiescence in his plots:

My Lord, for once you shall be ruled by me,
Hinder me not whate'er you hear or see.   (2.1.37–8)

Lorenzo begins by cross-questioning Pedringano, Bel-imperia's servant, and by a mixture of threats and promises extracts from him confirmation that Bel-imperia loves Horatio (2.1.41–106). This corruption of a servant is an object-lesson in how an intriguer undermines his target. Pedringano is persuaded to betray his mistress, who 'reposeth all her trust' in him (2.1.61), for Lorenzo offers him in exchange 'both friendship and reward', promising to 'shield [him] from whatever can ensue' (61, 72–3). On the basis of Lorenzo's offered protection, Pedringano

13. See Freeman, *Thomas Kyd*, pp. 56–9.

vows to deceive his mistress ('What I have said . . . shall for me | Be still [always] conceal'd from Bel-imperia'), and enters into a contract of secrecy with Lorenzo, to

> Be watchful when, and where these lovers meet,
> And give me notice in some secret sort. (99–100)

Lorenzo defines for Balthazar's benefit the intriguer's means of corruption:

> Where words prevail not, violence prevails.
> But gold doth more than either of them both. (108–9)

Praising his own 'stratagem' (110), Lorenzo urges Balthazar on to his goal of gaining Bel-imperia's love with the euphemism of 'removing' Horatio:

> Do you but follow me and gain your love,
> Her favour must be won by his remove. (135–6)

In the space of two scenes (1.4, 2.1) Kyd has economically established two intrigue plots, which may be summed up in tabular form (see Table 2.1).

By making Pedringano break his loyalty to Bel-imperia Lorenzo has gained a decisive superiority, for the accomplice will penetrate her secrets. Here Kyd springs a surprise on his audience, for where Pedringano had promised to report the lovers' meeting to Lorenzo, he unexpectedly shows it to him, and to us. The lovers confront each other, their 'hidden smoke . . . turned to open flame' (2.2.2), unaware that '*Pedringano shows all to the Prince and Lorenzo, placing them in secret*' (2.2.6, *stage direction*). This bold use of theatrical space sets up a remarkable overhearing scene. The love declarations between Bel-imperia and Horatio on the main stage are overlooked and commented on by Balthazar and Lorenzo on an upper level. In this situation the lovers' plot is exposed and negated by a far better organized, but morally depraved intrigue,

TABLE 2.1.

Intriguer	Helper	Goal
Bel-Imperia	Horatio	Fulfil their love, and so frustrate Balthazar's desire
Lorenzo	Pedringano	Fulfil Balthazar's desire: murder Horatio

involving a corrupt servant deceiving his mistress. This betrayal of the trust basic to the terms of service would arouse far more disapproval in an Elizabethan audience than it can do for us, with our impersonal contracts of hire and salary.[14] A horrible irony hangs over the lovers' plan to meet at the 'pleasant bower' in Hieronimo's garden: 'The court were dangerous, that place is safe' (2.2.44), as Bel-imperia innocently proposes. The ironies become overwhelming in the scene where the lovers have planned to go 'to the bower | And there in safety pass a pleasant hour' (2.4.4–5). The deceived Bel-imperia has no doubt concerning Pedringano's reliability—'he is as trusty as my second self' (8–9), and she asks him to keep a look-out. But in an aside to us Pedringano follows his own self-interest: 'I'll deserve more gold, | By fetching Don Lorenzo to this match' (2.4.12–13). Bel-imperia is soon disabused of her trust, as Pedringano returns with Lorenzo, Balthazar, and Serberine, another 'helper'. She realizes that 'we are betrayed' and can only watch helplessly while her 'second love' suffers the same fate as her first. Any doubt as to whether the spectator's response to Lorenzo is moral or purely intellectual, as Harbage proposed, is dispelled by the viciousness with which he treats his victim:

> LORENZO: O sir, forbear, your valour is already tried.
>   Quickly despatch, my masters.
>   *They hang him in the arbour.*
> HORATIO: What, will you murder me?
> LORENZO: Ay, thus, and thus, these are the fruits of love.
>   *They stab him.*

Lorenzo callously puns at Horatio's fate, hanged in his father's arbour:

> LORENZO: Although his life were still ambitious proud,
>   Yet is he at the highest now he is dead.   (2.4.52–5, 60–61)

Those who make jokes while murdering someone are marked out for special contempt, and often retribution.

---

14. On the notion of service in Elizabethan society see, e.g., Ann Kussmaul, *Servants and Husbandry in Early Modern England* (Cambridge, 1981); Mark Burnett, *Masters and Servants in English Renaissance Drama and Culture* (Basingstoke and New York, 1997); Judith Weil, *Service and Dependency in Shakespeare's Plays* (Cambridge, 2005).

Kyd's handling of these two inter-related intrigue plots achieves several goals. Bel-imperia's wish to revenge Andrea's murder has had the opposite result, the murder of Horatio. Lorenzo's superior plotting, aided by Pedringano's treachery, has notionally opened the way for Balthazar to marry Bel-imperia. This match has already been proposed by the Spanish King as a means of normalizing relations between his kingdom and Portugal (2.3.1–27, 41–50). But Bel-imperia, far from wishing to marry Balthazar, now has a redoubled reason for wanting revenge on him. Lorenzo did not consider that his sister might take any violent action against him (naturally enough, given women's subordinate status), but he nonetheless took the precaution of having her locked up. She is more resourceful than he thinks, however, and manages to send a letter to Hieronimo, identifying Lorenzo and Balthazar as Horatio's murderers. When Hieronimo goes to question Pedringano on his mistress's whereabouts, this arouses Lorenzo's mistaken fear that Serberine has 'revealed Horatio's death' (3.2.70–71). The Machiavel is forced to 'repent | That e'er I used him in this enterprise' (76–7). Having decided to destroy his helper turned harmer, Lorenzo bribes Pedringano to

> Meet Serberine at Saint Luigi's Parke . . .
> There take thy stand, and see thou strike him sure,
> For die he must, if we do mean to live.   (83–6)

Lorenzo promises that he and Balthazar will also be at the assignation, and hints ambiguously at Pedringano's reward: 'Then shalt thou mount for this' (93). Pedringano understands this as a promise of promotion, not thinking of the executioner's scaffold. Having sent his Page to Serberine with orders to meet him at the arranged place, Lorenzo reveals his final move to 'confirm the complot' he has cast 'Of all these practices', by sending the Watch there to catch Pedringano in the act (100–104). Addressing the audience, Lorenzo justifies his intrigue sophistically, in terms of using one evil to expel another, although he is responsible for both:

> Thus must we work that will avoid distrust,
> Thus must we practise to prevent mishap,
> And thus one ill another must expulse.   (105–7)

As for his accomplices, who have 'for coin their souls endangered', Lorenzo dismisses them contemptuously:

> And better 'tis that base companions die,
> Than by their life to hazard our good haps.
> Nor shall they live, for me to fear their faith:
> Ile trust myself, myself shall be my friend,
> For die they shall, slaves are ordained to no other end.   (115–19)

This has been, so far, a textbook example of intrigue, using one accomplice to kill the other and then be caught himself. In theory, nothing can go wrong. But Lorenzo has forgotten the possibility that Horatio's family might wish to have retribution or, failing that, revenge for his death. The murder has brought Hieronimo into the action, devastated by his loss and seeking justice. Further, the disposal of Pedringano was not as watertight as Lorenzo had imagined. Far from his conviction that 'one ill another must expulse', he should have known the indisputable truth, the logic of revenge, that violence generates violence.

Intrigues in Kyd's plays usually succeed in the short term but produce unforeseen consequences. Kyd shows this process in brief, as it were, by a thematically related subplot which takes place in the Portuguese court, in two matching scenes. In the first we see Balthazar's father, the Portuguese Viceroy, emotionally traumatized by his son's reported disappearance in battle, uncertain whether he has been captured or killed (1.3.1–42). Alexandro, one of his courtiers, assures him that Balthazar is alive, a prisoner of war in Spain (43–52). Villuppo, however, another courtier (the name means 'confusion, entanglement'[15]) denies his account, accusing Alexandro of lying to cover his own culpability in having accidentally shot Balthazar in the back during the battle (53–75). Alexandro protests—'O wicked forgery! O traitorous miscreant'—but he is carried off to prison, to await execution. Careful to leave us in no

---

15. Schick, *Spanish Tragedy*, 1898, p. 140, who also refers to a play by Girolamo Parabosco, called *Il Viluppo*.

doubt as to the nature of this intrigue, Kyd makes Villuppo stay behind at the end of the scene to reveal himself:

> Thus have I with an envious forgèd tale,
> Deceived the King, betrayed mine enemy,
> And hope for guerdon of my villainy. (1.3.93–5)

Villuppo is a small-scale version of Pedringano, but acting on his own initiative. In the matching scene, we see Alexandro bound to the stake, about to be executed, when the Portuguese Ambassador returns, bringing news that

> Your highness' son, Lord Balthazar, doth live;
> And, well entreated in the Court of Spain,
> Humbly commends him to your Majesty. (3.1.64–6).

The Viceroy orders Villuppo to release the prisoner—'Let him unbind thee that is bound to death, | To make a quittal for thy discontent', and Alexandro expresses relief that his 'innocence hath saved | The hopeless life' that the villain tried to destroy (82–4). Villuppo's intrigue was extremely short-sighted, since its success depended wholly on the Portuguese court not learning that Balthazar is alive. Once this fact emerges, he has no cover-up, being led away to suffer 'the bitterest torments and extremes' (99–101).

As two perceptive scholars have pointed out,[16] this subplot showing the Viceroy's near-fatal readiness to believe a false accusation provides a thematic contrast justifying Hieronimo's reaction when he receives the letter from Bel-imperia accusing Lorenzo and Balthazar of Horatio's murder (3.2.24–31). Unable to understand what motive they might have had for this deed, nor why Bel-imperia should be accusing her brother, Hieronimo urges caution on himself:

> Hieronimo beware, thou art betrayed,
> And to entrap thy life this train is laid.

---

16. See Freeman, *Thomas Kyd*, pp. 84–6, and G.K. Hunter, 'Ironies of Justice in *The Spanish Tragedy*', in Hunter, *Dramatic Identities and Cultural Tradition. Studies in Shakespeare and his Contemporaries* (Liverpool, 1978), pp. 215–29 (220–21).

Advise thee therefore, be not credulous:
This is devisèd to endanger thee,
That thou by this Lorenzo shouldst accuse,
And he, for thy dishonour done, should draw
Thy life in question and thy name in hate.
Dear was the life of my beloved Son,
And of his death behoves me be revenged.
Then hazard not thine own, Hieronimo,
But live t'effect thy resolution! (37–47)

While I agree that Kyd intended this parallel and contrast, justifying Hieronimo's delay until he receives confirmation of the allegation, I see a further significance in the Alexandro-Villuppo episode. Kyd shows us that intrigue plots may succeed for a while but can eventually produce an outcome opposite to that which the intriguers intended.

From the point when he receives Bel-imperia's letter Hieronimo is on the alert to find proof that Lorenzo and Balthazar should be the object of his revenge. His attempt to discover the truth 'by circumstances'— that is, 'circumstantial evidence', is at first blocked. His enquiry as to Bel-imperia's whereabouts is not only fruitless but arouses Lorenzo's suspicion that one of his accomplices has revealed Horatio's death (3.2.50– 119). But indirectly, via the comic subplot involving Pedringano (to be discussed later in this chapter), Hieronimo receives confirmation of the murderers' identity (4.1.19–68) and can begin to contemplate revenge. For the spectator or reader who has followed the success of Lorenzo's plot against Horatio, there is a grim pleasure in seeing a counterplot taking shape, following the rules of 'the syntax of intrigue' that I outlined earlier. Hieronimo has already realized that he must not reveal his purposes—'To listen more, but nothing to bewray' (3.2.52). Once he knows who murdered Horatio, he vows

I will revenge his death!
But how? not as the vulgar wits of men,
With open, but inevitable ills,
As by a secret, yet a certain mean,
Which under kindship will be cloakèd best. (4.7.20–24)

This is a formal announcement of the need to dissemble, an essential prerequisite for intrigue, feigning both 'kindship' (kindness) and 'simplicity' (innocence):

> Thus, therefore will I rest me in unrest,
> Dissembling quiet in unquietness,
> Not seeming that I know their villainies,
> That my simplicity may make them think
> That ignorantly I will let all slip.   (30–34)

Hieronimo soon has a chance to display his 'kindship' and 'courtesy', for he is summoned to court by the Duke of Castile, Lorenzo's father. The Duke has challenged Lorenzo with the rumour that he prevented Hieronimo from making complaints to the King, an accusation which Lorenzo denies with consummate hypocrisy (4.8.52–94). Confronted with Lorenzo, Hieronimo matches him in pretence, feigning effusive respect for 'mine honourable friend' (120–67), and dispelling all suspicion. But left alone he reassures us that he has not been fooled by this false courtesy with a proverb drawn from Guicciardini, another master of *ragione di stato*: '*Chi mi fa piu carezze che non suole, | Tradito mi ha, o tradir mi vuole*'.[17]

Hieronimo the intriguer now receives a helper, in the form of Bel-imperia, whom we have seen chafing at his failure to take revenge (4.3.7–11). She now upbraids him in person for showing 'such ingratitude unto thy son', and vows to take revenge herself if need be (5.1.1–29). Using the vocabulary of intrigue, Hieronimo welcomes Bel-imperia's resolve: 'I see that heaven applies our drift' (32)—where 'drift' means plot.[18] They each swear a solemn oath (42–8), and Kyd ends the scene by creating the impression that Hieronimo is master of everything that will happen:

> On then, whatsoever I devise,
> Let me entreat you grace my practices;
> For why, the plot's already in mine head.   (49–51)

---

17. Edwards translates: 'He who shows unaccustomed fondness for me has betrayed me or wants to betray me' (*Spanish Tragedy*, p. 97).

18. Edwards described 'applies our drift' as 'a most difficult phrase', failing to see its relation to intrigue (*Spanish Tragedy*, p. 101). I take 'apply' to mean 'comply, adapt to'.

The usual practice in intrigue plots, carefully observed by Kyd for Lorenzo's machinations, is for the intriguer to keep the audience informed at each stage of his plotting, describing the means used and the anticipated outcome. In the denouement of *The Spanish Tragedy*, however, Kyd withholds this information, preferring surprise. All we know is that Hieronimo is going to put on an entertainment to celebrate Belimperia's wedding to Balthazar, which will take the form of a tragedy devised by Hieronimo on the story of Erastus, 'a knight of Rhodes'. As he summarizes the plot: Erastus married Perseda,

> Whose beauty ravished all that her beheld,
> Especially the soul of Soliman,   (5.1.108–14).

Soliman, Emperor of the Turks, had tried in vain to win Perseda's love, and conveyed his frustration to one of his bashaws. This 'grandee' advised him, as Lorenzo had advised Balthazar, that the lady was 'not otherwise to be won | But by her husband's death, this Knight of Rhodes, | Whom presently by treachery he slew' (115–22). However, that intrigue resulted in an outcome unforeseen by the plotters, in the violence of Perseda's reaction:

> She, stirred with an exceeding hate therefore,
> As cause of this slew Soliman.
> And to escape the Bashaw's tyranny,
> Did stab herself; and this the Tragedy.   (123–6)

'O excellent!', Lorenzo exclaims—thinking that 'they do but jest, poyson in jest, no offence i'th'world'.[19]

By not disclosing Hieronimo's plan to the audience, Kyd denies us foreknowledge of the intrigue and its anticipated outcome. At least we know more than do the actors in the play, or the royal spectators—whom Hieronimo has locked in this room—that is, on the upper stage (5.3.11–14). We have been promised that this entertainment will somehow further a double revenge, by the father who has lost both his son and his wife—for Isabella has since gone mad and killed herself

---

19. *Hamlet*, 3.2.234–5.

THE SPANISH TRAGEDY 67

(4.2.1–25; 5.2.1–38), and by the woman who has lost her lover. Kyd gives Hieronimo two sequences of direct address to the audience, but neither of them reveals his plot. In the first he anticipates the 'confusion' (chaos) that will shortly ensue—

Now shall I see the fall of Babylon,
Wrought by the heavens in this confusion   (5.1.195–6),

while in the other he urges himself to remember all 'former wrongs', and to complete the plot he has 'laid of dire revenge' (5.3.21–30).

When the play takes place, the audience in the theatre, like the one within the play, is utterly astonished as this intrigue plot reaches fruition. Hieronimo, acting the part of the Bashaw, advises the Turkish Emperor Soliman (played by Balthazar) to 'Remove Erasto' [Erastus]—the same euphemistic verb used by Lorenzo to urge Horatio's death (2.1.32, 136), so that he can enjoy Perseda's love. Balthazar, as Soliman, protests that Erasto is his friend, but the Bashaw urges that 'if he be your rival, let him die'. At this Hieronimo turns to Lorenzo (acting the unfortunate Erasto), and carries out his instructions with one of those jests used by Kyd's murderers, very similar to the one Lorenzo had used in killing Horatio:

Erasto, Soliman saluteth thee,
And lets thee wit by me his highness' will,
Which is, thou shouldst be thus employed: (5.4.50–52).

'Stab him', the stage direction laconically orders, and Hieronimo does so. Bel-imperia, acting the heroine Perseda, laments Erasto's death, rejects Soliman's love, stabs him, and—to our great surprise—then stabs herself (52–67). The royal audience applauds, but Hieronimo steps forward to disabuse their pleasure in the feigned spectacle:

Haply you think, but bootless are your thoughts,
That this is fabulously counterfeit [based on a story],
And that we do as all Tragedians do.
To die today (for fashioning our scene)
The death of Ajax, or some Roman peer,

And in a minute starting up again,
Revive to please tomorrow's audience.   (76–82)

This is a wonderfully self-aware exploitation of the double nature of the fiction of the play-within-the-play (the first in English drama) and the fact of the three deaths.[20]

The reality behind the feigning, and its history, are too complex to be described in a few words, so Kyd gives Hieronimo a long, marvellously orchestrated speech, full of intense feeling (5.4.73–152). Hieronimo first draws a curtain to make a 'discovery', as in a play (we think of Miranda and Ferdinand playing chess), only to reveal the as yet unburied body of Horatio—'See here my show, look on this spectacle'. Hieronimo expresses grief for his son's death, which has destroyed his parents' lives, in a densely paradoxical expression of the love that makes the happiness of parents and children interdependent:

From forth these wounds came breath that gave me life,
They murdered me that made these fatal marks.   (96–7)

Hieronimo's narrative of the sequence of cause and effect which has brought everyone to this point includes an apt comment on the errors of Lorenzo. The intriguer was so confident that his plotting would go unnoticed that he 'Marched in a net and thought himself unseen' (118)—'a common phrase for palpable deceit and pretence', as Philip Edwards noted.[21] But Lorenzo failed to deceive those he had harmed, and Hieronimo's dissembled 'kindship' lulled Lorenzo into such a sense of security that he never suspected the counter-intrigue which destroyed him.

If one thing is clear from the harm given and returned in *The Spanish Tragedy* it is that the success of intrigue plots is only provisional. The intriguer deceives and manipulates to achieve a goal, but he seldom looks far enough ahead to evade a counter action. By killing Horatio, Lorenzo achieved his goal of clearing the way for Balthazar to marry Bel-imperia,

---

20. See, e.g., Anne Barton, *Shakespeare and the Idea of the Play* (London, 1962).
21. Edwards, *Spanish Tragedy*, p. 115.

but laid himself open to retaliation from Bel-imperia and Hieronimo. Bel-imperia is the only character who shows foresight, having looked far enough ahead to realize what would happen after she had killed Balthazar, and so decided to kill herself rather than live on. As Hieronimo explains to the Portuguese Viceroy, his son played the part of

> That Soliman, which Bel-imperia
> In person of Perseda murdered,
> Solely appointed to that tragic part
> That she might slay him that offended her.
> Poor Bel-imperia missed her part in this,
> For though the story saith she should have died,
> Yet I of kindness, and of care to her
> Did otherwise determine of her end.
> But love of him whom they did hate too much,
> Did urge her resolution to be such.   (5.4.137–45).

The psychological devastation that Bel-imperia endured through the murder of Andrea and Horatio has left her with nothing to live for. Hieronimo's life has also been ruined, and he too has looked beyond the success of his intrigue to a life not worth living. So, '*He runs to hang himself*', the stage direction says. But he had not predicted that he would be restrained, and from this point on he is forced to improvise. Amazingly (no one could have predicted this) Hieronimo first bites out his tongue, ostensibly to avoid any further cross-examination (187–91), a 'refusal to speak' which some scholars dismiss as 'inexplicable'.[22] But Kyd invents a last intrigue for Hieronimo to deceive the expectations of his captors. Being unable to speak, he offers to write down what they want to know. Finding his pen too blunt, he receives a knife to sharpen it, with which he kills the Duke of Castile, and then himself. His suicide is a stunning theatrical experience, but also a triumph of invention, the ability to react to unexpected circumstances that marks out the superior revenger.

22. Ibid., p. 117.

Unknown to him, Hieronimo's successful intrigues are overseen by the ghost of Don Andrea and the spirit of Revenge, who have been onstage throughout. Before he dies Hieronimo reminds his captors that

> My guiltless Son was by Lorenzo slain,
> And by Lorenzo and that Balthazar,
> Am I at last revengèd thoroughly.
> Upon whose souls may heavens be yet avenged
> With greater far than these afflictions!   (171–5)

His wish comes true in the following scene, where the frame around the play closes with Revenge recapitulating all the deaths before returning with Andrea to Hell:

> Then haste we down to meet thy friends and foes,
> To place thy friends in ease, the rest in woes.
> For here, though death hath end their misery,
> I'll there begin their endless Tragedy.   (5.5.45–8)

Recent critics are notably silent about this concluding scene, evidently embarrassed at its unabashed glorying in a satisfying revenge. But this is our problem, for modern scholars who express a Christian moral disapproval of revenge ignore the fact that the Old Testament God claims revenge—not justice—as his monopoly. They also ignore the age-old belief that moral action in society consists in 'Helping friends and harming enemies'.[23] Given the successful plotting of the destructive characters in this play, and the absence of any likelihood of legal retribution, those harmed have no other recourse but to this 'kind of wild justice', as Bacon called it.[24] But Bacon also noted that

> The most tolerable sort of revenge is for those wrongs which there is no law to remedy; but then let a man take heed the revenge be such

---

23. See, e.g., Mary Whitlock Blundell, *Helping Friends and Harming Enemies. A Study in Sophocles and Greek Ethics* (Cambridge, 1989).

24. See Bacon's essay 'Of Revenge', in Vickers (ed.), *Francis Bacon. A Critical Edition of the Major Works* (Oxford, 1996), p. 347.

as there is no law to punish; else a man's enemy is still before hand, and it is two for one. (p. 348)

To be 'before hand' is to be in the advantage, and one of the fascinating experiences of this play is to watch how characters gradually gain, only to lose the upper hand. Hieronimo and Bel-imperia time and execute their revenge so well, taking the logical choice of suicide as the final stage of revenge, that in the final scene they deprive those harmed of any chance of retribution. Readers and critics who feel discomfort with this apogee of violence, transcending all the harm and counter-harm plots in the play, impose their own morality on it, and deprive themselves from appreciating its remarkable coherence of action and ethics.

The marvellously constructed interlocking intrigue plots in *The Spanish Tragedy* form only part of the play's complex design. The action takes place at several levels, each moving at its own tempo. Earlier, in the uppermost plot strand, the King of Spain and the Viceroy of Portugal had concluded to their own satisfaction arrangements for the marriage of Balthazar and Bel-imperia, 'For strengthening of our late-confirmed league' (2.3.11). In fact, the planning of the marriage stretches across the play, regularly juxtaposed with scenes of violence and its aftermath. A meeting between the two parties (4.6.25–110) is prefaced and interrupted by the madness of Hieronimo, who '*digs with his dagger*', trying to 'rip the bowels of the earth' to bring Horatio back and 'show his deadly wounds' (70–73). The first confrontation between the two rulers (4.8.1–39) is preceded by the marvellous 'mirror scene' between Hieronimo and the old man Bazulto, grieving for his dead son (4.7.67–175). It is followed by one in which Hieronimo feigns friendship with Lorenzo, demonstrating that he has recovered from his mad fit. Hieronimo is so successful in dissembling his feelings that he is invited to produce some 'pleasing motion' to 'grace the wedding festivities' (5.1.60–67). The two courtiers deputed to arrange the entertainment discuss Hieronimo condescendingly, unaware of his real intentions:

BALTHAZAR How like you this?
LORENZO Why thus my Lord:
     We must resolve to soothe his humours up.   (5.1.190–93)

Hieronimo's apparently good-humoured compliance establishes a mood of pleasurable anticipation in the royal audience—'These be our pastimes in the Court of Spain' (5.4.8), the King proudly assures his guest, blissfully unaware of the irony—which persists even after the deaths of Balthazar, Lorenzo, and Bel-imperia.

KING: Well said, old Marshal, this was bravely done!   (5.4.68)

The courtiers' total unpreparedness for the scenes they have just witnessed accounts for the time it takes them to realize what has happened and start questioning Hieronimo (5.4.153–67). Kyd finally brings together all the plot levels that he has sustained, each at its appropriate tempo, courtly diplomacy side-by-side with mayhem. Those scholars who have best studied this play are justified in praising its plotting. As Arthur Freeman judged,

> Kyd's manner of spinning out the plot reveals nothing less than genius for altering, intensifying, blending, and augmenting story lines only hinted at by known precedents. In the absence of any further known sources, we must credit him with powers of invention unparalleled among the dramatists of his time. (p. 50)

None of Kyd's other plays matches *The Spanish Tragedy* in complexity, but each of them contains elements found there, and in similar constellations.

Tragic Comedy

In terms of Renaissance literary theory, Elizabethan tragedy was a mixed genre, if not a bastard. Where classical tragedy supposedly dealt with rulers and great families (there is, however, a watchman in Aeschylus' *Agamemnon*, and a nurse in *Choephoroe*, not to mention Euripides' collection of ordinary people), the Elizabethans mixed classical and native traditions, bringing together rulers and plebeians, verse and prose, tragedy and comedy. Although critics in previous generations were content to describe scenes involving lower-class characters as 'comic relief', in modern times we have come to realize that Elizabethan dramatists often related notionally comic scenes to the serious concerns of tragedy. In this, as in so many respects, Kyd was a pioneer. Alfred Harbage credited him not only with establishing intrigue in English drama, but with applying it to comic purposes:

> Perhaps Kyd's greatest innovation was to employ comic methods with tragic materials, thus creating a species of comi-tragedy. Manoeuvres traditionally associated with the petty ends of petty tricksters are given a sensationally lethal turn so as to win a new and oddly mixed response—of amusement and horror, revulsion and admiration.[25]

Briefly discussing the plot sequence in *The Spanish Tragedy* in which Kyd's Lorenzo manoeuvres 'Pedringano into slaying Serberine, the authorities into arresting Pedringano, and the latter into remaining silent until the moment of his execution because of the hope of a pardon', Harbage described Lorenzo's methods as 'the traditional ones of comic intrigue', citing *Gammer Gurton's Needle* and *Ralph Roister Doister* as examples of dramatic complications produced by such simple means as a lost needle or a mispunctuated letter (p. 38). Douglas Cole also credited Kyd with having 'invented ironic tragedy through adapting comic intrigue'.

Our appreciation of the skill with which Kyd adapted comedy to tragedy makes the term 'comic relief', still used by some critics,[26] inadequate. However, in addition to their function in a larger scheme, Kyd's comic characters exist in their own right as entertainers who hold the stage, talk directly to the audience, give an amusing running commentary on events. They are used as commentators on other characters, ridiculing their pretensions and providing more amusement. Their role might be described as simultaneously comic and serious.

---

25. Alfred Harbage, 'Intrigue in Elizabethan Tragedy', in Richard Hosley (ed.), *Essays on Shakespeare and Elizabethan Drama. In honour of Hardin Craig* (London, 1963), pp. 37–44, at p. 37. See also Douglas Cole, 'The comic accomplice in Elizabethan revenge tragedy', *Renaissance Drama*, 9 (1966): 125–39.

26. See e.g., Freeman, *Thomas Kyd*, p. 91.

74   CHAPTER 2

The Pedringano-Serberine plot strand in *The Spanish Tragedy* begins when the intriguer Lorenzo uses Pedringano to kill Serberine. As we know, Lorenzo has also forewarned the Watch to be at the assignation place so that the assassin can be caught in the act. Readers and theatregoers witness this plot at two levels. Seeing it from Lorenzo's superior perspective, Pedringano's view is that of the gulled, for whom we feel no sympathy. All his naive utterances are tinged with an irony of which he remains unaware. When he reaches the assignation, still confident that 'my noble Lord | Will stand between me and ensuing harms' and that 'this place is free from all suspect' (3.3.13–16), Pedringano carries out his contract, shooting Serberine with a 'dag' (a heavy pistol or handgun), and is promptly arrested. As soon as Balthazar learns of Serberine's death, he goes off to arrange an immediate trial, to be carried out by Hieronimo in his role as Knight Marshal, leaving Lorenzo to gloat over the success of his Machiavellian 'policy':

> I lay the plot, he prosecutes the point,
> I set the trap, he breaks the worthless twigs,
> And sees not that wherewith the bird was limed.
> Thus hopeful men, that mean to hold their own,
> Must look like fowlers to their dearest friends.   (3.4.40–44)

Lorenzo's concluding lines take the form of a maxim or aphorism, a stylistic device cultivated by Machiavelli and Guicciardini in the *ragione di stato* tradition.[27] Again we note the intriguer's specious euphemism: for 'hopeful men' read ruthless egoists, who hunt down their prey. To follow this successful 'reaching fatch' (46), or 'far-seeing stratagem' (Edwards), Lorenzo has some more devices to destroy his accomplice. He sends his Page to the imprisoned Pedringano, assuring him that 'his pardon is already signed', and that the Page will attend his trial with a pardon:

> Show him this box, tell him his pardon's in it,
> But open't not, an' if thou lov'st thy life.   (3.4.72–3)

---

27. See Brian Vickers, *Francis Bacon and Renaissance Prose* (Cambridge, 1968), pp. 68–70.

Left alone, Lorenzo considers taking one further precaution, 'And that's to fee[28] the executioner' (81), but decides that the secrecy needed for a successful intrigue will not let him

> trust the Air | With utterance of our pretence therein,
> For fear the privy whisp'ring of the wind
> Convey our words amongst unfriendly ears,
> That lie too open to advantages.   (82–5)

Lorenzo is an accomplished plotter, of whom Alfred Harbage wrote that 'the intricacy of his methods must be recognized as entertainment for its own sake' (p. 39). However, theory alone is not enough. Despite his own awareness of the dangers of trusting accomplices, Lorenzo is unable to control the further behaviour of the Page and Pedringano. Kyd brilliantly exploits the resources of the theatre by writing a soliloquy in prose (as befits a comic or low-life character) for the Page, who has promptly disobeyed his master's injunction not to open the box:

> My Master hath forbidden me to look in this box, and by my troth 'tis likely, if he had not warned me, I should not have had so much idle time, for we men's-kind in our minority are like women in their uncertainty: that they are most forbidden, they will soonest attempt—so I now. [*Opens the box.*] By my bare honesty, here's nothing but the bare empty box! Were it not sin against secrecy, I would say it were a piece of gentlemanlike knavery. I must go to Pedringano, and tell him his pardon is in this box, nay, I would have sworn it, had I not seen the contrary. I cannot choose but smile to think how the villain will flout the gallows, scorn the audience, and descant on the hangman, and all presuming of his pardon from hence. Will't not be an odd jest, for me to stand and grace every jest he makes, pointing

---

28. Philip Edwards suspected 'that "see" [long s] is a misprint for "fee"; the remark would be more in character and more powerful', but he refused to 'tamper' with the text (*Spanish Tragedy*, p. 62). That misreading was common, but more important are Kyd's other uses of 'fee', such as the King's reward of Horatio: 'His ransom therefore is thy valour's fee' (1.2.183), or Black Will's 'Tell me of gold, my resolution's fee' (3.91). The decisive usage is Alice's interest in London's 'alehouse ruffians' who 'will murder men for gold. | They shall be soundly fee'd to pay him home' (1.442–4), using 'fee' as a verb. In their 2013 edition Calvo and Tronch still read 'see'.

my finger at this box: as who would say, 'Mock on, here's thy warrant'? Is it not a scurvy jest, that a man should jest himself to death? Alas poor Pedringano, I am in a sort sorry for thee, but if I should be hanged with thee, I cannot weep. *Exit.* (3.5.6–19)

This speech is a masterpiece of comic irony, at one level expressing the Page's disillusionment with his master's 'gentlemanlike knavery', but at another anticipating Pedringano's unawareness of the discrepancy between Lorenzo's promise and performance in terms of a comic act, 'an odd jest', even 'a scurvy jest', but still one to 'smile' at. The Page expresses our own feelings towards this gull, ready to murder someone for money but so easily cheated: 'I am in a sort sorry for thee, but . . . I cannot weep'.

The execution scene is brilliantly staged, with more surprises. Pedringano enters *'with a letter in his hand, bound'*, as the stage direction puts it, and expresses his relief that the Page boy has at last come from Lorenzo,

> For I had written to my Lord anew
> A nearer matter that concerneth him,
> For fear his Lordship had forgotten me.
> But sith he hath remembered me so well   (3.6.18–21)

Pedringano is confident that his pardon is at hand. He freely confesses his crime to the Lord Marshal, Hieronimo, in verse (3.6.28–32), descending to prose in order to abuse the Hangman, with his lower social status—observing the decorum governing the use of prose in drama which Shakespeare was shortly to follow.[29] Indeed, Pedringano shows outrageous arrogance in jesting with the Hangman, as it must seem to everyone present—except the audience, and the Boy holding the empty box. The joke is on Pedringano, however:

> PEDRINGANO: Sirrah, dost see yonder boy with the box in
>   his hands?
> HANGMAN: What, he that points to it with his finger? . . .
> PEDRINGANO: What hath he in his box, as thou
>   think'st?   (3.6.65–6, 73)

29. See Brian Vickers, *The Artistry of Shakespeare's Prose* (London, 1968; 2005).

Pedringano still believes that 'it may be, in that box is balm for both' his body and soul, and he is still clutching at Lorenzo's assurances even after Hieronimo has left the courtroom in disgust at his impudence, ordering the execution to take place:

> PEDRINGANO: Nay soft, no haste.
> DEPUTY: Why, wherefore stay you, have you hope of life?
> PEDRINGANO: Why ay.
> HANGMAN: As how?
> PEDRINGANO: Why rascal, by my pardon from the King.
> HANGMAN: Stand you on that, then you shall off with
> this.   (3.6.99–104)

And the hangman *'turnes him off'* in full view of the audience, a unique stage direction in early modern drama.[30] As Arthur Freeman observed, 'the hangman's contemptuous reply to the prisoner's hope of pardon ("Stand you on that?") implies that at this point the boy has finally thrown open the box and revealed it quite empty'.[31] The gull's folly in trusting his master's promises is all too evident. Yet Lorenzo has also been too trustful, or complacent, in not conceiving that his dupe might be capable of independent action. In the following scene the Hangman delivers to Hieronimo the letter that Pedringano had addressed to Lorenzo, on 'A nearer matter that concerneth him', revealing that Pedringano killed Serberine on Lorenzo's orders, and that he had also helped Lorenzo and Balthazar murder Horatio. Here, finally, is the evidence that settles Hieronimo's doubts about Bel-imperia's allegations:

> Now see I what I durst not then suspect,
> That Bel-imperia's letter was not feigned,
> Nor feigned she, though falsely they have wronged
> Both her, myself, Horatio, and themselves.   (4.1.49–52)

---

30. See Alan C. Dessen and Leslie Thomson, *A Dictionary of Stage Directions in English Drama, 1580–1642* (Cambridge, 1999), p. 240.

31. Freeman, *Thomas Kyd*, p. 113.

In this respect then, Harbage was wrong to describe Lorenzo's Machiavellian plotting as 'entertainment for its own sake'. The empty box, with all the layers of comic irony that it carries, is a great stage gag, but Lorenzo might have better employed his wits in disposing of Pedringano immediately after the murder, as truly efficient villains do. The gull's posthumous disclosure has given Hieronimo the knowledge he had lacked, allowing him to accept Bel-imperia as accomplice in the revenge which will destroy Lorenzo, Balthazar, and other innocent bystanders. Collateral damage is not a modern invention.

Female Agency

Kyd is unusual among his contemporaries in the active roles he writes for women. In the plays of Marlowe, women play distinctly subordinate parts. Dido is an exception, as a major character, although her behaviour is constrained by Virgil's narrative. In *Edward I* Peele wrote a short but violent role for Queen Eleanor, transforming her into a virago. In Kyd, when we consider the important parts played by Bel-imperia in *The Spanish Tragedy*, Perseda in his Turkish tragedy, Alice in *Arden of Faversham*, Gonorill and Ragan in *King Leir*, Em (for Emily) in *Fair Em*, we see that he gives women autonomy of action almost equalling that of men, a power to make decisions on their own behalf and to carry them through. Kyd's decisions grant women greater prominence than they normally achieved either on the London stage or in real life.

If we look for predecessors in the drama for such active feminine roles, we find them, I suggest, not in English but in Latin drama, in the tragedies of Seneca. The influence of Seneca in English tragedy has often been observed, and occasionally disputed. Howard Baker urged the long-neglected case for Ovid, whose representations of violence had a visible influence on the drama, notably in the banquet scene of *Titus Andronicus*.[32] It is true that the *Metamorphoses* were widely read, but we should not reduce this matter to an either/or choice, for Seneca himself owed much to both Ovid and Virgil, and 'an interest in portraying the

---

32. Howard Baker, *Induction to Tragedy* (Baton Rouge, LA, 1939).

passions had long been central to Roman poetry at Rome, as seen in Vergil's *Aeneid*, and in Ovid's many passionate heroines'.[33] In a characteristically trenchant and scholarly essay, G. K. Hunter re-stated the case for seeing a parallel influence of Ovid and Seneca on the Elizabethans.[34] Several of Seneca's tragedies are in effect revenge plays, and in his pioneering study of that genre Fredson Bowers drew attention to those plays that portrayed 'great crimes and examples of the evil results of murder, as in *Thyestes*, *Medea*, and *Agamemnon*' as having 'made the greatest impression upon the Elizabethans'.[35] It is significant that each contains a central revenging character, 'Atreus, Medea, and Clytemnestra, those revengers beyond the pale of reason' (p. 42), and that two of these are women.

In her opening speech Medea, outraged that her husband Jason has abandoned her for a new bride, invokes the Furies, the 'goddesses who avenge crime' (14), and announces that 'My revenge is born, already born: I have given birth' (25–6). She addresses her innate 'spirit': 'if you are alive, if there is any of your old energy left', then 'drive out womanish fears', and contemplate 'savage, unheard-of, horrible things' (40–43). Creon, father of Jason's new bride, addresses Medea as a gender hybrid, 'you architectress of wicked crimes, who have a woman's evil willingness to dare anything, along with a man's strength' (266–8).[36] Medea exalts in the power within her: 'my rage will never slacken in seeking revenge but grow ever greater' (403–7). The revenge that Medea first planned was directed against the bride's father, Creon, but on reflection she realizes that the best way to hurt Jason would be to kill his bride. Having done so, Medea is not yet satisfied and decides to kill their two sons: 'The place to wound him is laid bare' (546–50).

---

33. John G. Fitch, Introduction to his translation of Seneca's tragedies in the Loeb Classical Library: *Seneca VIII (Tragedies 1)* (Cambridge, MA, and London, 2002), p. 22.

34. G. K. Hunter, 'Seneca and the Elizabethans: a case-study in "influence"', *Shakespeare Survey*, 20 (1967): 17–26; reprinted in and quoted from Hunter, *Dramatic Identities and Cultural Tradition. Studies in Shakespeare and his Contemporaries* (Liverpool, 1978), pp. 159–173; and 'Seneca and English Tragedy', ibid., pp. 174–213.

35. Fredson Bowers, *Elizabethan Revenge Tragedy* (Princeton, NJ, 1940), p. 41.

36. Cf. Macbeth's tribute to his wife: 'Bring forth men-children only' (1.7.73).

Seneca's presentation of her devastating revenge is curiously divided. On the one hand, showing events from Medea's perspective, he presents her exulting in the news that her revenge has succeeded, that Creusa and Jason have been killed, urging her 'spirit' on once more: 'Why are you slackening, my spirit? Follow up your successful attack! How small a part of your revenge is this that thrills you!' (895–6). Indeed, in this process it seems as if she is coming into her own, finally fulfilling her innate qualities: 'What great deed could be dared by untrained hands, by the fury of a girl? Now I am Medea; my genius has grown through evils' (908–10; '*Medea nunc sum: crevit ingenium malis*'). As the editor helpfully notes, her '*ingenium*' (inborn nature and talent) denoted by her name, which means "The thinking/inventive woman" has come to maturity'.[37] But while presenting Medea's sense of self-realization, Seneca continually uses the language of moral evaluation to make her describe what she plans to do as her spirit's 'ultimate crime' (923–4), repeatedly referring to infanticide as 'that unheard-of deed, that abomination' (929–32). Having killed the first, she feels exultation not shame (976–7), but Seneca restores the moral perspective as she tells herself: 'Depart, you have brought crime to fulfilment—but not yet so, revenge' (986–7). Although she regrets what she has done ('I feel ashamed'), she also feels 'a great sense of pleasure' stealing over her. Not 'content with one slaughter', she kills the second son: 'Good, it is finished' (1019). Medea has fulfilled herself to her own satisfaction.

Reading Seneca's *Medea* through the eyes of Thomas Kyd, as it were, who was drawing on the Latin masters to create his own distinctively Elizabethan form of tragedy, we can sense an ethical and aesthetic dilemma. Other dramatists were generally content to endorse contemporary gender attitudes, which defined woman's nature as softer than man's, hence unable to perform violent deeds.[38] Kyd could entertain the concept of a woman being as ready as any man to take personal revenge, equal in anger and in desire to punish those who have irrevocably harmed her. But two factors differentiate his presentation of revengeful

---

37. Fitch (tr.), *Seneca VIII*, p. 423 n.

38. See, for example, Ian Maclean, *The Renaissance Concept of Woman* (Cambridge, 1980).

women from Seneca's, one moral, the other aesthetic. Kyd's active women—Bel-imperia, Perseda, Gonorill, Ragan, Alice Arden—may, at the final moment, seize a dagger to kill their harmer, but they lack the larger-than-life power of a Medea or a Clytemnestra. Until the decisive moment it seems that they will bow to Elizabethan norms and hire a man to the deed. Aesthetically, the dramatic forms available to the two dramatists differed considerably. Seneca's tragedies resemble spoken narratives interspersed with lyrical moralizing, one consequence of the small number of characters onstage being that Medea must function both as an agent and as a moral commentator on her own actions. In contrast, the mimetic nature of English popular drama made it highly unlikely that a character bent on revenging an injury would consistently judge their actions as crimes.

In the tragic dramas of the English Renaissance the great revengers are all men: Hieronimo, Barabas, Hamlet, Hoffman, Othello, Vindice. I have not made an extensive survey, but in all these plays women are far more likely to be victims rather than agents. In *The Spanish Tragedy*, however, as in *Soliman and Perseda*, women play an important role in the revenge action. Bel-imperia's sufferings antedate the action of the play, for the Ghost of Andrea tells Revenge in the opening scene how,

> By duteous service and deserving love
> In secret I possessed a worthy dame,
> Which hight sweet Bel-imperia by name.
> But in the harvest of my summer joys
> Death's winter nipped the blossoms of my bliss,
> Forcing divorce betwixt my love and me.   (1.1.10–14)

Andrea's ghost describes how, having been outnumbered and unchivalrously killed during the wars between Spain and Portugal, he descended to Pluto's court, and received from Proserpine permission to gain the help of Revenge in punishing his murderers. Revenge then brings the situation up to date:

> Then know, Andrea, that thou art arrived
> Where thou shalt see the author of thy death,

Don Balthazar the Prince of Portugal.
Deprived of life by Bel-imperia.   (86–9)

For an Elizabethan audience experiencing this play for the first time it would have been startling to learn that they would shortly see a woman killing a man in revenge. Perhaps this is the point being made by Revenge's next line: 'Here sit we down to see the mystery'.

As a woman, Bel-imperia cannot take direct and violent action against a man, much as she would want to. But after Horatio has told her how Andrea was killed by Balthazar, Bel-imperia begins to see Horatio as a replacement lover, with a new role in her life:

> Had he not loved Andrea as he did,
> He could not sit in Bel-imperia's thoughts.
> But how can love find harbour in my breast
> Till I revenge the death of my beloved?
> Yes, second love shall further my revenge.   (1.4.62–6)

This is a remarkable utterance coming from a woman, and it gives the lie to those critics who think that the play's revenge action only begins with Hieronimo's pursuit of Horatio's murderers. G. K. Hunter, author of several penetrating discussions of Kyd, disputed an earlier critical verdict that *The Spanish Tragedy* has a 'unity of action, and . . . also unity of motive, for it all centres round revenge', objecting that 'Revenge as a motive, or a psychological propellant to action, only appears halfway through the play'.[39] The truth is, rather, as Philip Edwards pointed out, that

> *The Spanish Tragedy* is a play about the passion for retribution, and vengeance shapes the entire action. Revenge himself appears as a character near the beginning of the play, a servant of the spiritual powers, indicating what a man may find in the patterns of existence which are woven for him. Retribution is not only the demand of divine justice but also a condescension to human wants. Andrea seeks

39. Hunter, 'Seneca and English Tragedy', p. 194.

blood for his own blood; though he died in war, Balthazar killed him in a cowardly and dishonourable fashion, and not in fair fight (1.4.19–26, 72–5; 1.2.73). (1959, p. li)

Where some commentators believe that 'the real action starts only with the death of Horatio', Edwards observed that in fact 'Balthazar's killing of Andrea . . . begins the action' (p. liv), and that 'the murder of Horatio in the bower' initiates

> the *fourth* of the interlocked revenge-schemes . . . . : Andrea's the first, then Bel-imperia's, then Lorenzo's and Balthazar's, and finally Hieronimo's. Kyd may seem to take some time to reach this most important of his revenge-schemes, but he chose to set layer within layer, wheels within wheels, revenge within revenge. (p. lv)

The plot is a unity, built around the pattern of harm and counter-harm, much of the action being taken up with the threefold process of identifying the harmer; finding the appropriate time, place, method of retribution; and trying to preserve oneself from becoming a victim in turn.

In this sequence of harm and retribution, Kyd gives Bel-imperia an unusually prominent role, creating, as Edwards described her, 'a woman of strong will, independent spirit, and not a little courage (witness her superb treatment of her brother after her release, first furious and then sardonic, making Lorenzo acknowledge defeat; 3.10.24–105)' (p. liv). As I showed above, her (rather vague) plan to use Horatio in an intrigue designed to frustrate Balthazar's desire is blocked by Lorenzo's counter-intrigue, resulting in Horatio's murder. Bel-imperia is then locked up by Lorenzo, but her desire for revenge is so strong that she manages to smuggle a letter to Hieronimo, written in her blood:

> 'For want of ink receive this bloody writ.
> Me hath my hapless brother hid from thee.
> Revenge thyself on Balthazar and him!
> For these were they that murderèd thy son.
> Hieronimo, revenge Horatio's death,
> And better fare than Bel-imperia doth.' (3.2.26–31)

Hieronimo at first distrusts this message, but, as we have seen, his attempt to reach her drives Lorenzo into getting rid of both Serberine and Pedringano, an intrigue which ultimately confirms the truth of Bel-imperia's allegations (3.7.50–54). Thus, her letter plays a crucial role in the revenge action.

Kyd keeps Bel-imperia's role as accomplice in revenge before us by making good use of the Elizabethan theatre's flexibility. She is shown alone '*at a window*' of Lorenzo's house, complaining of the 'outrage' of being 'sequestered from the Court' by her 'Accursed brother, unkind murderer', and addressing Hieronimo from afar:

> Hieronimo, why writ I of thy wrongs?
> Or why art thou so slack in thy revenge?   (4.3.7–8)

Here Bel-imperia seems to have stepped out of the main action into the framing scenes, where Andrea's Ghost consorts with Revenge, impatiently desiring satisfaction:

> Awake, Erichtho! Cerberus, awake! . . .
> Awake, Revenge, for thou art ill-advised
> To sleep. Awake! What, thou art warned to watch!   (4.9.1,10–11)

While many commentators focus on Hieronimo's suffering and search for revenge, Kyd sustains Bel-imperia's retributive role on a parallel plane, not letting us forget that a desire for 'wild justice' has been driving her on since Act 1, scene 4. When Lorenzo finally releases her, foolishly judging Horatio's murder to be 'as a nine days' wonder, [now] o'erblown', (4.4.11), Bel-imperia becomes the moral centre of the play. She denounces Lorenzo to his face as 'no brother, but an enemy' (25), and accurately informs Balthazar that 'you, my Lord, were made his instrument' (65). Bel-imperia's function as the articulate embodiment of moral outrage at her brother's crimes reaches its high point in the opening scene of Act 5, where her long-desired meeting with Hieronimo finally takes place. Here she delivers a swingeing reproach to this father who, it seems, has done nothing to avenge his son's death:

Is this the love thou bear'st Horatio?

. . . .

With what excuses canst thou show thyself,
With what dishonour, and the hate of men,
From this dishonour and the hate of men?[40]   (5.1.1, 8–10)

No longer addressing him from afar, as if part of the play's framing action, but face to face, Bel-imperia heaps up recrimination: 'Be not a history to after times | Of such ingratitude unto thy son' (14–16). Bel-imperia could rank Hieronimo with 'monstrous fathers [who] forget so soon', but she prefers to shame him into action by taking action herself:

Myself, a stranger in respect of thee,
So loved his life, as still I wish their deaths,
Nor shall his death be unrevenged by me,
Although I bear it out for fashion's sake.
For here I swear in sight of heaven and earth,
Shouldst thou neglect the love thou shouldst retain,
And give it over and devise no more,
Myself should send their hateful souls to hell
That wrought his downfall with extremest death!   (22–29)

This is surely the most remarkable speech yet uttered by a female character on the English stage. In its unquenchable determination, directness of utterance, and self-confidence—'My self' is twice placed as the first word of a line—it outdoes most speeches given to men. Hieronimo is astonished, as any man would be in that era, but her strength of purpose finally convinces him that she can be relied on as a helper. Having asked pardon for his 'fear and care' (caution) in not having believed her letter, he swears himself to their joint cause:

---

40. Editors wrongly omit this line, deeming it a printer's error, when it is Kyd's deliberate use of rhetoric. See my note 'Epistrophe and the "lost line" in *The Spanish Tragedy*', *Notes and Queries*, 268 (2023): 160–64.

And here I vow (so you but give consent
And will conceal my resolution)
I will ere long determine of their deaths,
That causeless thus have murderèd my son.   (42–5)

Bel-imperia accepts the secrecy needed for this intrigue, ready to act with him as an equal, repeating his exact words, as if in a religious ritual:

Hieronimo, I will consent, conceal,
And aught that may effect for thine avail,
Join with thee to revenge Horatio's death.   (96–8)

Hieronimo entreats her, 'whatsoever I devise', to 'grace my practices' (49–50). Lorenzo's Machiavellian word for treachery (3.2.101, 106) is now reclaimed for the just revengers.

As we have seen, Bel-imperia's role in Hieronimo's revenge consists in playing the role of 'Perseda, chaste and resolute', as Hieronimo describes her (5.1.140). The love triangle in Hieronimo's entertainment parallels that in the play itself: Lorenzo as Erastus, Balthazar as Soliman, and Bel-imperia as Perseda. As the 'play of Hieronimo' unfolds, life seems to be imitating art, for just as 'in real life' Balthazar had been persuaded by his confidant (Lorenzo) to kill Horatio, the rival for his beloved, so in the play, acting the role of Soliman, Balthazar accedes to his confidant's suggestion to kill his rival: only the confidant is now Hieronimo (as Brusor), and the victim is Lorenzo. The irony that this parallel afforded was no doubt one of the reasons why Kyd chose the story of Soliman and Perseda for his inset play. As for Bel-imperia, she kills Soliman/Balthazar, as predicted, but with one unexpected verbal detail when she confronts the tyrant:

Yet by thy power thou thinkest to command,
And to thy power Perseda doth obey.
But were she able, thus she would revenge
Thy treacheries on thee, ignoble Prince: *Stab him.*
And on herself she would be thus revenged!
    Stab herself.   (5.4.63–7)

The conditional tense—'were . . . would . . . would'—seems at first sight to be out of place here, considering that Bel-imperia is able to kill Balthazar, and does the deed before our eyes. But it is appropriate, I believe, in that women in Elizabethan society were not considered able to kill men or carry out revenge in a man's world. In creating Bel-imperia Kyd broke that convention, establishing women's rights to be considered equal with men, as revengers, whether good or evil. Shakespeare learned from his example.

3

Soliman and Perseda

THE THIRD OF Kyd's plays to find entry in the Stationers' Register in 1592 did so on 20 November:

> *Edward White. Entred for his Copie under thandes of the Bisshop of London: and m' warden Styrropp the tragedye of Salomon and Perceda*[1]

Shortly afterwards (presumably) White engaged Edward Allde to print his new acquisition, undated:

> *The Tragedye of Solyman and Perseda. Wherein is laide open, Loues constancy, Fortunes inconstancy, and Deaths Triumphs.*

Only one copy of this Quarto has survived, now in the British Library, and on bibliographical evidence it has been dated '1592'. White published a second edition in 1599, with a further issue that year, on which 'an additional line of type was stamped in, apparently by hand, after the sheet was printed', with the claim 'Newly corrected and amended'. Thomas Hawkins was the first scholar to identify Kyd's authorship, since 'it carries with it many internal marks of that author's manner of composition'. Hawkins noted that 'in *The Spanish Tragedy* the story of Erastus and Perseda is introduced by Hieronimo' in the play-within-the-play. Hawkins was the first editor to divide the play into five acts and he made

---

1. All bibliographical information is taken from Greg, *BEPD*, 1.8, 186–7 (no. 109).

a number of valuable emendations.[2] Gregor Sarrazin was the first scholar to show that Kyd's source, as for the playlet in *The Spanish Tragedy*, was the opening novella in Henry Wotton's collection, *A Courtlie Controversie of Cupids Cautels Containing five tragicall Historyes by 3 gentlemen, 2 gentlewoman* (1578), translated from Jacques Yver's *Le Printemps d'Yver* (1572).[3] Sarrazin demonstrated the many verbal details that the author of *Soliman and Perseda* had borrowed from Wotton, but also showed that several close parallels existed between the novella and *The Spanish Tragedy*, strong evidence that Kyd had written both plays.[4] His attribution was endorsed by F. S. Boas in 1901 with a range of additional evidence that made it definite. It was additionally confirmed by Arthur Freeman (1967) and Lukas Erne (2010), both of whom added still more detail.[5] Sarrazin argued that it antedated *The Spanish Tragedy*, citing its frequent use of the archaic expression 'for to' followed by the infinitive.[6] Freeman argued for a dating in around 1593; Erne placed it in 1588–9; J. J. Murray argued for 1587, perhaps with a later re-working in 1591;[7] Wiggins dates it 1588.[8]

Elizabethan dramatists regularly took the plots of their plays from printed sources. The Bible, ancient history, English chronicles, Italian novella and their French imitations, recent narrative poems, real-life crimes, all were pressed into service.[9] Thanks to the intensive study of

2. See Thomas Hawkins (ed.), *The Origin of the English Drama*, 2 vols (London. 1783), 2.195–284, cited in Lukas Erne (ed.), *Soliman and Perseda [1592/93]* (Manchester, 2014; Malone Society Reprints), pp. viii–x. In his appendix, Erne lists 18 of Hawkins's emendations, all of which have been accepted by subsequent editors.

3. See Sarrazin, *Thomas Kyd und sein Kreis*, pp. 1–48, including a partial reprint (pp. 12–40) of the source, Wotton's *Courtlie controversie of Cupids Cautels* (1578). Unless otherwise noted, translations from the German are mine.

4. Ibid., pp. 42–4.

5. See Boas, *Works of Thomas Kyd*, pp. liv–lvi; Erne, *Beyond* The Spanish Tragedy, pp. 157–202; Freeman, *Thomas Kyd*, pp. 140–66.

6. Sarrazin, *Thomas Kyd und sein Kreis*, p. 58. The phrase is used six times.

7. See John J. Murray (ed.), *The Tragedye of Solyman and Perseda* (New York and London, 1991), pp. vii–ix.

8. Wiggins, *British Drama*, 2.403–6.

9. See Max Bluestone, *From Story to Stage. The Dramatic Adaptation of Prose Fiction in the Period of Shakespeare and his Contemporaries* (The Hague, Paris, 1974).

Shakespeare's sources, we have a good idea of the range of material available to an industrious—and, fortunately, long-lived dramatist.[10] The main reason for studying a play's sources is to see how the dramatist creatively transformed them. Kyd added fresh characters to his source plot, introduced extant characters earlier in the play, to link them more closely to the action, and added parallel plots.

Kyd took the story from Wotton but introduced many changes.[11] As I have shown elsewhere, he borrowed from his friend, Thomas Watson, the triad of allegorical figures representing Love, Fortune, and Death who act as a Chorus to the play.[12] Their contest to claim the absolute power over human actions is presented in the opening scene and hangs over the entire play, reappearing at the end of each Act, with Death finally claiming the prize in the Epilogue. Thus, as in *The Spanish Tragedy*, human actions expressing the conflict of human desires and the law of cause and effect, are placed within a framework suggesting that they are influenced by superior forces. The catastrophe is essentially the same as in *The Spanish Tragedy*, in the fatal love triangle by which Soliman kills his friend Erastus in order to enjoy Perseda, only to be killed by her. This is already a re-shaping of the source, where Perseda is killed in the siege of Rhodes, having failed to achieve revenge, and Soliman erects a splendid marble tomb to the lovers' memory (Wotton, pp. 67–72)—a conclusion that Kyd evidently regarded as undramatic. Faced with the task of expanding this rather simple story of jealousy and violence to a full-length play, Kyd's main change was to add two new characters, Basilisco and Piston, to form a comic underplot. He broke up the block-composition of the source, in which the first part of the story takes place in Rhodes, the second in Constantinople, by introducing a scene with the Turkish Emperor early on (1.5), and by freely moving between the

10. See Geoffrey Bullough (ed.), *Narrative and Dramatic Sources of Shakespeare*, 8 vols (London, 1957–75), and the excellent compendium, freshly updating and evaluating the primary and secondary literature, Stuart Gillespie, *Shakespeare's Books. A Dictionary of Shakespeare's Sources* (London and Brunswick, NJ, 2001).

11. Quotations from Wotton come from the selection printed by Sarrazin (*Thomas Kyd und sein Kreis*, pp. 12–40), but giving the page references of the original edition (London, 1578).

12. See Vickers, 'Embedded Poetry'.

two locales in Acts 3 to 5. Of many other changes, well analysed by Lukas Erne,[13] I wish to focus on the elements of intrigue that Kyd added.

Intrigue: Winners and Losers

In the source (set on the island of Rhodes) Erastus falls in love with Perseda, they exchange presents (he gives a jewel, she a golden chain or 'carcanet'), and they live happily together for ten months (Wotton, pp. 34–7). Then a tournament is held to celebrate the wedding between a local nobleman's daughter and the Prince of Cyprus, at which an unknown knight defeats all comers (pp. 37–9). The bridegroom removes the victorious knight's helmet, revealing Erastus, but in the process accidentally dislodges the carcanet, which falls to the ground. It is found by 'a Gentleman of the town', who gives it to a 'countrey Damosel named Lucina' (pp. 39–45). When Perseda happens to see this girl wearing the chain she concludes that Erastus has betrayed her, and returns his love token, breaking off their relationship (pp. 45–50). Desperate to regain the carcanet, Erastus becomes friendly with Lucina, manages to win back the chain at some 'playe' or wager, only to be confronted by her jealous lover, who attacks Erastus and is killed by him (pp. 51–3).

Erastus flees to Constantinople, where he is accepted into Soliman's military elite, and is victorious in several battles, winning the Emperor's regard. When the Turks decide to attack Rhodes, however, Erastus refuses to fight against his native town, and Soliman himself leads the victorious army, returning with Perseda as his prisoner (pp. 53–6). The Emperor falls in love with her, but Perseda rejects his advances and tries to commit suicide, being foiled by Soliman (pp. 56–8). When Erastus meets Perseda again they greet each other with such signs of 'unseperable love' that Soliman gives the woman who has refused him to his friend Erastus 'as Lover and lawfull espouse, although I am enforced to confesse, that her beautie . . . hath untill this presente hadde auchthoritye to commaunde me' (p. 60).

---

13. See Erne, *Beyond* The Spanish Tragedy, pp. 168–82, a perceptive account.

Soliman generously makes Erastus governor of Rhodes, and life returns to normal. But Soliman was haunted by Perseda's beauty, a 'greefe that little by little grew so greate' until he felt 'bitter repentance of his . . . unadvised liberalitie' (p. 61). Some time later he decides 'to impart his greefe unto his Cousin Brusor', who, as it happened, 'envied Erastus extremely' for having been so favoured by the Emperor. After 'long deliberation and counsell in the matter' Brusor tells Soliman that he will not succeed with Perseda 'unlesse she were first deprived of Erastus' (p. 65). He advises Soliman to recall Erastus to Constantinople and then accuse him of

> revolt and rebellion, whereupon being committed to prison for the
> offence, judgement and execution of death may ensue. The Emperour
> joyfully embracing this wicked counsellor, commended exceedingly
> his invention, and dispatched him presently to practise the execution
> of his divelish device. (p. 65)

(The narrator's anger at 'this wicked counsellor' and 'his divelish device' reminds us of the moral expectations on which Elizabethan drama depends, although it often foregoes formulating them.)

Having travelled to Rhodes, Brusor, 'under colour of secret and waightie affaires allured and ledde poore Erastus to Constantinople', where he is accused 'by false witnesse, of purpose provided', and beheaded (p. 66). Struck down with grief, Perseda plans to kill herself, but her servant urges her not to do so 'untill you have revenged the death' of Erastus. Perseda puts on Erastus' armour, ascends the castle battlements, denounces Soliman as a 'cruell and ungratefull wretch', and exposes herself to 'a volee of shot, among the which two bullets sent from a Musket stroke hir through the stomack' (p. 67). Having erected a magnificent monument to the two lovers, Soliman 'caused the traitor Brusor to bee hanged, in the guerdon of his wicked counsell' (p. 72).

With our knowledge of *The Spanish Tragedy*, it is easy to see what attracted Kyd to this story of violence and betrayal, a fatal conflict between love and friendship. But the novella lacked several elements necessary to Kyd's conception of an effective plot. The 'gentleman' who found Lucina's chain is unnamed, and Lucina disappears from the story as soon as Erastus has regained it. The novella devotes a great deal of space to the lovers' laments in the privacy of their chambers, but seldom brings them face to face. It gestures at the friendship between Soliman and Perseda, but hardly shows them together, and gives no insight into the Turk's mentality. Above all, in the novella the climactic intrigue is introduced late, by a character we have never seen before, and is perfunctorily despatched in a few lines of narration, passing over a scene of great dramatic potential.

Kyd rectifies these failings by giving Lucina's friend a name, Ferdinando, and creating a destructive triangular relationship which echoes that in the main plot, with Erastus involved in both. His killing of Ferdinando gives Lucina a motive for taking revenge on him, just as Soliman's execution of Erastus gives Perseda a motive for wanting revenge (a motive that the source signally fails to exploit). Where the source allows Lucina to disappear from the story, Kyd makes her the companion of Perseda in Rhodes, when they jointly lament the loss of their lovers (3.2.1–15). Kyd has both women captured by Soliman's forces attacking Rhodes, but in his play the Turkish army is led by Brusor (now the Emperor's 'bashaw'). Kyd took pains to develop Brusor into a character who is involved in the play from first to last. He is one of the Knights whom Erastus defeats in the tourney at Rhodes (1.3.47–63, 194–5), a humiliation that provides Brusor with his first motive for revenge. Brusor subsequently brings Soliman news of Erastus's victory in the tourney (3.1.16–30) and presents Erastus to the Emperor in person (3.1.68). In the play Kyd has Brusor sent to attack Rhodes, which means that Soliman can spend more time in Erastus' company, and thoroughly establishes the friendship between the two men (3.1.143–9, 4.1.7–57), with Soliman as the more appreciative one. When Brusor returns with two female captives, Perseda and Lucina, Soliman reserves Perseda for himself and gives Lucina to Brusor (4.1.71–2): they form a couple each of whom has a motive for harming Erastus, as we see in the final intrigue.

94   CHAPTER 3

When Soliman gives the governorship of Rhodes to Erastus, this arouses Brusor's displeasure:

> Must he reap that for which I took the toil?
> Come, Envy, then, and sit in friendship's seat!
> How can I love him that enjoys my right?   (4.1.182–4)[14]

By adding Brusor's sense of ingratitude and resentment to the story, Kyd has provided the motivation for Brusor's wish 'to stumble him | That thrust his sickle in my harvest corn!' (4.1.221–2), a motive that appears suddenly in the source, and late on. Brusor's first advice is to woo Perseda 'with secret letters . . . and with gifts', and when Soliman rejects this as ineffective Kyd brings into action the other character whom Erastus has harmed, as Lucina offers her services:

> Hear me, my lord, let me go over to Rhodes,
> That I may plead in your affection's cause.
> One woman may do much to win another.   (4.1.228–30)

The Emperor counters that so long as Erastus lives 'there is no hope in her', from which Brusor draws the obvious conclusion that Erastus must die. The loyal servant outlines a plot to falsely accuse Erastus of treason, 'And then he shall be doomed by martial law'. (4.1.245–50). 'O fine device!', Soliman exclaims, echoing Lorenzo's pleasure on hearing Hieronimo's description of the plot of *Soliman and Perseda*, 'O excellent!' (*Sp. T.* 4.1.127). In the source the trial and execution of Erastus receives a few perfunctory lines, but Kyd makes out of it a most affecting scene.[15]

---

14. I cite the edition by Matthew Dimmock in Vickers (ed.), *The Collected Works of Thomas Kyd*, vol. 1, pp. 333–485.

15. See Erne, *Beyond* The Spanish Tragedy, p. 179, for an excellent analysis of 4.1, 'both a trial and an eavesdropping scene. The staging is of a sophistication that goes beyond Kyd's predecessors and is rare even in early Shakespeare. The scene displays the same interest in multilayered action as the play-within-the-play in *The Spanish Tragedy*. The central action—involving the Lord Marshal, the two false witnesses, the Janissaries, and Erastus—is watched over by the hidden Soliman. Simultaneously, the trial and Soliman are spied on by Piston, who escapes when Erastus is strangled'. Erne rightly places it, 'as a two-layered eavesdropping scene' alongside *Troilus and Cressida* 5.2, 'where Diomedes and Cressida are spied upon by Troilus and Ulysses and all four are watched by Thersites'.

Soliman allows the Lord Marshal to conduct the trial of 'our perjured friend' and conceals himself to observe it: 'Here will I stand to see and not be seen' (5.2.4). This is another eavesdropping-with-commentary scene, just like that in *The Spanish Tragedy* (2.2.7–57), where Lorenzo and Balthazar spy on the love-encounter between Horatio and Belimperia, their vicious commentary accompanying the lovers' words. But Kyd gives an added dimension to this scene in that Soliman's asides display a changing state of mind quite unlike the superiority that the eavesdropper normally enjoys over his victims. Soliman's intrigue has given him a privileged position, but as he witnesses the proceedings his divided reactions, expressed in asides to us, reveal a huge internal crisis of feeling, passing through three stages:

(i)   See where he comes, whom though I dearly love,
      Yet must his blood be spilt for my behoof.   (5.2.12–13)
(ii) My self would be his witness, if I durst,
      But bright Perseda's beauty stops my tongue.   (32–3)
(iii) O unjust Soliman; O wicked time,
      Where filthy lust must murder honest love!   (82–3)

That final comment shows the complexity of feeling that Kyd has developed from a few hints in the source, with Soliman's moral sense gaining the upper hand as he denounces himself as guilty of 'filthy lust'—before proceeding with the execution. His intrigue, suggested and abetted by Brusor, Lucina, and all those who have taken part in the rigged trial, had as its aim the elimination of Erastus, a goal which is attained in the source without any complications. But Kyd has noted other places in the novella where Soliman's behaviour was violent and irrational, as when, after Perseda's death from a musket's bullet, the Emperor first 'a thousand tymes kissed hir colde mouth', then 'drew his faulchion, and brandishing his poysie brond [weighty sword] about him, he hurt and slew as many of his people as would abide, but speedily they fled hys presence and lefte hym alone' (Wotton, p. 69). Having formed from this description a conception of Soliman's violent swings of mood, Kyd invented a scene (1.5) displaying a quarrel between his two brothers, in which Amurath kills Haleb. In return Soliman, mourning Haleb—angrily kills Amurath—but he then mourns Amurath. This spectacle may have prepared the audience for what is otherwise a stunning volte-face, one of those surprises Kyd liked to keep in store. No sooner has Soliman witnessed Erastus being strangled than he emerges from his hiding-place:

> Ah, poor Erastus, art thou dead already?
> What bold presumer durst be so resolved
> For to bereave Erastus' life from him,
> Whose life to me was dearer than mine owne? (5.2.102–5)

The 'recoil on the self' which we have already witnessed in Soliman now takes its logical development, as, forgetting his own agency, he orders all those who have helped to carry out his previous wishes by killing Erastus to be executed. Soliman himself kills the two Janissaries who strangled Erastus (5.2.104–7). Then the Lord Marshal takes the two perjured witnesses—'Your self procured us', one of them complains, 'Is this our hire?', wails the other (115)—and *bears them to the tower top*, as the stage direction puts it, from whence *they are both tumbled down* (116–24). Like the hanging of Pedringano in *The Spanish Tragedy*, Kyd creates a daring dramatic effect, exploiting the structural resources of the Elizabethan theatre. That only leaves 'the wicked Judge' to be disposed of—a deed that Soliman subcontracts to his Bashaw:

> Brusor, as thou lovest me, stab in the Marshal,
> Lest he detect us unto the world
> By making known our bloody practices (133–5)

There Kyd shows Soliman unusually sensitive to public opinion; or perhaps it reflects the Elizabethans' received image of the Ottoman empire, wishing to conceal their crimes against humanity.

The normal goal of an intrigue plot, as we have seen, is to harm others and benefit yourself. Soliman imagined that he would gain Perseda by killing Erastus, but Kyd has built up the friendship between the two men so convincingly that we recognize the ironic reversal by which the intrigue yields the opposite result to that expected: Soliman damages himself. He has failed to think beyond the immediate gratification of his desires and becomes an almost tragic figure in his divided reactions, the most complex character in the play.[16] Lucina has also failed to project into the future the consequences of aiding and abetting Soliman. When Perseda learns of Erastus' betrayal and murder, she realizes that Lucina has been an accomplice in the plot against him, and kills her (5.3.39–43), another instance of the chains of causation which are so strong in Kyd's plays. Harm generates counter-harm: no one escapes.

Comedy in Tragedy

The three changes that Kyd made to Wotton's narrative, involving additional appearances for Brusor, Lucina, and Soliman, are all success-ful, strengthening each role. But less successful were his other extensive additions to the plot, involving two new characters, who form a loosely related comic underplot. Kyd took advantage of the joust in Wotton's novella to introduce the anti-type of knightly virtue, Basilisco, a 'Brag-gart Soldier' or *miles gloriosus*. He appears in nine scenes, six of them with Piston, who doubles up as the cheeky servant familiar from Plautus and Terence, mocking and teasing his master. As comic characters, they essentially belong in the medium of prose, reserved in Elizabethan drama for servants, clowns, drunkards, mad people, and foreigners.[17]

Kyd observed—indeed, helped to create—this convention, but none of the early editions observed it, possibly due to the untidiness of the manuscript. Editing the play in 1901, F. S. Boas failed to recognize the appropriate medium and mostly set Basilisco's part as verse. It was left to a German scholar, Walther Miksch, to point out that the Basilisco scenes must be treated as prose, since if set as blank verse they seem so clumsy or jerky ('holperig') as to suggest that the dramatist was trying to make the character look ridiculous through his speech.[18] It is greatly to the credit of John J. Murray, in his edition of *Soliman and Perseda*, that

---

16. See Arthur Freeman's comment: 'Kyd has . . . converted Soliman from a simple and passionate tyrant to a complex character in whom rage and remorse alternate with heroic rapidity . . .' (p. 147). For 'heroic' I would suggest 'frenetic'.

17. See, e.g., Vickers, *Artistry of Shakespeare's Prose*.

18. Walther Miksch, 'Die Verfasserschaft des *Arden of Feversham* (Ein Beitrag zur Kydforschung)', Ph.D. Diss., Universität zu Breslau (1907), pp. 59–60.

he treated Basilisco's speeches as prose, and Arthur Freeman's otherwise justified criticism of Murray's textual inaccuracies is defective on this point.[19] It is especially disappointing that Ladan Niayesh, in her 2018 edition of the play, followed Boas.[20] Inability to 'read' this convention means that editors and readers fail to appreciate the delicious scene where Kyd allows Basilisco to adopt the dignity of Petrarchan verse in attempting to woo Perseda (2.1.30–82).

Needing new material to fill out his plot to the appropriate length for a public theatre play, Kyd made great use of Basilisco. His dependence can be seen from the remarkable amount of space he gave to creating 'a substantial character', as Lukas Erne terms him: 'His part is about as large as Erastus's in terms of the number of lines, but significantly bigger in terms of stage presence. Whereas the lovers are largely static characters who speak and lament, Basilisco performs the type of actions spectators are likely to remember.'[21] True enough, he enters riding on that lowly animal, a mule; he climbs a ladder, is pulled down by Piston and is made to swear an oath on the page's dagger, a scene that Shakespeare alluded to in *King John*.[22] Perseda, wishing to get rid of him, sends him to put on his armour, in which he makes a doubtless awkward reappearance.

Memorable though he may be in these farcical scenes, Basilisco is hardly of equal importance to Erastus, and some of the long speeches

19. Originally a Ph.D. Dissertation (New York University, 1959), subsequently published as *The Tragedye of Solyman and Perseda*, ed. J.J. Murray (New York, 1991). In 1967 Freeman dismissed Murray's edition as 'extremely undependable, both textually and critically' (p. 156; also pp. 145, 154 note, 158), and added this scornful footnote: 'In Murray's edition a considerable quantity of blank verse is printed, for no reason presumably but that it scans a little roughly, as prose' (p. 156 n.). However, Murray had good reason to do this.

20. See Ladan Niayesh (ed.), *Three Romances of Eastern Conquest* (Manchester, 2018), p. 42. This is otherwise a useful edition, including Greene's *Alphonsus, King of Aragon* and Heywood's *The Four Prentices of London*.

21. Erne, *Beyond* the Spanish Tragedy, p. 192.

22. Piston formulates an oath referring simply to 'Basilisco' without his title, who objects: '—Knight, good fellow, knight, knight!', to which Piston replies 'Knave, good fellow, knave, knave!' In *King John*, when Lady Faulconbridge describes her bastard son as an 'untoward knave' he replies: 'Knight, knight, good mother, Basilisco-like' (1.1.242–3).

that Kyd gave him are inadequately energized by the dramatic context. One way of achieving this goal was demonstrated by Plautus, who used the comic stereotype of a braggart soldier in seven of his twenty extant plays. In his *Miles Gloriosus* the braggart soldier Pyrgopolynices ('terrific tower-taker', in Plautus' invented name) is accompanied by his parasite, or hanger-on, Artotrogus ('bread-muncher'). As Eric Segal observes, they represent the 'quintessential comic opposites' defined by Aristotle, the *alazon* and the *eiron*.[23] The *alazon* is 'the overstater, the bluffer, the great balloon of hot air', summed up in the word *alazoneia* (our nearest equivalent is *braggadocio*), while the *eiron* is 'the ironic man, the understater, the needle of "I know nothing" which takes the air out of the *alazon*'s "I know everything"'. In their opening exchange Plautus conveys some typical boasts of Pyrgopolynices by making the interlocutor seem to elicit them from the boaster while adding his own ironic comments. In Segal's lively translation:

> ARTOTROGUS: And then that elephant in India—
> The way your fist just broke his arm to smithereens.
> PYRGOPOLYNICES: What's that—his *arm*?
> ARTOTROGUS: I meant his leg, of course.
> PYRGOPOLYNICES: I gave him just an easy jab.
> ARTOTROGUS: A jab, of course!
> If you had really tried, you would have smashed his arm
> Right through his elephantine skin and guts and bone!
> PYRGOPOLYNICES: No more of this.
> ARTOTROGUS: Of course. Why bother to narrate
> Your many daring deeds to me—who knows them all.
> [*Aside.*] It's only for my stomach that I stomach him.
> While ears are suffering, at least my teeth are suppering.
> And so I yes and yes again to all his lies.[24]

---

23. See Eric Segal's translation, *Plautus, Four Comedies* (Oxford, 1996), pp. xxiii–xxvi. For Aristotle, see *Nicomachean Ethics*, 4.5. This binary category was revived in modern times by Northrop Frye, in *Anatomy of Criticism* (Princeton, NJ, 1957), pp. 40ff.

24. Segal, *Plautus, Four Comedies*, p. 4.

Plautus also gives his braggart a slave as servant, Palaestrio, who makes direct criticism of his employer. He delivers the prologue, informing us that

> This play is called the *Alazon* in Greek,
> A name translated 'braggart' in the tongue we speak.
> This town is Ephesus; that soldier is my master,
> Who's just gone to the forum. What a shameless crass bombaster!
> He's so full of crap and lechery, no lies are vaster.
> He brags that all the women seek him out *en masse*,
> The truth is, everywhere he goes they think he's just an ass.[25]

Kyd ignored Plautus's first, indirect method, but followed the second, giving Piston a speech directly describing his master's faults, ridiculing Basilisco as he sets off to the tilt:

> Truly, I am sorry for him. He joust like a knight? He'll jostle like a jade! It is a world to hear the fool prate and brag! He will jet as if it were a goose on a green! He goes many times supperless to bed, and yet he takes physic to make him lean. Last night he was bidden to a gentlewoman's to supper, and because he would not be put to carve,[26] he wore his hand in a scarf and said he was wounded. He wears a coloured lath in his scabbard, and when 'twas found upon him, he said he was wrathful, he might not wear no iron. He wears civet, and when it was asked him, where he had that musk, he said all his kindred smelt so. Is not this a counterfeit fool?   (1.3.85–94)

(Since civet is a powerfully smelling fluid from the anal glands of the genus *Viverra*, Basilisco is declaring an unfortunate kinship.) But these are comments made in Basilisco's absence, not in direct confrontation with an ironic interlocutor. Instead, Kyd gave us the boaster on his own, heaping up extravagant claims with no independent perspective that

---

25. Ibid., p. 6.

26. Strangers at a feast might be invited to carve the main meat dish, but Basilisco considers this beneath his dignity. The 'coloured lath' in his scabbard is a thin piece of wood painted to look like a sword, traditionally worn by the Vice figure of the medieval morality plays.

could 'place' him. In his first appearance Basilisco delivers a thirty-three-line speech, from which I choose this typical excerpt:

> Upon a time in Ireland I fought on horseback with an hundred kerns [soldiers], from Titan's eastern uprise, to his western downfall, insomuch that my steed began to faint. I, conjecturing the cause to be want of water, dismounted in which place there was no such element. Enraged therefore, with this scimitar [I], all on foot, like an Herculean offspring, endured some three or four hours' combat, in which process, my body distilled such dewy showers of sweat that from war-like wrinkles of my front by palfrey cooled his thirst.   (1.2.91–110)

That is one of several fantastic claims that Basilisco makes, rather like another *miles gloriosus*, Baron Münchausen, but it is not amusing. It lacks a comic context. The function of the ironic commentator is to represent a norm by which we can estimate the extravagance of the boaster's lies.

Kyd is more successful in a scene where Basilisco tells Piston how he intends to defeat Erastus in combat, in which his shield will be strong enough to deflect cannon shot (very likely!):

> That, once put by, I roughly come upon him, like to the wings of lightning from above. I with a martial look astonish him. Then falls he down, poor wretch, upon his knee, and all too late, repents his surquidry. Then do I take him on my finger's point, and thus I bear him thorough every street, to be a laughingstock to all the town. That done, I lay him at my mistress' feet, for her to give him doom or life or death.
>   PISTON Ay, but hear you sir, I am bound, in pain of my master's displeasure, to have a bout at cuffs, afore you and I part.   (2.3.56–64)

There, at least, the element of fantasy is clearly defined by introducing the future tense (rather like Malvolio's soliloquy in *Twelfth Night*) but Kyd fails to use Piston's presence to deflate the boaster.

Basilisco risks becoming a stand-up comedian, his solo performances unrelated to the dramatic action. His next soliloquy avoids this danger, being a comment on what has been happening since we saw him last.

Brusor and his soldiers have captured Rhodes and taken as prisoners Perseda, Lucina, and their entourage. Two of her party refuse to 'turn Turk', loyal to their Christian beliefs, and are promptly executed. Basilisco ignobly cries out 'I turn, I turn! O save my life I turn!' Brusor protects him, announcing that 'When we land in Turkey, | He shall be circumcised and have his rites' (3.5.25–7).[27] Given that information, playgoers and readers are well placed to evaluate Basilisco's bizarre account of the event, which he takes as proving that

> the Christians are but very shallow in giving judgement of a man at arms, a man of my desert and excellence! The Turks, whom they account for barbarous, having fore-heard of Basilisco's worth, a number underprop me with their shoulders, and in procession bare me to the church, as I had been a second Mahomet. I, fearing they would adore me for a god, wisely informed them that I was but man, although in time perhaps I might aspire to purchase godhead, as did Hercules; I mean by doing wonders in the world. Amidst their church they bound me to a pillar, and to make trial of my valiancy, they lopped a collop off my tenderest member. But think you Basilisco squitched[28] for that? Even as a cow for tickling in the horn! That done, they set me on a milk white ass, compassing me with goodly ceremonies. That day, methought, I sat in Pompey's chair and viewed the Capitol, and was Rome's greatest glory. (3.5.1–19)

This speech, for once, draws on the immediate dramatic context, giving us the norm against which the *alazon*'s version can be judged. It would be a pity to disturb Basilisco's blissful ignorance, believing that the ritual was 'a trial of my valiancy', which he passed. An impressive detail, showing that Kyd had succeeded in creating a character with a life of its own, is the glimpse he gives us of Basilisco's self-estimate, on a level with Mahomet and Pompey, unaware of his vanities and delusions.

---

27. Niayesh, *Three Romances*, p. 30, lists several sixteenth-century accounts of Turkish circumcision rituals.

28. *OED* defines 'squitch' as 'To twitch or jerk (*away*)', with a first citation from 1680. However, the word also occurs in John Dolman's 1561 translation of Cicero's *Tusculan Disputations* (*STC* 5317).

Having invented Basilisco, Kyd linked him with the main action as an unwanted suitor for Perseda. After his lengthy public boast, left alone Basilisco reveals his inner self:

I am melancholy: an humour of Venus beleagereth me. I have rejected with contemptible frowns the sweet glances of many amorous girls, or rather ladies. But certes, I am now captivated with the reflecting eye of that admirable comet, Perseda. I will place her to behold my triumphs and do wonders in her sight.   (1.3.1–5)

Already the possessive lover, Basilisco becomes indignant when he hears Erastus call her 'My sweet Perseda', announcing 'I will follow for revenge' (24–5). Basilisco thinks himself into the role of Perseda's lover, a self-transformation that Kyd marks by allowing him to speak verse, the lover's medium, flourished in his effusive greeting for Ferdinando and Lucina:

All hail, brave cavalier! Good morrow, madam!
The fairest shine that shall this day be seen,
Except Perseda's beauteous excellence,
Shame to Love's queen, and empress of my thoughts.   (2.1.30–33)

A decade later such a pronounced pentameter would receive a scathing reaction:

ORLANDO: Good day and happiness, dear Rosalind.
JAQUES: Nay then, God b'wi' you an you talk in blank verse.
[Exit]   (As You Like It, 4.1.31–2).

Kyd expected that his audience, and readers would instantly recognize that Basilisco was 'putting on the style', without drawing attention to it. He has a more serious issue to deal with, Perseda's shocked reaction on recognizing Lucina's new ornament: 'she wears my carcanet! | Ah, false Erastus, how am I betrayed!' (2.1.48–9). Basilisco, worried that she might have been offended by his praise of Lucina, notices her upset: 'Say, world's bright star, | Whence springs this sudden change?' Assured of not being to blame, he launches himself as the newly minted Petrarchan lover:

What is it then, if love of this my person,
By favour and by justice of the heavens,
At last have pierced through thy tralucent[29] breast,
And thou misdoubts, perhaps, that I'll prove coy?

In this period the word 'person' still referred to the human body,[30] so the actor might preen himself while looking upwards to heaven. With his 'person' in mind, Basilisco reassures his beloved that he won't be 'coy'—that is, as the *OED* defines it: 'Displaying modest backwardness or shyness (sometimes with emphasis on the displaying); not responding readily to familiar advances'. The notion of Basilisco displaying modest backwardness is instantly risible, as Dr Johnson might have said, but for Perseda he is just an obstacle to be removed: '[*Aside*] Now must I find the means to rid him hence!' She orders him to arm 'from top to toe' and return in an hour's time, 'when thou in my behalf shalt work revenge'. Basilisco is delighted to be given employment suitable for 'men of valour':

This is good argument of thy true love.
I go, make reckoning that Erastus dies,
Unless forewarned, the weakling coward flies!

When he is out of hearing Perseda exclaims: 'Thou foolish coward! "Flies"?' This scene is far more successful than Basilisco's first self-presentation because Kyd has provided a second level of perception and judgment. He allows the braggart to continue his self-deluding role as lover while juxtaposing him with Perseda's irritation and disgust. By not

---

29. Kyd used 'translucent' in *The Spanish Tragedy*. The *OED* lists this as the first usage in English of 'tralucent' (a variant, meaning 'to shine through'). The second instance comes from Jonson's *Masque of Beautie* (1608) describing his stage setting: 'In the centre of the throne was a tralucent Pillar, shining with several-coloured lights that reflected on their [the masquers'] backs'. What can be shining through Perseda's breast? Basilisco flaunts a new word without knowing what it means.

30. Cf. Jonathan Swift: 'Last Week I saw a Woman *flay'd*, and you will hardly believe, how much it altered her Person for the worse', *The Tale of a Tub*, chapter 9, 'A Digression concerning Madness', in Herbert Davis (ed.), *The Prose Writings of Jonathan Swift*, 14 vols (Oxford, 1939–65), 1.109.

letting her reveal her true feelings Kyd maintains the gap between them, as appropriate for a comic butt.

Vengeful Woman

From the outset Kyd conceived Perseda as a resourceful woman, always ready to act boldly in her own interests. As Lukas Erne pointed out, Kyd changed his source in making her take the initiative in exchanging love tokens with Erastus (1.2.30–38).[31] Having seen Lucina wearing the carcanet, Perseda wrongly deduces that Erastus has betrayed her. Seeing him approaching, she declares her intention to 'frame myself to his dissembling art', but after a few moments of Erastus's explanation she finds herself unable to sustain the pretence, uttering her grief and unrestrained anger against him:

> If heavens were just, thy teeth would tear thy tongue
> For this thy perjured false disloyalty!   (2.1.124–5)

The threefold repetition of *thy*, coupled with the matching *th* of *this* and the alliteration on *teeth* and *tear* forces the actor to spit out these lines. She reproaches him with an enormously powerful speech (2.1.112–49), ten lines longer even than Bel-imperia's denunciation of Hieronimo's inaction. In this speech Perseda becomes, like her, the unchallengeable arbiter of right and wrong: 'The fault is thine!' (144). She breaks off their relationship on a note of finality: 'Perseda now is free, | And all my former love is turned to hate' (153–4).

The finality is only temporary. When Piston presents the chain that Erastus had won back, with the instruction to 'give it you, for perfect argument that he was true, and you too credulous', Perseda realizes that she has been 'too cruel' (2.2.8). When she learns of Erastus' desperate measures in regaining the chain, killing Ferdinando and being forced to flee Rhodes, Perseda accepts responsibility:

> My heart had armed my tongue with injury,
> To wrong my friend, whose thoughts were ever true.   (22–3)

31. Erne, *Beyond* The Spanish Tragedy, p. 170.

Kyd's presentation of her is always sympathetic, a figure of feminine dignity and sincerity. But he could still make fun of her in the scene where she and Lucina, sharing the same situation, express it in identical terms:

PERSEDA: Accursèd chain! Unfortunate Perseda!
LUCINA: Accursèd chain! Unfortunate Lucina!
My friend is gone, and I am desolate.
PERSEDA: My friend is gone, and I am desolate.
Return him back, fair stars, or let me die.
LUCINA: Return him back fair heavens, or let me die,
For what was he, but comfort of my life?
PERSEDA: For what was he, but comfort of my life?   (3.2.1–8)

That sequence—which Kyd continues for another ten lines—mixes pathos with a degree of ridicule, as if they were singing an operatic duet, lovers having the same stereotyped reactions. (Da Ponte and Mozart use this device brilliantly in *Così fan Tutte*.)

Three short scenes later, Brusor conquers Rhodes and the two women are shipped off to Constantinople as the booty of war. Kyd shows Soliman's infatuation with Perseda by making him praise her beauty with a stock device from Renaissance love poetry, the blazon, the formulaic cataloguing of a woman's beauty, starting with the head and moving downwards. Thanks to Kyd's familiarity with the poetry of Thomas Watson, Soliman uses all the appropriate resources of Petrarchism.[32] His persuasions having failed, he uses threats:

SOLIMAN: Why, thy life is done, if I but say the word.
PERSEDA: Why, that's the period that my heart desires.
SOLIMAN: And die thou shalt, unless thou change thy mind.
PERSEDA: Nay then, Perseda grows resolute.
Soliman's thoughts and mine resemble
Lines parallel that never can be joined.

---

32. In 1898 Sarrazin, *Thomas Kyd und sein Kreis*, (p. 6) quoted sonnet 21 of Watson's *Hekatompathia* for a close parallel to this blazon. Boas, in *Works of Thomas Kyd* (p. lix), dismissed it as just a 'stock Renaissance catalogue of feminine charms', but the similarity is striking.

Having warned him that her affections are 'like pillars of adamant' (97), she rejects him with a decisive analogy from geometry, all the more remarkable in a woman's mouth (possibly unique in Elizabethan drama). That word 'resolute' characterizes all of Kyd's strong-hearted women, whether their actions be good or bad.

Rebuffed, in an act of high drama, Soliman prepares 'the stroke of death', ordering Brusor to cover Perseda with a cloth so that he won't be distracted by her beauty. However, in the event he is unable to go through with it, the only time in the play that he fails to deliver death with his scimitar. Indeed, in a total change of direction typical of this whimsical ruler, he admits that he has submitted to the power of Cupid ('Love would not let me kill thee'). He voluntarily retreats to the status of a conventional lover, vowing 'in honest sort to court thee', that is, to respect her chastity (4.1.148). This is the behaviour of any decent young bachelor, but incongruous in the autocratic ruler of an empire. A moment later Erastus appears, and Kyd gives us another example of lovers echoing each other's thoughts and words:

> PERSEDA: My sweet and best beloved!
> ERASTUS: My sweet and best beloved!
> PERSEDA: For thee, my dear Erastus, have I lived.
> ERASTUS: And I for thee, or else I had not lived.   (155–8)

They continue for another seven lines, making Soliman (in an aside) deduce that 'heavens and heavenly powers do manage love', and that he should best allow them to marry. This is Soliman's greatest volte-face, acknowledging a power stronger than his own. He crowns this unexpected generosity by appointing Erastus governor of Rhodes, only requesting that, for urgent personal reasons, they should set sail immediately. We alone know what this 'privy cause' is.

Soliman's generosity in yielding her to Erastus seems to be the happy turning point in their lives. But the intrigue proposed by Brusor results in Erastus' murder, and when Piston brings the news of his death, Perseda realizes that she has been betrayed by the woman closest to her:

> Lucina, came thy husband to this end,
> To lead a lamb unto the slaughterhouse?

Hast thou for this, in Soliman's behalf
With cunning words tempted my chastity?
Thou shalt abye for both your treacheries [pay]
It must be so. (5.3.40–44)

Basilisco being present during this exchange, Perseda follows Elizabethan norms by turning to a man for help in performing a violent act:

Basilisco, dost thou love me? Speak!
BASILISCO: Ay, more than I love either life or soul. What, shall
I stab the Emperor for thy sake?
PERSEDA: No, but Lucina. If thou lovest me, kill her.
    Then Basilisco takes a dagger and feels upon the point of it.
BASILISCO: The point will mar her skin.

Her request is as dramatic as Beatrice's to Benedict: 'Kill Claudio!' The braggart warrior, having fatuously offered to kill Soliman, now confronts reality. Basilisco's feeble pretence to evaluate the consequences of such an act—as if he didn't know—having revealed his cowardice, Perseda takes on the man's role:

What, darest thou not? give me the dagger then—
There's a reward for all thy treasons past.
    Then Perseda kills Lucina. (50)

As with all the onstage deaths in this play, the speed and lack of preparation creates a shock effect that leaves theatregoers and readers momentarily dazed. Basilisco breaks the silence by expressing willingness to perform a menial task far below his chivalric pretensions, offering to 'bear her hence, to do thee good', help contemptuously rejected: 'No, let her lie, a prey to ravening birds'.

That must have been a horrifying, almost unnatural, event to an Elizabethan audience. Basilisco's silence may have been due to shock, or disbelief that Perseda was capable of such a thing. It still astounds modern readers, even an enlightened editor, such as Ladan Niayesh:

The play also introduces Perseda as the stock figure of the delicate and loving heroine, but the vengeful cruelty she eventually exercises in stabbing Lucina when learning how the latter's beloved Brusor caused Erastus's fall, jars with that picture. The barbarousness of the act in 5.3 is felt even more through the contrasting attitude of Basilisco, whose refusal to commit the murder pushes Perseda to do it herself. For Freeman, this mixed scene brings out both the seriousness of Perseda's transgression and 'the essential humaneness of the comic crew, caught up in the web of tragic intrigue'.[33]

With due respect, it seems to me that neither scholar understands Kyd. In the world of his plays, a woman who has been betrayed, causing the death of her loved one, is entitled to take her own revenge. Who else will do it? And Basilisco's 'contrasted attitude' springs from a distinctly unworthy motive, cowardice.

Perseda instantly resolves to fortify Rhodes and deprive 'proud, insulting Soliman' of public victory and private pleasure:

> I know the letcher hopes to have my love,
> And first Perseda shall with this hand die,
> Then yield to him and live in infamy.   (5.3.55–60)

Like Bel-imperia, Perseda is ready to die for the man who was worthy of her, unlike 'the letcher' Soliman. After his vapid hyperboles on her beauty her use of that word is refreshingly direct, resolute, unforgiving.

In the theatre, as on the page, those thirty-five lines represent an experience of great intensity, which few dramatists could better. I find it all the more puzzling that Kyd should follow it with another long soliloquy from Basilisco on the 'ubi sunt' topic:[34]

> I will ruminate. Death, which the poets feign to be pale and meagre, hath deprived Erastus' trunk from breathing vitality. A brave cavalier, but my approved foeman. Let me see. Where is that Alcides, surnamed Hercules, the only club man of his time? Dead.

---

33. Niayesh, *Three Romances*, p. 31, citing Freeman, *Thomas Kyd*, p. 166.

34. So named after medieval poems beginning 'Where are . . . ?', used for meditations on mortality.

And so on though a conventional list of classical heroes. When Basilisco returns to himself he delivers further commonplaces:

> I am myself strong, but I confess Death to be stronger; I am valiant, but mortal; I am adorned with nature's gifts, a giddy goddess, that now giveth and anon taketh. I am wise, but quiddits [quibbles] will not answer Death. To conclude: in a word, to be captious, virtuous, ingenious, Or to be nothing when it pleaseth Death to be envious. (5.3.63–82)

This whole speech is also thirty-five lines but seems much longer and can only seem an anti-climax. It is 'in character' insofar as Basilisco puts himself in the same categories as famous classical warriors, but I find it out of place here. Perhaps Kyd wrote it as a farewell speech for the actor who had succeeded in the role; or perhaps he thought it desirable to have a contrast of mood after the sudden, unexpected revenge killing. But he left till last the most important insight into Basilisco's character, delivered by the man himself:

> I love Perseda as one worthy, but I love Basilisco as one I hold more worthy, my father's son, my mother's solace, my proper self. Faith, he can do little that cannot speak, and he can do less that cannot run away. Then, sith man's life is as a glass, and a filip [a smart tap] may crack it, mine is no more and a bullet may pierce it. Therefore I will play least in sight. (5.3.78–84)

As ever, Basilisco's logic is transparently defective, designed to protect his 'proper self', whatever other grandiose claims he may make. To 'play least in sight' sounds like an Elizabethan children's game (like hide and seek), at which he feels no shame. Unfortunately, Basilisco's timing is wrong, for he gets trapped in the castle as Soliman's forces attack.

Kyd has set the scene for his grand finale, where he makes the most effective alteration to his source. In Wotton, Perseda appears on the defensive walls as the Turks are preparing to attack, shouts angrily at Soliman, and is killed by a musketeer's bullets. That conclusion is unsatisfactory in every way, reducing her death to a mere incident of war. In *The Spanish Tragedy* Kyd had given Perseda a different role to play in Hieronimo's fatal entertainment, where she first kills Soliman, then herself. For the dénouement of his Turkish tragedy Kyd invented a third outcome. In the preceding scene Perseda had resolved to kill herself rather than 'yield to him and live in infamy' (5.3.57–8). Now the Turkish army arrives, led by Soliman, still deluded, still imagining that 'yet Perseda lives for Soliman' (5.4.13). A warrior appears *'upon the walls'*, wearing man's armour, and answers his questions boldly:

> SOLIMAN: Why, what art thou that dares resist my force?
> PERSEDA: A gentleman and thy mortal enemy,
> And one that dares thee to the single combat.
> SOLIMAN: First tell me, doth Perseda live or no?
> PERSEDA: She lives to see the wreck of Soliman.
> SOLIMAN: Then I'll combat thee what ere thou art.
> PERSEDA: And in Erastus' name I'll combat thee,
> And here I promise thee on my Christian faith,
> That if thy strength shall overmatch my right
> Then will I yield Perseda to thy hands.

To the audience the double meaning in her speech is clear, but Soliman is unable to see it. She comes down from the gallery to the main stage, accompanied by Piston and Basilisco, who each intervene in character:

> PISTON: Ay, but hear you, are you so foolish to fight with him?
> BASILISCO: Ay, sirrah, why not, as long as I stand by?
>
> *Then they fight, Soliman kills Perseda*

With her dying words she reveals her identity with a finely ironic verdict on this 'letcher':

> Ay, now I lay Perseda at thy feet,
> But with thy hand first wounded to the death.
> Now shall the world report that Soliman
> Slew Erastus in hope to win Perseda,
> And murdered her for loving of her husband.   (60–64)

The selfishness of the unwanted lover who destroys his rival has seldom been expressed so pithily. (It sounds like a chapter title in a Renaissance collection of tales.) The succeeding passage of dialogue marks a decisive moment in the play, as Soliman realizes that the intrigues he has launched to satisfy his desires have resulted in a second self-harming:

> SOLIMAN: What, my Perseda, ah what have I done!
> Yet kiss me, gentle love, before thou die.
> PERSEDA: A kiss I grant thee, though I hate thee deadly.
> SOLIMAN: I loved thee dearly and accept thy kiss.
> Why didst thou love Erastus more than me,
> Or why didst not give Soliman a kiss
> Ere this unhappy time? Then hadst thou lived!

For Soliman the kiss has a trophy (or booty) value, proof that he has finally managed to overcome the barrier of Perseda's chastity. It is, however, a futile achievement to kiss the lips of a dying woman. There can be little future in it. Spontaneously, her two companions join in, first Basilisco, another deluded wooer:

> BASILISCO: Ah, let me kiss thee too before I die.
> SOLIMAN: Nay, die thou shalt for thy presumption,
> For kissing her whom I do hold so dear.
> *Then Soliman kills Basilisco*
> PISTON: I will not kiss her, sir, but give me leave to weep over her,
> for while she lived, she loved me dearly, and I loved her.
> SOLIMAN: If thou didst love her, villain, as thou saidst,
> Then wait on her thorough eternal night.
> *Then Soliman kills Piston*

Piston and Basilisco are comic figures who have strayed into a tragedy by mistake. Their deaths are more upsetting than those of other bystanders in tragedy since they are unheroic, harmless, and silly. Piston does not carry a sword with which he could defend himself; Basilisco may have one but would be too scared to use it. Kyd has used comic irony to bring out the discrepancy between their being and their ends. It is not an outcome that one could generalize or moralize, any more than one could for Mercutio's death in *Romeo and Juliet*, another entertaining figure who is caught in the wrong place at the wrong time. But in blending comic intrigue and comic figures with a tragic dénouement, Kyd enlarged the scope of English tragedy.

Now there are three corpses onstage and only two characters left alive. Our attention is fixed on Soliman as he agonizes over Perseda's death:

Ah, Perseda, how shall I mourn for thee?
Fair springing rose, ill plucked before thy time.   (80)

Kyd has created Soliman as an autocrat who has a reflex reaction of evading responsibility for misfortune, to the extreme point of killing those who have carried out his orders. At first he blames 'the heavens' for this double disaster, but soon his focus changes:

Even for Erastus' death, the heavens have plagued me.
Ah no, the heavens did never more accurse me,
Than when they made me butcher of my love.
Yet justly, how can I condemn myself,
When Brusor lives that was the cause of all?   (89–93)

The weasel word there is 'justly'. True, Brusor suggested the stratagem for getting rid of Erastus, but Soliman endorsed it, and only he is to blame for Perseda's death. The Emperor launches a kind of catechism questioning Brusor about Perseda: 'Is she not fair?', 'Was she not constant?', 'Was she not chaste?'[35] Brusor answers each question in the affirmative, and praises Erastus for his many virtues. Then Soliman turns on him:

Ah, was he so? How durst thou then, ungracious counsellor,
First cause me murder such a worthy man,
And after tempt so virtuous a woman?
Be this therefore the last that ere thou speak.
Janissaries, take him straight unto the block,
Off with his head, and suffer him not to speak!   (106–10)

When Erastus was executed, Kyd recreated the Turkish method of strangling, which involves tying the victim to a post. Since that would cause a delay here, Kyd has him whisked away.

---

35. There is an echo of this catechism in the dialogue between Othello and Iago reviewing Desdemona's admirable qualities (*Othello* 4.1.175–90).

Having vented his anger by disposing of Basilisco, Piston, and Brusor, Soliman has nothing left to do but, in a romantic gesture, to lie down next to Perseda. He is still the conventional lover, indulging himself with grand phrases:

And on thy beauty still contemplate
Until mine eyes shall surfeit by my gazing.

(How would you recognize the symptoms of surfeit?) But as he does so he notices a paper affixed to her corpse with a last message for him:

'Tyrant my lips were sauced with deadly poison,
To plague thy heart that is so full of poison.'
—What, am I poisoned?   (117–19)

Soliman spoke from a position of imagined superiority when he said 'I . . . accept thy kiss', not realizing that Perseda, displaying the same foresight as Hieronimo with his request for a knife, must have anticipated Soliman's wish that he should finally receive a kiss, and made it a deadly one. Soliman's plots have been undermined by an intriguer who looked further ahead, and who, like Hieronimo, had nothing left to live for. In Kyd's plays such people are the most dangerous enemies.

Kyd's invention has drawn on two motifs from European fiction: the woman disguised in armour who is killed in combat by the man who loves her,[36] and the poisoned kiss. His placing of them in this final scene is skilful, satisfying the reader and audience that retribution awaits even tyrants. Soliman's reaction to learning that Perseda has outwitted him, is violent:

Then Janissaries,
Let me see Rhodes recovered ere I die.
Soldiers, assault the town on every side.
Spoil all, kill all! Let none escape your fury!

---

36. See, e.g., the fight between Tancred and Clorinda in Tasso's *Gerusalemme Liberata*, set to music by Monteverdi; Spenser, *The Faerie Queene*, and Ariosto, *Orlando Furioso*.

To wish total destruction on every human being within his reach is perfectly suited to his megalomaniac personality. Kyd balances it with another detail completely in character, the persistence of a frustrated lover:

> Yet something more contentedly I die,
> For that my death was wrought by her device,
> Who living was my joy, whose death my woe.   (130–32)

After the satisfaction of finally being able to kiss Perseda, this is another fatuous self-consolation: 'At least she killed me! That shows I was someone special to her'.

In his dying speech Soliman wishes his body to be buried with those of Erastus and Perseda. He apologizes posthumously to Erastus, somehow claiming to have 'revenged thy death with many deaths'—but since it was he who had Erastus killed, it is absurd logic to claim that other people were to blame, or that the murder of those who obeyed his orders can constitute revenge. Kyd gives the last word to the unreformed, disappointed lover:

> And sweet Perseda, fly not Soliman,
> When as my gliding ghost shall follow thee,
> With eager mood, through eternal night.

Spectators and readers know what a nightmare it would be for Perseda, to be stalked by Soliman!

In his own way, Soliman has the same faults as Basilisco. Neither man has any idea of what his adored lady thinks of him. Perseda calls the one a 'lecher', the other a 'foolish coward'. Both suitors play out a would-be romance in which the woman is expected to fill the slot available for her. Kyd created two parallel portraits of the narcissistic, self-deluded lover, matching Balthazar in *The Spanish Tragedy*.

Looked at as a whole, *Soliman and Perseda* succeeds in expanding the brief treatment of Hieronimo's play-within-the-play, a mere sixty lines, into a fully articulated tragedy. The opening scenes of the two lovers' mutual declaration and exchange of love tokens, followed by Erastus's loss of the chain and Perseda's bitter complaints, are treated confidently and with verbal energy. In strict dramatic theory, accidents are an inferior cause of tragedy since they do not derive from personal responsibility. Kyd took over from his source two accidents, the loss of the carcanet and the fact that Erastus, having regained it, happens to meet Ferdinando, leading to their fight and the latter's death. However, as Erne has argued, in constructing his plots, Kyd's aim was 'to highlight a process of cause and effect'.[37] Ferdinando's death is a harming that gives Lucina a motive for revenge, which she carries out by persuading Perseda to remain in Rhodes while Erastus returns to Constantinople, to be killed by Soliman. Lucina's betrayal of Erastus is a harming which gives Perseda a motive for revenge by killing Lucina. Returning to the joust scene in Act 1, Erastus's defeat of Brusor gave the latter a (smaller) motive for revenge, which he duly executes.

Kyd ties together the various plot strands with the simple but fundamental narrative structure of harm followed by revenge. The three plot sequences that he creates interlock with each other. Erastus first gave Brusor a motive for revenge by defeating him in the tourney and by becoming Soliman's favourite. Erastus also gave Lucina a motive for revenge by killing her lover Ferdinando. Now she can help her husband Brusor in his manipulation of Soliman to have Erastus sent back to Constantinople, to his death. The most prolific user of the Harm-Revenge causation is Soliman, who first kills his brother Amurath for having murdered Haleb. In Act 5 Soliman has his revenge on Erastus, Basilisco, Piston, Brusor, and the population of Rhodes. But having been the agent in the deaths of four people who have harmed him, together with an unknown number of Rhodian citizens, Soliman is tricked into killing the one person he values above all others, Perseda. Having been the revenger and agent in all these plots, in an ironic reversal he becomes Perseda's victim. The only characters who stand outside this nexus are the braggart soldier and the witty servant. Although sources of comedy, they are marginal to the plot structure. They get sucked undeservedly into the Harm-Revenge sequence at the end, killed in Soliman's homicidal fury.

37. Erne, *Beyond* The Spanish Tragedy, p. 172.

Viewed in relation to the three plot strands that Kyd used in the first version of this story in *The Spanish Tragedy*, we can see that he has given most space to the murderous intrigues, in which Soliman and Brusor are set against Erastus and Perseda. These fill most of the action in the Constantinople scenes. As they come to a first climax in the murder of Erastus, Perseda emerges as the vengeful woman, ready to stab her harmer, but using subterfuge and physical combat to kill Soliman. As for the third element in Kyd's dramaturgy that I have distinguished, the use of comedy in a tragic context, in the person of Basilisco, at times the comedy becomes inflated as a thing in itself. It is only in a few shocking moments at the end that comedy turns into tragedy. *Soliman and Perseda* is a play of great variety, if less complex and less unified than *The Spanish Tragedy*, but no other Elizabethan dramatist could have written it.

Authorship Markers

The excellent facsimile edition of the play by Lukas Erne in the Malone Society Reprints series (2014) carries the subtitle 'Attributed to Thomas Kyd'. I mentioned earlier that the evidence presented by F. S. Boas in 1901 and other scholars, down to the monographs by Arthur Freeman (1967) and Erne himself (2001) left no doubt about Kyd's authorship. Professor Erne may well claim that he added the subtitle in his role as a textual editor, an austere discipline that requires a higher stage of proof than other areas of scholarship. I would reply that such proof has long been available if scholars knew where to look.

As long ago as 1909, J. E. Routh published a little-known essay in which he showed that Kyd used some unusual forms of rhyme.[38] He began: 'It is now generally conceded, on internal evidence, that Thomas Kyd wrote *Soliman and Perseda*', but offered additional evidence 'from certain rime schemes' that it shared with *The Spanish Tragedy* and *Cornelia*. Routh referred to 'the sporadic appearance in all three plays of three regular rime schemes; *aca*, where *c* is an unriming line; *abab*, and

---

38. J.E. Routh, 'Thomas Kyd's Rime Schemes and the Authorship of *Soliman and Perseda* and of *The First Part of Jeronimo*', *Modern Language Notes*, 20 (1905): 49–51.

aaa' (p. 49). The basic form of *Cornelia* is decasyllabic couplets, Kyd's preferred medium for Garnier's alexandrine couplets, but Routh identified four instances of the *aca* scheme: *best/stand/rest* (1.1.35–7); *libertie/honors/tyrannie* (3.1.30–32); *jarres/earth/warres* (4.1.35–7); and *libertie/house/antiquitie* (5.5.436–8). Routh identified thirteen *aca* rhymes in *The Spanish Tragedy*, of which I select four: *successe/newes/happinesse* (1.2.17–19); *yoake/lure/Oake* (2.1.3–5); *day/heavens/allay* (3.6.5–7); and *misdone/stabd/sonne* (4.5.6–8). Routh found seven of these rhymes in *Soliman and Perseda*, of which I cite four: *dwell/woe/tell* (2.1.104–6); *progenie/misdone/treacherie* (2.1.299–301); *me/lippes/knee* (4.1.113–15); and *againe/Soliman/paine* (5. 4.123–5). Routh found the *abab* rhyme nineteen times in *Cornelia*, six times in *The Spanish Tragedy*, and once in *Soliman and Perseda*: *simplicitie/thee/perjury/free* (2.1.145–8), although that seems to me, rather, an *aaaa* rhyme. Routh found the *aaa* rhyme twice in *Cornelia*, three times in *The Spanish Tragedy*, and once in *Soliman and Perseda*: *extremitie/clemencie/peremtorie* (3.4.7–9), to which I add another: *liberall/affable/heroyacall* (5.4 103–5). Routh also listed less frequent rhyme patterns, with only one or two instances. He found three in *Cornelia*, five in *The Spanish Tragedy*, and three in *Soliman and Perseda*. Those in *Soliman and Perseda* are *acaa*: *Emperie/affections/thee/maladie* (4.1.143–6); *aaca*: *me/sea/would/infancie* (1.2.1–4); and *acbab*: *know/welcome/Germanie/foe/enemy*. Routh concluded his pioneering 1903 essay with a comment on the possible influence of Garnier's *Cornélie*, with its profusion of rhyme schemes in the choric odes, which Kyd had certainly read before writing *The Spanish Tragedy*. To illustrate his point that 'Kyd's rimes exhibit great mobility of form', Routh pointed to the presence of eight distinct patterns in *The Spanish Tragedy* (p. 51). *Soliman and Perseda* has seven different rhyme schemes, showing that it was written by the same idiosyncratic rhymer.

Another pioneering study ignored by Freeman, Erne, and previous Kyd scholars appeared in 1936, a Princeton doctoral dissertation by Philip Timberlake on the feminine ending in Elizabethan drama.[39] As

---

39. Timberlake, *Feminine Ending in English Blank Verse*.

I explained in chapter 2, the regular blank verse line, the iambic pentameter, has a 'masculine ending' with a stress on its final word:

Now is the winter of our discontent

The feminine ending (so called in French prosody) is an extra, unstressed syllable:

To be or not to be, that is the ques/tion

Timberlake showed that the feminine ending was rarely used by Tudor dramatists. It began to be used by the 'University Wits', but infrequently: Peele, Lodge, and Greene averaged between 0.5 and 1.8 percent, while Marlowe's usage ranged from 1.3 in *Tamburlaine* to 1.7 in *Dr Faustus* and 3.7 in the highly derivative *Edward II* (1592). Kyd was the great innovator here, developing from the rate of 1.2 percent in *The Spanish Tragedy* (1585) to 10.2 percent in *Soliman and Perseda* (1589) and even 9.5 in *Cornelia* (1594), despite translating from the French. Timberlake concluded that 'Kyd was following nobody, and that he freely admitted feminine endings because he saw their fitness for dramatic speech'.[40] His great beneficiary was Shakespeare, who reached 10.4 percent in his first two plays, *2 Henry VI* and 10.7 in *3 Henry VI*, both performed in 1592, 16.8 percent in *Richard III* (1593), and 15.7 percent in *The Two Gentlemen of Verona* (1594).[41]

These two empirical studies were major contributions to placing *Soliman and Perseda* among Kyd's authentic plays. Another legitimate approach has been to cite the many structural and verbal similarities it shares with *The Spanish Tragedy*, as the work of Boas, Freeman, and Erne has demonstrated. Given the material conditions of the Elizabethan theatre, with several companies operating repertory systems, each competing for new plays, and dramatists often writing to a short delivery time, it is inevitable that writers should have repeated their favourite phraseology.[42] Previously scholars researching self-repetition had to

---

40. Ibid., pp. 46–53.

41. Ibid., pp. 88–94, 100–104.

42. See, e.g., Brian Vickers, 'Identifying Co-Authors,' especially 'Dramatists repeat themselves', in Vickers (ed.), *The Collected Works of John Ford*, 5 vols (Oxford, 2012–), 2.33–75.

rely on their own reading and noting, but, as I mentioned earlier, in 2017 Pervez Rizvi created an invaluable new resource, a database of 547 plays performed between 1537 and 1642, in modern spelling. He then wrote software programs to document every repetition of phrases three to ten words long, in every play. Users can easily compare any play with any other for a quantitative analysis of the unique phrases that they share, very strong proof of common authorship.[43]

The greatest number of complex phrases (those extending for three or more consecutive words) that *Soliman and Perseda* shares with any other play is with *The Spanish Tragedy*. They have in common 230 matches in total (that is, unfiltered for rarity), of which thirty-eight are unique in Rizvi's corpus. Of the other play in Kyd's accepted canon, *Soliman and Perseda* shares eight matches with *Cornelia* (seventy-three in total), and of the plays I have newly attributed to him it shares twenty-five unique n-gram matches with *Arden of Faversham* (181 matches in total), and twelve with *King Leir* (185 matches in total). Readers can also analyse this data qualitatively by tracing a match back to its dramatic context. Doing so will reveal a closeness of phrasing and function in these selected parallels. Soliman's epitaph for Perseda echoes Hieronimo's for Horatio

SOLIMAN Fair springing **rose, ill plucked before thy time** *SP* 5.4.81

HIERONIMO Sweet lovely **Rose, ill plucked before thy time** *Sp. T.* 2.5.109

When Perseda greets Erastus on arriving in Constantinople she echoes the Portuguese Viceroy's lament fearing that his son has died in battle:

43. See 'Shakespeare's Text. A collection of resources for students of the original texts of Shakespeare's plays', https://www.shakespearestext.com/can/index.htm. First-time users should select 'Download Collocation and N-gram Matches', enter the play title *Soliman and Perseda* in the search box, and then select 'N-grams/Maximal matches/List of Matches/HTML'. This will bring up a link at the foot of the page to download ngrams-soliman_and_perseda.htm .zip. Then each play needed can be entered in the search box. More advanced users of spreadsheets can choose the CSV option.

SOLIMAN AND PERSEDA   121

PERSEDA **My sweet and best beloved**
ERASTUS **My sweet and best beloved**   *SP* 4.1.155–6
VICEROY ... **my** joy **and best beloved,**
My best beloved, my sweet and only son.   *Sp. T.* 1.3.37–8

Soliman's generous reply to Perseda's request for a favour (that she may retain her Christian faith) uses the same form of words as the Viceroy's grateful reception of news (in fact, false) about his son from Villuppo:

PERSEDA Grant one boon that I shall crave of **thee,**
SOLIMAN **Whate'er it be,** Perseda **I** grant it **thee**   *SP* 4.1.139–40
VICEROY Speak on, **I'll** guerdon **thee whate'er it be**   *Sp. T.* 1.3.55

Kyd uses the same phrasing in three plays to describe the different experience of a minority of men within a military group:

Rhodes is taken, and **all** the men are slain.
Except some few that turn to Mahomet.   *SP* 4.139–40
All well my sovereign Liege, **except some few,**
That are deceased by fortune of the war   *Sp. T.* 1.2.2–3
Well forth to field they marchèd **all** at once,
Except some few that stayed to guard the trench.   *Corn.* 5.1.92–3

The braggart Basilisco and the true soldier Hieronimo express the same belief in heavenly justice:

BASILISCO By favour and **by justice of the heavens**   *SP* 2.1.61
HIERONIMO May come (**by justice of the heavens**)
    Sp. T. 3.6.6–7

Two characters witnessing the imminent death of a beloved try to prevent it:

SOLIMAN **O save his life,** if it be possible   *SP* 5.2.100
BEL-IMPERIA **O save his life** and let me die for   *Sp. T.* 2.4.60

Two characters newly bereaved call on others to help them express their grief:

SOLIMAN Come janissaries and **help me to lament** *SP* 1.6.112
HIERONIMO Here Isabella, **help me to lament** *Sp. T.* 2.5.39

Two young men express the value they place on a beloved, one living, the other dead:

ERASTUS Therefore to thee I owe **both love and
     life**. *SP* 2.1.113
ANDREA And by war's fortune lost **both love and
     life** *Sp. T.* 1.1.41

Two characters lament the death of the person they loved best:

SOLIMAN **Who living was my** joy, whose death my
     woe *SP* 5.4.132
BEL-IMPERIA **Who living was my** garland's sweetest
     flower, *Sp. T.* 1.4.4

Erastus and Cornelia know the grief of loss, but she is more sanguine about restoration:

ERASTUS Ah no, **great losses** seldom **are restored.**
What if my chain shall never **be restored**? *SP* 1.4.75–6
CORNELIA **Great losses** greatly **are** to be deplored,
The **loss** is **great** that cannot **be restored** *Corn.* 2.1.175–6

Both Basilisco and Caesar admire bravery in battle:

Or Pompey **that brave warrior** *SP* 5.3.70
And **that brave warrior** my brother-in-law *Corn.* 4.2.57

In the closing scene of Kyd's Turkish tragedy, the choric figure Death, victorious over his rivals Love and Fortune, exults at his triumphal journey down to hell and back. In *Cornelia* Cicero, given Christian attributes like all the characters in Garnier's play, also uses hell as a distance marker:

DEATH: Ay, now will Death in his most haughty pride,
Fetch his imperial car **from deepest hell,**
And ride in triumph through the wicked world, *SP* 5. Epil. 33–5

CICERO: And those great cities whose foundations reached
From deepest hell, and with their tops touched
    heaven   *Corn.* 2.1.267–8

That parallel between two such different plays shows how Kyd could adapt his lexicon to whatever dramatic context he created. Readers wanting to check more parallels between *Solyman and Perseda* and the accepted Kyd canon can find them in the Rizvi database. Although its authorship has been doubted by Kyd's enemies, it is an integral part of Kyd's canon, a varied and stimulating play.

4

Cornelia

THE ONE WORK by Kyd for which his full name appeared in the records during his lifetime was a translation of Garnier's *Cornélie*. The play was entered in the Stationer's Register on 26 January 1594:

> Ent. N. Linge and J. Busbye: lic. Dickins: Cornelia, Thomas Kydd beinge the author.[1]

When it was published later that year Kyd's name was printed not on the title page but following the text, in the Explicit, a painfully appropriate classical text for his present condition:

> *Non prosunt Domino quae prosunt omnibus; Artes.* Tho: Kyd.[2]

The reissue in 1595 gave a full—but by now posthumous—acknowledgement:

> *Pompey the Great, his fair Corneliaes Tragedie: Effected by her Father and Husband's downe-cast, death, and fortune. Written in French, by that excellent poet Ro: Garnier; and translated into English by Thomas Kid.*

Cornélie (1574) was the third of Garnier's tragedies, much influenced by Seneca in dramatic situations, characterization, choruses, stichomythic dialogue, epic narration, *sententiae*, and rhetorical figures. For

---

1. Greg, *BEPD*, 1.195–6 (no. 116).

2. Ovid, *Metamorphoses*, tr. A.D. Melville (Oxford, 1986), p. 16, 1.524: 'skills which help afford | To all mankind fail now to help their lord.'

the choral lyrics with their varied strophic patterns, as Raymond Lebègue has observed, Garnier modelled himself on the Pléiade poets, especially Ronsard.[3] The play has seven scenes (four of the five Acts consisting of a single scene), and five choric odes, four of which are spoken by a Chorus of Roman women, the fifth by a group of Caesar's friends. The first Act consists of a long monologue by Cicero, deploring the decline of Rome under Julius Caesar. In Act 2 Cornelia laments the death of her second husband, Pompey the great, murdered as he was returning in defeat from the battle of Pharsalia. In Act 3 Pompey's servant Philip arrives, bearing an urn containing his master's ashes, and the heroine laments once more. Act 4 scene 1 presents a heated discussion between Cassius and Decimus—not Marcus—Brutus on Caesar's victory, Cassius urging he be assassinated, Brutus temporizing. In the following scene we see their opponents, Caesar and Mark Antony, who debate whether to treat Caesar's enemies with mercy or punishment. As Lebègue pointed out, 'as in other tragedies of this period, neither of the two speakers convinces the other, and no decision emerges from the debate.'[4] In the final act an enormously long messenger's speech (513 lines in the original) brings news that Cornelia's father, Metellus Scipio, has been killed in the battle of Thapsus. Having heard 'the piteous manner of her father's end', as Kyd concludes 'The Argument' prefixed to the play, 'she took, as she had cause, occasion to redouble both her tears and lamentations: wherewith she closes the catastrophe of this their tragedy.'[5]

In his dedicatory epistle to the Countess of Sussex Kyd conceded that, in the desolate state in which he found himself in the winter of 1593–94, 'it may be wondered at by some, how I durst undertake a matter of this moment, which both requires cunning, rest and opportunity'. Those three epithets (where 'cunning' means skill, aptitude) show that Kyd was perfectly aware of the qualities needed by a translator. Some Kyd scholars, however, have denied him these skills, pronouncing his translation defective. F. S. Boas judged that 'Kyd's blunders are at times

3. Ibid., p. 27.

4. Ibid., p. 264.

5. All quotations from *Cornelia* are taken from the modern-spelling edition by Lucy Rayfield and Adam Horsley in Vickers (ed.), *The Collected Works of Thomas Kyd*, vol. 2.

ludicrous', and in his extensive Notes frequently accused Kyd of having misunderstood Garnier's French.[6] Alexander Witherspoon, in studying Garnier's influence on Elizabethan drama, unkindly described *Cornelia* as 'a paraphrase rather than a translation of Garnier's tragedy', suggesting that this was due in part to Kyd's 'faulty knowledge of the French language and classical literature. Some of his renderings of Garnier's allusions are amusingly wide of the mark'.[7] Félix Carrère, the only Francophone among Kyd's critics, recorded his surprise on discovering 'des inéxactitudes, des méprises, voire des béunes grossières' and 'les erreurs de sens, souvent graves'. Carrère listed some of these unsatisfactory translations in passing, then added a complete list of 'Erreurs de traduction commis par Thomas Kyd'.[8]

Anyone who compares the two texts line by line will undoubtedly find deviations which betray Kyd's imperfect knowledge of French. But their extent has been exaggerated; moreover, critics have overlooked evidence of Kyd's coherent rationale in choosing English equivalents. It is to the credit of Josephine A. Roberts and James F. Gaines to have undertaken a systematic re-evaluation of Kyd's performance that frees him from several of these charges.[9] Their careful comparison documented 'nearly 400 amendments' that he had made to the text (p. 125), revealing some significant patterns in the translation. Kyd's critics claimed that he 'confused "trespas", a popular synonym for "mort" and an important rhyming word dating back to Villon, with the common English meaning of "trespass", or sin' (p. 126). However, Roberts and Gaines cite three

6. See Boas, *Works of Thomas Kyd*, pp. lxxi, 414–36.

7. Alexander Witherspoon, *The Influence of Robert Garnier on Elizabethan Drama* (New Haven, CT, and London, 1924), pp. 94, 97.

8. Félix Carrère, *Le Théâtre de Thomas Kyd. Contribution à l'Étude du drame Elizabéthain* (Toulouse, 1951), pp. 315–20, 439–43.

9. Josephine A. Roberts and James F. Gaines, 'Kyd and Garnier: The Art of Amendment', *Comparative Literature*, 31 (1979): 124–33. The authors adopted the following procedure: '(1) identification of all amendments without arbitrary classification as "errors," (2) verification of the author's knowledge of the language by consulting entire word groups throughout the work, (3) regrouping of the amendments to find significant image clusters, and (4) inter- as well as intra-textual analysis of the image clusters' (p. 133).

passages where Kyd correctly renders 'trespas' as meaning 'death',[10] so that he cannot be accused of ignorance when rendering Garnier's 'Des effroyables nuits où les trespassez vont' (G 242) as 'Of dead-sad night, where sins do mask unseen' (K 2.1.20). Rather, they judge, 'the etymological connection between the words, reinforced by religious equations of sin with death, suggested to him an entirely new, more vivid image—that of sins secretly cavorting in the night' (p. 126). Moreover, as they point out, 'the association of night and sin had existed in Kyd's mind long before he undertook this translation',[11] for he had used it in *The Spanish Tragedy* for Hieronimo's words over his slain son, which they describe as 'among the most inspired in the great revenge play': 'O heavens, why made you night to cover sin?' (2.4.88). Roberts and Gaines show that Kyd used the term '*sin* as one of the most important elements of his amendments', citing four instances of his deliberate and consistent use of the word.[12]

Elsewhere Kyd amended Garnier's neo-classical Rome by transforming a pagan concept into a Christian one. Roberts and Gaines note that he 'usually replaces references to the gods or to simple fatality with direct evocations of heaven' (p. 130), introducing the phrases 'as heavens please' and 'heaven's will',[13] and even emphasizing the change:

Nos jours sont limitez qu'òn ne sçauroit estendre   (G 1441)
Heaven sets our time, with heaven may nought dispense.
    (K 4.2.147)

10. Roberts and Gaines quote *Cornélie* in the edition of Garnier's *Œuvres Complètes* by Lucien Pinvert, 2 vols (Paris, 1923) which numbers neither scenes nor lines. My French quotations are from Lebègue, *Robert Garnier. Porcie, Cornélie*, which uses through-line-numbering. I have added the prefix 'G' for Garnier. References to Kyd's *Cornelia* are from the Rayfield and Horsley edition, prefixed by 'K' for Kyd. Compare G 390 and K 2.2.272; G 477–8 and K 2.1.258–9; G 1923–4 and K 5.1.450–51.

11. This is to beg the question of the play's date. Since Kyd shows knowledge of *Cornélie* already in *The Spanish Tragedy* (see chapter 1, note 76, this volume, and Erne, *Beyond* The Spanish Tragedy, pp. 54–5), I think his translation may well be earlier.

12. Cf. G 205–6 and K 1.1.206–7; G 278 and K 2.1.56; G 1737–8 and K 5.1.227–8; G 1784 and K 5.1.388–9.

13. Cf. G 589 and K 2.1.376; G 386 and K 2.1.170.

Where Garnier reproduces a Stoic acceptance of death and disapproval of suicide (G 505–6), Kyd puts that idea into a Christian context:

> Death's always ready, and our time is known
> To be at heaven's dispose, and not our own.   (K 2.1.288–9)

Even Lucretia's virginity is rendered in Christian terms: 'That erst was clear as heaven's Queen' (G 607; K 2.1.401). Conversely, and 'perhaps the most widespread feature in Kyd's amendments is the addition of images of hell', which 'erupt everywhere in this tragedy' (p. 132). Kyd refers to 'lowest hell', 'hell's infectious breath' (2.1.230), and creates the antithesis 'grief to hear and hell for me to speak' (2.1.201).[14] As Roberts and Gaines note, it may be the connotations of hell, or it may be the conventions of Senecan tragedy that caused ghosts to 'play a crucial role in [Kyd's] amendments. Garnier's *Cornélie* is replete with "ombres", but Kyd seizes on each opportunity to create more'. Garnier's reference to 'tant de gens, morts pour nostre franchise' (G 1103) becomes 'their ghosts that died to do us good' (K 4.1.40). Garnier's heroine refers to a dream in which she sees 'pres de mon lict moiteux | Le funebre Pompé d'un visage piteux' (G 677–8), but Kyd adds the sinister detail of its incorporeal movement:

> And lo (me thought) came gliding by my bed
> The ghost of Pompey with a ghastly look   (K 3.1.75–6).

Kyd introduces into Garnier still further references to the ghosts of Pompey, Prometheus, and even Caesar,[15] all symbols 'for any illusion that leads to distress and despair'.

Even this brief summary is enough to show that Kyd rendered Garnier's French not in a state of ignorance but with a specific and consistent set of artistic goals. Kyd regularly amplified the force of lamentations by adding gestures to tears. Where Garnier's heroine recalls how, after

---

14. Cf. G 1736–7 and K 5.1.225; G 535 and K 2.1.320; G 415 and K 2.1.201. Kyd uses the word 'hell' fifteen times.

15. Cf. G 743 and K 3.1.146; G 1530 and K 4.2.239; G 1136 and K 4.1.74.

seeing her second husband Pompey the Great murdered before her eyes, she had wanted to commit suicide, but 'trois fois retenuë avec larmes et cris, | Avec force de bras, à plaindre je me pris' (G 413–4), Kyd adds an expressive gesture:

> And thrice detained, with doleful shrieks and cries,
> With arms to heav'n upreared I 'gan exclaim   (K 2.1.197–8)

There Kyd transferred the arm movement from the retainers trying to hold Cornelia back to the heroine lamenting her fate, introducing, as Roberts and Gaines showed, 'an image cluster' also found in *The Spanish Tragedy*: 'With mournful eyes and hands to heaven upreared' (4.7.68). Their careful study reveals that 'Kyd also uses this obsessive picture of sadness in other amendments to *Cornélie*' (p. 128):

> With blubbered eyes and hands to heaven upreared . . .
> With folded arms I sadly sit and weep . . . [16]

Readers will have noticed the identical syntactical and metrical template underlying those four descriptions of grief. My analysis, later in this chapter, of collocations shared between *Cornelia* and Kyd's other works, will reveal the homogeneity of his linguistic resources.

Kyd's translation of Garnier was an exercise of sustained judgment. Roberts and Gaines show that it necessitated a form of 'cultural angliciz-ing', where Kyd had 'to eliminate obscure foreign elements in favor of references more familiar to the English reader' (p. 128). Kyd also gave fresh life to some of Garnier's 'often commonplace nautical descrip-tions, as when he transforms "A jamais tourmentez par les meurtières vagues" [G 1926] into "Tossed with the salt waves of the wasteful seas" [K 5.1.454]'. In such passages Kyd enlarges the emotional scope of Gar-nier's words, turning a bland listing of elements—'La Peste, La Famine,

---

16. Cf. G 1651, which only describes the matrons' eyes ('Les yeux battus de pleurs') and K 5.1.130; G 426, which describes three different reactions ('Je ne fay que plorer, que plaindre et que gemir') and K 2.1.207.

et l'orage des eaux' (G 1169) into this more resonant and expressive collocation:

> Th'infectious plague, and famine's bitterness,
> Or th'ocean (whom no pity can assuage)
> Though they contain dead bodies numberless
> Are yet inferìor to Caesar's rage.   (K 4.1.110–13)

Equally deliberately, Kyd tones down 'the high-flown mythology of Garnier's verses', simply omitting 'such adjectives as "romulides" walls (G 793) and "pylien" Nestor' (G 1439). Where Garnier uses mythological names, Kyd substitutes 'the qualities they represent: "Adrastée" (G 1869) becomes "revenge"' (K 5.1.382), 'and "Cerbère . . . qu'on ne peut amorcer" (G 742) becomes "a fell remorseless monster"' (K 3.1.195). Garnier's conventional plea to the classical Parcae or Fates—'Venez me prendre, ô Parque'—(G 1571), becomes the much more vivid appeal, 'O earth, why op'st thou not?' (K 5.1.39).

The whole tenor of Kyd's amendments to Garnier is to achieve a more concrete utterance, domesticated and familiarized to an everyday English context. Where Garnier marks the passing of time by reference to the constellation Boötes, or the Herdsman, driving his oxen across the sky:

> Et desja le Bouvier sous le ventre de l'Ourse
> De ses boeufs lens pressoit la paresseuse course   (G 671–2)

Kyd transforms the distant constellation to a homely English waggoner:

> And now the sleepy wainman softly drove
> His slow-paced team, that long had travellèd   (K 3.1.69–70)

(English readers will appreciate Kyd's use of Spenserian alliteration and euphony there.) Roberts and Gaines also note that 'Kyd turns to the realm of nature for many of the images in the amendments'. Where Garnier uses the conventional term 'ondoyer' for the billowing movement of liquids, Kyd transforms it to 'the image of a land transformed to marsh' (p. 131), as in these two instances:

And with their blood made marsh the parchèd plains
Th'earth that the Euxine sea makes sometimes marsh[17]

As they point out, 'this image had already become part of Kyd's tragic universe in *The Spanish Tragedy*': 'Made mountains marsh with spring tides of my tears' (4.1.8).

Kyd's translation of Garnier can now be seen as a coherent intellectual and artistic enterprise, cutting back expression in some areas, enlarging it in others. Of particular interest are the passages of his own writing that Kyd inserted, of which even the scholars who criticized his knowledge of French gave more favourable accounts. Translating this essentially static drama, with its plangent rhetoric and stereotyped laments, might seem to offer Kyd little scope for adding personal touches. However, where his predecessor in the task of translating Garnier, the dutiful Countess Pembroke followed her text most diligently, Kyd took many liberties. As A. M. Witherspoon observed, rather caustically:

> The translator of *Marc Antonie*, in her efforts to reproduce it as exactly as possible, adds only one couplet to the original, and omits only one line. Kyd omits half a hundred lines, and adds a hundred others, many of which are not even suggested by the original.[18]

Witherspoon judged *Cornelia* to be more a paraphrase than a translation but excused the divergences on the grounds that Kyd's great 'poetic ability' and 'originality' would make it difficult for him to follow Garnier closely (p. 94). Indeed, sometimes Kyd 'uses the original only to furnish him with the skeleton of a thought, which he then clothes with muscle and sinews of his own making' (p. 95). The passages that Witherspoon quoted to illustrate 'the characteristic freedom which he exercises whenever a suggestion of the French poet's appeals especially strongly to his fancy', such as these descriptions of night, always an evocative topic for Kyd:

---

17. Cf. G 39 and K 1.1.40; G 1349 and K 4.2.51.
18. Witherspoon, *Influence of Robert Garnier*, p. 98.

The silent night that long had sojournèd,
Now 'gan to cast her sable mantle off   (3.1.67–8)

But ye sad powers that rule the silent deeps
Of dead-sad night, where sins do mask unseen:
You that amongst the darksome mansìons
Of pining ghosts, twixt sighs, and sobs and tears,
Do exercise your mirthless empery.   (2.1.19–23)

In the first passage, Kyd's epithet for Night's 'sable mantle' is more inventive than Garnier's rather wooden account, in which the night 'Tournoit plus loing du soir que de l'Aube du jour'. In the second, Kyd's rendering of Garnier's unimaginative appeal to the gods, 'Exercez vostre Empire, o Dieux maistres de tous',—'Do exercise your *mirthless* Empory'—gives them a more sinister tinge, which reminds me of Epicurus's image of the gods as indifferent to human affairs.

Kyd's invention showed itself in the many piecemeal additions to Garnier that display some of his own preoccupations. Where Garnier has the colourless phrase, 'qui ne nous doivent rien', Kyd expands the line to read 'That owed us nothing but revenge for wrongs' (1.1.140), a 'characteristic' Kydian concern, as Boas observed (p. 417). Kyd increases the emotional level of one passage by adding the words 'to our eternal moans' (2.1.273 note) and transforms Garnier's 'Les serpens de Cyrene' into 'aspics, serpents, snakes' (3.3.43 note). Kyd condensed several passages in the Messenger speech, but added one analogy with nature to describe the power of Caesar's attack, able to 'beat down' his adversaries,

And lay them level with the chargèd earth,
Like ears of corn with rage of windy show'rs   (5.1.281–2)

Josephine Roberts and James Gaines, having shown how Kyd consistently adapted Garnier's text to include references to heaven and hell, note that the dramatist's 'ethical concerns become apparent when he adds five lines at a key point in the fifth act to magnify the role of Cornelia's filial devotion to her dead father':

Thy death, dear Scipio, Rome's eternal loss,
Whose hopeful life preserved our happiness;
Whose silver hairs encouragèd the weak;
Whose resolutions did confirm the rest;
Whose end, sith it hath ended all my joys . . .   (5.1.361–5)

As they rightly comment, 'Whereas self-destructive revenge was the motive force of the action in *The Spanish Tragedy*, ennobling endurance is at the heart of *Cornelia*. When the heroine is contemplating immediate death at the end of the play, she realizes she must first bury her father and place duty above her own personal desires' (p. 131). These two defenders of Kyd also note (p. 132) that where Garnier had compared Rome's treatment of Caesar to a farmer who destroyed a family of wolves but saved one whelp as a pet, only for it to destroy his whole flock of sheep, Kyd substitutes an Aesopic fable which gives a more direct instance of ingratitude harming a benefactor:

Like moral Aesop's misled country swain,
That found a serpent pining in the snow,
And full of foolish pity took it up,
And kindly laid it by his household fire,
Till, waxen warm, it nimbly 'gan to stir,
And stung to death the fool that fostered her.   (3.2.39–44)

In addition to these piecemeal alterations, Kyd added a long passage of his own (largely in blank verse) at the start of Act 3, beginning with the transition from night to dawn:

The cheerful cock, the sad night's comforter,
Waiting upon the rising of the sun,
Doth sing to see how Cynthia shrinks her horn,
While Clytie takes her progress to the east,
Where, wringing wet with drops of silver dew,
Her wonted tears of love she doth renew.
The wandering swallow with her broken song,
The country wench unto her work awakes;
While Cytherea, sighing, walks to seek

Her murdered love transformed into a rose,
Whom, though she see, to crop she kindly fears;
But, kissing, sighs, and dews him with her tears.
Sweet tears of love, remembrancers to time;
Time past with me that am to tears converted,
Whose mournful passions dull the morning's joys,
Whose sweeter sleeps are turned to fearful dreams,
And whose first fortunes, filled with all distress,
Afford no hope of future happiness. (3.1.1–18)

In the third line Kyd alludes to Ovid's account (*Metamorphoses*, 4.256) of Clytie, daughter of Oceanus, who was deserted by her lover Apollo and pined away, being changed into a sunflower, always rotating to face the sun-god. That emblem of unhappy love is followed by an allusion to Venus and Adonis, with the variant that the unfortunate beloved is turned into a rose. As Roberts and Gaines observed,

> The mythological elements, Cynthia, Clitie, and Citherea, contrast sharply with the humbler elements, such as the Cock, the Swallow, and the Country-wench. Although the dawn poem, or *aubade*, is generally joyous, this one is dolorous throughout. While it is more lyrical than most of Cornelia's speeches, this original poem coincides in its sadness with her emotions at this stage of the action, and Kyd may have added it to compensate for Garnier's brusque beginning of the act (p. 130).

Alternatively, it could be said that Kyd moves from unhappy myth to unhappy reality, in a marvellously direct and simple evocation:

> Sweet tears of love, remembrancers to time;
> Time past with me that am to tears converted

The lines are appropriate to Cornelia, but they may also describe Kyd's own mental and physical state at this time, as he described it in the play's dedication to the Countess of Sussex, 'Having no leisure, most noble Lady, but such as evermore is travailed with the afflictions of the mind, than which the world affords no greater misery', hoping that the finished labour will transcend 'those so bitter times, and privy broken passions that I endured in the writing it'. Although subjecting himself, as best he could, to the translator's impersonal art, *Cornelia* contains enough of Kyd's individual voice to repay a modern reader.

Kyd had more opportunity to put his individual poetic stamp on *Cornelia* when it came to the Choruses. As Witherspoon observed, Kyd 'showed much ingenuity in reproducing the varied effect of the original by the use of different strophe-forms, each of his choruses having its own peculiar metrical arrangement'.[19] In some cases Kyd conscientiously followed the French, leading to awkward inversions and unidiomatic English (e.g., 1.1.159–172, 3.3.176–80). In other cases, he deployed some of his own stylistic preferences, such as alliterating on the letter *h*, with his favourite epithet 'hapless' (used nine times in this text):

> but we, by war,
> Must seek in *h*ell to have a *h*apless room
> Or . . . foolish men . . . by murder of themselves, must *h*ie,
> *H*opeless to *h*ide them in a *h*apless tomb?   (1.1.211–14)

In addition to such sarcastic alliteration Kyd can impress us with his control of a stanza's music and movement, as in this evocation of Fortune:

> Her feet, more swift than is the wind,
> Are more inconstant in their kind
>   Than autumn blasts,
> A woman's shape, a woman's mind,
>   That seldom lasts.   (3.3.151–5)

A French scholar suggested that, in stanzas using shorter lines, Kyd may have been favoured by the English language, which can offer many more short words, and especially monosyllables, than French.[20] Nonetheless, it demands no small poetic gifts to transform Garnier's moralizing verse

---

19. Witherspoon, *Influence of Robert Garnier*, p. 97.
20. Carrère 1951, p. 321.

into such a freely flowing English stanza as this, written in the relatively rare trochaic metre:

> Oh, how many mighty kings
> Live in fear of petty things.
> For when kings have sought, by wars,
> Stranger towns to have o'erthrown,
> They have caught deservèd scars,
> Seeking that was not their own.   (4.2.234–9)

The most assured of these Choruses is the final one (also in trochaic octosyllabics), in which 'Caesars friends' wish their leader success. (Marvell, the master of this form in English poetry, would not have been ashamed to own them.)

> O fair sun, that gently smiles
> From the orient-pearlèd isles,
> Gilding these our gladsome days
> With the beauty of thy rays:
> Free from rage of civil strife,
> Long preserve our Caesar's life.
> That from sable Afrique brings
> Conquests whereof Europe rings.
> And fair Venus, thou of whom
> The Eneades are come,
> Henceforth vary not thy grace
> From Julus' happy race.
> Rather cause thy dearest son,
> By his triumphs new begun,
> To expel from forth the land
> Fierce war's quenchless fire-brand;
> That of care acquitting us,
> Who at last adore him thus,
> He a peaceful star appear,
> From our walls all woes to clear.
> And so let his warlike brows

Still be decked with laurel boughs,
And his statuès new set
With many a fresh-flow'red coronet.
So in every place let be
Feasts, and masques, and mirthful glee,
Strewing roses in the street,
When their emperor they meet.   (4.2.168–95)

As Félix Carrère generously commented, 'Dans les dernières stances, enfin, il arrive que l'art du traducteur dépasse celui de son modèle'.[21]

The Place of *Cornelia* in Kyd's Canon

At first sight, one might expect that a writer translating a text would find a wholly new lexicon to render the original. On further thought we may realize that, although he may refer to a dictionary to translate unusual foreign words, his own language—his phrasal lexicon, his preferred syntactical structures—will remain the same. However hard we try to adapt our style to a different goal, over a lengthy text it is inevitable that our habitual linguistic usages will show through. The evidence of unique collocations shared between *Cornelia* and the other texts in the extended Kyd canon, as I am redefining it, shows how deep these usages lie.

My findings contradict the attitudes of those critics who have attempted to exclude *Cornelia* from Kyd's canon for being a translation (see Table 4.1).[22]

21. Carrère, *Le Théâtre de Thomas Kyd*, p. 323.

22. For example, two editors of the *New Oxford Shakespeare* (no friends to Kyd), Gary Taylor and Rory Loughnane, discussing the identity of Shakespeare's co-author of *Edward III*, dispute one part of my evidence for Kyd, the number of matching phrases that Kyd's section of the play shares with *Cornelia*. They cite the estimate made by Gaines and Roberts that Kyd made '400 "amendments" . . . in his *loose translation*' [their phrase] and object that 'a second layer of authorship—not only a reworking, but also a translation—creates uncertainty about the play's value in attesting authorship'. 'The Canon and Chronology' in Taylor and Egan (eds), *New Oxford Shakespeare Authorship Companion*, p. 504. This may sound plausible, but it overlooks the obvious point that both the translation and the reworking display Kyd's lexicon and phraseology.

138 CHAPTER 4

TABLE 4.1. Matches between *Cornelia* and the extended Kyd canon

Work	No. of matches	No. of lines	Every x matches
The Housholders Philosophie	12	1504	125
The Spanish Tragedy	33	2739	83
Soliman and Perseda	24	2200	92
King Leir	22	2588	118
Arden of Faversham	10	2410	241
Fair Em	2	1485	743
1 Henry VI	16	1821	113
Edward III	21	1490	71
Total	140		

By comparing *Cornelia* with works undoubtedly written by Kyd we can validate this new method of matching collocations to establish common authorship, so that we can apply it to texts of unknown authorship with some confidence in its validity. Secondly, we can build up our own lexicon of Kyd's phrasal repertoire. To begin with his prose translation from Tasso, since *The Housholders Philosophie* is not a play sharing similar dramatic situations, I list the twelve unique matches without commentary.[23] Passages set in bold type are exact verbal parallels; those underlined use identical semantic or syntactical elements.

<u>accomplished with the graces</u> **of the body**	*Corn.* Argt. 2
<u>busied in those exercises</u> **of the body**	*HP* 1323–4
into the hands **of his so** <u>mighty</u> enemy	*Corn.* Argt. 28–9
the weight **of his so** <u>famous monarchy</u>	*HP* 415–16
More **than the most** <u>infected filthiest part</u>	*Corn.* 2.1.80
then the most <u>incontinent and suffering companion</u>	*HP* 630–31
Hys hayre and beard, deform'd with blood and sweat	*Corn.* 3.1.82
by the whiteness of **his hayre and beard**	*HP* 97–8
And ne're **returneth to the** <u>Corse</u> interd	*Corn.* 3.1.140
howe it turneth and **returneth to the** <u>wife</u>	*HP* 1425
Why then you thinke there is **no praise in** <u>war</u>	*Corn.* 4.1.118
that Shamefastnes which merits **no praise in** <u>a man</u>	*HP* 550
To expell **fro forth the** <u>Land</u>,	*Corn.* 4.2.182

23. I cite this text from the edition by Domenico Lovascio in Vickers (ed.), *The Collected Works of Thomas Kyd*, vol. 1, with through-line-numbering.

Thrust me **fro forth the** <u>world</u>, that mongst the spirits	5.1.336
never ranne arrowe **fro forth the** strongest <u>bow</u>	*HP* 48
Of creeping Emmets, **in a Countrey** <u>Farme</u>	*Corn.* 5.1.73
amongst the woods and **in a Countrey** <u>Towne</u>	*HP* 81–2
For **true it is, that** Caesar brought at first	*Corn.* 5.1.88
True it is, that who so taketh the position	*HP* 366–7
So that dispayring **to defend themselves**	*Corn.* 5.1.269
as not only serveth **to defend themselves**	*HP* 808–9
Looking upon his <u>weapon</u> dide with blood	*Corn.* 5.1.313
he laughed so hartilie, **looking upon his** <u>wife</u>	*HP* 313

These matches, whether noun-phrases (nos. 1, 4, 6, 8), verb-phrases (nos. 5, 9, 10, 11), or collocations of function words (nos. 2, 3, 7) constitute part of Kyd's phrasal lexicon. Linguists can make analyses according to various grammatical and syntactic categories, and would undoubtedly find more instances of each phrasal pattern in Kyd's writings.

As for collocational links with Kyd's plays, *The Spanish Tragedy*, being Kyd's most characteristic work, furnishes most matches. The beginning of a verse line is a favoured place for symmetrical utterances:

and in the presence of his young son Sextus	*Corn.* Argt. 13
And in the presence of the Court of Spain	*Sp. T.* 4.6.45
And with their blood made marsh the parchèd plains	*Corn.* 1.1.40
And with their blood, my joy and best beloved	*Sp. T.* 1.3.37
Amongst the rest of mine extreme mishaps	*Corn.* 3.3.1
Amongst the rest of what you have in charge	*Sp. T.* 2.3.32
And last, not least, bereft of my best Father	*Corn.* 5.1.424
The third **and last not least** in our account	*Sp. T.* 1.4.162

Those collocations of four and five words were all continuous; elsewhere Kyd sustains a collocation's structure but allows other words to intervene:

And made them <u>subject</u> **to** our <u>Roman Lawes</u>	*Corn.* 4.1.123
And made them <u>bow their knees</u> **to** <u>Albion</u>	*Sp. T.* 1.4.171
O earth, why <u>op'st</u> **thou not?**	*Corn.* 5.1.39
O earth why <u>didst</u> **thou not** in time devour	*Sp. T.* 2.5.26
Now I see the heavens | Are heaped with rage	*Corn.* 5.1.37–8
Why so, **now** shall **I see the** fall of Babylon	*Sp. T.* 5.1.194–5

Conversely Kyd places some collocations at the end of a line, or even over-runs the line ending:

displeasd with Pompey and <u>my</u> **self,	And do**	*Corn.* 2.1.52–3
Content <u>thy</u> **self, and do** not trouble me	*Sp. T.* 3.5.12
**But thus	We see** it fareth with the envious	*Corn.* 4.2.91–2
But thus we see our innocence hath saved	*Sp. T.* 3.1.82
And faire <u>Venus,</u> **thou of whom	The** Eneades are come	*Corn.* 4.2.176
Wast **thou** <u>Lorenzo,</u> <u>Balthazar,</u> and **thou	Of whom** my Son	*Sp. T.* 4.1.42–3
Never leaving till **they fled	And**	*Corn.* 4.2.197–8
all the rest **they fled	And**	*Sp. T.* 1.2.81
He doth, deviseth, sees, nor dareth **ought	That may**	*Corn.* 4.11.177–8
And **ought that may** effect for thine avail	*Sp. T.* 5.1.47
I stepped **to him	To** have embraced him	*Corn.* 5.1.324–5
Let me alone, I'll send **to him to** meet	*Sp. T.* 3.2.88

As we have seen, Kyd regularly amended his version of Garnier to include references to heaven and hell, usually in terms of divine aid or punishment:

I fear the **heavens will not** <u>hear</u> our prayer	*Corn.* 3.3.55
Heavens will not let Lorenzo err so much	*Sp. T.* 4.8.51
Must seek **in Hell to** <u>have</u> a hapless room	*Corn.* 1.1.211
the fiends **in Hell,	To** <u>be</u> avenged	*Sp. T.* 4.6.77–8

But at other times he invokes the heavens in astronomical or cosmological terms. Two separate lines in *Cornelia* echo a collocation that Kyd had introduced in *The Spanish Tragedy*:

Or like **the sun that** . . . as the heavens	Do **coast the earth**	*Corn.* 2.1.127–9
The sun, that lends **the earth** his light	3.3.166
The sun, | That hourly **coasts** the centre of **the earth**	*Sp. T.* 3.1.22–3

As Roberts and Gaines showed, Kyd often made Garnier's references to the sea more vivid or added his own phrasing. Where Garnier had written 'tourmenté par les meurtrieres vagues' (G 1926), Kyd substituted a line which begins with a more exact term for the movement of the waves, adding the more immediate epithets 'salt' and 'wasteful', also creating an expressive alliteration:

Tossed with the salt <u>waves</u> of the <u>wasteful</u> <u>seas</u>	*Corn.*5.1.454

The resulting line looks back to a passage in *The Spanish Tragedy*, but outdoes it in emotional force:

Whenas a raging <u>sea</u>, | **Tossed with the** <u>wind</u> and <u>tide</u>   *Sp. T.* 4.7.102–3

There would be another twenty unique parallels between the early and the late play.[24] Despite their many differences, both are tragedies, involving malicious plotting, the use of weapons, revenge, and death, as these collocations show:

If he had died, **his** <u>faulchion</u> **in his fist**	*Corn.* 2.1.172
Bearing **his** latest <u>fortune</u> **in his fist**	*Sp. T.* 5.4.148
He almost felt the poniard **when he fell**	*Corn.* 2.1.185
And **when he fell** then we began to fly	*Sp. T.* 1.3.70
And cast the plot to catch him in **the trap:**	**He**	*Corn.* 3.3.84
I set **the trap, he** breaks the worthless twigs	*Sp. T.* 3.4.41
Whom (to be King himself) he soon <u>removed</u>	*Corn.* 4.1.140
Glad, that I know on **whom to be** <u>revenged</u>	*Sp. T.* 2.1.114

One aspect of *Cornelia* that might have attracted Kyd is its nature as a tragedy involving love. Cornelia is the embodiment of female love, both as a daughter and a wife, and Garnier gave great place to her laments. In *Soliman and Perseda* the lovers lament the absence, or death of their beloved in terms similar to those that Kyd re-used for *Cornelia*. His Roman heroine is condemned to passive suffering, in a phrase of Kyd's invention:

Sorrow consumes me, and instead of rest
With folded arms **I** sadly <u>sit</u> **and weep;** | **And**   *Corn.* 2.1.206–7

Kyd had used this phrase before, when Ferdinand's father, powerless to claim redress, could only lament his son's murder:

But whilst **I** <u>stand</u> **and weep, and** spend the time
In fruitless plaints   *SP* 2.1.303–4

Erastus, falsely accused by Perseda of being unfaithful, finds himself unable to act:

What then **remains for my** <u>perplexed heart</u>   *SP* 2.1.164

---

24. For a complete list of these matches see my website: https://brianvickers.uk/.

Scipio, confronting defeat and humiliation, decides to commit suicide:

> **What** refuge now **remains for my** <u>distress</u>
> But thee, my dearest, ne'er-deceiving sword?   *Corn.* 5.1.316–17

The same collocation can mark sharply contrasting situations. Having recounted the dream in which she saw 'The ghost of Pompey, with a ghastly look; | All pale and brawn-fall'n' (3.1.75–6), Cornelia longs for the time when 'sweetest death' will stop her suffering, 'And **bless me with** <u>my Pompey's company'</u> (*Corn.* 3.1.108–10). Soliman, when Perseda is brought before him as a captive, uses the same phrase to register his love at first sight, 'Then sweeting **bless me with** <u>a cheerful look'</u> (*SP* 4.1.91). The Chorus of Roman citizens hopes that Caesar will be defeated, so that

> the sun-bright crown
> That now the tyrant's head doth deck
> **May turn to** Rome with true renown   *Corn.* 2.1.382–4

Soliman enjoys a tyrant's power, and hopes that Perseda will yield him pleasure:

> That her captivity **may turn to** bliss   *SP* 4.1.74

In her despair Cornelia hopes to be reunited with her husband, and

> Come visit thee in **the Elysian shades**   *Corn.* 3.1.107

Soliman uses the same collocation, but as part of an erotic blazon describing the parting between Perseda's breasts,

> Twixt which a vale leads to **the Elysian shades**   *SP* 4.1.83

In these plays of suffering and disappointment it is natural to seek consolation,

> The **loss** is **great** that <u>cannot be</u> **restored**   *Corn.* 2.1.25

But hope can also yield to despair, as Erastus realizes, having lost Perseda's love token:

> Ah no, **great losses** seldom <u>are</u> **restored**   *SP* 1.4.130

Soliman and Perseda, like *Cornelia*, includes much violence, both private, in Soliman's unpredictable mood swings, that result in the death of those dearest to him, and public, in the Turkish ruler's attacks on Rhodes. Both plays share collocations describing conflict, war, and the exercise of power. In the 'Argument' to *Cornelia*, Kyd records how Pompey sent his wife to safe keeping,

> **upon the first** fires **of** the civil wars betwixt him and *Caesar*
> Corn. Argt. 6

That collocation recurs in the ritualized context of the jousting at which Erastus gains the victory but loses Perseda's carcanet:

> **Upon the first** encounter **of** your **foe**   *SP* 1.3.67

In conflict situations the parties concerned often utter their defiance, as does Cicero:

> Caesar, **thou shalt not** vaunt thy conquest long,
> **Nor** longer hold us in this servitude.
> **Nor shalt thou** bathe thee longer in our blood   *Corn.* 3.2.66–8

Kyd had used the same extended collocation in his Turkish tragedy for the reassurances Soliman gives Erasmus, unwilling to lead a force against Rhodes:

> **Nor** suffer this or that to trouble thee
> **Thou shalt not** need Phylippo **nor** his isle
> **Nor shalt thou** war against thy Countrymen   *SP* 3.1.138–41

In the opening scene of Garnier's play Cicero asks, 'What right had our ambitious ancestors . . . | To enter Asia' (1.3.132–4) and to create so much suffering, 'our power t'extend | Or over-run **the world from East to West**' (1.3.14–8). In the attack on Rhodes, Brusor has no compunction in describing Soliman as 'Monarch and mighty Emperor of **the world,** | **From East to West**' (3.5.4–5). In describing past or future losses on the battlefield, 'a thousand' is a convenient number, not least for its iambic stress:

> But we shall see **a thousand of** them dead   *Corn.* 5.1.77
> O that **a thousand of** our Turkish souls   *SP* 1.5.88

Yet, behind the official statistics are many instances of suffering:

> The plaints **of men oppressed** do pierce the air   *Corn.* 3.3.56
> What millions **of men oppressed** with ruin and scath
> The Turkish armies did o'erthrow in Christendom.   *SP* 3.5.4–5

As we have seen, Kyd frequently amended the text of Garnier to include references to heaven. These often take the form of collocations, already used in *The Spanish Tragedy*, and repeated in *Soliman and Perseda*. Cicero hopes that 'flatt'ring Chance' may again favour Rome, 'where so long ago | Heav'ns did their favours lavishly bestow', and Cornelia agrees:

> 'Tis true, **the heav'ns, at** least wise if they please,
> May give poor Rome her former liberty   *Corn.* 2.1.158–9

After victory, a pious gratitude is in order, 'by favour and by justice of **the heavens at** last' (*SP* 2.1.158–9). In Kyd's Christian world, the existence of heaven presupposes its opposite, whether in a Roman or a Mohammedan context. Cicero, describing the vicissitudes of history, reflects on the instability even of

> And those great cities, whose foundations reached
> **From deepest hell**, and with their tops touched heaven   *Corn.*
> 2.1.267–8

The action of *Soliman and Perseda* is punctuated by the appearance of the allegorical figures, Fortune, Love, and Death. After the final catastrophe, as the corpse of Soliman is carried out, Death claims the victory:

> Ay, now will Death, in his most haughty pride,
> Fetch his imperial car **from deepest hell**   *SP* 5.5.34–5

Other collocations shared by the Roman and the Turkish tragedies may not show thematic links, but they do reveal more of Kyd's phrasal lexicon:

> May <u>light</u> upon them **once for all**   *Corn.* 2.1.405
> But by myself <u>lament</u> me **once for all**   *SP* 4.1.46

<u>Judge</u> others, **as thou wouldst** be <u>judged</u> again	*Corn.* 1.1.128
<u>Keep</u> it, quoth she, **as thou wouldst** <u>keep</u> my self	*SP* 1.4.124

Could never <u>have been curbed</u>, **but by** itself.	*Corn.* 1.1.58
Which **never can** <u>be parted</u> **but by** death	*SP* 2.1.25
And **never can** <u>be quenched</u>, **but by** desire	*KL* 3.60

Ships to pass the main, | **Upon the shore**	*Corn.* 3.3.182–3
So sings the Mariner **upon the shore**	*SP* 5.1.15
Since first she set her foot **upon the shore**	*KL* 18.40

Time past with me **that am to** tears <u>converted</u>	*Corn.* 3.1.14
that am to <u>make enquiry</u> after it	*SP* 1.4.96–7
Or govern me **that am to** <u>rule</u> my self	*AF* 10.84

Whatever problems modern readers have had with *Cornelia*, these were not shared by Kyd's contemporaries. When Lady Helen Branch (wife of the Lord Mayor) died on 10 April 1594, one 'W. Har' composed an *Epicedium* to her memory, which jointly invites Shakespeare and Kyd to consider her as a comparable subject for poetry:

> You that have writ of chaste *Lucretia*,
> Whose death was witness of her spotless life,
> Or pen'd the praise of sad *Cornelia*,
> Whose blameless name hath made her fame so rife,
> As noble Pompeys most renowned wife:
> Hither unto your home direct your eyes,
> Whereas, unthought on, much more matter lies. (Boas, p. lxxvi)

(It is appropriate to find Kyd and Shakespeare bracketed together in 1594, when they had just collaborated on *Edward III*.) A year later, in his *Polimanteia, or the meanes lawfull and unlawfull, to judge of the fall of a common-wealth*, William Covell looked forward to some future time when literary merit would be recognized: 'Then should not tragicke *Garnier* have his poore *Cornelia* stand naked upon every poste: a work, howsoever not respected, yet excellently done by Th. Kyd' (Boas, p. lxxvi). The phrase 'stand naked upon every post' refers to the practice of stationers posting up title pages of their ware on posts in the book-shop area surrounding St Paul's.

146　CHAPTER 4

Further evidence of the popularity of Kyd's play is the fact that two anthologies published in 1600, Robert Allott's compilation, *England's Parnassus*, and John Bodenham's *Bel-Vedére* between them include more than forty excerpts from *Cornelia*.[25] Readers will discover much to enjoy in a play that has yet to enter the modern consciousness.

25. Charles Crawford (ed.), *England's Parnassus* (Oxford, 1913), p. 377, identified twenty-one quotations from *Cornelia*, leaving two ascribed to Kyd but untraced. The recent edition by Lukas Erne and Devani Singh, *Bel-Vedére or the Garden of the Muses. An Early Modern Printed Commonplace Book* (Cambridge, 2020) noted that 'Kyd is exceptional in having a significant presence in *Bel-vedére* that is based on a purely dramatic corpus', with twenty-one quotations from *The Spanish Tragedy*, ten from *Solyman and Perseda*, and twenty-two from *Cornelia* (p. lxiv).

5

King Leir

Date and Sources

The first record of this play is an entry in the Stationers' Register for 14 May 1594:

> Ent. E. White [replacing A. Islip]: a booke entituled the moste famous chronicle historye of Leire Kinge of England and his Three Daughters.[1]

In his so-called 'Diary', the ledger recording his dealings with the theatre companies, Philip Henslowe noted two performances of 'Kinge leare' on 7 and 8 April 1594 at the Rose theatre, when two companies were acting together, Queen Elizabeth's Men and the Earl of Sussex's Men.[2] As we have seen, other evidence connects Kyd with Elizabeth's Men.[3] Nothing more was heard of the play in official documents until an entry in the Register for 6 May 1605:

---

1. See Greg, *BEPD*, 1.337–8 (no. 213). An earlier entry in Volume A of the Register (*BEPD*, pp. 10–11) lists *King Leir* among five plays transferred on that day from Islip to White, who had published three plays by Kyd in 1592: *Arden of Faversham*, *Soliman and Perseda*, and *The Spanish Tragedy*. Presumably Kyd sold the plays to White directly, not having previously sold them to any of the theatre companies.

2. See Foakes and Rickert (ed.), *Henslowe's Diary*, p. 21.

3. Unfortunately, two recent historians of the company were unaware of this evidence. See McMillin and MacLean, *The Queen's Men*. They refer to the passage in Dekker's *A Knight's Conjuring* for its mention of Atchelow and Bentley (pp. 143, 195) without recognizing the significance of Kyd's name in this context.

Ent. S. Stafford: a booke called the tragicall historie of Kinge Leire and his Three Daughters, &c., as it was latelie acted.

This time publication quickly followed, with a more expansive claim about its staging:

The True Chronicle History of King Leir, and his three daughters, Gonorill, Ragan, and Cordella. As it hath bene divers and sundry times lately acted.

As Greg observed, the 'lately acted' claim 'was probably intended to lead the public to suppose that it was none other than Shakespeare's *King Lear*', following the recent popularity of that play, performed by the King's Men.[4] But Shakespeare's *Lear* did not appear in print until 1608.

The best account of the sources of *King Leir* remains Wilfrid Perrett's unsurpassed survey of the Lear story.[5] Perrett established that the author of this play 'selected materials from the three most recent metrical versions of the story',[6] that is, William Warner's poem *Albion's England* (1586), the enlarged edition of *The Mirror for Magistrates* published by John Higgins in 1587, and the first three books of *The Faerie Queene* (1590).[7] Perrett showed that smaller details come from Gascoigne's *Supposes* (1566), Richard Edwardes's *Damon and Pythias* (1565), and Lodge's *Rosalynde* (1590). As to the authorship, Perrett noted that 'Malone ascribed it to Kyd, an opinion which Boas and Schick do not attempt to refute' (p. 117), an impressive agreement between the leading Kyd scholars of their day, German and English. For himself, Perrett observed that 'there are a hundred signs in diction, rhyme, tendency, knowledge of the fable etc. that [*King Leir*] is the work of one man throughout' (p. 118), but he offered no suggestion as to his identity.

4. See W.W. Greg (ed.), *The History of King Leir 1605* (Oxford, 1907; Malone Society Reprints).

5. See Wilfrid Perrett, *The Story of King Lear from Geoffrey of Monmouth to Shakespeare* (Berlin, 1904), pp. 95–121.

6. Ibid., p. 99.

7. All three sources are reproduced in, and here quoted from Bullough (ed.), *Narrative and Dramatic Sources of Shakespeare*, vol. 7, *Major Tragedies* (London and New York, 1973). See pp. 269–308 for an excellent discussion of the play in relation to Shakespeare, and 323–36 for the texts.

In this chapter I shall justify my attribution to Kyd in two stages.[8] First I discuss the presence in this play of the three characteristic elements of Kyd's dramaturgy that I identified in *The Spanish Tragedy*: the use of intrigue, the introduction of comedy into tragedy, and the creation of a vengeful female character. In addition, I point out the unique nature of *King Leir* in Kyd's canon, the switch of genre, from tragedy to romance. Secondly, I shall analyse the linguistic and stylistic features that confirm Kyd's authorship.

Intriguers and Victims

In *King Leir* Kyd introduces the element of intrigue surprisingly early and in a surprising form. In his other plays it emerges out of the interaction between characters as a response to events, often linked with harm suffered and the desire for revenge. Further, intrigues are normally launched in private conversation between the intriguers, sometimes joined by associates or instruments who will carry out the deed. In this play Leir himself announces the intrigue in the opening scene, addressing his assembled court. Kyd differs from tradition again for the process of division. In the three sources the King simply announces that he intends to divide his kingdom according to his daughters' professions of love, but Kyd shows the King trying to manipulate the proceedings in advance. Leir wishes to make the division dependent on his daughters' choice of husbands. Gonorill and Ragan already have royal suitors, Leir tells his courtiers, but 'My youngest daughter, fair Cordella vows | No liking to a monarch, unless love allows' (1.59–60).[9] Unlike every other intriguer in Kyd's plays, Leir has not suffered any harm. For purely political reasons he is anxious to marry her to the King of Ireland, as we subsequently learn, so that 'our state | May be protected 'gainst all foreign hate' (2.43–4). Cordella's marriage will strengthen the country's security. Leir hopes to do this, 'if my policy may her beguile', or deceive

8. See also Brian Vickers, 'Kyd's authorship of *King Leir*', *Studies in Philology* 115 (2018): 433–71.

9. All quotations are from the edition by Eugene Giddens in Vickers (ed.), *The Collected Works of Thomas Kyd*, vol. 1.

(1.66). Anyone sensitive to the Machiavellian connotations of 'policy' in Elizabethan drama will be surprised that a father should use such a dubious term in planning to make his daughter marry the man of his choice, without consulting her. The good counsellor Perillus urges him to 'Lose not the title of a loving father. | Do not force love where fancy cannot dwell' (1.72–3) but Leir ignores his advice, declaring that he intends to lay a plot for Cordella:

> I am resolved, and even now my mind
> Doth meditate a sudden stratagem
> To try which of my daughters loves me best,
> Which, till I know, I cannot be in rest.   (75–8)

Kyd exposes Leir's ill-judged policy by the specious arguments he uses. 'This granted', he says, using a term from dialectic, when a speaker states his basic assumptions—but Leir is not engaged in dialogue—

> when they jointly shall contend
> Each to exceed the other in their love,
> Then at the vantage will I take Cordella,
> Even as she doth protest she loves me best,
> I'll say then, 'Daughter, grant me one request:
> To show thou lovest me as thy sisters do,
> Accept a husband whom myself will woo'.   (82–5)

Kyd has given Leir a fully formed scenario in which he plans to overwhelm Cordella—to 'take' her 'at the vantage' is to seize an opportunity of catching your opponent off balance, say; but Cordella is no opponent. Leir assumes that he can predict his daughter's reactions, adding the grotesque idea that she will allow him to 'woo' her husband. Utterly unconcerned about her own wishes, he is equally insensitive to the terms he uses: 'This said'—another debating ploy—

> she cannot well deny my suit,
> Although, poor soul, her senses will be mute.
> Then will I triumph in my policy
> And match her with a king of Brittany.   (86–9)

In order to win his 'suit', a legal term fitting the fictive contest that Leir has imagined (except that he is both suitor and judge), he will 'mute' her senses (as if anaesthetizing an animal used in an experiment), depriving his daughter of her powers of judgment—'poor soul.' He sympathizes as if this decision has been made by someone else, evading his own responsibility.

In the drama of Kyd such words as 'policy' and 'stratagem' are usually associated with characters like Lorenzo in *The Spanish Tragedy* or Brusor in *Soliman and Perseda*. Leir is not in this class, of course, since he does not intend to kill anyone, but his unfatherly manipulation is wrong in itself, and is likely to backfire. (Elizabethan audiences were well aware of the bad effects of parental interference, summed up in the title of a play by George Wilkins, *The Miseries of Enforced Marriage*, 1606.) Kyd has set up the King's self-pleasing stratagem so that he can counter it with another, far more effective intrigue. He has added to the small cast of characters found in his sources two matching counsellors, Skalliger, a corrupt courtier, and Perillus, a loyal servant of the King. Leir ended his speech with a rhyming couplet ('policy' | 'Brittany'), but the audience alone hears Skalliger add a third rhyme in his aside to us, before visiting Gonorill and Ragan: 'I'll to them before, and bewray your secrecy' (90). In the vocabulary of intrigue, to 'bewray' or reveal an intrigue is to destroy the intriguers' power and superiority over their targets. Leir's plot is already doomed to failure.

The next scene shows Leir's eldest daughters discussing Cordella with jealous resentment, looking for a way 'To be revenged upon her unperceived' (2.75)—although she has not harmed them. Skalliger offers them the opportunity, revealing that Leir desires 'to know | Which of you three do bear most love to him', adding that 'whose answer pleases him the best, | They shall have most unto their marriages' (59–60). Where other versions have Leir planning to divide the kingdom equally, Kyd evidently realized that the possibility of gain will give Gonorill and Ragan an added motivation. They anticipate Cordella's categorical refusal of 'the Irish King' and plan to exploit her irritation:

So will our father think, she loveth him not,
Because she will not grant to his desire,

Which we will aggravate in such bitter terms,
That he will soon convert his love to hate:
For he, you know is always in extremes.   (2.95–8)

Working from the single hint in the 1587 text of *The Mirror for Magistrates* ('my sisters did despise | My grace and gieftes, and sought my wrecke to wage'), Kyd has developed in convincing detail the older sisters' motives for wishing to harm Cordella, making use of Skalliger's betrayal of his king. Ragan's closing words express the intriguers' semi-aesthetic admiration for their stratagem—'Not all the world could lay a better plot', a regular feature of Kyd's intrigues. The division of the kingdoms now takes place, resulting in Leir disowning Cordella, and dispossessing himself. Undaunted, resolving that 'These hands shall labour for to get my spending' (2.133), Cordella leaves this plot strand. When she returns it will be in a different genre, tragicomedy.

Kyd pursues Leir's story, returning to the sources for his daughters' treatment of him. In *Soliman and Perseda* Kyd had introduced early on Brusor, Soliman, and Lucina, characters who are going to be important later in the action. Similarly, in the opening scene of this play he introduced two characters of his own invention, the evil courtier Skalliger and the good counsellor Perillus (the model for Shakespeare's Kent).[10] Kyd used Perillus as a commentator on Lear's folly in trying to 'beguile' (deceive, cheat) their children (1.91–3), and for his failure to distinguish 'vain flattering words' from 'the hidden tenor of [Cordella's] humble speech' (3.135–8). Kyd increased Perillus's role as an authoritative commentator by giving him his longest solo appearance on stage (8.1–29), telling us that Cordella has disappeared and that Leir is now staying 'in Cornwall with the eldest'. We are dismayed, but hardly surprised, to learn of Gonorill's sudden volte-face once she had gained power, maltreating her father 'in most opprobrious sort', and calling him 'fool and dotard to his face' (8.14–15).

---

10. Perrett described *Leir* as 'the offspring of the native stage. Perillus and Skalliger may be the good and bad spirits of the Moralities, materialized' (*Story of King Lear*, pp. 109–10).

In scene 9 we see Gonorill confiding her anger to the politic courtier Skalliger, who advises her to reduce Leir's train of followers by half, 'kind advice' which she promises to reward (9.32–3). Kyd exploits the flexibility of Elizabethan drama by making Skalliger step out of character into a choric role, denouncing both himself and his mistress:

Go, viperous woman,[11] shame to all thy sex:
The heavens, no doubt, will punish thee for this:
And me a villain, that to curry favour,
Have given the daughter counsel 'gainst the father.   (9.39–44)

This device, the villain isolated on stage at the end of a scene in order to reveal his evil doing, having been promised a reward, is exactly what Kyd did with the malicious intriguer Villuppo (*Sp. T.* 1.3.92–5). Skalliger, however, having denounced himself, has reached the limits of his usefulness: a politic courtier is no longer needed, passions are sufficiently inflamed. The character leaves the play, but the actor may return in the role of Messenger.[12]

Kyd now brings Perillus back as a loyal helper to Leir, a pairing which persists to the end of the play, both characters always appearing together. Leir finally realizes his 'unkindness to Cordella', and has no choice but to go to Ragan, who may 'be kinder, and intreat me fair' (10.95, 102–3).

These direct conflicts are now supplemented by a new intrigue, directed against Leir. In enlarging and diversifying his source material, for the first time in the Lear story, Kyd differentiated the sisters' husbands. Cornwall shows himself sympathetic to Leir—'Father, what aileth you to be so sad?' (10.1), and he is so upset when Gonorill abuses Leir that he leaves them, unable 'to hear this discord sound' (10.33). The effect of his good nature is to emphasize his wife's evil. When he hears that Leir

---

11. Where the briefest hint in Warner indicts one daughter as attempting her father's death, Kyd conceives of them having the same viciousness, describing them five times over as 'vipers' (Perrett, *Story of King Lear*, p. 107).

12. Perrett made the acute suggestion that 'Skalliger's post of "serviceable villain" is taken later by the Messenger, who might well be Skalliger in disguise. There is the same suggestion of undue familiarity with Gonorill in Scene 12 as in Scene 3. The two parts were certainly written for the same actor' (p. 112).

has gone to Ragan in Cambria, Cornwall resolves to 'send a Post immediately' to learn 'whether he has arrived safely' (12.21–2). But Gonorill decides to 'intercept the Messenger' and corrupt him (just as Lorenzo corrupted Pedringano) 'With sweet persuasions, and with sound rewards' (12.23–5). In the figure of '*the Messenger that should go to Cambria*', as the stage direction helpfully identifies him, Gonorill finds a willing accomplice. Appealing to him simultaneously with erotic advances and money (12.57–9, 83, 100–102),[13] Gonorill seizes Cornwall's letter to Leir, substituting one of her own to Ragan. In it she alleges that Leir 'hath detracted her, given out slanderous speeches against her', created discord. Then, almost as an after-thought, she mentions 'a further matter':

> GONORILL: If my sister thinketh convenient, as my letters
>   importeth, to
> make him away, hast thou the heart to effect it?
> MESSENGER: Few words are best in so small a matter: these are but
>   trifles.
> By this booke I will. [*Kisses the paper*]   (12.109–11)

Gonorill has twice described the content of her letter but has withheld this shocking detail, dressed up in euphemisms ('convenient', 'make him away'). Kyd has taken over from the brief account in Warner's poem a plot element that, with his interest in vengeful women, may have attracted him to this story in the first place:

> Gonorill . . . not only did attempt
> Her fathers death, but openly did hold him in contempt.[14]

As Perrett observed, Warner's 'fruitful idea of the daughters' attempt on Leir's life . . . forms the basis of four scenes (12, 15, 17, 19) and causes the introduction of a new character, "*the Messenger or murtherer*."'[15]

Here Kyd's characteristic plot structures overlap. The need for a character who can easily move between Gonorill and Ragan as they plot

---

13. Just as Alice Arden does to Black Will (*AF* 14.112–16).

14. Bullough (ed.), *Narrative and Dramatic Sources*, vol. 7, p. 335.

15. Perrett, *Story of King Lear*, p. 100.

their father's murder suggests the role of a Messenger, who can multi-task as a contract killer. In making this decision Kyd shifts from intrigue to what a Renaissance critic might describe as 'indecorous' or inappropriate comedy, eliciting laughter in situations where someone's life is at stake, as with Pedringano's execution. From the outset Kyd conceives the Messenger as an entertainer. When Gonorill suggestively assures him, 'I tell thee, we make a great account of thee', he makes the bawdy undertone clear:

> This sword, this buckler, this head, this heart, these hands, arms, legs, tripes, bowels, and all the members else whatsoever are at your dispose. Use me, trust me, command me.   (12.64–7)

When Gonorill praises his 'good tongue' he starts boasting of his exaggerated past exploits, like Basilisco:

> And as bad a tongue, if it be set on it, as any oyster-wife at Billingsgate hath. Why, I have made many of my neighbours forsake their houses with railing upon them, and go dwell elsewhere, and so by my means houses have been good cheap in our parish.   (76–8)

Despite his wit, with his casual readiness to be hired as an assassin ('so small a matter'), the Messenger should come across as an unpredictable figure, comic but also sinister.

Sandwiched between Gonorill's two scenes, Kyd introduces Ragan to us in a soliloquy in which she proudly presents herself as a woman challenging masculine power:

> I rule the King of Cambria as I please.
> The states are all obedient to my will,
> And look whate'er I say it shall be so.
> Not anyone, that dareth, answers no.   (11.5–10)

Her callousness towards her father matches her sister's: 'I'd send him packing some where else to go'.[16] When Lear and Perillus arrive at her

---

16. Gonorill had used the same language: 'You may go pack and seek some other place'.

house, 'two old men', tired and unattended, we observe the intriguer's habitual hypocrisy as Ragan disguises her hatred:

No, I mistake not—sure it is my father!
[*Aside*] I must dissemble kindness now of force.
  She runs to him and kneels down, saying:
Father, I bid you welcome full of grief . . .   (14.30–32).[17]

After her fulsome greeting, Kyd isolates Ragan for another soliloquy, expressing her mounting hatred for Leir and impatience to get rid of him:

Yet will I make fair weather to procure
Convenient means, and then I'll strike it sure.   (14. 58–9; my
    italics)

Ragan uses the same term as Gonorill, an uncanny parallel in both sisters using identical euphemisms when discussing terms with a hired killer.

According to Kyd's presentation, the Messenger's motive is primarily financial. When Ragan is reading Gonorill's letter, he interprets her visible anger as a good omen for a new contract:

See how she knits her brow and bites her lips
And stamps and makes a dumb show of disdain,
Mixed with revenge and violent extremes.
Here will be more work and *more crowns for me.*   (15.16–19; my
    italics)

A corrupt servant rejoicing at his employer's anger as a sign of more work and more reward: this is a situation that we have seen in Kyd's acknowledged oeuvre in Pedringano's realization that 'Instead of watching [keeping watch] I'll deserve *more gold*, | By fetching Don Lorenzo to this match' (*Sp. T.* 2.4.12–13; my italics). Having consistently emphasized Ragan's pride in ruling her husband, Kyd takes care to show her

---

17. Mosby reacts in the same way when he sees Alice coming: 'But here she comes and I must flatter her' (*AF*, 8.44).

especially annoyed by Gonorill's false report that Leir 'means to alter so the case | That I shall know my lord to be my head' (15.25–6). As in many sibling relationships, one sister knows the best way to upset the other. This imagined threat to her female supremacy makes Ragan decide 'to cut [Leir] off in time' (42), so she turns to the Messenger, just as Goneril had done:

> RAGAN: Hast thou the heart to act a stratagem
> And give a stab or two, if need require?
> MESSENGER: I have a heart compact of adamant,
> Which never knew what melting pity meant . . .
> If you will have your husband or your father
> Or both of them sent to another world,
> Do but command me do't. It shall be done.   (15.54–5, 58–60)

He receives a down payment, delighted to have

> A purse of gold given for a paltry stab.
> Why, here's a wench that longs to have a stab.
> Well, I could give it her and ne'er hurt her neither.   (67–9)

Bawdy jokes are appropriate to his role as entertainer, getting the audience on his side.

Kyd presents the daughters' intrigue to kill their father from both viewpoints. We next see the Messenger expecting Ragan's instructions, so that he will 'know her mind | And hope for to derive *more crowns from her*' (17.6; my italics). But Ragan is curiously hesitant, almost embarrassed:

> RAGAN: It is a thing of right strange consequence
> And well I cannot utter it in words . . .
> Ah, good my friend, that I should have thee do
> Is such a thing as I do shame to speak—
> Yet it must needs be done.
> MESSENGER: I'll speak it for thee, queen. Shall I kill thy father?
> I know 'tis that, and if it be so, say.
> RAGAN: Ay.

But there is an additional target:

> RAGAN: Thou must kill that old man that came with him.
> MESSENGER: Here are two hands; for each of them is one.
> RAGAN: And for each hand here is a recompense.
> *Gives him two purses.*

If it seems out of character for Ragan to be ashamed of any violent action that will further her desires, Kyd's purpose is to contrast her diffidence with the Messenger's joy at earning more money for such a 'paltry thing':

> Oh, that I had ten hands by miracle!
> I could tear ten in pieces with my teeth,
> So in my mouth you'd put a purse of gold.

Kyd is building up his hired assassin as a callous murderer who will do anything for money. Ragan outlines the time and place where the killer shall meet his targets: before dawn tomorrow at the thicket about two miles from the court, where she will promise to meet them herself (17.37–40)—of which she clearly has no intention. To arrange an assignation, but then to send a murderer instead, this is the device that Lorenzo uses to get rid of Serberine (*Sp. T.* 3.2.68–91). After her hired killer has left the stage, Ragan reveals her cold-blooded plan to kill him once he has done the deed—'About it then, and when thou hast dispatched, | I'll find a means to send thee after him' (17.57–8). This is another echo of Lorenzo's plan to have his 'base companions die' for his preservation (*Sp. T.* 3.2.115–6).[18] Kyd's Machiavellian intriguers are all cut from the same cloth.

Tragedy into Comedy

Kyd has carefully set the stage for a double murder. The intrigue that Gonorill and Ragan have launched seems guaranteed to succeed. Leir and Perillus reach the assignation place at an early hour, recognize their vulnerability, pray together, and fall asleep (19.1–19). Then the

---

18. Cf. Mosby's callous readiness to kill Greene, Michael, Clarke, and even Alice, so that he can be 'sole ruler of mine own' (*AF*, 8.23–43).

Messenger appears, 'pat like the catastrophe in the old comedy', his change of role being signalled by the stage direction:

Enter the Messenger or murderer with two daggers in his hands.

(19.19)

Since we have seen how serious Ragan was about the murder, his ostensive role is sinister, but his comic persona wins through. Indeed, it is oddly reassuring when he starts to entertain us by imagining what might happen if he were as vulnerable as the two old men:

> *Were it not a mad jest* if two or three of my profession should meet me and lay me down in a ditch and play rob-thief with me and perforce take my gold away from me whilst I act this stratagem, and by this means the greybeards should escape?   (19. 20–23; my italics)

That would indeed be 'a mad jest'—we recall the Boy carrying Lorenzo's 'pardon' for Pedringano, commenting on his role:

> *Will't not be an odd jest* for me to stand and grace every jest he makes, pointing my finger at this box, as who would say: 'Mock on, here's thy warrant.' *Is't not a scurvy jest* that a man should jest himself to death?
>
> (SP. T. 3.5.13–17; MY ITALICS)

This 'mad jest' begins the longest (some 360 lines) and most memorable scene in the play on an oddly jocular note. The Messenger ascends to the more serious medium of verse, but Kyd still allows him scope for comedy. As he comes across his victims asleep, the stage direction orders him to do a double take:

> *See them and start.*
> But stay, methinks my youths are here already
> And with pure zeal have prayed themselves asleep.
> I think they know to what intent they came
> And are provided for another world.   (26–9)

By giving the Messenger a basically comic role, Kyd keeps the audience in suspense. He jests continually, but he is also ready 'to stab', and we cannot predict what he will do next. When Leir and Perillus wake up he stands aside, and comments to us on their conversation, as Leir reports the bad dream he has had:

> PERILLUS: Fear not, my Lord, dreams are but fantasies,
> And slight imaginations of the brain.
> MESSENGER: [*Aside*] Persuade him so; but I'll make him and you
> Confess that dreams do often prove too true.
> PERILLUS: I pray, my Lord, what was the effect of it?
> I may go near to guess what it pretends.
> MESSENGER: [*Aside*] Leave that to me, I will expound the
> dream.   (43–9)

It seems at that point as if Kyd is about to break through the convention of the aside and let the unobserved character engage in conversation with the main speaker, as Shakespeare did for the exposure of Malvolio in *Twelfth Night*, and that of Parolles in *All's Well that Ends Well*.[19] This is another one of Kyd's special 'split scenes', with a commentator only visible to the audience. In *The Spanish Tragedy* Lorenzo and Balthazar comment from their hiding-place on the love scene between Horatio and Bel-imperia (2.2.26–31). In *Soliman and Perseda* Soliman comments from the safety of his hiding-place on the fake trial which leads to Erastus being strangled (5.2.21–3, 65–8). In all three plays the commentators have a superiority over the overheard speakers.

As in those two tragedies, since we share with the Messenger full knowledge of his commission, we experience the scene on two levels, that of the unprotected victims and that of the predator, master of the situation. When he finally reveals himself to Leir and Perillus '*They reele*' (65), as another expressive stage direction instructs the actors, and express their deference:

> LEIR: My friend, thou seem'st to be a proper man—
> MESSENGER: [*Aside*]'Sblood, how the old slave claws me by
> the elbow.
> He thinks, belike, to 'scape by scraping[20] thus.   (19.77–9)

---

19. See Vickers, *Artistry of Shakespeare's Prose*, pp. 232–3, 305–8.
20. My emendation.

Like any experienced clown figure in Elizabethan drama, the Messenger has always one eye on the audience. When Leir gives him his purse, the authorial stage direction instructs '*Take it*', and when Perillus adds his purse too, the action is described:

Takes his and weigh them in both his hands.

MESSENGER: I'll none of them. They are too light for me.

Puts them in his pocket.   (85–6)

The stage direction gives the actor a chance to show his comic timing. Having pocketed their purses, despite their being 'too light', the Messenger asks both men to agree to do something for him. After a long build-up (90–108) he finally discloses the favour, in a comic anti-climax, sure to arouse laughter:

Do me the pleasure for to kill yourselves
So shall you save me labour for to do it.   (19.109–10)

Drawing attention to what he is doing, the playwright makes Leir beg: 'Play not the cat which dallieth with the mouse' (116).

Unlike any other intrigue plot known to me, the crucial figure in this decisive episode is not an intriguer who has given the contract, but the instrument paid to carry it out. Leir and Perillus are at his mercy: their purses are in his pocket, the two daggers in his hands can 'make away with' their lives. He has also pocketed the purses of Gonorill and Ragan, whose happiness depends—perversely enough—on him killing their father. In a different way, theatre goers and readers are also dependent on him to resolve the question, can the instrument be trusted? There are not many scenes in early modern drama in which so much power is invested in one character.

When the victims were asleep the Messenger revealed that Ragan has prepared a letter, with orders to give it them before he kills them. Now Leir tries to find out who has ordered their murder, convinced that Cordella, 'whom I have offended' (135), has done so. He is truly shocked when the Murderer reveals that

Thy own two daughters Gonorill and Ragan,
Appointed me to massacre thee here.   (19.165–6).

Kyd's purpose in revealing this is partly to make Leir realize the truth about the evil daughters, and partly to emphasize Cordella's innocence in preparation for a later scene, when Leir and Cordella are reunited.

When asked to swear the truth of this report, the Messenger first swears 'by heaven', but Leir rebukes him: 'Swear not by heaven, for fear of punishment. | The heavens are guiltless of such heinous acts'. He then swears by earth, but Leir again objects: 'Swear not by earth, for she abhors to bear | Such bastards as are murderers of her sons'. The Messenger takes the only remaining option:

MESSENGER: Why, then, by hell and all the devils I swear.
LEIR: Swear not by hell, for that stands gaping wide
To swallow thee an' if thou do this deed.

   Thunder and lightning.   (189–91)

This completely unprepared for event was a 'popular theatrical device' on the Elizabethan stage, signifying the supernatural.[21] In their excellent study of stage directions Dessen and Thomson note that thunder 'is several times interpreted as the voice of the gods', especially 'as a sign that heaven is angry'. Kyd was able to draw on Renaissance Christian beliefs when needed, perhaps responding to an early Christian flavour in the source, but modern readers will have to suspend their disbelief.

In a long aside the Messenger reveals the effect that the thunder had had on him:

I would that word were in his belly again.
It hath frighted me even to the very heart.
This old man is some strong magician.
His words have turned my mind from this exploit.   (191–4)

Having shown them Gonorill's letter, he hastens to share his dilemma with us:

---

21. See Dessen and Thomson, *A Dictionary of Stage Directions*, pp. 230–31.

Shall I relent, or shall I prosecute?
Shall I resolve, or were I best recant?
I will not crack my credit with two queens
To whom I have already passed my word.
Oh, but my conscience for this act doth tell
I get heaven's hate, earth's scorn, and pains of hell.   (197–202)

He is an old-fashioned Elizabethan villain, with Christian beliefs (unlike his Jacobean successors) and Kyd still has him speak in verse. But as the two old men increase their appeals, each asking for the other to be spared, Kyd brings him down to prose, as if his dignified role as executioner is beginning to weaken. When Perillus claims that his death doesn't matter, the Messenger replies: 'Marry, but it doth, sir, by your leave. Your good days are past. Though it be no matter for you, 'tis a matter for me' (245–6), since 'the queen commands it must be so'. When Leir makes a more eloquent appeal to save Perillus, the strain becomes visible:

LEIR: Oh, if all this to mercy move thy mind,
Spare him. In heaven thou shalt like mercy find.
MESSENGER [*aside*]: I am as hard to be moved as another,
    and yet methinks the strength of their persuasions stirs
    me a little.   (270–73)

The good counsellor then deploys the most telling arguments, advising him to keep his 'hands still undefiled from blood', and to consider his own situation as accomplice of two daughters who paid him to kill their own father: can they be trusted to spare his life?[22] Perillus first frightens the Murderer with the consequences of 'this outrageous act', and the 'horror' that will surely 'haunt' him 'for the deed' (285–6). Then he identifies the vulnerability of the hired assassin in a Christian universe:

---

22. This is exactly Mosby's reasoning in his soliloquy, when he decides that, since he can't trust Alice, he must kill her: 'You have supplanted Arden for my sake, | And will extirpen me to plant another' (*AF* 8. 40–41).

> Think this again: that they which would incense
> Thee for to be the butcher of their father,
> When it is done, for fear it should be known,
> Would make a means to rid thee from the world.
> Even in the hottest hole of grisly hell,
> Such pains as never mortal tongue can tell.
> *It thunders. [The Messenger] quakes and lets fall the dagger next to*
> *Perillus.* (19.287–94)

We already know how accurate this prediction is, and the thunder reinforces the deterrent. The Messenger '*lets fall the other dagger*'. When Leir asks him why he delays killing them he preserves his confident persona, ever master of the situation:

> MESSENGER: I am as willful as you for your life.
> I will not do it, now you do entreat me.
> PERILLUS: Ah, now I see thou hast some spark of grace.
> MESSENGER: Beshrew you for it. You have put it in me,
> The parlousest old men that e'er I heard.
> Well, to be flat, I'll not meddle with you.
> Here I found you, and here I'll leave you.
> If any ask you why the case so stands,
> Say that your tongues were better than your hands. *Exit*
> *Messenger.* (19.300–308)

And with a rhyming couplet he leaves them, unfazed as ever.

Vengeful Woman

Kyd has unfinished business with Ragan. He had already innovated twice over, in bringing on to the Elizabethan stage vengeful female characters. Bel-imperia declares herself ready to kill with her own hands the man who had murdered her beloved, and she does so in the bloody masque that ends the play, before stabbing herself. Perseda stabs Lucina, who had betrayed Erastus to Soliman's revenge, and poisons Soliman. Bel-imperia and Perseda were both good women, sympathetic characters. Having awarded the female sex the rights to violence for a good cause, previously a male prerogative, Kyd gave the same licence to women pursuing an evil cause. One of his sources recorded an actual (but unspecified) attempt by Gonorill to cause 'Her father's death'. Having planned to emphasize this unnatural behaviour, Kyd started the preparation for this plot strand already in the second scene, by showing her two sisters' resentment of Cordella. Gonorill describes her as 'that proud pert peat', who

> is so nice and so demure,
> So sober, courteous, modest, and precise,
> That all the court hath work enough to do
> To talk how she exceedeth me and you.   (2.1–4, 10–12)

Gonorill sounds like one of Cinderella's jealous sisters, but for Ragan jealousy naturally generates a desire to harm:

> RAGAN: What should I do? Would it were in my power
> To find a cure for this contagious ill.
> Some desperate medicine must be soon applied
> To dim the glory of her mounting fame   (2.13–16)

The metaphor 'desperate medicine' refers to a condition which is 'despaired of, irremediable, not to be saved; or at least extremely dangerous', as Alexander Schmidt defines it.[23] In the mouth of a sister complaining of a sibling's beauty, it is an omen of vicious things to come.

Their opportunity to harm Cordella arrives when the politic courtier Skalliger 'bewrays' or reveals their father's intrigue, the ceremony Leir has planned. Forewarned, these two sisters already have an unfair advantage, but Kyd makes them legitimize their strategy in terms which suggest that Cordella has done them an injury:

> RAGAN: Now have we fit occasion offered us
> To be revenged upon her unperceived.
> GONORILL: Nay, our revenge we will inflict on her,
> Shall be accounted piety in us.   (74–7).

---

23. Alexander Schmidt, *Shakespeare Lexicon and Quotation Dictionary*, 3rd edn., rev. Gregor Sarrazin, 2 vols (Berlin, 1902; New York, 1971), 1.300.

The only harm that Cordella has done her sisters is to be more popular than them, no justification for the revenge they plan to 'inflict on her'.

The word 'revenge' in a woman's mouth was always unusual on the Elizabethan stage, and in Kyd's plays women use it when they feel personally harmed, for instance by the murder of her lover or husband, as in the cases of Bel-imperia and Perseda. Gonorill and Ragan had no more serious motive for seeking revenge on Cordella than their envy of her beauty, but their resentment provided Kyd with an opportunity to establish his characters' natures early in the play, as he generally preferred. Having brought about the disinheriting of Cordella, and gained her share of the kingdom, Gonorill is the first to receive a visit from the father whom she flattered so much, and she soon drives Leir away to live with her sister. Left alone on stage, in one of the first ever soliloquies in Elizabethan drama for a female character planning to take action against a man, Gonorill vows to 'intercept the Messenger' and 'temper him ... | With sweet persuasions and with sound rewards' (12.23–5) to endorse her claim that Leir has gone to visit Ragan of his own accord, not driven away by her. Contemplating her father's journey, she speculates that

> He haply may, by travelling unknown ways,
> Fall sick and as a common passenger
> Be dead and buried. Would God it were so well.   (12.30–32)

It is rather upsetting to see a daughter contemplating her father's death so coldly. However, Gonorill is too impatient to wait for such an uncertain accident and hires the Messenger to kill Leir.

Kyd found it logical to extend the same *ressentiment* to Ragan, who is revealed as even more violent. Having read Gonorill's letter, with its 'slander' and fabricated tales against him, Ragan also threatens to kill her father:

> Well, it were best for him to take good heed,
> Or I will make him hop without a head
> For his presumption,   (15.27–9)

Unable to act without a man's help, Ragan now hires the Messenger, but, as we have seen, the combination of advance payment, his victims' appeals for pity, and heavenly thunder caused him to renege on his contract. Having witnessed this failed attempt, the audience enjoys superior knowledge to Ragan, and can appreciate the hypocrisy with which she voices to her husband the 'suspicion' that Cordella has used the power of 'wicked spirits or infernal fiends' to do away with Leir. If she were sure that this 'detested witch' had been responsible for killing her father, Ragan vows,

> Myself to France would go in some disguise
> And with these nails scratch out her hateful eyes   (12.20–27).

We believe her, and Shakespeare may have taken notice of that threat. But all she can do is to insult the Ambassador who has come from the Gallian King, Cordella's husband. She describes Cordella as 'the young murderess', and threatens to release her anger on the unfortunate official:

> And were it not, it is 'gainst law of arms
> To offer violence to a messenger,
> We would inflict such torments on thyself
> As should enforce thee to reveal the truth   (12.66–9)

The Ambassador, defending 'My King and Queen', tells her that 'you have done them wrong' (72–4), at which point Ragan calls him a 'saucy mate' and '*strikes him*' (86), a remarkably violent act for a female character in Elizabethan drama, especially one of such high rank. Cambria declines his wife's request that he punish the Ambassador, for to 'infringe the law of Arms, | Were to my everlasting obloquy'; but he resolves to 'take revenge' on Gallia (95–8).

Kyd has presented Ragan as a woman of uninhibited anger, attacking Cordella both behind her back and to her face, plotting the death of Leir and Perillus, and even assaulting an Ambassador. He extends his treatment of her to consider what it must be like to have so much anger but be unable to take direct action. Ragan vents her frustration to her husband:

> How shall I live to suffer this disgrace
> At every base and vulgar peasant's hands?

It ill befitteth my imperial state
To be thus used and no man take my part.   *She weeps.*   (91–4)

The vulnerability of her position as a female would-be revenger, dependent on a man to 'take my part', is vividly exposed three scenes later. Having seen Leir reunited with Cordella, the audience again enjoys a superior knowledge over Ragan, allowing us to view her self-revelation in soliloquy with some detachment, or even enjoyment. She discloses that she is suffering 'a hell of conscience . . . with horror for my fact' (evil deed), suffering an 'agony of doubt' lest she be found out (25.1–4). This is, however, a momentary twinge of conscience. She has no remorse about paying a murderer to kill her father: what disturbs her is the risk taken by every intriguer who trusts an accomplice to do the nasty work, the uncertainty whether she has been betrayed. (Although a constant element in all intrigue plots, this is one of the few occasions that a dramatist brings it into the open.) Ragan's uncertainty derives from the disappearance of the Messenger—who, we know, has fled with both her gold and that of his intended victims:

The slave whom I appointed for the act,
I ne'er set eye upon the peasant since.
Oh, could I get him for to make him sure,
My doubts would cease, and I should rest secure.   (25.5–8)

(We know what she means by 'make him sure'.) But if Leir and Perillus have escaped to the court of France, she fears, then they will be trumpeting her 'shame' (11–12).

Catching up that word at the beginning of her next line, Ragan widens her indictment to include all men, and the injustices of a social order that subordinates her:

A shame on these white-livered slaves, say I,
That with fair words so soon are overcome.
O God, that I had been but made a man,
Or that my strength were equal with my will![24]

---

24. Cf. Beatrice's (misplaced) anger at Claudio for having rejected Hero: 'O that I were a man! . . . O God, that I were a man! I would eat his heart in the market-place . . . O that I were

These foolish men are nothing but mere pity
And melt as butter doth against the sun.
Why should they have preeminence over us
Since we are creatures of more brave resolve?   (25.13–20)

Ragan's frustrated wish for revenge expresses itself in a form that would invert Renaissance concepts of woman as being of a more tender nature than man. Her assault on conventional ideas puts her in a rare class, but lest we should be tempted to label Ragan an early exponent of women's rights, we should note the direction her 'liberation' would take:

I swear I am quite out of charity
With all the heartless men in Christendom.
A pox upon them when they are afraid
To give a stab or slit a paltry windpipe,
Which are so easy matters to be done.   (21–7)

It is already shocking to normal morality to have a 'Messenger or Murtherer' accepting a murder contract as if it were a trifle, but to have a woman talking as if she were Marlowe's Lightborn, and coldly expressing regret that she could not have been her father's 'executioner' is an outrage—but one entirely in character for Ragan. A pragmatic realist, she quickly comes to terms with the likelihood that her murder attempt will be exposed—as it soon is, and she looks beyond to a wished-for future, in which men had better watch out:

Well, had I thought the slave would serve me so,
Myself would have been executioner.
'Tis now undone, and if that it be known,
I'll make as good shift as I can for one.
He that repines at me, howe'er it stands,
'Twere best for him to keep him from my hands.
Exit.

When Ragan spoke those words in the Elizabethan theatre, both men and women should have been frightened.

---

a man for his sake! Or that I had any friend would be a man for my sake! But manhood is melted into cur'sies . . .' *Much Ado about Nothing*, 4.1.303–19.

CHAPTER 5

Ragan is one of the most remarkable female characters in English drama up till this point, a creature of 'brave resolve' matching that of Bel-imperia and Perseda, women not afraid to stab their enemies when the opportune moment arises. Although denied physical action, Ragan's frustration articulates the anger felt by those heroines of Kyd's acknowledged plays, all three ranking with men in their determination to satisfy the desire for revenge, whether justified or not.

Comedy into Romance

Anyone who believes the accounts of *King Leir* given by modern commentators, without reading the play itself, will imagine it to be a pious Christian fable, lacking humour. E. B. Everitt described it as 'most rudimentary in art', 'advanced little beyond the Morality play', the characters being 'very close to generalizations. Cordella is *grace*, theologically understood', while Leir is 'a Prodigal Father', and there is a 'very apparent . . . ritualistic flavour of the dialogue'.[25] Other critics concur in this lukewarm estimate: Irving Ribner described it as 'a sentimental fairy tale with no historical pretensions'; David Bevington saw it as 'a sentimental romance'; while R.A. Law called it 'not a history but a romantic comedy, in which the characters follow conventional patterns, the tedious exposition results in a large number of scenes, and the diction is naive'.[26] However, despite these strictures, *King Leir* is a thoughtful and inventive play, with vigorous characterization and some original features. It also includes much verbal comedy, at several social levels. Despite their nobility, characters in the upper plot freely exchange bawdy puns, as when the Kings of Cambria and Cornwall receive news from Leir that they

25. E. B. Everitt, *Six Early Plays Related to the Shakespeare Canon* (Copenhagen, 1965), p. 11. (R. L. Armstrong is acknowledged as editor of the sixth play, *Edward III*.) Everitt (who believes that all six plays reprinted were early works by Shakespeare) finds it 'probable that the story came directly from Holinshed' (p. 11). But Wilfrid Perrett showed more than a century ago that the playwright drew on exclusively poetic sources: *The Mirror for Magistrates*, *The Faerie Queene*, and *Albion's England* (*Story of King Lear*, p. 99–109).

26. Cited by Anne Lancashire, in Terence P. Logan and Denzell S. Smith (eds), *The Predecessors of Shakespeare. A Survey and Bibliography of Recent Studies in English Renaissance Drama* (Lincoln, NE, 1973), p. 224.

are to be given Gonorill and Ragan in marriage, along with half the kingdom:

CORNWALL: If I have one halfe, and you have the other,
Then between us we must needs have the whole.
CAMBRIA: The hole! how meane you that? Zblood; I hope
We shall have two holes between us.
CORNWALL: Why, the whole Kingdome.   (5.49–52)

That is an awful pun, but it raises the immediate issue, 'What then is left for his third daughter's dowry, | Lovely Cordella . . . ?' (53–4). Gonorill and Ragan also joke, if only at Cordella's expense:

RAGAN: She were right fit to make a Parsons wife:
For they, men say, do love fair women well,
And many times do marry them with nothing.
GONORILL: With nothing! marry God forbid; why, are there
    any such?
RAGAN: I mean, no money.
GONORILL: I cry you mercy, I mistake you much.   (6.20–25)

The author of *King Leir* was not writing a Christian allegory.

The Romance plot begins when King of Gallia arrives in Brittany to see for himself the famed beauty of Leir's daughters. In the sources Gallia sends an ambassador, but Kyd makes him come in person, accompanied by the bluff Lord Mumford. Disguised as pilgrims, they come across the solitary Cordella, lamenting that she has been 'turned into the world to seek my fortune' (7.20). They hide and overhear her, in a 'split' scene where they comment in asides, unnoticed by her (7.15–51). The King is instantly taken with her beauty and virtue. He tests her values, finding her 'mind' to be superior to fortune, proposes marriage, and is accepted (7.52–155). Having energized the abbreviated conventions of Romance, by which a sudden meeting can result in a happy-ever-after life decision, Kyd develops this plot strand speedily. After five scenes of hectic activity in the main plot, we see Cordella again in a soliloquy in which she revels her gratitude to God and her happiness with her 'kingly husband, mirror of his time | For zeal, for justice, kindness, and for care' (13.9–10). As we know from many sources, most obviously Shakespeare's last plays, Romance seldom deals with any but ideal beings.[27] Her main concern is to find her father and earn his forgiveness. Two scenes later Kyd continues this strand with Cordella's husband, the King of Gallia, pleading with her to disperse 'these clouds of sorrow' (16.1). She explains that she cannot 'stop the course of nature's power' that makes her love her father (35–45), and Gallia awards her the matching status of Romance Ideal: 'Mirror of virtue. Phoenix of our age' (46). He decides to send an ambassador to Cornwall, where he thinks Leir 'keepeth now his residence', so that he and Cordella can be 'firmly reconciled | In perfect love as erst you were before' (59–60), the promised end of Romance.

Spectators and readers will know that Leir and Perillus have already left Cornwall's house, driven out by Gonorill's cruelty, to seek refuge with Ragan (scene 10); that Gonorill has suborned the messenger to substitute her letter for Cornwall's, and contracted him to kill her father (scene 12); that Leir and Perillus have reached Ragan's house, much to her displeasure (scene 14). We have also seen that Ragan's anger was allayed by the Messenger's arrival (scene 15), which produces a reinforcing second murder contract (scene 17). Thus, we know that Gallia's despatch of an ambassador to Gonorill in scene 16 is a fruitless errand, which Kyd could have dealt with by bringing the ambassador back to report his failure. Instead, Kyd chose to dramatize his unsuccessful mission in a scene of pure comedy. The ambassador announces that he has letters and presents for Leir, 'if I might speak with him'. Gonorill seems to take offence: 'If you might speak with him? Why, do you think | We are afraid that you should speak with him?' (18.24–8). The ambassador manages to pacify her irritation until she asks after Cordella's health:

> GONORILL: How doth my sister brook the air of France?
> AMBASSADOR: Exceeding well, and never sick one hour
> Since first she set her foot upon the shore.
> GONORILL: I am the more sorry.
> AMBASSADOR: I hope not so, madam.

27. See, e.g., Jean Alvares, *Ideal Themes in the Greek and Roman Novel* (Abingdon and New York, 2022).

GONORILL: Didst thou not say that she was ever sick
Since the first hour that she arrivèd there?
AMBASSADOR: No, madam, I said quite contrary.
GONORILL: Then I mistook thee.
CORNWALL: Then she is merry, if she have her health?
AMBASSADOR: Oh, no, her grief exceeds, until the time
That she be reconciled unto her father.
GONORILL: God continue it.
AMBASSADOR: What, madam?
GONORILL: Why, her health.
AMBASSADOR: Amen to that.   (18.38–50)

Kyd juxtaposes the Ambassador's shocked responses to these violations
of diplomatic decorum with Gonorill's involuntary revelations of her
true feelings about Cordella. It seems as if she has a built-in negativity
towards her sister, or that her unconscious is forcing her tongue to tell
the truth despite herself. When Cornwall offers to be 'a mediator in her
cause' and 'expiate' Leir's reported 'wrath', the poor Ambassador seizes
the opportunity to restore the norms of public discourse:

AMBASSADOR: Madam, I hope your grace will do the like.
GONORILL: Should I be a mean to exasperate his wrath
Against my sister, whom I love so dear? No, no.   (55–7)

In a peculiar psychological reflex her mind automatically converts any
positive outcome wished for Cordella into its opposite. Kyd has constructed an amusing scene by juxtaposing the Ambassador's expectation
of the norms of conversation, with Gonorill's deep-seated hatred of her
sister. Our laughter also renders Gonorill less frightening, a figure of
ridicule, not fear. Two scenes later he brings back the Ambassador '*solus*'
to report on his experience of 'the stately queen' who took 'exceptions'
to every word he spoke,

And fain she would have underminèd me
To know what my ambassage did import.
But she is like to hop without her hope
And in this matter for to want her will   (20.11–14)

The word 'hop' is contemptuous, ridiculously inappropriate for this stately queen, but expressing his indignation.[28]

Kyd has been gradually pulling together all the threads of his plot to bring about the defeat of evil that is such a reassuring feature of Romance. Scene 19, immediately preceding the Ambassador's soliloquy, had ended with Leir and Perillus, aided by divine thunder, neutralizing the murder contracts set up by Gonorill and Ragan. The scene following shows Gallia responding to Mumford's request 'that the next fair weather, which is very now, you would go in progress down to the seaside, which is very near' (21.50–53). Gallia and Cordella will disguise themselves as 'a plain country couple', with Mumford as their servant, which will make them unrecognizable to anyone expecting to see royal vestments. While they are getting ready for a picnic, we see Leir and Perillus, having just arrived on the same coast. (We recall the importance of Milford Haven as a focus of action in *Cymbeline*). Unable to pay the mariners who have brought them there, they are forced to exchange their own clothes for the seamen's much coarser garb, so that they 'may escape unknown' until they reach Cordella's 'court' (22.39–54).

The royal party now arrives, with a basket of food and drink, when Leir and Perillus also arrive '*very faintly*', in seamen's clothes, also unrecognizable. Kyd uses the device of a 'split scene' again, as Cordella and Gallia 'stand aside' to overhear the two men's conversation (24.16–71). At the point of exhaustion, Perillus even offers to feed Leir with blood from the veins in his arms, a device that Kyd borrowed from Lodge's *Rosalynde*. Cordella finally recognizes her father's voice, gives them food and drink, and a long, emotional recognition scene follows (86–200). At its climax Cordella kneels to her father, asking forgiveness, and he kneels to her with the same request. Having set up this symmetry, Kyd builds on it with daughter and father exchanging matching speeches:

CORDELLA: I pardon you? The word beseems not me,
But I do say so, for to ease your knee.

28. Her sister had used it in a soliloquy to utter another threat to Leir: 'it were best for him to take good heed | Or I will make him hop without a head | For his presumption' (15.28–31).

You gave me life. You were the cause that I
Am what I am who else had never been.
LEIR: But you gave life to me and to my friend,
Whose days had else had an untimely end.
CORDELLA: You brought me up whenas I was but young
And far unable for to help myself.
LEIR: I cast thee forth whenas thou wast but young
And far unable for to help thyself.   (24.211–20)

Kyd achieves a wonderfully eloquent simplicity in Cordella's acknowl-edgment of the gifts of existence: 'You gave me life. You were the cause that I | Am what I am who else had never been', and of parentage: 'You brought me up whenas I was but young | And far unable for to help myself', in each case contradicted by her guilty father. The brief reunion of Cordelia and Lear in Shakespeare's *King Lear* has greater resonance, given what came before, but in terms of direct statements of gratitude, Kyd yields nothing to Shakespeare.

As the reader or theatregoer experiences the final scenes of *King Leir*, it is hard to remember that we were once in the world of tragedy, with two daughters hiring a contract killer. Everything is now moving towards the restoration of Leir to his throne. Gallia prepares his army (scene 26), which then makes the four-hour sea crossing to Brittany, arriving at night and catching the inhabitants 'dead asleep':

Here shall we skirmish but with naked men,
Devoid of sense,[29] new waked from a dream.   (28.7–8)

Having captured the town, they soon meet the joint army of Cornwall and Cambria, accompanied by Gonorill and Ragan. The confrontation between the opposed parties reveals a use of prepared false propaganda by the guilty side that sounds remarkably modern:

---

29. Kyd had used a similar phrase when Leir announced how he planned to 'overwhelm' Cordella with his marriage settlement for her, 'Although, poor soul, her senses will be mute' (1.87).

GONORILL: They lie that say we sought our father's death.
RAGAN: 'Tis merely forgèd for a colour's sake
To set a gloss on your invasion.
Methinks an old man ready for to die
Should be ashamed to broach so foul a lie.   (29.89–93)

The 'flyting' that follows is more of its period, with a satisfying outcome as the two evil daughters are outmatched:

CORDELLA: Fie, shameless sister, so devoid of grace
To call our father liar to his face!
GONORILL: Peace, Puritan, dissembling hypocrite,
Which art so good that thou wilt prove stark naught!
Anon, when as I have you in my fingers,
I'll make you wish yourself in purgatory.
PERILLUS: Nay, peace thou monster, shame unto thy sex,
Thou fiend in likeness of a human creature!
RAGAN: I never heard a fouler-spoken man.
LEIR: Out on thee, viper, scum, filthy parricide,
More odious to my sight than is a toad!
[*Showing scrolls*] Knowest thou these letters?
    She snatches them and tears them.
RAGAN: Think you to outface me with your paltry scrolls?
You come to drive my husband from his right
Under the colour of a forgèd letter.   (29.94–108)

That last point is another familiar claim in the modern wars of disinformation ('the document is a clever forgery'). Gallia halts the altercation: 'To't gallants, to't. Let's not stand brawling thus', and a happily brief combat follows. Mumford has the satisfaction of chasing away both Cambria and Cornwall, Leir is restored to his throne but yields it to Gallia. The closing speech is given to Leir, who repairs his original fault:

Ah, my Cordella! Now I call to mind
The modest answer which I took unkind.
But now I see I am no whit beguiled.
Thou lov'st me dearly and as ought a child.   (33.17–20)

Despite the frantic activity of the closing scenes, Kyd kept a clear control of his design in transforming what might have been a tragedy into a romance. The destructive intrigue of Skalliger, Gonorill, and Ragan aroused Leir's hatred to the point where he dispossessed Cordella, and himself. But in driving Cordella out of her kingdom they produced an outcome opposite to their intent. By the operation of coincidence, a potent weapon for a dramatist, Kyd allowed her to meet Gallia, a King who satisfies her wish to love and be loved for her innate goodness. In this benevolent outcome, proper to Romance, Kyd allowed all the destructive elements to express themselves but finally disarmed them, restoring the abused and manipulated characters to their well-earned peace and happiness.

Authorship Markers: Phraseology

The identity of the play's author attracted little attention before the nineteenth century, although Malone detected traces of Kyd.[30] Victorian scholars proposed the usual suspects (Peele, Greene, Marlowe), without any evidence. The first to convincingly identify Kyd as the author of *King Leir* was William Wells in 1939, whose successes in attribution studies included identifying Middleton's hand in *Timon of Athens*.[31] Regrettably, his claim was ignored by the leading modern authorities on Kyd, Félix Carrère, Arthur Freeman, and Lukas Erne.[32] But his brief essay deserves more than total obscurity, since it made a surprisingly

30. See Edmond Malone, ed., *The Works of Shakespeare*, 21 vols (London, 1821): 'Kyd was also, I suspect, the author of the old plays of *Hamlet* and *King Leir*' (2.316).

31. William Wells, 'The Authorship of "King Leir"', *Notes and Queries*, 177 (16 December 1939): 434–8. Further references will be incorporated into the text. On his Middleton attributions, see Vickers, *Shakespeare, Co-Author*, pp. 264–67, 269–89.

32. See Carrère, *Le Théâtre de Thomas Kyd*, pp. 436ff.; Freeman, *Thomas Kyd*, p. 179, who does not even mention Wells's essay. Erne, *Beyond* The Spanish Tragedy, p. 223, lists *King Leir* among the plays with which Kyd has been 'wrongly credited', but his supporting footnote refers not to Wells's 1939 essay in *Notes and Queries* but to a later (and much weaker) piece, 'Thomas Kyd and the Chronicle History', *Notes and Queries* 178 (30 March 1940): 218–23. If Erne had ever seen the earlier paper, he would surely have considered Kyd's authorship of *King Leir* more seriously.

strong case. Wells began with a perceptive characterization of the play and its verse style:

> *Leir* is a play of simple, undisguised realism, with few flights of fancy. Its sentiment is extraordinarily naive, in content and expression, and yet, in its way, powerful. This accords with Kyd's characteristics. Its verse is 'pedestrian', but it is . . . abounding in feminine endings, and this points directly to Kyd, for none but he, among the pre-Shakespearian dramatists, wandered far from the normal ten-syllable line. Kyd does so to a great extent, both in *Cornelia* and in *Soliman and Perseda*. (p. 434)

Like most English scholars—it was published in some obscurity—Wells seems not to have known the authoritative 1931 study by P. W. Timberlake which established that Kyd in fact introduced feminine endings to English drama (see below). But Wells had studied Kyd's phraseology attentively and could declare with some authority that 'more cogent parallels' with *King Leir* can be found in Kyd's *Soliman and Perseda* than in any other Elizabethan play. I cite some of these:

> Brave knights, of Christendom and Turkish both,
> Assembled here in thirsty honour's cause,
> **To be enrollèd in** the brass-leaved book
> Of **never**-wasting **perpetuity**   (*SP* 1.3.1–4)
> Of us and ours, your gracious care, my lord,
> Deserves an everlasting memory
> **To be enrolled in** chronicles of fame
> By **never**-dying **perpetuity.**   (*KL* 1.67–70)

The significance of that parallel lies in the playwright's varying of the verb form expressing permanence—'never wasting | never dying'—while retaining the impressively polysyllabic word 'perpetuity' to end the line. The following examples noted by Wells will show that Kyd often recalled the physiognomy of a verse line, so to speak, the placing of key words at the beginning and/or ending.

> **First, thanks to heaven**; and **next to** Brusor's valour.   (*SP* 4.1.60)
> **First to the heavens, next, thanks to** you, my son.   (*KL* 33.3)

The sight of this shall show Perseda's name,
And add fresh courage **to my fainting limbs**. (*SP* 1.2.52–3)
Methinks your words do amplify, my friends,
And add fresh vigour **to my** willing **limbs**. (*KL* 32.37–8)

Wells noted that the phrase 'fainting limbs' recurs in *Leir*: '**And** never ease thy **fainting limbs** a whit' (14.10).

The case for Kyd's authorship of *King Leir* made by William Wells was also based on several significant parallels with *The Spanish Tragedy*. As he observed, 'It was an idea peculiar to Kyd that dead men required passports'. Thus, in the Induction to the *Spanish Tragedy*, the Ghost of Andrea is made to describe his visit to the underworld:

Not far from hence, amidst ten thousand souls,
Sat Minos, Æacus and Rhadamant,
To whom no sooner gan I make approach,
To crave a passport for my wandering ghost (*Sp. T.* 1.1.32–5)

In *Leir* the Messenger says of Perillus, whom he says he is going to kill:

Why, he must go along with you to heaven
Nay, presently to bear you company.
I have a passport for him in my pocket
Already sealèd, and he must needs ride post (*KL* 19. 219, 232–6)

In *Soliman and Perseda*, Piston, caught rifling the raiment of the dead Fernando, tries to excuse himself:

seeing he was going towards heaven, I thought to see if he had a
    pasport to S. Nicholas or no. (2.1.307–9).

Another striking resemblance between *King Leir* and Kyd's accepted canon, as Wells observed, is that 'Kyd's characters almost invariably anticipate disaster by premonitions', as Leir does:

And yet, me thinks **my mind** presageth still
I know not what; and yet I fear **some** ill (3.18–19)

In exactly the same phrasing, Bel-imperia in the *Spanish Tragedy* reveals her fear:

> **I know not what** myself;
> **And yet my heart** foretells me **some** mischance.   (2.4.14–15)

Another striking repetition that Wells noticed involved an identical ending and a mid-line expression in the form of a superlative. Kyd had used it earlier for Piston's mockery of Basilisco as '**the** bragging**est** knave **in Christendom**' (*SP* 1.3.84). He used it twice in this play, for Leir's praise of Gonorill and Ragan as '**the** kind**est** girls **in Christendom**' (*KL* 6.91) and the Messenger's celebration of his new career of taking purses as '**the** gainfull**est** trade **in Christendom**' (*KL* 15.66). It is an odd construction, but Shakespeare liked it.[33] Kyd used it again for Ragan's soliloquy in which she expressed herself to be 'quite out of charity | With all **the** heartless men **in Christendom**' who are 'afraid | To give a stab or slit a paltry windpipe' (25.21–4). Clearly the word 'heartless' has a special meaning in her lexicon.

The parallels that Wells cited between *King Leir* and Kyd's Turkish tragedy included an elaborate analogy based on the breeding habits of eagles. If Wells had looked at the context, he might have noticed a detail that strongly suggests Kyd's authorship of both passages, for in both cases the speaker uses it to declare their own sense of honour. Erastus does so in affirming his loyalty to Soliman:

> If any ignoble or dishonourable thoughts
> Should dare attempt, or but creep near my heart,
> **Honour** should force disdain to root it out;
> As air-bred eagles, if they once perceive
> That any of their brood but close their sight
> When they should gaze against the glorious sun,

---

33. Cf. 'sit there, the lying'st knave in Christendom' (*2H6* 2.1.124), 'he is the bluntest wooer in Christendom' (*3H6* 3.2.83), and two instances in *The Taming of the Shrew*: 'me up for the lying'st knave in Christendom' (Induction 2.24), and 'but Kate, the prettiest Kate in Christendom' (2.1.187). All postdate *King Leir* in performance.

They straightway seize upon him with their talons,
That on the earth it may untimely die,
For looking but askew at heaven's bright eye   (*SP* 3.1.85–90)

Leir does so when refusing to re-consider the division of the kingdom, having already despatched 'letters of contract' to Cambria and Cornwall:

Then do not so **dishonour** me, my lords,
As to make shipwreck of our kingly word.
I am as kind as is the pelican
That kills itself to save her young ones' lives
And yet as jealous as the princely eagle
That kills her young ones if they do but dazzle
Upon the radiant splendor of the sun.   (*KL* 512–16)

The second use of the analogy is briefer than the first, as if Kyd's memory had compressed it.

Wells cited several other striking parallels between *Soliman and Perseda* and *King Leir*:

So **it is** my lord, that **upon great affairs**   (*SP* 5.1.25)
No doubt, **it is** about **some great affairs**.   (*KL* 5.24)

Wells reported: 'I have noted the occurrence of "great affairs" in eight plays, assignable, on other grounds, to Kyd' (p. 436).

The great Danish scholar Paul Rubow, writing a few years after William Wells (whose work he did not know), pointed out many significant parallels between *King Leir*, *The Spanish Tragedy*, and *Soliman and Perseda* which formed the basis of his case that Kyd wrote *Leir*.[34] Some of these duplicated the parallels Wells had noted—in authorship attribution studies, such a convergence between two independent studies is especially significant—but Rubow added others derived from his

---

34. Paul Rubow, *Shakespeare og hans Samtidige* ('Shakespeare and his Contemporaries') (Copenhagen, 1948), pp. 145–55. I am grateful to Dr Lene Petersen, of the University of Southern Denmark (Odense), for providing me with translations of relevant passages in this remarkable study. Fortunately, the texts that Rubow quotes are in English.

own extensive reading. As he noted, Leir's announcement that 'my mind | Doth meditate a sudden **stratagem**' (*KL* 1.76–7) echoes Erastus's appeal to Love, to 'Inspire **me** with some present **stratagem**' (*SP* 2.1.183), where 'present' means 'instant' or 'immediate'—and where the same polysyllabic word is placed at the line ending (the rhetorical figure *epistrophe*). Cordella, at a low point in her life, is reluctant to explain why she is so sad:

> CORDELLA: Ah, pilgrims, **what** avails to show the cause
> **When there's no** means to find a **remedy**? (7.55–6)

That phrasal structure recurs in a light-hearted situation, when Belimperia tries to discourage Balthazar from wooing her:

> **What** boots complaint **when there's no remedy**? (*Sp. T.* 1.4.92)

But it also appears in a tragic one, as Erastus laments just before he is executed:

> **What** boots complaining **where's no remedy**? (*SP* 5.2.78–9)

Some verbal parallels suggest that Kyd may have subconsciously used a phrasal structure because it had deeper associations for him, recalling family relationships. This exchange between two rival sisters occurs at the beginning of a breakdown:

> CORDELLA: My tongue was never used to **flattery**
> GONORILL: **You** were not best say I **flatter:** if you do,
> My deeds shall shew, **I flatter not** with you. (3.103–5)

Kyd had used this structure once before, in the dispute between two rival brothers, each appealing to their older sibling, the Turkish emperor Soliman:

> AMURATH: Your highness knows I speak in duteous love.
> HALEB: Your highness knows I spake at your command
> And to the purpose, far from **flattery**.
> AMURATH: Thinks **thou I flatter**? Now **I flatter not**!
> *Then he kills Haleb* (1.6.74–7)

The similarity consists not only in the phrasing but in the dramatic situation.

For another contextual parallel that Rubow noted, take the reasons that Leir gives to his daughters for dividing the kingdom:

Ye flourishing branches of a kingly stock,
Sprung from a tree that once did flourish green,
Whose **blossoms** now are **nipped** with **winter's** frost   (*KL* 3.26–8)

That is an eloquent, rather self-pitying analogy compared to the utterance of Andrea's ghost describing how, in the 'prime and pride of all my years', he was cowardly murdered by Balthazar:

But in the harvest of my summer joys
Death's **winter nipped** the **blossoms** of my bliss (*Sp. T.* 1.1.9–13)

Leir continues in the same theatrical vein:

And pale grim **Death** doth wait upon **my** <u>steps</u>   (*KL* 3.29)

Soliman, who is really dying, poisoned by Perseda, declares

And now **pale Death** sits on **my** panting <u>soul</u>   (*SP* 5.4.152)

Hieronimo, having had his revenge, recalls how Horatio was 'butcher'd up'

In black dark night to **pale** dim cruel **Death**   (*Sp. T.* 4.4.106–7)

Kyd clearly derived his epithet from Horace but gives it more force.[35]

In several of the matches that Rubow noticed we can see Kyd reusing a phrase in a very different situation. When, towards the end of the play, Leir and Perillus re-enter the scene '*faintly*', having escaped death, Leir offers Perillus his arm to lean on, but the good old counsellor refuses:

Ah, good my Lord, **it** ill befits that I
Should lean upon **the person of a King**.   (14.5–6)

---

35. Cf. *Odes* 1.4: '*Pallida Mors aequo pulsat pede pauperum tabernas | regumque turris*'. 'Pale death knocks with impartial foot on the poor man's cottage and the rich man's castle': Horace, *Odes and Epodes*, tr. Niall Rudd (Cambridge, MA, and London, 2004), pp. 32–3.

The same idea recurs in *Soliman and Perseda*, but in the heated quarrel between the Emperor's two brothers, as Haleb insults Amurath:

> **It** is not meet that one so base as thou
> **Shouldst** come about **the person of a King**.   (1.5.71–2)

Like many Elizabethan dramatists, Kyd's memory could call up the semantic and syntactical structure of a sentence and 'fill in' new material. The Messenger in *Leir* seeks assurance from the contract-giver that he will be protected from punishment:

> I hope your grace **will stand between me and** my
>   neck-verse   (12.50–51)

Lorenzo, about to hire Pedringano to kill Serberine, reminds him of previous protection, when 'I **stood betwixt thee** and thy punishment' (*Sp. T.* 2.1.49). His instrument, about to carry out the contract, still feels secure:

> I know, if need should be, my noble lord
> **Will stand between me and** ensuing harms   (3.3.13–14)

On the scaffold the Hangman shows Hieronimo Pedringano's letter, admitting his guilt, and seeks and receives assurance from the Marshal to carry out a legitimate death-sentence:

> You **will stand between** the gallows **and me**?   (4.1.26)

Rubow also pointed out matches between *King Leir* and *Cornelia*, showing—in case anyone has ever doubted the fact—that a translator necessarily relies on the same phraseology that he uses for his own compositions. Gonorill, bandying words with the Ambassador, twists the phrase 'expiate his wrath' to its opposite:

> Should I be a mean to **exasperate his wrath | Against**
>   my sister   (19.56–7)

In fact, that is the collocation Kyd prefers in his other usages:

> **His wrath against** you 'twill **exasperate**   (*Corn.* 3.3.128)
> My father's old **wrath** hath **exasperate**   (*Sp. T.* 4.4.70)

When Ragan discovers that Leir has left her house, disheartened by her cruelty, she immediately blames some 'invocation' or charm

> Of wicked spirits or infernal fiends,
> Stirred by Cordella, moves this innovation
> **And** brings my father **timeless to** his end.   (22.20–22)

Rubow pointed out that, in translating Garnier,[36] Kyd had introduced a phrase of his own, describing how Death

> doth make the passage free;
> **And timeless** doth our souls **to** Pluto send.   (2.1.281–2)

Perhaps Kyd even remembered his rhyme word. A few lines later in this scene Ragan dramatizes her feigned anger at Leir's disappearance:

> Oh, but my grief, like to a swelling tide,
> **Exceeds** the **bounds** of common patience.   (23.34–5)

Rubow noticed that Kyd had echoed *Leir* in *Cornelia* again, bringing some fluency to a rather stiff stanza in one of the Choric odes[37]:

> Those fountains do to to floods convert,
> Those floods to waves, those waves to seas,
> That oft **exceed** their wonted **bounds**   (2.1.374–5)

In nine pages of text Rubow listed nearly 70 matches between *Leir* and Kyd's other plays.

William Wells and Paul Rubow were outstanding attribution scholars, widely read, blessed with excellent memories and efficiently organized note-taking systems. They represent the heights that manual methods can reach.[38] In recent years the rise of electronic computing has vastly increased the speed and range of data retrieval. In particular, a database

---

36. Garnier's text reads: 'la mort ... desja nous ouvre | Le chemin effroyant du Plutonique gouffres' (499–500)

37. Garnier's text reads: 'Enfantent les belles fontaines, | Et les fontaines les ruisseaux, | Les ruisseaux les grosses rivières, | Les rivières aux flots chenus' (585–8).

38. For further parallels that Wells and Rubow discovered between *Leir* and Kyd's canon, see Vickers, 'Kyd's authorship of *King Leir*', pp. 452ff.

created by Pervez Rizvi has revolutionized the identification of matching phrases in early modern drama. As I mentioned in the preface, Rizvi established a corpus of 527 plays for the public theatre performed between 1550 and 1642, enabling users to identify n-grams of various lengths, and collocations. Users can set a date-range of plays and compare the repeated phrases in any play within that time span and check how often a phrase recurs.[39]

In the first ever edition of *The Collected Works of Thomas Kyd*, each newly attributed play text is accompanied by an 'Authorship Commentary', consisting of a selection of the rare or unique matches with other plays in Kyd's accepted canon. The edition of *King Leir* by Eugene Giddens has been annotated by myself and Darren Freebury-Jones, with notes documenting 145 phrasal matches with the accepted Kyd canon, which include a considerable number of longer n-grams.[40] Rizvi's extensive researches have shown that the most reliable sizes for authorship attribution are three and four words long, and the more such rare or unique matches that can be identified the more likely an ascription will be. Since longer matches are rarer, they seldom feature in attributions. But *King Leir* shares some remarkably long matches with Kyd's canon. Here is Mumford's request to accompany the King of Gallia on his trip to Brittany:

> I **would your grace** would **favour me so much**
> **As** make **me** partner of **your** pilgrimage   (4.14–15)

That innocent request recycles much of the extremely polite request that Hieronimo makes to Lorenzo and Balthazar to take leading roles in the play he is preparing:

> Now **would your** lordships **favour me so much** |
> **As** but to **grace me** with **your** acting it.   (*Sp. T.* 5.1.81–2)

---

39. See Rizvi's interactive database, https://www.shakespearestext.com/can/, which contains several important essays, including The Counting of N-grams and some interesting 'experiments' with the data.

40. See Vickers (ed.), *The Collected Works of Thomas Kyd*, 1.465–525.

That is a ten-word collocation, the longest in this play. Such lengthy matches are either plagiarisms (very unlikely at such length) or instances of self-repetition. I have already quoted several examples of six-word matches between *Leir* and *The Spanish Tragedy*, such as the premonition that Leir and Bel-imperia share, and the security of having a patron 'stand between' you and punishment after you have committed a crime. Other hexagrams include the oaths sworn by the fearful Messenger: 'That to be true, **in sight of heaven I swear**' (18.182), and Bel-imperia's solemn vow to avenge Horatio's death if necessary: 'For here **I swear, in sight of heaven** and earth' (*Sp. T.* 5.1.25). The many pentagrams and five-word collocations shared between *Leir* and other Kyd plays include

And **never can be** quenche**d, but by** desire	(3.60)
Which **never can be** parted **but by** death	(*SP* 2.1.25)
Could never have been curbed, **but by** itself	(*Corn.* 1.1.58)

Reference to the contexts will show Kyd's skill in adapting a phrase to a new dramatic context and a new user.

To sum up this newly acquired evidence of the rightful place of *King Leir* in Kyd's canon, the rare or unique matching phrases we have collected between it and Kyd's accepted plays, whether n-grams or collocations, include one of ten words, ten of six words, twenty of five words, fifty-seven of four words, and twenty-eight of three words. Only one conclusion is possible: Kyd wrote *King Leir*.

Authorship Markers: Prosody

Additional evidence for Kyd's authorship of *King Leir* comes from studies of the play's prosody (verse structure) and rhyme. One prosodic feature that can differentiate dramatists is their use of the feminine ending—that is, an extra, eleventh syllable ending a decasyllabic line (as in 'To be or not to be, that is the ques'tion'). As mentioned in chapter 3, Timberlake showed that the feminine ending was rarely used by Tudor dramatists. Marlowe's usage ranged from 1.3 in *Tamburlaine* to 1.7 in *Dr Faustus* and 3.7 in the highly derivative *Edward II* (1592), a

188 CHAPTER 5

TABLE 5.1. Feminine endings in *King Leir* and in Kyd plays

	Total verse lines	Feminine endings	Percentage
The Spanish Tragedy	2,137	26	1.2
Soliman and Perseda	1,762	180	10.2
King Leir	1,198	208	10.8
Cornelia	1,179	119	9.5

further sign of his debt to other dramatists.[41] Timberlake accepted the case made by Charles Crawford and others that Kyd wrote *Arden of Faversham*,[42] which averages 6.2 percent, and observed that 'in the early nineties Kyd was customarily using feminine endings with a frequency surpassing that of any other' dramatist. Although Timberlake noted its high proportion of feminine endings (10.8 percent), he had already placed *King Leir* among 'certain anonymous plays' and failed to make the connection with Kyd. If his figures for *Leir* (61–2) are set beside those for other Kyd plays, the similarity is inescapable (see Table 5.1).

If Kyd, the acknowledged pioneer in this respect, 'used feminine endings with a frequency surpassing that of any other dramatist' in this period, that is further evidence that he wrote *King Leir*.

Another quantifiable prosodic feature in early modern verse drama is the position of pauses within the verse line, the placing of which reveals an author's distinctive preferences. In place of the usual procedure—computing the number of pauses in relation to the total number of lines in a work—the pioneering Estonian scholar Ants Oras followed the innovations of Russian quantitative prosody by studying 'the incidence of internal pauses in each of the nine possible positions within an iambic pentameter in relation to the totals of such pauses, regardless of the amounts represented by such totals'.[43] Oras counted the pauses—as defined by punctuation—in about 100,000 lines of verse drama, computing for each play the number of pauses in each position. This computation

41. See Alfred Hart, *Stolne and Surreptitious Copies. A Comparative Study of Shakespeare's Bad Quartos* (Melbourne, 1942; 2017), pp. 354–5, 361–2, 369–71, etc.

42. See the essays cited in note 26 above.

43. Oras, *Pause Patterns in Elizabethan and Jacobean Drama*, p. 2.

TABLE 5.2. Pause-patterns in *The Spanish Tragedy* and *King Leir* (in percentages)

Play	First half	Even	1	2	3	4	5	6	7	8	9
Sp. T	78.9	67.5	7.1	15.0	5.7	39.1	15.2	11.4	4.2	1.9	0.4
Leir	78.9	63.0	13.3	13.7	4.2	36.6	14.0	8.7	5.1	3.9	0.4

yielded two percentage figures, the first 'indicating the ratio of such pauses before the fifth position, i.e., in the first half of the line, to pauses after that position' (under *First Half* in the table), the second 'showing the percentage of pauses ... after an even-numbered syllable' (under *Even*). Across the period from the Tudor dramatists to the closing of the theatres in 1642, Oras traced a 'gradual shift of pauses from the earlier to the later part of the line', typically from position 4 to position 6, and 'the decreasing importance of pauses in the normally stressed even positions' (p. 4).

In his analysis Oras documented a remarkable similarity between *King Leir* and *The Spanish Tragedy*, which has passed unnoticed by scholars, even those interested in attribution studies. Oras's statistics for the two plays are strikingly close (see Table 5.2).[44]

Oras also produced 'frequency polygons' for each play, in which the vertical axis represents the percentage figures, while the horizontal 'indicates the position in the five-stress, ten-syllable verse line—the first position, the second, third, and so on though the ninth' (p. 5). The similarity between the pause patterns in the two plays emerges still more clearly in this figure (see Figure 5.1):

Such a profound similarity can hardly be coincidental.

As noted, Oras based his work on pauses as defined by punctuation. The recent, more comprehensive study by Marina Tarlinskaja, another exponent of the Russian method, covers in meticulous detail every aspect of prosody that can be quantified.[45] Without attempting to describe her complex method, I shall summarize her conclusions regarding *Leir*

44. Ibid., pp. 65–6.

45. Tarlinskaja, *Shakespeare and the Versification of English Drama*. Her analysis of 'Kyd's versification' (pp. 87–116) endorses my attribution of *King Leir* and *Fair Em* to the Kyd canon, together with substantial portions of *1 Henry VI*, *Edward III*, and *Arden of Faversham*.

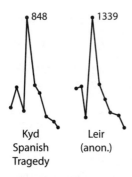

FIGURE 5.1. From Ants Oras, *Pause Patterns in Elizabethan and Jacobean Drama*, pp. 41–2.

in relation to the accepted canon. Her count for feminine endings differs slightly from Timberlake's but preserves the same contours. According to her calculations, the percentage score for *The Spanish Tragedy* is 1.5; for *Soliman and Perseda* it is 11.1 percent; for *Cornelia* it is 7.6 percent; and for *Leir* it is 10.4. Like Timberlake, Tarlinskaja found that Kyd 'was indeed the first dramatist to experiment with feminine endings' (p. 104), indeed, she judged that '*King Leir* could be attributed to Kyd on the basis of feminine endings alone' (p. 105). In using *enjambement*, Tarlinskaja found that Kyd anticipated Shakespeare with a more flexible line-structure: '*The Spanish Tragedy, Soliman and Perseda,* and *Leir* create a cluster of indices: 9.2–9.9 percent of the lines are run-on' (p. 103). In its use of the 'pleonastic *do*' to pad out a verse line, Kyd's *Cornelia*, translated from the rhymed Senecan tragedy *Cornélie*, has a score of 5.2 percent and *Leir* 6 percent, the result of the play's 'many rhymed lines (they create versification challenges for the author)' (p. 103). Finally, considering two more technical aspects of prosody, in his use of 'proclitic micro-phrases', the 'range of 200–250 per 1,000 lines characterizes all texts of the tentative Kyd canon', including *Fair Em* and *Leir* (96–7, 102). As for the preferred location of 'strong syntactic breaks', in most Elizabethan texts 'the major break falls after position 4. The three acknowledged texts by Kyd as well as *Fair Em* and *King Leir* create a homogeneous cluster' in the placing of such breaks after syllable 4: '*The Spanish Tragedy* 22.7, *King Leir* 22.6, *Fair Em* 22.4, *Soliman and Perseda* 20.1, and *Cornelia* 20.7 percent' (p. 102). The evidence from prosody supports that from the play's dramaturgy and its verbal texture, suggesting that *King Leir* may be safely admitted to Kyd's canon.

Authorship Markers: Rhyme

A dramatist's prosodic practices lend themselves to quantitative analysis much more readily than rhyme. Scholars have long been able to count the number of rhymes in a play, but since the use of rhyme is affected by character and dramatic context (such as the convention of using a

KING LEIR 191

TABLE 5.3. Rhymes in *King Leir* and in Kyd plays

Play	Total lines	Blank verse	Rhyme	Prose	Percentage of rhyme
Sp. T	2,702	2,633	399	72	15.2
SP	2,180	1,605	173	575	10.8
Corn.	2,027	1,685	374	0	22.2
Leir	2,587	2,415	473	172	19.6

rhyming couplet to end a scene), such information is not always indicative of an author's individual preferences. *King Leir* resembles Kyd's acknowledged plays both in its frequent use of rhyme and in its liking for non-couplet rhymes. Its overall proportion of rhyme is higher than *The Spanish Tragedy*, but slightly below that for *Cornelia*, almost midway between the two (see Table 5.3).

The basic verse form for early modern drama was the unrhymed decasyllabic line, with occasional use of couplet rhymes for sententious passages and to close a scene. Kyd, however, used a variety of rhymes within blank verse—indeed it was precisely this feature of *Soliman and Perseda* that, more than a century ago, allowed James Routh to attribute the play to Kyd.[46] Comparing *Soliman and Perseda* with *The Spanish Tragedy* and *Cornelia*, Routh drew attention to 'the sporadic appearance in all three plays' of three irregular rhyme schemes. The first and most unusual is the insertion of an unrhymed line into a couplet, giving the pattern *aca*. (It is as if Kyd were searching for a matching rhyme but went on writing until the rhyme appeared.) The other two forms that were liable to appear in his blank verse without warning were the alternating rhymes in a quatrain *abab*, and the triplet rhyme *aaa* (p. 49). Having cited instances of these rhymes in all three plays, together with several other anomalous forms, Routh concluded that '*Soliman and Perseda* is . . . at one in its use of such unusual and whimsically varied rime schemes set at random in the texture of the verse' (p. 50).

---

46. Routh, 'Thomas Kyd's Rime Schemes'. Arthur Freeman, a scholar notably cautious over attribution claims, welcomed Routh's analysis of the rhyme schemes in *Soliman and Perseda* as a proof of Kyd's authorship, and suggested that 'an extension of Routh's tabulation to include other playwrights of the late eighties and early nineties might render almost unimpeachable the case for Kyd' (*Thomas Kyd*, p. 146). That remains a desideratum.

192   CHAPTER 5

In *The Spanish Tragedy*, Routh cited thirteen instances of the interrupted couplet, some of which mirror large elements of the play's action, such as 'lunacy'/'Hieronimo'/'catastrophe' (5.4.119–21), or 'misdone'/ 'stabbed'/'son' (5.5.6–8). Routh failed to notice that many of these were either preceded or followed by a couplet rhyme, as if, having got into a rhyming frame of mind, Kyd found it easier to continue for a while before reverting to blank verse. Thus 'yoke'/'lure'/'oak' (2.1.3–5) is preceded by a couplet, as is 'son'/'you'/'done' (4.8.127–9), while 'death'/'straight'/'breath' (4.6.13–15) and 'ill'/'unrepaid'/'will' (4.7.2–4) are both followed by a couplet. In some densely rhymed passages, the interrupted couplet is both preceded and followed by a complete instance of that form, as in 'tossed'/'resort'/'lost' (2.2.12–14) and 'awhile'/'feigned'/'wile' (4.9.22–4). From *Soliman and Perseda* Routh cited six instances of the interrupted couplet: 'dwell'/'woe'/'tell' (2.1.102); 'progeny'/'misdone'/'treachery' (2.1.303–5); 'street'/'town'/'feet' (2.2.66–8); 'me'/'lips'/'knee' (4.1.115–7); 'way'/'hence'/'stay' (4.2.71–3); 'again'/'Soliman'/'pain' (5.4.123–5). As with the acknowledged plays by Kyd, the dominant rhyme form in *King Leir* is the couplet, but there is a wide range of other rhymes. I find eight instances of the interrupted couplet, including 'memory'/'fame'/'perpetuity' (1.68–70), 'three'/'dowries'/'mystery' (2.47–9); 'head'/'heed'/'head' (15.26–8); 'race'/'behold'/'place' (19.122–4); and 'bear'/'sons'/'swear' (19.186–8). In the interrupted couplet, the rhyming words are separated by one unrhymed. In other rhyme patterns in *King Leir*, as in Kyd's other plays, the couplet can be interrupted by two unmarked lines, in the form *abca*, as in 'again'/'ash'/'lips'/'disdain' (15.14–18). Also, the unmarked ending can separate a unit of three lines, in the form *abaa*, as in 'me'/'cause'/ 'thee'/'charity' (19.223–6).

The second type of Kyd's use of 'whimsically varied rime schemes set at random in the texture of the verse' is the familiar quatrain, *abab*, of which Routh cited six instances in *The Spanish Tragedy*, including 'port'/ 'tossed'/'resort'/'lost' (2.2.12–15), 'more'/'trudge'/'gore'/'judge' (4.6. 5–8), and 'confusion'/'understood'/'conclusion'/'good' (5.1.179–82).[47] In *King Leir* Kyd used rhyme to characterize Ragan. The quatrain *abab*

---

47. Routh noted only one instance of the quatrain in *Soliman and Perseda*, but he failed to observe that all four lines have the identical rhyme: 'simplicity'/'thee'/'perjury'/'free' (2.1.148–51).

demands that the speaker has formulated all four lines before she utters the first—unexceptional in poetry but somewhat artificial in drama, and not calculated to convey spontaneity. It is highly appropriate for Ragan, feigning grief over Leir's sudden departure from her house. Combined with one regular couplet (14–15), the dramatic effect is to convey a sense of falseness, that a daughter should be able to use prepared rhymes while claiming to grieve so much that she can barely speak:

> All sorrow is but counterfeit to mine,
> Whose lips are almost sealèd up with grief.
> Mine is the substance, whilst they do but *seem*
> To weep the less, which tears cannot *redeem.*
> Oh, ne'er was heard so strange a *misadventure,*
> A thing so far beyond the reach of *sense,*
> Since no man's reason in the cause can *enter.*
> What hath removed my father thus from *hence?*
> Oh, I do fear some charm or *invocation*
> Of wicked spirits or infernal fiends,
> Stirred by Cordella, moves this *innovation*
> And brings my father timeless to his end.   (22.12–23)

Kyd gives Ragan another quatrain (this time in the form *abba*) just before the play's climax, as she discloses her remorse for having hired an assassin to murder her father, coupled with frustration that she has been unable to dispose of him:

> (Scene 25) *Enter Ragan sola.*
> RAGAN: I feel a hell of conscience in my breast
> Tormenting me with horror for my *fact,*[48]
> And makes me in an agony of *doubt*
> For fear the world should find my dealing *out.*
> The slave whom I appointed for the *act,*
> I ne'er set eye upon the peasant since.
> Oh, could I get him for to make him *sure,*
> My doubts would cease, and I should rest *secure*   (1–8)

---

48. Here used in the meaning 'evil deed'.

194 CHAPTER 5

TABLE 5.4. Rhyme forms in Kyd's plays and *King Leir*

Rhyme	*Sp. T*	*Cornelia*	*SP*	*Leir*
aca	11	3	6	8
abab	7	20	0	2
aaa	3	4	1	3
abba	0	3	0	1
acaa	1	0	2	1
aaaa	1	0	0	2
Totals	23	30	9	17

The concluding couplet there mimics a resolution that Ragan will look for in vain.

The third of Routh's 'whimsical' rhyme schemes occurring unexpectedly in Kyd's blank verse is the triplet, seldom used. In *The Spanish Tragedy* he found three instances, including 'knight'/'fight'/'delight' (1.4.74–6), and 'equity'/'me'/'gravity' (4.7.54–6), and one in *Soliman and Perseda*: 'extremity'/'clemency'/peremptory' (3.4.7–9).[49] In *King Leir* Kyd used several triplets, including 'policy'/'Brittany'/'secrecy' (1.88–90), 'ensue'/'do'/'woo' (7.107–9), and 'thee'/'see'/'thee' (24.233–5). He even sustained a rhyme over four lines (*aaaa*), giving it additional point through syntactical symmetry: 'unto me'/'honesty'/'to me'/'adversity' (24.241–4). Leir's final speech, a succession of eight couplets, includes a triplet rhyme with one unrhymed element (*abaa*): 'today'/'Cambria'/'say'/'play' (29.171–4).

In sum, *King Leir* contains instances of all the rhyme patterns found in the three plays ascribed to Kyd. Indeed, it alone includes instances of every rhyme pattern Kyd is known to have used (see Table 5.4).

The evidence from feminine endings, pause patterns, and rhyme schemes, together with the dramaturgical and phrasal resemblances, collectively confirm Kyd's authorship of *King Leir*.

49. But Routh missed another triplet rhyme in this play, 'liberal'/'affable'/'heroical' (5.4.103–5).

PLATE 1. The Murder of Thomas Arden, from the 1633 Quarto of *Arden of Faversham*.

PLATE 2. The Murder of Horatio, from the 1615 Quarto of *The Spanish Tragedy*.

6

Fair Em

THE THIRD PLAY THAT I newly ascribe to Kyd is described on the undated Quarto title page as *A Pleasant Commodie of faire Em the Millers daughter of Manchester: With the loue of William the Conqueror: As it was sundrie times publiquely acted in the honourable citie of London, by the right honourable the Lord Strange his seruants*. The printer was perhaps John Danter, the publishers Thomas Newman and John Winnington.[1] The fact that Strange became Fifth Earl of Derby on 25 September 1593 would provide the *terminus ad quem* for the play's publication. The single surviving copy of the first Quarto, part of the Malone collection in the Bodleian, is undated, but W.W. Greg's analysis of the title-page ornament and other typographical details suggests that '*Faire Em* was put on the stage between 1589 and 1591'.[2] The Stationers' Register has no record of *Fair Em*, but this is hardly significant, since it has been estimated that only one-third of the publications listed in the *Short Title Catalogue of English Books 1475–1640* were formally entered in the Register.[3] However, the lack of an entry makes it difficult to date the play. Henslowe's diary lists the London performances of Strange's Men between February 1592 and February 1593 (when the outbreak of plague drove them out of London on a provincial tour) and *Fair Em* is not among them. Apart from outstanding successes, such as *The Spanish Tragedy*, the

1. W.W. Greg, *BPED* 1.192–3 (no. 113).

2. W.W. Greg (ed.), *Faire Em* (Oxford, 1928; Malone Society Reprints), p. viii. Quotations are from Brian Vickers (ed.), *Fair Em*, in Vickers (ed.), *The Collected Works of Thomas Kyd*, vol. 2.

3. See Leo Kirschbaum, *Shakespeare and the Stationers* (Columbus, OH, 1955), pp. 61–2.

vigorous competition between the companies, and the incessant demand for new attractions, meant that many plays did not stay in the repertory for long. Yet, as Greg observed, if we take literally the title page's reference to the 'citie of London' it might refer to the performances that Strange's Men gave at the Cross Keys, Gracechurch Street, in November 1589, violating a Privy Council Order 'for the stay of all plays within the City'.[4] Or it might have been in their repertoire earlier.

More light may be cast on the date of *Fair Em*, and on its authorship, from the attack that Robert Greene directed against the play in the address 'to the Gentlemen Students of both Universities' prefixed to his moralizing fable, *Greenes farewell to Folly. Sent to Courtiers and Schollers as a president* [precedent] *to warne them from the vaine delights that drawes youth on to repentance.* This pamphlet was entered in the Stationers' Register on 11 June 1587 to E. Aggas,[5] but the earliest known edition is the Quarto of 1592 (printed for T. Gubbin and N. Newton). Greg acutely observed that the term 'Martinize', which Greene uses in the dedication, dates the text to 1589 or later, since that was when the first Martin Marprelate tracts appeared. As other scholars have argued, Greene's diatribe against *Fair Em* gains a further significance when we recognize that it was personally directed against its author. As we saw in chapter 1, Kyd had already been the object of satire by Nashe in his Preface to Greene's *Menaphon* (1589).

Greene fulminated against those writers, who, when 'they come to write or publish anie thing in print, it is either distild out of ballets or borrowed of Theologicall poets . . .'. A ballad of 'The Millers daughter of Manchester' had been entered in the Stationers' Register on 2 March 1581 but has not survived, while Torquato Tasso, whose prose tract Kyd translated as *The Householder's Philosophy*, was a poet of wide interests, which—for all that Greene knew—might have included theology.

---

4. See Glynne Wickham, Herbert Berry, and William Ingram (eds), *English Professional Theatre, 1530–1660* (Cambridge, 2000), p. 302; and Chambers, *Elizabethan Stage*, 2.118–27.

5. Edward Arber, *A Transcript of the Registers of the Company of Stationers of London, 1554–1640 AD*, 6 vols (London, 1875–1894), 2.219.

Greene warms to his task, abusing the author of *Fair Em* both for lacking 'art' and for misusing scripture:

> And he that can not write true Englishe without the helpe of Clearkes of parish Churches, will needes make him selfe the father of inter-ludes.[6] O tis a jollie matter when a man hath a familiar stile and can endite a whole year and never be beholding to art! but to bring Scripture to prove any thing he sayes, and kill it dead with the text in a trifling subject of love, I tell you is no small peece of cunning. As for example two lovers on the stage arguing one an other of unkindnesse, his Mistris runnes over him with this canonicall sentence, A mans conscience is a thousande [*sic*] witnesses, and hir knight againe excuseth him selfe with that saying of the Apostle, Love covereth the multitude of sinnes, I thinke this was but simple abusing of the Scripture.[7]

As Greg pointed out, Greene alluded to certain speeches in *Fair Em*, namely the heroine's remark, "Thy conscience Manvile [is] a hundred witnesses"' [17.159], and the earlier lines, spoken not by Manvile as a lover but by Zweno as father:'[8]

> Yet love that covers multitudes of sins
> Makes love in parents wink at children's faults.   (17.124–5)[9]

Like his friend Nashe, Greene mocked rival playwrights who had only had a grammar-school education for lacking 'art' (*ars* or *technē*), a vast concept perhaps implying the technical skills that they deemed necessary to a dramatist. Ever since Malone, critics have accepted Greene's accusation, themselves ignorant of the fact that the Elizabethan

---

6. In 'Possible light on the Authorship of Fair Em', *Notes and Queries*, 262 (June 2017): 252–4, Darren Freebury-Jones suggests that Greene may have been referring to the fact that Kyd's father had been a churchwarden at St Mary Woolnoth's in Lombard Street, near Cripplegate.

7. Robert Greene, *Greenes farewell to Folly* (London, 1591), Sig. A 4ˇ.

8. Greg (ed.), *Fair Em*, p. viii, citing lines 1424 and 1385–6 from his edition. See also Romans 2:15: 'which shewe the effect of the Lawe written in their heartes: while their conscience beareth witness unto them, and also their thoughtes accusing one another, or excusing' (Geneva Bible).

9. Cf. 1 Peter 4:8: 'But above all things have fervent love among you: for love covereth the multitude of sins' (Geneva Bible).

198 CHAPTER 6

grammar school delivered seven years intensive study of Latin (only) to a level of proficiency enabling boys to read selected texts by major Latin authors, and to compose Latin verse. Moreover, the university B.A. curriculum included no literary subjects, being based on the works of Aristotle in Latin translation. Greene's claim that Shakespeare, or Kyd, had an inferior education should have been dismissed ages ago. As for Greene's jibe against this unwelcome dramatist who 'hath a familiar stile', or pen, since Kyd probably learned his father's trade as a scrivener, he must be the intended target. Greene particularized his attack in the continuation: 'and can endite a whole yeare and never be beholden to art'. Here 'endite' can mean both the physical act of writing, and literary composition, while 'art' remains the undefined quantity that Kyd lacks. It has been suggested that Greene's attack might even date the play to 1587,[10] but that would not fit the known activities of Strange's Men.

Although I shall cite much verbal and other evidence indicating Kyd's authorship, discussion of *Fair Em* is hampered by the poor condition of its text. As Greg noted, 'the printed text is very short', running to 1,485 lines in my computation (the Malone Society edition's through-numbering includes the stage directions), 'and may not preserve the play in its full form' (p. ix). Greg concluded that 'the play has been abridged almost to the point of obscuring the action' but suggested that not even 'rather drastic cutting' could explain 'the bold crudity of the later scenes. Some of these, though printed as verse, seem to consist for the most part of a mere prose summary which gives the essential meaning of the speeches with little attempt to reproduce the original wording. Occasional lines of verse are preserved', but with no attempt to regularize the whole, as usually occurs 'in most cases of reconstruction from memory' (p. x). To be recognized as an unauthorized or 'bad Quarto', however, it would have to display the three characteristics of such texts: the presence of *anticipations*, pre-echoes of an authentic phrase that appears later in the play, in its correct position; *repetitions* of

---

10. In 'The authorship of *Fair Em* and *Martin Mar-Sixtus*', *Notes and Queries*, 225 (1960): 8–10, H.D.S. Mithal suggested that 'if the prefatory matter to Greene's *Farewell to Folly* was written along with the text of the pamphlet before' its registration with the Stationers on 11 June 1587, then 'the play might well have been written earlier in 1587' (p. 8 n. 2).

an authentic phrase after its correct position; and *reminiscences* of other plays in the theatrical repertoire.[11] Those are not present here, and the textual incoherences can be accounted for by the fact that, at just under half the length of a standard Elizabethan play, *Fair Em* has been ravaged by cuts. One motive for these may have been the need to prepare an abbreviated version for touring. Lawrence Manley, joint author with Sally-Beth MacLean of a much-needed study of Lord Strange and his players, has analysed the casting requirements. Whereas other plays in the company's repertory that were performed in London have large casts—*The Spanish Tragedy* needs 15 adults and 4 boys, as does 1 *Henry VI*; *The Jew of Malta* and *The Massacre at Paris* each need 14 adults and 3 boys—*Fair Em* can be performed with 9 men and 4 boys. Manley has shown that 'the text has clearly been adapted for a reduced cast, since at least three important character roles have been cut in order to permit doubling'.[12] The cuts produce considerable confusion in the closing scenes, where characters called for by the action cannot appear, since their roles have been shortened to allow for doubling, and a promised confrontation between the English and Danish armies does not take place. In the following account of the play, I shall try to make sense of the action as it survives, without speculating on what might have been lost.

As a romantic comedy, *Fair Em* lacks several features found in other Kyd plays, such as a vengeful woman or a mixture of comedy and tragedy. It includes intrigue, deception, and disguise but with no vicious motives. There are two characters who disguise their true identities for most of the play, the first being King William the Conqueror, who adopts the name of Sir Robert of Windsor, 'to aspire the bliss | That hangs on quick achievement of my love' (1.71–2). The second is Sir William Goddard, who, having lost his lands at the Norman Conquest, is now forced to 'undertake this homely miller's trade . . . to save our wretched lives, |

---

11. For an extreme example, the first Quarto of *Hamlet* (1603) contains over 150 echoes of contemporary plays, ranging in date from 1579 to 1602: see Brian Vickers (ed.), *Hamlet: The Unauthorized Edition* (forthcoming).

12. Manley and MacLean, *Lord Strange's Men and Their Plays*, pp. 104–6.

200 CHAPTER 6

Threatened by conquest of this hapless isle' (2.4–6). There are two plots, both concerned with romantic love, which alternate until the final scene brings both strands together. One plot involves 'historical' characters, King William, Zweno, King of Denmark, and the Marquis of Lubeck, a Danish noble. In this plot there are two female characters who supply the love interest, Blanch, daughter of Zweno, who falls in love with William, and Mariana ('princess of Swethia'), who is loved by Lubeck. In the 'romantic' plot the focus of attention is Em (abbreviated from Emma), daughter of Sir William, who is wooed by three of William's courtiers: Manvile, Mountney, and Valingford. The plots are disposed as follows:

> *William*: scenes 1, 3, 6, 8, 10, 12, 13, 15, 17.
> *Em*: scenes 2, 4, 5, 7, 9, 11, 14, 16, 17.

As can be seen, the two plot strands alternate until they come together at the end.

The title plot has no known source, but, as Josef Schick pointed out in 1898,[13] the 'historical' plot of this 'pseudo-Shakespearian play'[14] derives from a source that Kyd used for the 'Solyman and Perseda' masque that concludes *The Spanish Tragedy* and for the subsequent play *Solyman and Perseda*, namely Sir Henry Wotton's translation from the French of Jacques Yver, *A Courtlie controversie of Cupids Cautels: Conteyning five Tragicall Histories* (1578).[15] The 'fourth Historie' (pp. 188–238) tells how

---

13. Schick (ed.), *Spanish Tragedy* (London, 1898). p. xxvi. More recently, this has been noted by Hunter in *English Drama 1586–1642. The Age of Shakespeare*, p. 107.

14. Schick gave it this epithet because at some point during the reign of Charles II, *Fair Em* was bound, together with *Mucedorus* and *The Merry Devil of Edmonton*, into a volume marked on the cover 'Shakespeare' and added to the royal library. That ascription was vigorously debated by English and German critics during the nineteenth century and led to the collection edited by Nicolas Delius, *Pseudo-Shaksperesche Dramen* (Elberfeld, 1854–74) and to the more substantial one, with fuller introductions, textual collations, and notes by Karl Warnke and Ludwig Proescholdt, *Pseudo-Shakespearian Plays*, 5 vols (Halle: 1883–88; reprinted in one vol., New York, 1973). C.F. Tucker Brooke included the play in his collection, *The Shakespeare Apocrypha Being a collection of fourteen plays which have been ascribed to Shakespeare* (Oxford, 1918).

15. All quotations are from the text of Wotton contained in the database, *Literature Online*.

King William the Conqueror, taking part in a grand tourney, and about to joust with the Marquis of Lubeck, was so struck with the picture of a lady painted on his opponent's shield that he broke off the combat and demanded to know her identity (pp. 191–2). He learns that she is Amir, Princess of Denmark [in the play her name is Blanch] and sends the Marquis on an embassy to win her love (pp. 193–8). Too impatient to await his envoy's return, King William resolves 'to transporte hymself into Denmark in disguysed habite' (p. 199). However, arrived on the continent, he happens upon 'the famous fountaynes' in 'the Country of Arden', which 'invite the passengers to drinke, engendrying in them the one love, the other hate, sure with such alteration, as it is impossible ever to extinguish their forces, whereof by a wanton curiositie the King woulde drinke . . .' (p. 200). The Princess of Denmark had passed that way some days previously, and 'hadde dronke onely of the fountayne of love'. Unfortunately, William 'pleased to tast of the one and the other', so that when, now disguised as 'the Knight of Meffy . . . the better to achieve his amorous conquest' (p. 202), he comes face to face with Amir, the 'enforced enmitie' he had acquired from this magic fountain produces a sudden aversion: 'nowe he viewed hir, hee hated hir to the death' (p. 203).

As a further twist in the plot, the King then falls hopelessly in love with 'a damoisell, which sate face to face against him' at supper. He declares his love to her (pp. 204–6), but she rudely rebuffs him (pp. 206–7), and the King enquires of another 'Damoysell' who it is that has treated him so roughly. She explains that the woman he is now enamoured of is Parthenia, Princess of Suses, [in *Fair Em* her name is Mariana] abducted from her native city Ectabanes by pirates and kept in the Danish court against her will (pp. 207–10). Despite describing his 'Tragicall Histories' as 'very pithie', Jacques Yver happily introduces subplots and other divertissements into his narrative, 'entermedled with divers delicate sonnets and Rithmes', as the title page promised. So King William now begins to utter a lengthy 'complaint of his dolours' in a series of verses, including an echo poem (pp. 212–16), finally plucking up the courage to declare his love to Parthenia, or 'Virginia' as the narrator now calls her

(p. 217). But Yver complicates his plot further, getting William imprisoned for brawling with another courtier, who turns out to be his friend, the Marquis of Lubeck; who is himself in love with Virginia. As a great exemplum of friendship, duly celebrated by the narrator, Lubeck gives up his beloved to William and helps him escape with her to England. But the Danish King discovers the accomplice responsible, and Lubeck is 'put to the torture: whereupon making open confession, he was convicted, and as a traytour to his Prince beheaded in his own castle . . .' (pp. 218–24). A somewhat improbable reality breaks in on this romantic comedy of disguise and sudden switches of affection, allowing Yver to wrap up this plot.

It is well known that Elizabethan dramatists scoured a wide range of histories and romantic tales to provide themselves with plots.[16] As we work slowly through this verbose and shapeless narrative, we realize how much they must have read and rejected. From this point on, Yver's concoction takes a new and even more unexpected direction. 'Behold our Lovers now sufficiently satisfied for all the paynes endured, and it may rightly be judged, they now dispised Fortune . . .' (p. 225). However, 'the smiling of Fortune is but a beyte to deceive us', as King William soon discovers, for the King of Denmark sends him the head of the Marquis of Lubeck, threatening revenge (p. 227). William promptly sets sail, routs the Danish forces, conquers Westphalia, Freesland, and 'the whole country lying betweene the mouth of Rheine and the river of Alba' (pp. 227, 230). His victories stand in sharp contrast to events in England, where 'many sedicious princes' plot an uprising, to begin with the murder of Queen Virginia. Alerted to the danger, the Queen invites all the nobles to a splendid banquet, at which she appears dressed in royal splendour and carrying four 'mortall instruments', or means of death, offering them to her enemies so that they may take her life. Moved by her eloquent innocence, the nobles make peace (pp. 227–9). However, a messenger who had quit the hall before that point carries to King William the erroneous news that his Queen is dead, and so the

16. See, e.g., Bluestone, *From Story to Stage*.

distraught King kills himself (pp. 230–33). Having prepared a triumphant welcome for her returning husband, Queen Virginia is shocked by the sight of his corpse, and embraces it so forcefully that 'a greate pinne, wherewith the lefte corner of hir partlet was pinned, had by reason of the stricte embracing of the harde body, entred under hir left pappe', killing her (p. 234). After which Yver wraps up his tale with a flurry of classical examples of sudden deaths, reiterating his concern with 'the miseries happening in love' (pp. 234–8).

Modern readers of Elizabethan plays may often feel dissatisfied with their plots, given our neo-Aristotelian concept of dramatic unity. Even if we allow, with Madeleine Doran, that Renaissance authors were more concerned to provide variety,[17] it must be conceded that many plays include uncoordinated actions, plots with loose ends, and unsatisfactorily quick resolutions. Faced with a chaotically disorganized source, Kyd took over the opening sequence of Yver's plot but gave it a distinctly new emphasis. The play begins with William having just broken off the joust because of the 'flames of beauty' emanating from the portrait on Lubeck's shield. The King is made to comment on this strange reversal, that 'a conqueror at arms' should be overcome by 'unarmèd thoughts, | And, threatened of a shadow, yield to lust' (1.33–5). The moralizing word 'lust' anticipates a later scene in the play, unconvincing though it may sound in the mouth of a man who has just fallen in love. Unlike Yver's leisurely and disjointed narrative, William instantly plans to 'travel in disguise | To bring this lady to our Britain court' (1.73–4).

Introducing himself as Robert Windsor, William is welcomed by King Zweno and his daughter Blanche, the lady he has come to woo. To follow out this plot strand for a while, when we next see William, two scenes later, we are surprised by the aside in which he confesses to us his sudden revulsion:

> [*Aside*] May this be she for whom I crossed the seas?
> I am ashamed to think I was so fond [foolish]—
> In whom there's nothing that contents my mind:

---

17. Doran, *Endeavors of Art*.

Ill face, worse featured; uncomely, nothing courtly,
Swart, and ill favoured, a collier's sanguine skin—
I never saw a harder favoured slut!
Love her? For what? I can no whit abide her!   (3.23–9)

In the source the King's sudden reversal is due to his having drunk from the magic fountain that produces both hate and love. In the play it seems wholly unmotivated: either a scene has been lost, or Elizabethan playwrights and audiences could easily accept such sudden psychological changes.

The next development is equally sudden. Faithful to the source, in which the Danish princess had drunk only of the fountain that engenders love, as the direction instructs, Blanche *speaks this secretly at one end of the stage*, confiding in us her love for the disguised King:

Unhappy Blanche, what strange effects are these
That works within my thoughts confusedly,
That still methinks affection draws me on
To take, to like—nay, more—to love this knight?   (3.43–6)

Using quite simple dramatic means, Kyd follows her aside with another from William, which complicates the situation still further. He reveals to us that he has now fallen in love with Mariana, the counterpart of Parthenia/Virginia in the source, here a Swedish princess kept at the Danish court against her will:

A modest countenance, no heavy sullen look,
Not very fair, but richly decked with favour;
A sweet face, an exceeding dainty hand,
A body, were it framed of wax
By all the cunning artists of the world,
It could not better be proportionèd.   (3.47–52)

Questioned by Lubeck, the King confesses to 'a certain odd conceit | Which on the sudden greatly troubles me' (55–6), namely his love for Mariana. This establishes the so-called 'chain motif', popular since the Greeks: *A* loves *B* who loves *C*, etc.: here Blanche loves William who loves Mariana. This chain receives an additional source of conflict, for Lubeck reveals that he too loves Mariana. Protesting to William, 'That is my love', he declares that it 'stands [not]with the honour of my state | To brook co-rivals with me in my love' (67, 79–80).

The discordant ending of that scene is carried over to the next one between them, where Lubeck tells Mariana that he has been involved in a brawl, resulting in 'Robert of Windsor' being imprisoned overnight. In the source the familiar opposition between Love and Friendship was easily resolved, for William's release became the catalyst for Lubeck pledging him eternal friendship and willingly yielding his beloved to the King (Wotton, pp. 218–20). Kyd deviates from the source twice, to good effect. First, the two men become friends again, but without Lubeck yielding up his beloved (6. 25–35). Secondly, Kyd adds a scene in which Blanche, in love with William, intercepts the letter he has written to Mariana, declaring his new love for her. Blanche angrily tears it up and rushes off, leaving Mariana to put the pieces together and read William's declaration of love to her (6.51–63). In the source her counterpart Virginia happily received the King's declaration that he no longer loves Amir without compunction, either for the rejected princess or for her loyal lover, Lubeck (Wotton, pp. 220–21). In *Fair Em*, however (the medium having changed from verse to prose),[18] Mariana avows that if William were

> the monarch of the world, he should not dispossess Lubeck of his love. Therefore I will to the court, and there, if I can, close to be friends with Lady Blanche, and thereby keep Lubeck, my love, for myself, and further the Lady Blanche in her suit as much as
> I may   (6.64–7)

Mariana is another of Kyd's resourceful women, always ready to take her destiny in her own hands. We next see her in another scene that he invented. In the source Lubeck ceded his beloved to the King directly,

---

18. The uncertain nature of the medium here and elsewhere, printed as verse in the Quarto, was rightly set as prose by Standish Henning in *Fair Em. A Critical Edition* (New York and London, 1980).

not informing her himself. In the play Kyd makes him confront her with his decision that, in order to demonstrate his friendship for William, he is formally renouncing his love for her:

> For him I speak, for him do I entreat,
> And with thy favour, fully do resign
> To him the claim and interest of my love.
> Sweet Mariana, then deny me not:
> Love William, love my friend and honour me,
> Who else is clean dishonoured by thy means.　(8.44–9)

In Kyd's eyes, the weakness of such a great gesture in the Renaissance scenarios of Love versus Friendship is that it ignores the woman's wishes or feelings. This time he ensures that she can speak her mind. Mariana vigorously questions Lubeck's affirmation of his continuing love for her—'Why do you post me to another, then?' (59), a pertinent question, and bluntly rejects his attempt to woo by proxy: 'Speak for your self my Lord: let him alone' (63). Mariana is not content merely to complain, she decides on action. Her problem is how to retain Lubeck's love yet avoid William's designs on her. Deciding on an intrigue for which she will need an accomplice, she invites Blanche to 'follow the complot[19] I have invented' (75). The next time that Sir Robert of Windsor comes 'to solicit me with Love', she will 'seem to . . . like' what he demands, provided 'it be no impeachment to my chastity' (84–8). She confidently describes her 'complot', which depends on correctly predicting how her wooer will react. She will arrange some place to meet Sir Robert

> for my conveyance from the Denmark court. Which determined upon, he will appoint some certain time for our departure; whereof you having intelligence, you may soon set down a plot to wear the English crown.　(88–91)

---

19. This word recurs in *The Spanish Tragedy*, spoken by Lorenzo: 'Now to confirm the complot thou hast cast', and in *Arden*, spoken by Black Will: 'We have devised a complot underhand', and by Mosby: 'will you two | Perform the complot that I have laid?'

Not revealing further details of her plot, Mariana assures Blanche that 'I will work to your desire and my content' (97–8). Sir Robert—William in disguise, readers must sometimes remind themselves, theatregoers having the advantage of seeing the personage—appears on cue, to pursue his courtship of Mariana. She seems to encourage him but objects that, being a prisoner, she is unable to leave the Danish court. He explains that he has a ship ready to take her to England, where they will get married 'straight', and promises to respect her chastity. She suggests that it would be 'most convenient, | To mask my face, the better to 'scape unknown', and William approves, like so many of Kyd's intriguers: 'A good device!' (8.131–3). The next time we see him the stage direction reveals all: '*Enter William and Blanche disguised, with a mask over her face*' (10.0), and with renewed promises to respect her chastity they set off for England. Mariana's 'complot' has worked beautifully, and William carries off the one woman who in fact loves him. There we can leave them for a while and return to Manchester.

In their first scene together, Em was warned by her father of the possible dangers in being wooed by her first suitor Manvile, one of the King's courtiers. Like other anxious fathers, he urges her to 'Regard thine honour' [chastity], not letting 'vehement sighs' and 'earnest vows' render her 'subject to the wrath of lust' (2.56–8). This is a clear thematic parallel to William's fear, in the previous scene, that he might 'yeeld to lust' (1.38). We soon meet Manvile, '*alone, disguised*', as the stage direction instructs. As Standish Henning commented, 'The nature of Manvile's disguise is not clear. He may be wearing a cloak over his court dress (or plainer clothing) to adopt an incognito for wooing Em, which he does contrary to his father's wishes. No mistaken identity is involved'.[20] In a soliloquy we see him enthusing about Em, 'the subject of my restless thoughts, | The anvil whereupon my heart doth beat' (4.1–2). In direct address he promises to love her 'as my self, | So thou

20. Henning, *Fair Em*, p. 120. Shortly afterwards the other two suitors appear, also 'disguised'. Henning notes that they 'have two reasons to disguise themselves, 1) They have not gone to Denmark with William as ordered, and 2) they are wooing Em, which necessitates an incognito, because of the divergence in social station. Since, as with Manvile, there is no mistaken identity, the disguise is a simple cloaking of court dress' (ibid., p. 121).

be constant in thy plighted vow' (11–12). We have not seen them exchanging vows, which may suggest that a scene has been lost. The importance of constancy, introduced late in the 'historical' plot, is foregrounded here, and with good purpose. Kyd now introduces her second and third suitors, whom he gently mocks for their standard role as rival lovers:

> Enter Valingford at another door, disguised   (13)
> Enter Mountney disguised, at another door   (23)

Manvile '*stays, hiding himself*', as a marginal note directs, and overhears the two courtiers each declare his love for Em (4.14–39). Anguished, Manvile rushes off 'to forestall such foes' (41), leaving Valingford and Mountney to confront each other with their 'strange, unlikely passion', before amicably agreeing to 'yield to either's fortune in this choice' (42–70). Their friendly agreement is in sharp contrast to the jealous and possessive Manvile, who rushes to Em and accuses her of having abandoned him for the two courtiers, suspecting that they now enjoy 'what lately I possessed' (5.67). Em rejects his mistrust with a clear conscience, but her suitor petulantly bursts out:

> Ah, impudent and shameless in thy ill!
> That, with thy cunning and defraudful tongue,
> Seekest to delude the honest-meaning mind!   (5.71–3)

Manvile's sudden jealousy pushes him into a misogynistic fit, bitterly aggrieved

> To think my love should be rewarded thus,
> And, for thy sake, abhor all womankind!   (90–91)

Left alone, Em feels unjustly treated by her lover's 'frantic, bedlam jealousy' (111), but resolves to maintain her constancy to Manvile, whatever 'unkindness' he may show (114–15). As later events will show, constancy is not a universal good.

In his romantic plot strand, Kyd finds an ingenious way for the heroine to defend herself from her unwanted suitors. When Mountney urges his suit, she feigns deafness (5.118–71), and when Valingford follows, she claims to be blind (7.7–45). Mountne reacts to the news with sympathy and at once thinks of medical treatment: [*Aside*] 'What, is she deaf? A great impediment, | Yet remedies there are for such defects' (5.139–40). Left alone, he reflects that, if he can cure her 'infirmity' it might benefit his suit, so he resolves to consult one of 'the king's physicians'. But a thought suddenly strikes him:

> But Mountney: stay, this may be but deceit—
> A matter feigned only to delude thee.
> And, not unlike, perhaps by Valingford: (5.159–61)

Two scenes later we see Valingford being given the same treatment, Em claiming to have been 'stricken blind by mishap, on a sudden' (7.15). He reacts just like Mountney: 'Fair Em, I am not a little sorry to see this, thy hard hap. Yet, nevertheless, I am acquainted with a learned physician, that will do anything for thee at my request' (18–20). He offers her a jewel 'in token of my love' but she refuses, being unable to see it. Left alone, this suitor regrets the situation but has a sudden thought:

> But, Valingford, search the depth of this device. Why, may not this
> be feigned subtlety, by Mountney's invention, to the intent that
> I, seeing such occasion, should leave off my suit, and not any
> more persist to solicit her of love? I'll try the event: if I can by
> any means perceive the effect of this deceit to be procured by his
> means, friend Mountney, the one of us is like to repent our
>   bargain.   (7.44–50)

Kyd makes effective use of patterning and symmetry in this plot. In the theatre, especially, we are amused at the two lovers playing out their scenes in identical ways, as if they were puppets (as he had done with Perseda and Lucina). Their friendship now in danger, our next view of them is in scene 9, where Kyd brings the symmetry of his plotting to a head:

> *Enter Valingford and Mountney at two sundry doors, looking angrily
> at each other, with rapiers drawn.*   (9.0)

The situational comedy is increased by the disparity between the drawn swords and the verbal sparring match that follows, which shows that neither suitor is keen to fight.

But as they circle around each other they realize that they have been 'deluded both' by Em's pretended blindness and deafness (9.1–35). They make up their quarrel and resolve to establish whether Em has 'natural impediments', or 'merely counterfeit' ones by going 'straight unto her father' (36–42). Kyd has the ability, essential to dramatists, of managing plot lines so that the audience's expectation is aroused for the next scene between them. Manvile reaches the Miller before they do and complains of Em's deteriorating behaviour since the other two suitors have gained access to his house, at which point they arrive, complaining about Em's blindness and deafness. Em has managed to persuade the Miller's clownish servant, Trotter, to support her pretence and he leads her in, apparently helpless. She sustains the fiction of having lost two senses, much to her father's anguish, who feels 'the utter overthrow' of his 'joy and only solace' (54–5). Left alone, the three suitors decide on their futures. Manvile reveals his true nature:

> Both blind and deaf? Then is she no wife for me, and glad I am so good occasion is happened! Now will I away to Manchester and leave these gentlemen to their blind fortune.   (56–8)

That unfeeling piece of wordplay increases our dislike for him. Mountney, blaming fortune for having 'thus spitefully crossed our hope', sets off to rejoin King William, 'who is this day landed at Liverpool' (59–61). Their withdrawal leaves Valingford in the position of *tertius gaudens*, to the great satisfaction of theatregoers and readers. He alone has the emotional intelligence needed to intuit Em's deception:

> I'll stay behind to solicit my love, for I imagine that I shall find
> this but a feigned invention thereby to have us leave off our
>   suits.   (63–5)

Here again Kyd encourages the audience to think ahead: how will Valingford communicate with a maiden both deaf and blind?

But before that confrontation can take place Kyd introduces an unexpected scene, showing Manvile having quickly transferred his affections to a more marriage-worthy maiden. He has chosen Elner, daughter of a rich 'Citizen of Manchester', with whom he speedily comes to an understanding (14.1–9). But, equally unexpectedly, Valingford appears on the scene, having been following Manvile. He now tells father and daughter about Manvile's 'double dealing' with Em:

> For be it spoken to you, he hath been acquainted with a poor miller's daughter, and diverse times hath promised her marriage. But what with his delays and flouts, he hath brought her into such a taking that I fear me it will cost her her life. (17–29)

The shocked Elner vows that, if this be true, 'he should not be my husband, were he never so good' (34–5). Happy with his successful plot, Valingford reveals to us his double motive:

> [*Aside*] Now shall I be revenged on Manvile, and by this means get Em to my wife. And, therefore, I will straight to her father's and inform them both of all that is happened. (44–6)

If we are tempted to disapprove of Valingford's exaggeration, he has become the moral centre of this plot, and we might recall the saying that 'All's fair in love and war'.

In this sequence Kyd has set up a double level of dissimulation, with Valingford as the agent who will expose both Manvile's hypocrisy and Em's innocent pretence. In his next scene with the Miller, Valingford, pursuing his goal of gaining Em's hand, points up the contrast between Mountney, who 'quickly gave over' his courtship, thinking Em to be blind and deaf, and his own 'entire affection' to her: 'but I, by reason of my good meaning, am not so soon to be changed' (16.10–11). Constancy is his 'good meaning', as it is Em's. But in her case loyalty works to her own disadvantage: being unaware of the truth, she is still loyal to Manvile (18–20). When Valingford informs her that 'Manvile hath forsaken thee', as her father confirms, Em realizes with shock that her loyalty has been misplaced:

> But can it be, Manvile will deal so unkindly to reward my justice with such monstrous ungentleness? Have I dissembled for thy sake? And dost thou now thus requite it? (47–9)

By shifting to 'thou' Em seems to be rebuking him in person for having been the cause of her deceiving both her suitors and her father.

In other Elizabethan comedies dramatic plot reversals are sometimes carried through with only minimal reactions from the characters affected. But Kyd wrote two speeches for the heroine, amounting to thirty lines, in which she acknowledges her betrayal with a full emotional and moral response. She apologizes both to her father, for causing him 'grief, by overfond affecting a man so truthless', and to Valingford:

> My love to Manvile, thinking he would requite it, hath made me double with my father and you, and many more besides, which I will no longer hide from you. (61–3)

She had dissembled deafness and blindness so that no other suitor could affect her love for Manvile, but now 'I perceive my true intent hath wrought mine own sorrow; and, seeking by love to be regarded, am cut off with contempt, and despised' (68–71). By the standards of early Elizabethan comedy this is a remarkably full expression of remorse, giving Em greater depth than any other character in the play. Deeply regretting her mistake, she begs to be excused: 'Favour my departing at this instant, for my troubled thought desires to meditate alone in silence' (79–81). Few characters in the drama of the late 1580s show any sign of internal feeling-states, and Kyd is to be admired for registering Em's moral and emotional sensitivity in this moment of humiliation.

Leaving her in Manchester we can return to the historical plot, in which Zweno is angry that William has managed

> To steal away fair Mariana, my prisoner,
> Whose ransom, being lately 'greed upon,
> I am deluded of by this escape. (12.9–11)

He becomes even angrier to learn that William has in fact taken his daughter Blanche. Accusing Lubeck of being an accomplice, Zweno has him imprisoned, together with Mariana, and resolves to ask King William to send (his alias) 'that proud knight of Windsor', to Denmark, 'to suffer for his shame' together with Blanche,

Or I shall fetch her unto Windsor's cost—
Yea, and William's too, if he deny her me!   (47–8)

Having resolved the double pretence in this plot level, Kyd now unites both plots, and brings all his characters on stage. In scene 16 we have just seen Em reacting to the news of her deception by an inconstant lover with shame and dignity. In scene 17, as we saw earlier, William's reaction to the double surprise that Mariana has deceived him out of love for Lubeck, and that Blanche has taken part in the deception out of her love for him, is to express a misogyny directed against all women. Blanche rightly protests:

Unconstant knight: though some deserve no trust,
There's others faithful, loving, loyal and just.   (17.147–8)

It seems as if a stalemate has been reached, but there follows a completely unprepared for scene. (Either the text has been damaged or Kyd wants to surprise us.)

The text may be damaged at this point, but from the context we can reconstruct the new situation that has confronted William in England. During his absence civil discord has broken out, and on his return the disguised and unrecognized King is arrested by rebel soldiers led by Demarch (scene 13). He discloses his identity and resumes power, only to learn that Zweno, bent on retrieving his daughter, is preparing to invade England. William tells the Danish ambassador that he has not abducted Blanche (scene 15), a truce is arranged, and the two Kings confront each other (scene 17). Still unaware of the substitution trick, William insists that he has rescued Mariana, 'Who wrongfully thou detainest prisoner' (17.62). But Zweno declares that Mariana and Lubeck will be executed unless Blanche is restored. William expresses his shock: 'It cannot be I should be so deceived' (67), but at once he is confronted with the real Mariana, and a moment later, his 'Lady [is] sent for', who is revealed to be Blanche. At this realization William again lapses into misogyny:

Away, Demarch! What tellest thou me of ladies?
I so detest the dealing of their sex
As that I count a lover's state to be the base
And vilest slavery in the world.   (17.93–6).

The Danish King tartly enquires: 'Say, Duke William, is this Blanche or no? | You know her if you see her, I am sure', forcing William into an explanation: 'Zweno I was deceived, yea utterly deceived' (100).

The highly improbable romance plot of the source, involving magic fountains, gives way to an at least recognizable human reaction of bitterness at being gulled. If William's earlier recoil from Blanche in favour of Mariana had seemed unmotivated, Kyd has followed out the implications of the double love relationships with a better grasp of psychology than Yver. In the source Virginia (here Mariana), the object of the King's second infatuation, abandons her lover Lubeck without compunction and becomes William's queen. In the play, although William now berates her as 'cruel Mariana' and 'Unconstant Mariana' (104, 115), we see her as admirable in her constancy to Lubeck. But for William the shocked realization—'May this be true? It cannot be true. | Was it Lady Blanche which I conveyed away?' (113–14)—leads to another outburst. Mocking 'the fooleries' that men are expected to use when wooing, William vows to 'never subject myself | To any such as she is underneath the sun' (135–7). This vow brings him into instant conflict with Zweno, angry at his 'rash denial' of Blanche, but the deceived and disappointed man reiterates his misogyny:

> Conceit hath wrought such general dislike
> Through the false dealing of Mariana
> That utterly I do abhor the sex.
> They are all disloyal, unconstant; all unjust.   (17.141–4)

But as with Shakespeare's misogynists (Ford, Othello, Leontes, Posthumus), whose disgust is always shown to be unfounded, the behaviour of two characters onstage serves to disprove William's absolute dismissal of womankind. One is Mariana, constant in her love of Lubeck, the other Blanche, who expresses her point of view with some force:

> Unconstant knight: though some deserve no trust,
> There's others faithful, loving, loyal and just.   (17.147–8)

Blanche's rebuke is justified, but in terms of the plot situation it defines an apparently unbridgeable gulf between her and the man she loves.

At this point, in the play's final scene, Kyd unites the two plot lines. A surprising stage direction instructs: *Enter to them Valingford with Em and the Miller, and Mountjoy, and Manvile, and Elner.* Somehow, six characters who belong in the other plot, and then only in Manchester, have been persuaded to travel to Windsor for semi-judicial proceedings before the King. Valingford, the moral centre of that plot strand, takes charge, presenting to William 'two women', Em and Elner, 'that are contracted to one man' (151–2). Manvile is in effect cross-questioned, as if in court, as to which woman 'did he first give his faith' (156). He admits that he first wooed Em, but that 'some impediments . . . Made me forsake her quite', namely that 'she could neither hear nor see' (162–8). In most Elizabethan comedies the rejected suitor disappears into oblivion, never mentioned again, but Kyd has arranged a confrontation between all the characters. He gives Em a self-assured speech in which she describes how she had worshipped Manvile with true love and had only feigned these 'impediments' because of his unreasonable jealousy when he saw her with the other suitors (170–89). Manvile tries to save the situation with a grand gesture (ruthlessly ignoring his new love Elner standing by): 'Pardon me, sweet Em, for I am only thine'. Em replies with full moral authority, asking what would have happened if he had been really blind:

> I tell thee, Manvile, hadst thou been blind,
> Or deaf, or dumb,
> Or else what impediments might befall to man,
> Em would have loved, and kept, and honoured thee;
> Yea, begged if wealth had failed for thy relief.   (17.196–204)

Her speech echoes the Church of England marriage service, with a further echo of a famous Shakespeare sonnet.[21] Em rejects him (206–8), as does Elner (211–13), and in a spirited sequence of mockery Manvile is publicly shamed. Earlier, Em had said that if Manvile were to be punished 'for his treachery', she 'would think herself not a little happy'

---

21. 'Let me not to the marriage of true minds | Admit impediment' (Sonnet 116).

(16.76–8): the audience shares her pleasure at the discomfiting of this fickle lover.

This unusually detailed showing-up of Manvile, together with the union of Valingford and Em, would be enough for a satisfying denouement to an Elizabethan comedy. But Kyd has not finished with this episode juxtaposing true loyalty and its degradation, for it has an unexpected knock-on effect. Previously locked in disillusionment with all women, King William has an epiphany:

> I see that women are not general evils.
> Blanche is fair: methinks I see in her
> A modest countenance; a heavenly blush.   (17.222–4)

He asks Zweno for her hand in marriage, who gladly agrees, delighted to find him 'so tractable', the play ending with a double union, an unexpected and truly satisfying conclusion.

There cannot be many Elizabethan plays in which the events of one plot strand impinge on the other with such a decisive effect, making us realize how artfully the dramatist has orchestrated the whole. In the 'historical' plot strand we saw two loving women, Mariana and Blanche, remaining true to their men despite danger and difficulties. One of these men—the Marquis of Lubeck—was equally constant, the other—William—wilfully rejected Blanche for Mariana, fell into misogyny having been denied her, but has been recovered to health by Em's example. In her plot strand we saw a lukewarm suitor in Mountney, a totally constant lover in Valingford, and a wholly untrustworthy one in Manvile. Collectively, the three women emerge as the fixed points in this structure. The resourceful pair, Mariana and Blanche, take their fate into their own hands, and succeed. Em is less of a direct agent, being acted on and deceived, but her misplaced love for an evil man, her remorse at having grieved and deceived the truly good men, give her an exceptional moral stature. The control of two plots that could easily have reverted to the shapelessness of the source, and the fullness of moral sense given to the heroine, mark *Fair Em* as the work of a gifted comic dramatist.

Authorship Markers: Phraseology

As I noted earlier, in 1898 Josef Schick identified the 'historical' plot of *Fair Em* as deriving from the Solyman and Perseda story that Kyd had used in two plays, namely Wotton's *A Courtlie Controversie of Cupids Cautels* (1578), translated from the French of Jacques Yver. Neither Schick nor any other scholar suggested Kyd's authorship until Paul Rubow did so in 1948, citing several matches between it and *The Spanish Tragedy*.[22] First, the concluding attempt to establish Manvile's responsibility:

> WILLIAM: Stand forth, women, and say
> **To** whether **of you** he first gave his faith.
> EM: **To me,** forsooth.
> ELNER: **To me, my** gracious lord.
> WILLIAM: Speak, Manvile, **to whether didst thou** give thy faith?
> MANVILE: **To say the truth**, this maid had first my
>   love. (17.153–7)

Rubow compared the Spanish King's attempt to discover who had captured Balthazar:

> KING: But tell me—for their holding makes me doubt—
> **To** which **of** these twain art thou prisoner?
> LORENZO: **To me, my** liege.
> HORATIO: **To me, my** sovereign . . .
> KING: Say, worthy prince, **to whether did'st thou** yield? . . .
> BALTHASAR: And, **truth to say**, I yield myself to both.
>   (*Sp. T.* 1.2.160ff.)

Rubow compared two other passages from the same scenes:

> WILLIAM: Sir Thomas Goddard, welcome to thy prince:
> And fair Em, **frolic with thy** good father . . .

---

22. See Rubow, *Shakespeare og Hans Samtigide*, pp. 132–3. Earlier Rubow (p. 45) had quoted the phrase 'breathe their soules into the air' (*FE* 4.11), a match for 'Where shall I run to breathe abroad my woes' (*Sp. T.* 3.7.1).

MILLER: And longer let not Goddard **live** a day
Than he in honour loves his sovereign.   (17.262–7)

KING: But now, knight marshal, **frolic with thy** king . . .
HIERONIMO: Long may he **live** to serve my sovereign liege,
And soon decay, unless he serve my liege.   (*Sp. T.* 1.2.100–104)

Rubow's third match between the two plays was briefer:

that were a breach | Against **the Law of Arms.**   (17.20–21)
That were a breach to common **law of arms.**   (*Sp. T.* 1.2.50)

He also noted that the phrase '**In hope thine oath is true**' (*Sp. T.* 2.1.96) recurs exactly in *Fair Em*: '**In hope your oath is true**' (8.140) and is reworked on two other occasions beginning '**In hope** . . .' (10.14, 15.27). That was the extent of Rubow's observation, and he made no general argument for Kyd's authorship. My respect for his acuity in identifying Kyd's hand in *King Leir* and *Arden of Faversham* encouraged me to study the whole play, resulting in a firm attribution. Rubow was remarkably observant, relying on his reading memory, as all attribution scholars should do. But nowadays we have, in addition, many automated helps, above all the remarkable annotated corpus of 527 early modern plays created by Pervez Rizvi, which has helped me to compile a list of over 100 matches between *Fair Em* and Kyd's accepted canon. These are all unique or very rare matches. I present a selection here, always placing them in their dramatic context.

Being Kyd's only comedy, *Fair Em* has fewer links with the three accepted plays than the other new attributions. But since its main subject matter is the progress of romance, from its initiation, challenged by obstacles, on to success or failure, we find many similarities in the value that men place on 'mighty love'. In the opening scene William, smitten with love for Blanche, dismisses his council,

That we may parley of these private cares,
Whose strength subdues **me more than all the
    world.**   (1.29–30)

In the second chorus of *The Spanish Tragedy*, the Ghost of Andrea recalls Bel-imperia,

On whom I doted **more than all the world**,
Because she loved **me more than all the world**   (*Sp. T.* 2.6.5–6)

In scene 2 the Miller prepares Em for what awaits her in adult life:

lovely daughter, since thy youthful years
Must needs **admit** as young **affections**   (2.44–5)

His words partly echo those of Soliman to Perseda, just taken captive:

Virgin, how doth thy heart **admit**,
The pure **affection** of great Soliman?   (*SP* 4.1.95–6)

Kyd's lovers praise their beloved's beauty by using the highest points of comparison. In a soliloquy Manvile praises Em:

Full ill this life becomes thy **heavenly look**,
Wherein sweet love and virtue sits enthroned   (4.4–5)

Balthazar, in love with Bel-imperia feels himself 'Led by the loadstar of her **heavenly looks**' (*Sp. T.* 4.3.121). Trotter, the Miller's Man, like many servants in plays, has a secret love that emerges in a clumsy gesture, as the stage direction records: '*he offers to kiss*' Em. When she chides him: 'How now, Trotter? Your master's daughter?', he defends himself: 'I **aim at the fairest**' (5.23–4). Horatio recounts to Bel-imperia how he had seen Andrea, her 'worthy chevalier', fighting bravely, 'For glorious cause still **aiming at the fairest**' (*Sp. T.* 1.4.10–11). Lubeck, more eloquent, describes Mariana as 'Sole paragon **and mistress of my thoughts**' (12.17). The *miles gloriosus* Basilisco, another man with aspirations above his status, celebrates 'Perseda's beauteous exellence, | Shame to Love's queen, **and empress of my thoughts**' (*SP* 2.1.32–3).

In *Fair Em*, as elsewhere in Kyd, love can suffer rejection, loss, and other misfortunes. William, having fallen in love with Blanche after seeing her portrait on Lubeck's shield, suffers a sudden reversal when he sees her in the flesh: 'May **this be she for whom I** crossed the seas?' (3.23). A happier moment of recognition comes to Erastus when he is reunited with Perseda, presumed to be dead: 'for **this is she | For whom I** mourned' (*SP* 4.1.160–61). William, captured in battle and still under the illusion that the woman he conveyed from Denmark to England is Mariana, laments at being separated from her:

> Ah, Mariana, cause of my lament,
> Joy of my heart, and **comfort of my life!**
> For thee I breathe my sorrows in the air   (13.5–7)

He echoes the laments of two women separated from the men they love, Lucina from Ferdinando: 'For what was he, but **comfort of my life?**', Perseda from Erastus: 'For what was he, but **comfort of my life?**' (*SP* 3.3.7–8). As he did with Mountney and Walingford, Perseda and Lucina, Kyd sometimes likes to play with lovers who, like puppets, utter identical remarks. William is more original, diagnosing his suffering as he experiences it:

> or silently I **sigh**;
> My sorrows afflicts **my soul with** equal **passion**   (13.8–9)

He almost reaches the intensity of Hieronimo, mourning a beloved son:

> Yet still tormented is **my** tortur'd **soul**
> **With** broken **sighs** and restless **passions**   (*Sp. T.* 3.7.10–11)

Yet both plays contain attempts at consolation. Mariana explains to Zeno that, knowing of Blanche's love for William, she arranged the disguise plot that

> **I** did devise **to ease the grief** your daughter did
>   **sustain**   (17.108)

In the same scene from *The Spanish Tragedy* from which I have just quoted, Hieronimo, still grieving, thinks that reading Pedringano's letter to Lorenzo, just delivered by the Hangman, might be a comfort:

> **I** will, **to ease the grief** that I **sustain**,
> Take truce with sorrow while I read on this.   (*Sp. T.* 3.7.30–31)

That parallel may illuminate the workings of Kyd's memory, the process by which some obscure association connected King William's lament with Hieronimo's.

Other matches, not directly connected with love, show that *Fair Em* belongs in Kyd's canon. Em, still believing that Manvile loves her, angrily accuses Valingford: 'you would have me as **an** open **gazing-stock to all the** world' (16.40–41). Basilisco, angry that Erastus should be his rival for Perseda's love, constructs a fantasy in which he defeats Erastus 'and thus I bear him thorough every street, to be **a laughingstock to all the** town' (*SP* 2.2.59–60). Like many Elizabethan dramatists, driven to self-repetition by the theatre companies' demands for new scripts, often at short notice, Kyd was adept at re-working a phrase. Manvile's polite acknowledgment, 'I am **greatly beholding to you**' (4.55) is a variant of Phillipo's 'He is **beholding to you greatly**, sir' (*SP* 1.2.111). Mariana's '**be it in secret spoken** to yourself' (*FE* 8.74) reworks the corrupt witness's false testimony about Erastus the plotter: '"**For be it spoke in secret** here," quoth he' (*SP* 5.2.54). Having set the structure of a phrase, Kyd only needed to alter one word: '**I** knew **you not, and therefore**' (*FE* 6.25) becomes: '**I** kept **it not, and therefore**' (*SP* 1.5.68). A different pronoun transforms '**In hope** your **oath is true**' (*FE* 8.140) to '**In hope** thine **oath is true**' (*Sp. T.* 2.1.92).

As I mentioned before, *Fair Em* uses intrigue for innocent ends. Nevertheless, the form it takes is identical with that used for Kyd's murder plots. Mariana's appeal to Blanche '**to** follow **the complot** I **have** invented' (8.75), echoes Lorenzo's 'Now **to** confirm **the complot** thou **hast** cast' (*Sp. T.* 3.2.106), Black Will's 'We **have** devised a **complot** underhand' (*AF* 3.128), and Mosby's 'will you two | Perform **the complot** that I **have** laid?' (*AF* 14.84).

One truly unusual collocation, '**the wrath of** lust' (*FE* 2.58), had been used by Kyd in *The Householder's Philosophy* (1588), translated from Tasso: '**The wrath of** Fortune' (*HP* 43). Phrases from *Fair Em* (ca.1593) appear in his translation of Garnier's *Cornélie* (published in 1594, but perhaps written earlier), confirming that Kyd drew on the same lexicon when writing in English or translating. A contrite Em, realizing all the faults she created in trying to retain Manvile's love, judges it appropriate to

> ghostly give myself
> To sacred prayers for this, **my former sin**   (7.33–4)

When Kyd translated the climactic Messenger speech, narrating the utter destruction of the forces of Pompey, Cornelia's second husband, he enlarged the text. Having followed Garnier's description of Caesar moving among his troops, 'inflaming' them to anger, Kyd added this couplet to his translation:[23]

> Till outward rage with inward grief begins
> A fresh remembrance of **our former sins.**   (*Corn.* 5.1.228–9)

Kyd also drew on *Cornelia* in presenting William's frustration at being captured by the English rebels: 'Could any cross, could **any plague be worse?**' (*FE* 13.1) In a vehement self-accusing speech Cornelia describes herself as a 'hapless wife, thus ominous to all, | Worse than Megaera,[24] **worse than any plague**' (*Corn.* 2.1.111–12). One final match with *Cornelia* may be cited, from Mountney's wooing speech to Em, where he claims to be offering 'honourable love', the kind

> that unites in honourable **bands** of holy rites
> And **knits** the **sacred** knot that gods—   (5.133–4)

Em, still loyal to Manvile, cuts him off. Kyd used some of the same words for Cornelia's belief that some supernatural powers are displeased that she and Pompey had both been previously married,

> And do (with civil discord furthering it)
> Untie the **bands** that **sacred** Hymen **knit**   (*Corn.* 2.1.53–4)

Since *Fair Em* is a comedy, it would be a fault against decorum to end on that tragic note. We should rather revive the spirit of the Danish King entertaining William, 'To spend the time in solace and disport' (3.41), which links up with a similar stage in *The Spanish Tragedy*, 'Meanwhile let us devise **to spend the time** | **In** some delightful **sports** and revelling'

---

23. Cf. Raymond Lebègue (ed.), *Cornélie* (Paris, 1973), p. 229, verse 1739, which Kyd translates at 5.1.229.

24. Megaera was one of the three furies.

(1.5.108–9), or even more appropriate, King William's public acknowledgment of the Miller's true social status:

Sir Thomas Goddard, welcome to thy prince:
And fair Em, **frolic with thy** good father.　(17.261–2)

A truly happy ending, transcending those temporary festivities in the Spanish court:

But now, knight marshal, **frolic with thy** king,
For 'tis thy son that wins this battle's prize.　(*Sp. T.* 1.2.96–7)

Authorship Markers: Prosody

Fair Em has additional links with the Kyd canon in its verse structure. Marina Tarlinskaja has recently endorsed my attribution to Kyd, and although some of her analytical categories are complex, readers unfamiliar with prosodic theory can see from the relative scores how closely the play's verse resembles Kyd's norms.[25] As she records, 'the ratios of proclitic micro-phrases' in *King Leir* and *Fair Em* 'are very close and very "Kyd-like", at 220–250 per 1,000 lines'. For the complementary prosodic unit, 'the ratio of enclitic micro-phrases in *Fair Em* . . . is almost the same as in *The Spanish Tragedy*'. As for 'the preferred location of strong syntactic breaks', Tarlinskaja found that 'the three acknowledged texts by Kyd as well as *Fair Em* and *King Leir* create a homogeneous cluster' after syllable 4. The percentages are: *The Spanish Tragedy* 22.7, *King Leir* 22.6, *Fair Em* 22.4, *Soliman and Perseda* 20.1, and *Cornelia* 20.7. For run-on lines, the ratio for *Fair Em* is 11.7, comparable with *The Spanish Tragedy* (9.5), *Soliman and Perseda* (9.9), *King Leir* (9.2), and *Cornelia* (13.6). The percentage of pleonastic 'do' (superfluous use of that verb to fill out a decasyllabic line) 'in *Fair Em* (32.5) is close to that for *The Spanish Tragedy*' (17.1) and *Soliman and Perseda* (20.4). Finally, the ratio for feminine endings in *Fair Em* (8.4) is within the same range as *Soliman and Perseda*

---

25. See Tarlinskaja, *Shakespeare and the Versification of English Drama*, pp. 90, 101–4.

(11.1) and *King Leir* (10.4), far higher than that achieved by any other dramatist before Shakespeare.

I hope that my discussion of its dramatic structure, together with this evidence from authorship markers, will convince readers to approach *Fair Em* as an enjoyable addition to Kyd's authentic works and to Elizabethan comedy as a genre.

7

Arden Of Faversham

Date and Source

The Stationers' Register for 3 April 1592 contains an entry assigning 'The tragedie of Arden of Feuersham and Blackwill' to the London bookseller Edward White, who published the play later that year with a most descriptive title page:

> THE LAMENTABLE AND TRUE TRAGEDIE OF M. ARDEN OF FEVERSHAM IN KENT. *Who was most wickedlye murdered, by the meanes of his disloyall and wanton wife, who for the love she bare to one Mosbie, hyred two desperat ruffins Blackwill and Shakbag, to kill him. Wherin is shewed the great malice and discimulation of a wicked woman, the unsatiable desire of filthie lust and the shamefull end of all murderers.*[1]

As M.L. Wine pointed out in his Revels edition, this is an example of the unusually detailed title page intended to serve as an advertisement, to be pasted on posts in front of the booksellers' stalls in St Paul's churchyard.[2] The printer was Edward Allde, who also worked with White on *The Spanish Tragedy*. These two plays were linked together in the Stationers' Register on 18 December 1592, which recorded an offence by two members of the Company:

---

1. Greg, *BEPD*, 1.183–5 (no. 107).
2. M.L. Wine (ed.), *The Tragedy of Master Arden of Faversham* (London, 1973), pp. xix, 48–9.

Ordered in full Court that, whereas E. White has printed The Spanish Tragedy belonging to A. Jeffes, and Jeffes has printed the tragedy of Arden of Kent belonging to White, all copies be confiscated to the use of the poor of The Company, that each pay a fine of 10s.

It was a curious confusion, reflecting the fact that a number of Kyd's plays came on the market at the same time. Presumably Jeffes thought that *The Spanish Tragedy* would sell better, as it did, with ten editions by 1633, while *Arden* only reached two further editions, in 1599 and 1633.

In *Arden of Faversham* Kyd took a story found in Holinshed's *Chronicles* (the 1587 edition,[3] which added marginal glosses) featuring a fatal love triangle. Holinshed's account of how 'a gentlemen named Arden [was] most cruellie murthered and slaine by the procurement of his own wife' (p. 148), is extremely short, less than twelve pages in a modern edition, and offers the barest hints concerning characterization and motive. The basic situation is clear, one of '*Love and lust*', as a marginal note tells us. Alice Arden betrayed her husband, 'a man of a tall and comelie person-age', for a love affair with 'one Mosbie, a tailor by occupation, a blacke swart man'. Their affair was conducted under her husband's nose and partly with his connivance, for he hoped to receive material benefits from her connections. However, this *ménage à trois* eventually broke down, for Alice, 'at length inflamed in love with Mosbie, and loathing hir husband, wished and after practised the meanes how to hasten his end' (p. 149). First Alice asked 'a painter dwelling in Faversham, who had skill of poisons', to prepare one having a 'most vehement and speedie opera-tion', which she put in Arden's breakfast. But she failed to follow the in-structions for mixing it, her husband noticed the taste, and she managed to knock over the bowl in order to destroy the evidence. '*Arden is poi-soned by his wife, but recovereth*', the marginal note tells us (p. 149).

According to Holinshed's narrative, Alice then 'fell in acquaintance with one Greene', from whom 'Arden had wrested a piece of ground' by some dubious legal action, giving rise to 'blowes and great threats'

---

3. See Wine (ed.), *Tragedy of Master Arden of Faversham*, pp. xxxv–xliii. His Appendix II (pp. 148–59) reprints the source, from which my quotations are taken.

between them. 'Therefore she, knowing that Greene hated hir husband, began to practise with him how to make [Arden] awaie; and concluded, that if he could get anie that would kill him, he should have ten pounds for a reward' (pp. 149–50). Through a neighbour, Greene meets 'one Blacke Will, a terrible cruell ruffian', known to be 'as murthering a knave as anie is in England' (p. 150). Black Will accepts the offered fee, and the next day Greene points out Arden in St Paul's churchyard; 'but there were so many gentlemen that accompanied him to dinner, that he missed of his purpose' (p. 151). At this point the source mentions that 'Greene shewed all this talke to maister Ardens man, whose name was Michael', and adds, rather belatedly: 'The cause that this Michael conspired with the rest against his maister, was: for that it was determined that he should marrie a kinswoman of Mosbies', a detail that leaves much unclear. At all events, Michael now becomes the accomplice of Greene, agreeing to leave the house doors open at night so that Black Will can murder Arden in his bed. But Michael, who is already terrified of this 'notorious murthering ruffian', and 'fearing least Blacke Will would kill him as well as his maister, after he was in bed himselfe, he rose againe and shut the doores'. A moralizing marginal note tells us how *'One murthering mind mistrusting another, doo hinder the action whereabout they agreed'* (p. 152). Trust is indeed a fundamental element in conspiracies. Black Will gets 'in a great chafe' at this, but the following day Michael manages to pacify him.

A marginal note introduces the next phase of action: *'The fourth attempt to make Arden awaie disappointed'* (p. 152). Learning that Arden will soon set off for home, the plotters plan to kill him on Rainham Down, open land near Faversham. Michael, however, 'still fearing that Blacke Will would kill him with his maister, pricked his horsse of purpose, and made him to halt, to the end that he might protract the time'. Another, unexpected obstacle appears, for on his way home Arden meets 'diverse gentlemen of his acquaintance, who kept him companie: so that Blacke Will mist here also of his purpose' (p. 152). Alice Arden has not appeared in the action since engaging Greene to organize her husband's murder, but now she re-emerges, supplying the two ruffians with meat and drink. A marginal note underlines the significance of this act: '*Ardens wife visiteth, succoureth emboldneth, and directeth Black Will &c: how to accomplish his bloudie purpose*' (p. 153). Black Will is thus instructed to 'lie in wait' for his prey in 'a certaine broome close' (a coppice of yellow-flowered shrubs), which Arden will pass in going to take the ferry. But although he got up early, 'Blacke Will . . . mist his waie', and so 'maister Arden escaped yet once againe' the marginal note adding: '*Blacke Will yet againe disappointed*' (p. 153). At this point Mosby, whom the reader of Holinshed has never encountered, enters the action, planning to 'picke some quarrel' with Arden at 'Saint Valentines faire', in order 'to fight with him'. But this plot is abandoned when they recall that Arden had never allowed himself to be 'provoked by Mosbie to fight with him' (p. 154).

Finally, the conspirators—now comprising Mosby's sister, Mosby, Greene, Black Will, George Shakebag, and Alice—'accompanied with Michael hir man, and one of hir maids'—hit on a plot to kill Arden while he is playing 'a game at the tables' (backgammon). Mosby 'at the first would not agree to that cowardlie murthering of him', but Alice 'fell downe upon hir knees to him, and besought him to go through with the matter, as if hee loved hir he could be content to do'.—'*O importunate & bloudie minded strumpet!*', the marginal note exclaims (p. 154). So all the '*confederats joine their practices*', luring Arden 'into the parlor' for a game of backgammon. At the agreed signal 'Blacke Will stept foorth, and cast a towell about his necke, so to stop his breath and strangle him'. Mosby hit him on the head with 'a pressing iron of fourteene pounds weight' (just over 6 kilos), and Black Will finished him off with a knife. After Will's departure, 'mistresse Arden came into the counting house, and with a knife gave him seven or eight pricks into the brest'—'becawse she would make hym sure', as another source puts it (p. 155 note). 'Thus this wicked woman, with hir complices, most shamefullie murdered hir owne husband, who most entirelie loved hir all his life time'. Then Alice displays her hypocrisy, having invited some friends to supper: 'When they came, she said: I marvell where maister Arden is, we will not tarrie for him, come ye and sit downe, for he will not be long' (p. 156).

The discovery of the murder is a satisfying sequence of cause and effect. The conspirators carry Arden's corpse out into a field in haste, 'with his slippers on: and betweene one of his slippers and his foot, a long rush or two remained' (p. 156), indicating where he had been killed. Also, it had snowed, and the killers' footsteps can be seen 'betwixt the place where he laie, and the garden doore'. The mayor and other officials then find 'a piece of Ardens haire and his bloud spilt in the house', together with a knife, and a blood-stained cloth (p. 157). Mosby even has Arden's blood on 'his hose and pursse' (p. 158), such clumsy inattention to incriminating evidence causing them all to be caught and executed, including some who were quite innocent.

This is in many ways a wonderful plot for a dramatist, easy for the audience to understand with its sharp outline and clear division of personages. But it also offers challenges, to create fully drawn characters, not paste-board villains, and to embed them in a recognizably gradated social context.

Intriguers and Victims

Kyd gets this story under way even more quickly than in preceding plays, but from a different viewpoint. Where he had previously begun with the intriguer, here he begins with the victim. We find Arden in conversation with his friend Franklin, who is trying to lift his 'melancholy mood'. But Arden is overwhelmed by 'foul objects that offend mine eyes', the evidence of his wife's adultery:

> Love letters passed 'twixt Mosby and my wife,
> And they have privy meetings in the town.
> Nay, on his finger did I spy the ring
> Which at our marriage day the priest put on.
> Can any grief be half so great as this?   (1.14–18)

This is Kyd's first deviation from his source, in which Arden is complaisant in the affair. Franklin offers the unhelpful comment that 'women will be false and wavering', but Arden is additionally disgusted by Mosby's low status, a 'botcher', or mender of clothes, who has 'Crept into the service of a nobleman'. Arden is 'by birth a gentleman of blood', while Mosby is a 'ribald', 'a menial or dependent of low birth' (*OED*).

Arden threatens a violent punishment, with his enemy's 'dissevered joints and sinews torn', his body lying on the floor, 'smeared in the channels of his lustful blood' (1.35–42). Franklin's response to these angry but impotent threats is the advice to be patient and 'entreat her fair'.

By beginning with the victim Kyd ensures that, from the outset, we will regard Alice Arden and Mosby through his eyes, alert for any signs of falseness. Enter Alice, with a reproach:

> Husband, what mean you to get up so early?
> Summer nights are short, and yet you rise ere day.
> Had I been 'wake you had not rise so soon.   (56–9)

After her husband's account of her blatant infidelity, our disbelief is immediate, but Arden seems not to take offence, romantically recalling Elegy 1.13 from Ovid's *Amores*:

> Sweet love, thou know'st that we too, Ovid-like,
> Have often chid the morning when it 'gan to peep,
> And often wished that dark night's purblind steeds
> Would pull her by the purple mantle back
> And cast her in the ocean to her love.

Past memories are replaced by present anguish:

> But this night, sweet Alice, thou hast killed my heart:
> I heard thee call on Mosby in thy sleep.

Worse still, she 'started up suddenly, | Instead of him, caught me about the neck'. This detail gives credence to Arden's, and our suspicions. Kyd confirms them to us, when Arden announces that he and Franklin have business in London, asking her to prepare their breakfast,

> For yet ere noon we'll take horse and away.
>   *Exeunt Arden and Franklin.*

Left alone, Alice seizes on the line, repeating it as if it were some precious token: 'Ere noon he means to take horse and away!' Kyd gives her a short soliloquy that reveals so much about her, starting with her pent-up sexual desire for Mosby and resentment of Arden:

Sweet news is this! Oh, that some airy spirit
Would in the shape and likeness of a horse
Gallop with Arden 'cross the ocean
And throw him from his back into the waves!   (1.93–6)

That recalls Gonorill's wish that her father might just disappear:

He haply may, by travelling unknown ways,
Fall sick and as a common passenger
Be dead and buried. Would God it were so well.   (*KL* 12.30–32)

—except that Alice has not enrolled 'some airy spirit' to do the deed but her lover, praised in terms designed to shock an Elizabethan audience:

Sweet Mosby is the man that hath my heart;
And he [Arden] usurps it, having nought but this:
That I am tied to him by marriage.
Love is a god and marriage is but words,
And therefore Mosby's title is the best.
Tush! Whether it be or no, he shall be mine
In spite of him, of Hymen, and of rites.

The 'nought' that she dismisses is the sacrament of marriage, one that Elizabethan men and women took seriously. As David Cressy observed, marriage 'involved a series of literal actions with strong legal, cultural, and religious connotations that take us to the heart of Tudor and Stuart society'.[4] Alice feels 'tied' to Arden by marriage, a wholly negative version of the 'images of yokes, knots, and bonds' common in both religious and secular authors, metaphors for the process 'that secures harmony and balance between two forces while combining their effort to a common end'.[5] Alice tries to devalue the concept by stating that 'marriage is but words', putting her in the same class as that notorious sophist Falstaff.[6] But in the

---

4. David Cressy, *Birth, Marriage, and Death. Ritual, Religion, and the Life-Cycle in Tudor and Stuart England* (Oxford, 1997), p. 286.

5. Ibid., p. 297.

6. 'What is in that word "honour"? What is that "honour"? Air' (*1 Henry IV*, 5.1.134–5).

next line she claims that 'Mosby's title is the best', basing her argument on a word that she evidently misuses, a title being 'An established or recognized right to something, *esp.* a legal right to the ownership of land or other property; the aggregate of facts or evidence that give rise to such a right; a claim made on the basis of such evidence' (*OED*). What right does Mosby have? In the next line she dismisses all arguments with the resolve: 'he shall be mine'.

I cannot think of any female character in English drama before 1592 who expresses illegitimate desire and flouts social morality with such energy and self-belief. Alice's impatience to wrest her life to her own desires emerges in all its force when Adam, landlord of the local inn, informs her that Mosby is staying there but forbids her to visit him, being 'wondrous sad' (serious).

> ALICE: Were he as mad as raving Hercules,
> I'll see him. Ay, and were thy house of force,
> These hands of mine should raze it to the ground
> Unless that thou wouldst bring me to my love.   (1.112–18)

If those passionate lines were to be found in a fragmentary Elizabethan manuscript, few readers would imagine that a woman is speaking. Left alone, Alice utters her 'brave resolve' with as much power as Ragan, Perseda, or Bel-imperia, vowing to ignore her 'marrow-prying neighbours' and her jealous husband, addressing the absent Mosby in the intimate 'thou' form:

> But, if I live, that block shall be removed;
> And, Mosby, thou that comes to me by stealth
> Shalt neither fear the biting speech of men
> Nor Arden's looks. As surely shall he die
> As I abhor him and love only thee.   (1.132–40)

Arden is now reduced to a 'block' or obstacle that Alice plans to remove, three times using the verb form 'shall', with its stronger connotations of personal resolve.

In relatively brief space Kyd has created a character of enormous presence and credibility. Having registered her passionate elevation of

Mosby we are naturally curious to see for ourselves the man who has inspired this passion. The first view is a shock:

> MOSBY: Away, I say, and talk not to me now.
> ALICE: A word or two, sweetheart, and then I will.
> 'Tis yet but early days; thou need'st not fear.   (1.178-80)

The 'early days' refer to a previous scene, where Alice, having cultivated Michael, Arden's servant, as an accomplice in her plot to murder Arden, reminded him of their bargain:

> Ay, but, Michael, see you keep your oath
> And be as secret as you are resolute.
> MICHAEL: I'll see he shall not live above a week.
> ALICE: On that condition, Michael, here is my hand:
> None shall have Mosby's sister but thyself.   (1.143–7)

The brevity of this exchange shows that discussions have already taken place, a bride for Michael being the reward for betraying his master. It is from this contract, sealed with a handshake (an unusual act of authority for an Elizabethan woman), that Alice reassures Mosby, who knows nothing of this plot. But his mind is elsewhere:

> MOSBY: Where is your husband?
> ALICE: 'Tis now high water, and he is at the quay.
> MOSBY: There let him be. Henceforward know me
>   not.   (181-3)

Alice is deeply hurt:

> Is this the end of all thy solemn oaths?
> Is this the fruit thy reconcilement buds?
> Have I for this given thee so many favours,
> Incurred my husband's hate, and (out alas!)
> Made shipwreck of mine honour for thy sake?
> And dost thou say, 'Henceforward know me not'?   (184–9)

Kyd gives her a twenty-line protest which ends with her rejecting him: 'Base peasant, get thee gone ... And so farewell'.

If Mosby really loves her, we might think, he would apologize and make up, but he does the opposite:

Ungentle and unkind Alice, now I see
That which I ever feared and find too true:
A woman's love is as the lightning flame
Which even in bursting forth consumes itself.   (204–6)

This sounds like one of the many misogynistic tags that abound in Elizabethan collections of sententiae, or something that Orsino might have memorized.[7] Mosby uses it as a cold-blooded move to put Alice on the defensive, as women must have often been in that society. Only now does he offer some explanation for his cruel words:

To try thy constancy have I been strange.
Would I had never tried, but lived in hope!   (207–8)

He has indeed been 'strange', meaning 'unnatural', but to claim that he was only testing her constancy seems unlikely, especially when he follows it with such a self-pitying Petrarchism (as if to complain that 'cruel women fix men between hope and despair'). Kyd gives Alice enough resentment to reproach him—'What needs thou try me whom thou never found false?'—but his feeble reply—'Yet pardon me, for love is jealous', rings hollow. Kyd gives her a bitter comment and an ominous premonition:

So lists the sailor to the mermaid's song;
So looks the traveller to the basilisk.
I am content for to be reconciled,
And that, I know, will be mine overthrow.   (212–15)

She sets Mosby in two positions of destructive power, the mermaid or Siren that lures sailors to their death and the poisonous basilisk whose look kills.

---

7. Cf. e.g., Lysander's description of love: 'Brief as the lightning in the collied night . . .' (*Midsummer Night's Dream*, 1.1.145–9) and Shakespeare's Sonnet 73.12: 'Consumed with that which it was nourished by'.

Kyd has introduced a troubling possibility. Whereas the whole premiss of the play is that Arden will be the victim, Alice may yet be also a victim of Mosby. She seems to foresee, and accept, her own 'overthrow', before switching back to her optimistic mode—'Nay, Mosby, let me still enjoy thy love; | And, happen what will, I am resolute' (217–18). Kyd has constructed this brief exchange (a mere forty lines) to reveal Mosby's power and readiness to hurt and manipulate her. Alice has passion, and love, but he has a cold and calculating eye for the main chance. This scene is a rehearsal, or preparation for a later quarrel, which will reveal more of his true nature.

To turn from the victims to the intriguers, Kyd faithfully follows Holinshed's placing of Alice as the chief instigator of the murder plots. Thanks to her husband's frequent absences, mostly on business, she can use their home as a central clearing house for recruiting possible accomplices. In the unusually long opening scene, a whole troop of men come and go, some by her arrangement, others unexpected, at their own initiative. Excluding Arden and Franklin, who are present from 1–92, 290–416, the sequence (an asterisk marks accomplices) begins at line 105 with Adam the innkeeper. Then follow: 142 *Michael, 176 *Mosby, 246 *Clarke, 447 *Greene, 537 *Mosby and *Clarke, 591 *Clarke and Susan, many of whom are onstage for a long time. Scene 2 is wholly peopled by accomplices, apart from Bradshaw: *Greene, *Black Will, *Shakebag. Most of the characters in the play are intriguers and accomplices, who speak almost all of the dialogue. The only exceptions are Arden, Franklin, Lord Cheyne, the Mayor of Faversham, and a few minor characters.

The topics dominating their discussion are the ways and means of murdering Arden, and payment for services rendered. Kyd adds a possible mode of murder not chronicled by Holinshed. Mosby knows a painter, Clarke, 'The only cunning man of Christendom', who 'can temper poison with his oil' (227–8) so that if he paints a portrait of Alice, Arden will be killed when he looks at it. Alice doesn't like the idea of her image killing her husband, but they meet Clarke nonetheless. He understands that Alice loves Mosby and, just like the Messenger in *Leir*, accepts as an everyday fact that she naturally wishes to get rid of her 'block':

Let it suffice I know you love him well
And fain would have your husband made away;
Wherein, trust me, you show a noble mind,
That rather than you'll live with him you hate
You'll venture life and die with him you love.   (1.265–7)

That is hardly the outcome they are planning, but they accept some poison from the painter. This is the poison that Alice put it in Arden's broth, so ineffectually.

Kyd has taken from Holinshed a story with a strong but linear plot line, a series of attempted murders that keep failing. The challenge for a dramatist is to embed this sequence into a fully realized and credible dramatic context. One way that Kyd does so is by characterizing the accomplices. Clarke's idea that Alice and Mosby will be happy to die, provided they are together, is part of his curious mixture of cold pragmatism and derivative aesthetic theories. He is ready to prepare the poisonous portrait at any time, and has a favorable image of the painter to justify it:

Provided, as you have given your word,
I may have Susan Mosby to my wife.
For, as sharp-witted poets, whose sweet verse
Make heavenly gods break off their nectar draughts
And lay their ears down to the lowly earth,
Use humble promise to their sacred Muse,
So we that are the poets' favourites
Must have a love. Ay, love is the painter's Muse,
That makes him frame a speaking countenance,
A weeping eye that witnesses heart's grief.
Then tell me, Master Mosby, shall I have her?   (1.246–57;
    my italics)

The lines I have italicized could be from some contemporary *paragone*, a comparison between the arts, such as the common topic '*Ut pictura poesis*'. Kyd creates a striking contrast between the second-hand aesthetic theory and the ruthless contract that surrounds it: 'Provided I may have Susan Mosby to my wife . . . shall I have her?' It is as if two different people are talking.

As for payment, several commodities are offered to the accomplices. Susan is an unmarried servant, a desirable acquisition in terms of her earning and procreative powers. She has no power to choose her husband, for that lies with her senior male relative, Mosby. Later in this scene Mosby asks Alice if she has 'dealt and tempered with my sister' (539), that is, persuaded her to accept Clarke. Alice replies that he should 'woo himself', permission that he accepts, offering his return services 'to the uttermost' in 'either goods or life' (546–7). Forty lines later he reappears with Susan, who has been persuaded and is correctly docile, 'If you be willing that it shall be so'. Mosby then calls in his debt:

> Ah, Master Clarke, it resteth at my grant;
> You see my sister's yet at my dispose;
> But so you'll grant me one thing I shall ask,
> I am content my sister shall be yours.   (599–602)

The quid pro quo is the poisoned crucifix, subsequently vetoed by Alice, yet Clarke retains his side of the bargain. All through this sequence readers and playgoers know that, earlier in this scene, Alice had promised Susan to Michael as reward for his assistance in the murder (142–76). Michael is already aware that Clarke is a rival ('he hath sent a dagger sticking in a heart, | With a verse or two stolen from a painted cloth'), and in a later scene he confronts Clarke, only to come off with a broken head (10.46–73). Alice rightly understands—'I'll lay my life, this is for Susan's love'. Kyd is meticulous in fulfilling plotlines, but after this Clarke disappears from the play, his significance exhausted.

A second commodity dealt with in Alice's clearinghouse for accomplices is land. Holinshed had vividly described the process by which 'Arden had wrested a piece of ground' behind the Abbey from 'one Greene . . . and there had great blowes and great threats passed betwixt them . . . Therefore she knowing that Greene hated hir husband, began to practise with him how to make him awaie'.[8] So far all the visitors at the house have been wanting to see Alice or Mosby, and have been potential accomplices. Alice hopes that this visitor is 'one that comes | To put in practice our intended drifts' [plots], but Greene wants to see her husband, having heard that Arden has acquired the land on which he had been a tenant. Kyd arouses our sympathy for this victim of greedy landowners:

> Your husband doth me wrong
> To wring me from the little land I have.
> My living is my life; only that
> Resteth remainder of my portion.
> Desire of wealth is endless in his mind,
> And he is greedy-gaping still for gain   (1.468–73)

Greene didn't enter Arden's house as a willing accomplice in his murder but that is what he becomes. Alice increases his anger by claiming that Arden mistreats her and consorts with whores, strengthening Greene's desire for revenge: 'I'll pay him home, whatever hap to me' (513). Alice deters him from risking his own life—'hire some cutter for to cut him short', giving him money to hire killers and promising the 'restitution of his land' (519=23).

Land plus money is the appropriate reward for Greene, but most villains are content with cash. We recall Lorenzo's maxim:

> Where words prevail not, violence prevails.
> But gold doth more than either of them both.   (*Sp. T.* 2.1.110–11)

Alice has heard that 'in London many alehouse ruffians keep, | Which ... will murder men for gold' (444–5), and Greene instantly heads there, managing to recruit the 'two desperat ruffins Black Will and Shakebag' mentioned on the title page. He approaches them cautiously—just as Gonorill and Ragan had done to their 'Messenger or Murderer', with the request to murder their father. Greene begins with a euphemism, requesting their 'help ... in a matter of great consequence', offering

---

8. Wine (ed.), *Tragedy of Master Arden of Faversham*, p. 149.

them 'twenty angels' if they'll be 'secret and profound'. They instantly realize what he is looking for:

> WILL: How? Twenty angels? Give my fellow George Shakebag and me twenty angels and if thou'lt have thy own father slain that thou mayst inherit his land, we'll kill him.
> SHAKEBAG: Ay, thy mother, thy sister, thy brother, or all thy kin. (2.84–7)

(Following on from the Messenger in *Leir*, we might think that the Elizabethan underworld had a flourishing trade in murder for settling family disputes.) The would-be murderers' first attempt having failed, Greene tries to exert pressure on them:

> Remember how devoutly thou hast sworn
> To kill the villain; think upon thine oath.
> WILL Tush, I have broken five hundred oaths!
> But wouldst thou charm me to effect this deed,
> Tell me of gold, my resolution's fee. (3.79–83)

It is Will who gives the final polish to Mosby's plan of trapping Arden when he's playing backgammon and kill him.

> That done, bear him behind the Abbey,
> That those that find him murdered may suppose
> Some slave or other killed him for his gold. (14.115–17)

Once the murder is completed, Will has his 'fee' and departs: 'We have our gold. Mistress Alice, adieu', leaving them to discover that his plan to ditch Arden's body would be useless on a snowy day. The last villain we see is Shakebag, having failed to find shelter with a tapster's wife:

> I spurned her down the stairs, and broke her neck, and cut the tapster's throat; and now I am going to fling them in the Thames. I have the gold: what care I though it be known? I'll cross the water and take sanctuary. (15.6–9)

That plan turns out to be as useless as the others, for we learn in the Epilogue that Shakebag 'took sanctuary and, being sent for out, | Was murderèd in Southwark'. One rogue said: 'We have our gold', the other 'I have the gold', but earning your fee and keeping it are unlikely achievements for two such blunderers.

From Tragedy to Comedy

As we have seen, Holinshed's heavily moralized account is couched in tones of outrage and disapproval. But Kyd realized that this story of incompetence carried material for comedy, and he added incidents of his own invention to make the would-be murderers seem ridiculous. On their first outing Greene points out their prey, Arden, who has been walking a turn in St Paul's, a common rendezvous for business deals. But the churchyard of St Paul's was also lined with booksellers' stalls, and just as Will is preparing to 'run [Arden] through' with his sword, a printer's apprentice, wanting to prevent pilfering when the crowd comes out of the cathedral, shuts the stall:

> [*Then lets he down his window, and it breaks Black Will's head*
> WILL: Zounds, draw, Shakebag, draw! I am almost killed.
> PRENTICE: We'll tame you, I warrant.
> WILL: Zounds, I am tame enough already.   (3.46–50)

Will's self-deflating reply shows the comic nature of his role, as the audience laughs both with and at him. This would-be murderer is foiled by a banal accident, the harmer is harmed: 'my broken head grieves me not so much, as by this means Arden hath escaped' (60–61).

This setback is the first of Will and Shakebag's many failures to carry out their 'hit'. *Arden of Faversham* was a pioneering play in many respects, not least as the first black comedy, in which a pair of professional murderers, far from presiding over the Guild of London Assassins, can't even kill an unarmed man who is unaware of being their target. Instead of overcoming obstacles they are themselves obstacles. Will's utterances are terrifying—

> Seest thou this gore that cleaveth to my face?
> From hence ne'er will I wash this bloody stain,
> Till Arden's heart be panting in my hand.   (3.97–9)

but it turns out to be just sound and fury. Their next plot is to kill Arden in his bed, for which they need an accomplice within the household. They approach Arden's servant Michael, who has been unmoved by the attempts of Greene and Shakebag at persuasion, so Black Will takes over. Since they know from Greene that Alice has recruited Michael as an accomplice, Will first mocks his low status in the hierarchy of murderers:

> How comes it then that such a knave as you
> Dare swear a matter of such consequence?   (3.141–2)

(In this class-conscious society the issue of status is often invoked by superiors to put inferiors in their places.) Will warns Michael that 'We have devised a complot underhand' to reveal him as an accomplice in Alice's murder plot and 'send thee roundly to the devil of hell'. Having established their hold over Michael, Will puts him in his lowly place:

> And therefore thus: I am the very man,
> Marked in my birth-hour by the Destinies,
> To give an end to Arden's life on earth;
> Thou but a member but to whet the knife
> Whose edge must search the closet of his breast.
> Thy office is but to appoint the place
> And train [lead] thy master to his tragedy;
> Mine to perform it when occasion serves.   (150–57)

Other dramatists might have given a few lines to this villain, but Kyd has imaginatively realized that criminals have their own sense of relative importance. We have heard Will expressing his wish that one day 'murder would grow to an occupation', a term implying social respectability, as in the biblical injunction that 'every man should labour in his occupation'.[9] Will sees himself at the apex of the hierarchy, like a priest giving instructions to an acolyte. The function of Black Will's boasting is to mark the discrepancy between his self-image and reality. In fact, he is himself 'but a member' in a chain created by Alice, who employed

---

9. Cf. 1 Corinthians, 7:20: 'Let every man abide in the vocation wherein he was called'.

Greene, who employed Will, who has now employed Michael. Kyd knows, from his interest in intrigue, that the longer such a chain extends itself, the greater the risks. Michael's role in this attempt on Arden's life will be to leave the street door unlatched, but Black Will's threats to Michael are so terrifying that they have the opposite effect. The fearful Michael has a nightmare that disturbs the whole house, Arden discovers the unlocked door (4.90–101), and the murderers fail again. The weak link in the chain was not Michael but Black Will for being too intimidating.

Shakebag is another unreliable instrument. As we know, for a conspiracy to succeed it is essential for the plotters to work together. Far from presenting a unified destructive force, while they were waiting for Michael's signal Shakebag accuses Black Will of cowardice and they begin to quarrel (5.18–33). When we see them again the quarrel revives so violently that they come to blows and Greene must separate them (9.11–37). Everything in this murder plot seems to be going wrong, the intrigue becoming comic due to the mutual distrust and incompetence of its agents.[10] Later in this scene Arden is about to walk into the assassins' trap when the Lord Cheyne rides up, recognizes Black Will, and warns him to reform (9.95–125), a chance meeting in which Greene piously sees a providential force: 'The Lord of Heaven hath preserved him' (142), but Will disagrees: 'The Lord of Heaven a fig! The Lord Cheyne hath preserved him'. Holinshed describes two attempts failing because Black Will got lost, but Kyd transforms one of them by introducing a new unpredictable and uncontrollable agent, the weather, thick fog descending where they are hiding in some shrubs near the ferry. Will thinks that he is 'almost in hell's mouth, where I cannot see my way for smoke' (12.2–3), the two of them blundering around 'like a couple of blind pilgrims' (18). The general farcical level continues when Shakebag falls into a ditch (perhaps the stage trapdoor) and is 'almost drowned' (20). As Mosby bitterly comments, 'These knaves will never

---

10. Holinshed adds a marginal note: 'One murthering mind mistrusting another, doo hinder the action whereabout they agreed' (Wine, *Tragedy of Master Arden of Faversham*, p. 152).

do it, let us give it over' (12.64). When Greene next meets his hired killers, he reaches the same conclusion:

WILL: Sirrah Greene, when was I so long in killing a man?
GREENE: I think we shall never do it. Let us give it over.
SHAKEBAG: Nay. Zounds, we'll kill him though we be hanged at
   his door for our labour.   (14.1–4)

Alice took a risk by extending the intrigue chain, trusting Greene to hire competent murderers, but he has failed her badly. Will is the more talkative one, resembling Basilisco in fantastic boasting. Just as Kyd used Piston to puncture that braggart's pretensions, here he shows Greene unable to disguise his irritation:

WILL: Thou knowest, Greene, that I have lived in London this
   twelve years, where I have made some go upon wooden legs for
   taking the wall on me . . . I have cracked as many blades as thou
   hast done nuts.
GREENE: Oh, monstrous lie!
WILL: Faith, in a manner I have. The bawdyhouses have paid me
   tribute: there durst not a whore set up unless she have agreed
   with me first, for opening her shop windows. . . . I have broken
   a sergeant's head with his own mace and bailed whom I list
   with my sword and buckler. . . . To conclude, what have I not
   done? Yet cannot do this! Doubtless, he is preserved by
   miracle.   (14.5–24)

For Greene it was providence that frustrated their acts, for Will it was a miracle, another easy excuse for failure.

This speech resembles others by Basilisco in *Soliman and Perseda* and the Messenger in *King Leir*, but where they made their boasts at our first view of them, before we knew their weaknesses, Will makes his after he has failed, sounding like an empty vessel. Worse still, when Alice asks: 'Gentlemen, | How missed you of your purpose yesternight?', and Greene sourly answers ''Twas long of Shakebag, that unlucky villain', Will offers to defend his partner by reconstructing the fight in terms of sword-play, but in fact blames him—'he should have locked with both his hilts ... he bears his sword-point half a yard out of danger ... a buckler in a skilful hand is as good as a castle. Nay, 'tis better than a sconce ...' His acting out of the movements onstage makes an amusing scene. But Alice is not so easily deflected:[11]

> ALICE: Ay, but I wonder why you both stood still.
> WILL: Faith, I was so amazed I could not strike.   (14.45–61)

Will's feeble excuse must have aroused laughter, and perhaps contempt. It is typical of Kyd's care for detail that he found time to reveal how a braggart could use the 'terms of art' to conceal his cowardice.

The latest failure means that every attempt to kill Arden has been foiled by clumsiness, chance, and the incompetence of the hired assassins. They now suggest that they could 'dog [Arden] through the fair, | And stab him in the crowd, and steal away'. Having rejected this idea as 'unpossible', Alice welcomes the return of Mosby, who 'will, I hope, invent some surer means'. Starting a new intrigue, he turns to the contract killers: 'Black Will and Shakebag, will you two | Perform the complot that I have laid?' Mosby then outlines the method that will finally prove successful.

A Vengeful Woman (and Her Lover)

We have already seen Kyd's creation of two justifiably vengeful female characters, Bel-imperia, and Perseda. Unable to achieve justice, they take revenge at the climactic point of the action by stabbing to death a man who murdered their beloved. Kyd then created Ragan, who forms the unjustifiable desire to kill her father and hires an assassin to perform a task that she feels unable to do herself. But all three are outdone by Alice Arden, whose adulterous desire to do away with her husband extends through the whole play. And, like Ragan, Alice's crime is

---

11. In an earlier scene, where Clarke claimed the ability to blend poison with his paints, Alice asks the pertinent question, how can you use 'baleful and impoisoned' colours | And no ways prejudice yourself withal?' Mosby praises her, for once: 'Well questioned, Alice' (1.616–20).

unjustifiable: her husband's mere existence, blocking her desire for Mosby, is her only motive for wanting his death.

Kyd's treatment of Alice illustrates the advice (ascribed to the American playwright Mark Swan), 'Show, don't tell'. Holinshed's narrative is overloaded with condemnations of Alice, 'who most shamefullie murdered hir owne husband', extending to hysterical marginal notes ('O importunate & bloudie minded strumpet!'). A historian may be allowed indignation, but not a dramatist. Kyd scrupulously conceals his own opinions, allowing Alice to speak and act freely, showing her at her own valuation. With a flexible use of those vital resources of drama—asides and soliloquies—he shows her desires, hopes, and fears, 'inflamed in love with Mosby, and loathing her husband', as Holinshed put it. There are many expressions of love in Elizabethan drama, but no expressions of hate so intense and long sustained as hers, and few to equal it elsewhere.

As I have shown, Kyd likes to introduce important characters early in the play. In *Soliman and Perseda* he brought on Soliman in the first act, long before he appears in the source, and in *King Leir* did the same for Perillus, a character of his own creation. Holinshed mentions Mosby several times in the first two paragraphs, recording how he 'obtained such favour at [Alice's] hands that he laie with hir, or (as they terme it), kept hir, in abusing hir bodie', and often lodged in Arden's house (ed. Wine, p. 148). Thereafter he is not mentioned in the unsuccessful murder attempts and only reappears just before the final plot (pp. 153–4). Kyd brings Mosby on in the first scene, with the shock greeting to Alice: 'Away, I say, and talk not to me now' (1.178). As we have seen, they quarrel and make up, soon beginning to plot murder in earnest. Kyd uses Mosby's frequent presence to transform Alice's role, allowing her to reveal desire and tenderness. She reminds him of their earlier days together:

> Remember, when I locked thee in my closet,
> What were thy words and mine? Did we not both
> Decree to murder Arden in the night?   (1.190–92)

(The incongruity between the erotic setting and the ruthless conversation shows Alice's 'resolve'. But the term 'decree' can only be used by law-givers.) When Mosby is present, she seems more complete, they are 'an item'. It is altogether fitting that the long first scene should end in this way:

> MOSBY: Now, Alice, let's in, and see what cheer you keep.
> I hope, now Master Arden is from home,
> You'll give me leave to play your husband's part.
> ALICE: Mosby, you know who's master of my heart,
> He well may be the master of the house.   *Exeunt.*   (1.630–34)

That is one of the few occasions in Elizabethan drama where the audience is encouraged to think that a man and a woman leaving the stage are about to make love. Kyd allows his characters to be happy, whatever other people might think.[12]

Kyd also gives Alice frequent opportunities to release her hatred for Arden, especially when she is alone (1.95–6, 140–41). After Mosby has calmed their first quarrel, she anticipates Arden's imminent death:

> His time is but short;
> For, if thou beest as resolute as I,
> We'll have him murdered as he walks the streets.   (438–40)

Yet, despite Alice's self-confidence, Arden's removal belongs to some unrealized future. Despite her threefold 'shall' (1.136–9), the actual verb tense for the lovers' state remains the conditional, or 'counter-factual', as linguists call it. When Mosby announces that he has a plan to stop Arden returning to London, Alice cries 'Ah, would we could!' (1.224–6). When Mosby's accomplice Clarke, the painter and amateur poisoner, recognizes that Alice 'fain would have your husband made away', and praises her for showing 'a noble mind' (1.266–7), Alice acknowledges her dependence on her lover:

---

12. In her edition of *Arden of Faversham* (London, 2022), Catherine Richardson reminds us of how this would appear to an Elizabethan audience: 'As he rules her heart and enjoys her body, Mosby may fittingly take over control of the household. Involving taking Arden's rightful place as patriarchal head and usurping his rule over servants and property as well as Alice herself, this is a truly shocking situation' (158 n.)

Yet nothing could enforce me to the deed
But Mosby's love. [*To Mosby*] Might I without control
Enjoy thee still, then Arden should not die;
But seeing I cannot, therefore let him die.   (1.271–5)

Alice has moved from 'would' and 'could' to 'could . . . might . . . should
not . . . let', but to shift from the conditional to the optative is to be still
in the realm of indeterminacy. After her botched attempt to poison
Arden (1.362–425), Alice assures Mosby that Arden's 'time is but short',
but she has progressed no farther than a future tense qualified by the
word 'if': 'if thou beest as resolute as I . . '. Being 'resolute', however, is
not much use when the 'alehouse ruffians' they hire can be routed by a
printer's apprentice letting down the shop blinds.

Theatregoers and readers now follow the action to London, witnessing further failures by the would-be-murderers (3.120–7.20). All this
while Kyd has kept Mosby and Alice from us, but he brings them together in scene 8, in many ways the most powerful scene in the play—so
good, in fact, that some scholars have given it the highest honour, mis-
takenly attributing it to Shakespeare. It begins with a long introspective
soliloquy by Mosby, which reveals his hopes and fears, a recent development in Elizabethan drama, as the soliloquy was extended beyond communicating information. We await his words with great interest, for his
first appearance showed him to be cold and calculating with Alice, with-
holding love. He had seemingly picked a quarrel, to see how she would
react. When she showed hurt and indignation, he claimed that he had
been testing her constancy, but he was really reaffirming his power
and her dependence.

We have seen Mosby's accomplished mendacity in relationship with
others, but according to the conventions of Elizabethan drama, in soliloquy characters tell the truth. Kyd first reveals Mosby's unsettled
state: 'Disturbèd thoughts drives me from company | . . . Continual
trouble of my moody brain | Feebles my body', his 'troubled mind is
stuffed with discontent' (8.1–10). Kyd gives Mosby an eloquent description
of his state of mind but shows him searching for an explanation: perhaps
his 'golden time was when I had no gold', but slept well. Success—or is

it ambition?—has brought him the fear of failure: 'since I . . . sought to build my nest among the clouds, | Each gentlest airy gale doth shake my bed | And makes me dread my downfall to the earth' (15–18). Mosby is trying to describe his situation so that he can understand it, but seems to recognize that he has been avoiding the issue:

> But whither doth contemplation carry me?
> The way I seek to find, where pleasure dwells,
> Is hedged behind me that I cannot back,
> But needs must on, although to danger's gate.   (19–22)

Playgoers and readers are none the wiser. We know that 'pleasure', or *voluptas*, was often condemned in classical and Renaissance ethics as the goal of hedonists who scorn *virtus*, the true goal for good men and women.[13] But that is still too general, and Mosby's reference to danger is equally obscure.

Kyd has been using the tactics of delay, constructing over twenty lines of verse to build up our curiosity to know the cause of Mosby's unease. When he finally gets to the point, we realize that we are surprised to find that we know all the agents concerned:

> Then, Arden, perish thou by that decree,
> For Greene doth ear the land and weed thee up
> To make my harvest nothing but pure corn.
> And for his pains I'll heave him up awhile
> And, after, smother him to have his wax;[14]
> Such bees as Greene must never live to sting.   (23–8)

Mosby's 'decree', like Alice's 'title', refers to some law-giving body of their own imagination. His metaphors from farming, with Greene as a ploughman working for Mosby, and Arden reduced to a weed that would otherwise damage Mosby's harvest, followed by Greene being reduced to a bee that will produce honey before being suffocated, open

---

13. See Brian Vickers, 'Leisure and Idleness in the Renaissance: The Ambivalence of *otium*', *Renaissance Studies*, 4 (1990): 1–37, 107–54.

14. As Wine notes, Mosby refers to 'the practice of smoking out bees to reach their honey and their wax' (*Tragedy of Master Arden of Faversham*, p. 74).

new vistas into Mosby's psyche. The callousness of the metaphors by which he will use Greene as an instrument to gain his own ends and then liquidate him, identifies him as another of Kyd's Machiavellian plotters. They all descend from Lorenzo, who offered a rational justification for constructing murderous intrigues while protecting himself:

> They that for coin their souls endangered,
> To save my life, for coin shall venture theirs;
> And better it is that base companions die,
> Than by their life to hazard our good haps.
> Nor shall they live, for me to fear their faith:
> I'll trust myself, myself shall be my friend;
> For die they shall, slaves are ordained to no other end.
> (*Sp. T.* 3.2.131–7)

Mosby works by the same principle, with the same contemptuous valuation of his tools. Mosby reduces his other accomplices (the Painter and Michael) to dogs fighting over a bone—in this case, Susan:[15]

> I'll none of that, for I can cast a bone
> To make these curs pluck out each other's throat;
> And then am I sole ruler of mine own.   (34–6)

It is unsettling to think that all the time Mosby was being courteous to his hired assassins, he was planning to dispose of them. With a dramatist's creative privilege, Kyd lets us see into Mosby's vision of the future. We even follow him as he forgets, then remembers the last of his associates:

> Yet Mistress Arden lives; but she's myself,
> And holy church rites makes us two but one.

Mosby's first thought is to imagine that he is, or will be married to Alice,[16] and she is unlikely to testify against him. But we see his brain immediately identifying a risk and finding the remedy:

---

15. As pointed out by Keith Sturgess in his edition of *Three Elizabethan Domestic Tragedies* (Penguin, 1969).

16. Holinshed records that Alice 'had made a solemne promise to him, and he againe to hir, to be in all points as man and wife together, and thereupon they both received the sacrament

> But what for that I may not trust you, Alice?
> You have supplanted Arden for my sake
> And will extirpen me to plant another.
> 'Tis fearful sleeping in a serpent's bed,
> And I will cleanly rid my hands of her.   (39–43)

His first words, rejecting trust as a weakness, echo Lorenzo's paranoiac fears that Pedringano will betray him, despite his elaborate device with the empty box:

> One only thing is uneffected yet,
> And that's to fee[17] the executioner.
> But to what end? I list not trust the air
> With utterance of our pretence therein,
> For fear the privy whisp'ring of the wind
> Convey our words amongst unfriendly ears
> That lie too open to advantages.   (3.4.90–96)

Mosby completes the animal analogies for the associates he plans to kill by reducing Alice to a serpent stinging him in bed. But she enters, as if on cue, and there is a touch of comedy in his volte-face:

> *Here enters Alice [with a prayer book].*

> But here she comes, and I must flatter her.—
> How now, Alice! What, sad and passionate?
> Make me partaker of thy pensiveness;
> Fire divided burns with lesser force.
> ALICE But I will dam that fire in my breast
> Till by the force thereof my part consume. Ah, Mosby!

Mosby's formal, pompous terminology ('partaker of thy pensiveness') and glib *sententia* ('fire divided . . .') are part of his repertoire of

---

on a sundaie at London, openlie in a church there' (Wine, *Tragedy of Master Arden of Faversham*, pp. 153–4). But to stand next to a woman during the communion service is hardly an official contract.

17. My emendation for 'see' [long s]. For 'fee' as a verb, see Alice: 'They shall be soundly fee'd to pay him home' (1.444).

sincere-sounding phrases that may be profitably used when dealing with women, but Alice's deeply felt sigh is the true language of feeling. Kyd manages to make Mosby sound insincere and self-pitying when he tries to be eloquent. But he suddenly abandons sympathy, going on the offensive:

> Ungentle Alice, thy sorrow is my sore;
> Thou know'st it well, and 'tis thy policy
> To forge distressful looks to wound a breast
> Where lies a heart that dies when thou art sad.   (54–7)

It is a bold move, to make such an unpleasant accusation, that Alice uses 'policy' (devious pretence, often connected with Machiavelli), contriving or feigning distress so as to 'wound . . . a heart that dies when thou art sad'. (Mosby's heart has just been broken 'in thousand pieces' by her; now it has died. He has exhausted that metaphor.)

The problem Mosby faces is how to handle a woman with whom he has been committing adultery when she feels shameful and repentant. Alice tries to communicate her shame, starting from the beginning: 'Thou knowest how dearly Arden loved me'. Mosby interrupts impatiently: 'And then?' Alice repeats the phrase, as if she is about to continue a narrative *ex ovo*, but suddenly breaks off:

> And then—conceal the rest, for 'tis too bad,
> Lest that my words be carried with the wind
> And published in the world to both our shames.

It has not been noticed that Alice re-enacts Lorenzo's distrust of any audible 'utterance of our pretence',

> For fear the privy whisp'ring of the wind
> Convey our words amongst unfriendly ears
> That lie too open to advantages.   (Sp. T. 3.4.94–96)

Lorenzo's motive for secrecy is fear, Alice's motive is shame. She feels that her behaviour with Mosby has lost her previous 'title' of 'Arden's honest wife' and gained 'an odious strumpet's name', due to Mosby having 'enchanted' her. If Mosby were content to 'forget . . . what hath passed between us', he could stop at this point. But he has not finished with her, for Alice's money and her death—together with that of three other accomplices—will, so Mosby thinks, open 'The way I seek to find where pleasure dwells'. Critics sometimes accuse Alice of indulging in fantasy, but if she is guilty, Mosby is more so, imagining that he can arrange five deaths unscathed and live to enjoy the widow's money.

Mosby's strategy of regaining Alice's love is a twenty-five-line abusive tirade on all the material damage he has suffered for loving her, 'the credit I have lost', the neglected 'matters of import | That would have stated me above thy state', the 'Forslowed [missed] advantages', above all the lost social and financial opportunity:

> I left the marriage of an honest maid,
> Whose dowry would have weighed down all thy wealth,
> Whose beauty and demeanour far exceeded thee.
> This certain good I lost for changing bad   (87–90)

We may doubt whether there ever was such a 'good', but these are words chosen to hurt Alice, who, he claims—returning her insult— 'unhallowed [like a witch] hast enchanted me'. Connoisseurs of rhetoric may admire Mosby's peroration, but readers familiar with Kyd's method of allowing his personages to damn themselves out of their own mouths will suspect that his indignation is feigned, calculated to overwhelm Alice by its seemingly irrevocable insults:

> Thou art not fair: I viewed thee not till now.
> Thou art not kind: till now I knew thee not.
> And now the rain hath beaten off thy gilt
> Thy worthless copper shows thee counterfeit.
> It grieves me not to see how foul thou art,
> But mads me that ever I thought thee fair.
> Go, get thee gone, a copesmate for thy hinds!
> I am too good to be thy favourite.   (98–105)

After such a crushing demolition, we might think, there can be no going back; but Mosby knows what he is doing. Alice's first reaction is to pick up on Mosby's harping on the money he has forgone: her friends were right to tell her

> That Mosby loves me not but for my wealth,
> Which, too incredulous, I ne'er believed.

Now she knows, but it doesn't matter, for, as she plainly admits, she's desperate to regain Mosby's love:

> Nay, hear me speak, Mosby, a word or two;
> I'll bite my tongue if it speak bitterly.
> Look on me, Mosby, or I'll kill myself;
> Nothing shall hide me from thy stormy look.
> If thou cry war, there is no peace for me.

Now we see how well Mosby planned his attack. Presumably he has turned his back on her so that she cannot see his face, which upsets her most. His declaration of war brings her instant capitulation as she begs him to notice her:

> Wilt thou not look? Is all thy love o'erwhelmed?
> Wilt thou not hear? What malice stops thine ears?
> Why speaks thou not? What silence ties thy tongue?

Whatever Alice's plans to murder her husband, in this scene I can only feel sympathy for her, to be so dependent on this callous and brutal man. As she continues her appeal Alice rehearses his qualities, the capacities have made her fall in love with him:

> Thou hast been sighted as the eagle is,
> And heard as quickly as the fearful hare,
> And spoke as smoothly as an orator,
> When I have bid thee hear, or see, or speak.

These attributes are surely hyperbolical, far exceeding anything we have seen in Mosby, verging on bathos.[18] But of course, lovers' impressions

---

18. Compare Shakespeare's *Venus and Adonis* 1093–1104, where the Queen of Love comically celebrates her dead lover's qualities.

relate only to things that they have experienced. This wonderful scene leaves me feeling embarrassed at being party to this personal revelation. It is not always comfortable seeing into someone else's psyche. Alice has been crushed, begging Mosby to forgive her for 'this little fault', and then 'I'll ne'er more trouble thee'.

Mosby has re-established his hold over her, a demonstration of power in personal relationships that is upsetting, especially since we know his plans for her. He adroitly changes the subject, recalling her angry—and true—description of him as 'a base artificer', playing the class card for once from the inferior position:

> MOSBY: We beggars must not breathe where gentles are.
> ALICE: Sweet Mosby is as gentle as a king,
> And I too blind to judge him otherwise.

Having broken, and restored their relationship, Mosby makes another move out of the handbook for dealing with women, flattering their persuasive powers,[19] and adding a warning:

> Ah, how you women can insinuate
> And clear a trespass with your sweet-set tongue!
> I will forget this quarrel, gentle Alice,
> Provided I'll be tempted so no more.   (8.145–8)

They kiss and make up, then return to the matter on which their relationship is based, the murder of Arden:

> MOSBY: Well, were his date complete and expired!
> ALICE: Ah, would it were! Then comes my happy hour.
> Till then my bliss is mixed with bitter gall.

This has been the first meeting of these conspirators for several scenes, and some dramatists might have shown them recapitulating what has gone wrong and how to put it right. But Kyd took on a far more difficult task, to reveal Mosby's inmost thoughts, his contempt for all

---

19. Wine quotes a contemporary proverb: 'A woman's weapon is her tongue'.

the other conspirators and his plans to 'make away' with them, once they've helped hm achieve his goal, 'And then am I sole ruler of mine own'. That is a shocking revelation but far worse is his plan to give Alice the same treatment, to be heaved up awhile and then smothered to have her wax. Kyd makes great use of the resources of drama, the direct presentation of Mosby's intended use and destruction of Alice, so clearly exposed for playgoers and readers, immediately followed by her confrontation with a man who remains completely opaque to her. She is an instrument to be played on. Mosby feigns anger and righteous indignation, monitors Alice's upset as he calculatedly withdraws his (simulated) love, until he can gradually open a path of reconciliation by which she can happily revert to her previous dependence. This is a further development of Kyd's intrigue plot, intuited by Alice early on, by which one of the agents hunting a victim is marked down to be herself a future victim. For playgoers and readers Alice remains fatally ignorant of the precarious reality surrounding her.

Comedy into Tragedy

We left the progress of the action when Mosby, having failed and been wounded in an ill-conceived attempt to involve Arden in a street fight, offered a new 'complot' to the hired assassins. He will 'fetch Master Arden home' so that 'we, like friends, | Will play a game or two at tables [backgammon] here' (14.90–91). Alice, as ever, wants to get to the point: 'But what of all this? How shall he be slain?' Mosby plans to lock Black Will and Shakebag in the 'countinghouse' (a private chamber used as a business office) until a given signal, when they will 'rush forth' and kill Arden (93–101). Mosby and Greene go off to fetch Arden, leaving Alice alone with Black Will. She exercises her feminine charm on him to secure his help: 'Come, Black Will, that in mine eyes art fair; | Next unto Mosby do I honour thee' (104–5), offering him a fee of £20 up front and a further £40 'when he is dead' (huge sums of money), together with horses for their escape. Black Will explains how they will kill Arden 'bravely':

Place Mosby, being a stranger, in a chair,
And let your husband sit upon a stool,
That I may come behind him cunningly
And with a towel pull him to the ground,
Then stab him till his flesh be as a sieve.   (109–10)

Confronted with this vicious plan Alice exclaims 'A fine device!' She even offers her help, but Shakebag's conventional notion that women are 'too faint-hearted' makes him stick to the notion of murder as an exclusively male activity:

Here would I stay and still encourage you,
But that I know how resolute you are.
SHAKEBAG: Tush! You are too faint-hearted; we must do it.
ALICE: But Mosby will be there, whose very looks
Will add unwonted courage to my thought
And make me the first that shall adventure on him.
WILL: Tush, get you gone! 'Tis we must do the deed.
When this door opens next, look for his death.   (14.126–33)

The two assassins go into their hiding-place, leaving Alice alone onstage, waiting for Mosby to return.

Kyd has deliberately isolated her so that she he can reveal her current thoughts and feelings, impatient as ever to have her desires realized:

Ah, would he now were here, that it might open!
I shall no more be closed in Arden's arms,
That like the snakes of black Tisiphone
Sting me with their embracings. Mosby's arms
Shall compass me . . .   (14.134–8)

Kyd gives her two relevant classical allusions, first to Tisiphone, one of the three Erinyes (Furies), the Avenger of Murder. As Pierre Grimal recorded in his extensive handbook, 'there is no specific legend surrounding her, apart from the obscure episode which portrays her as in love with the young Cithaeron', according to which 'he spurned her love and she turned one of the locks of her hair into a snake, which bit him', causing his death.[20] Editors have suggested that the allusion is 'ironic', given Tisiphone's role as avenger of homicide.[21] I would argue, however, that Kyd chose this allusion for the idea of Arden's loathsome embraces. Otherwise. Kyd's presentation of Alice here is positive. She expresses the wish that, 'were I made a star, | I would have none other spheres but those', bounded by Mosby's arms, a conceit not too far from Donne's love poetry. Certainly, few dramatists would give such a wished apotheosis to an evil or unsympathetic character. Nor would they allow her this rapturous conclusion:

> There is no nectar but in Mosby's lips!
> Had chaste Diana kissed him, she like me
> Would grow lovesick and from her wat'ry bower
> Fling down Endymion and snatch him up.
> Then blame not me that slay a silly man,
> Not half so lovely as Endymion.   (134–45)

We now know that Kyd had a special relationship with Lyly's *Endymion*, which may give that allusion special relevance.[22] Although Kyd portrays Alice positively, at her own valuation, he focusses the problem for theatregoers and readers with her direct address (unusual in Elizabethan drama): 'blame not me that slay a silly [foolish; defenceless] man'. Mosby may be 'so lovely' in her own eyes, but a mythological allusion doesn't give her the right to murder Arden.

That was the last sympathetic view of Alice for some time, as she now takes her place with this crew of cowardly murderers. Michael fetches some wine, while Arden and Mosby begin their game of backgammon. When Will and Shakebag come out from the counting house there is a moment of black comedy as they see a problem not foreseen in their 'fine device':

---

20. Pierre Grimal, *The Dictionary of Classical Mythology*, tr. A.R. Maxwell-Hyslop (Oxford, 1996), pp. 105, 456–7.

21. Wine (ed.), *Tragedy of Master Arden of Faversham*, p. 118; Richardson (ed.), *Arden of Faversham*, p. 259.

22. See Darren Freebury-Jones, 'Exploring Verbal Relations between *Arden of Faversham* and John Lyly's *Endymion*', *Renaissance and Reformation* 41 (2018): 93–108.

258 CHAPTER 7

WILL: [*aside to Alice*] Can he not take him yet? What a spite is that!
ALICE: [*aside to Will*] Not yet, Will. Take heed he see thee not.
WILL: [*aside to Alice*] I fear he will spy me as I am coming.
MICHAEL: [*aside to Will*] To prevent that, creep betwixt my
    legs. (14.120–23)

At this climax of the often-attempted murder Kyd might be daring the audience to laugh at the sight of bulky Black Will creeping through the legs of the young servant Michael. If so, it will be only momentary, for Mosby gives the cue, a phrase normally used in board games, 'I can take you':

MOSBY: [*to Arden*] One ace, or else I lose the game.
    [*He throws the dice.*]
ARDEN: Marry, sir, there's two for failing.
MOSBY: Ah, Master Arden, 'Now I can take you.'
    Then Will pulls him down with a towel.
ARDEN: Mosby! Michael! Alice! What will you do?
WILL: Nothing but take you up, sir, nothing else.
    [*Mosby stabs Arden.*]
MOSBY: There's for the pressing-iron you told me of.[23]
    [*Shakebag stabs Arden.*]
SHAKEBAG: And there's for the ten pound in my sleeve.[24]
ALICE: [*to Arden*] What, groans thou? [*To Mosby*] Nay, then, give
    me the weapon.
[*To Arden*] Take this for hind'ring Mosby's love and mine.
    [*Alice stabs Arden and he dies.*]
MICHAEL: O mistress! (14. 221–31)

Alice finally gets her wish, becoming if not 'the first' to venture on Arden, then not far behind. Although we have long been aware of Alice's

---

23. Alluding to an earlier confrontation, in which Arden had removed Mosby's sword, claiming that, as an artisan (a tailor), he had no right to wear it and should rather carry 'your bodkin, | Your Spanish needle, and your pressing Iron' (1.310–13). In the source Mosby strikes Arden with the iron, which would be a risky weapon to use on stage.

24. This is the advance payment that Alice has given him.

hatred for her husband, it still comes as a shock to see her giving him the death blow, having found signs of life ('What, groans thou?'). Arden's pathetic exclamation, as he recognizes the three people most indebted to him as responsible for his murder—'Mosby! Michael! Alice! What will you do?'—is echoed by Michael's shocked, or incredulous words, 'O, mistress!' As a servant he would have been almost part of the family, and to see Alice killing her husband touches him more than anyone else present.[25] In having her revenge on the man who has hindered 'Mosby's love and mine', Alice Arden declares her identity with Bel-imperia, who stabs the man who killed her lover, and with Perseda, who stabs the woman who betrayed her husband to his death. Alice's urgent demand, 'Nay, then give me the weapon!', echoes Perseda's 'give me the dagger then' (5.3.49). She shares their readiness to usurp a man's place by killing the guilty party—except that Arden is not guilty of anything other than being her husband, superfluous to her lover. For that reason, she is the only one of Kyd's murderous women to be punished for a crime, suffering the dreadful death reserved for witches, to be burnt alive.

Our attitude to Alice fluctuates between sharing her romantic vision of her love for Mosby and being aware of the reality she ignores: the immediate one of Mosby manipulating and grooming her for the role of victim, and a larger and more threatening reality, the claims of law and order. Kyd received from Holinshed a concise account of the speedy process by which Arden's murder was discovered and the wrongdoers identified. His task as dramatist was to imagine how each of the characters will react to their guilt.

The person most deeply affected is Alice. Only a few moments after the euphoria of killing Arden she feels guilt, as she and Susan fail to erase the blood on the floor:

---

25. In an earlier scene, when Black Will had frightened Michael into agreeing to betray his master, Kyd gave him a remorseful soliloquy: 'Ah, harmless Arden, how, how hast thou misdone, | That thus thy gentle life is levelled at? | The many good turns that thou hast done to me | Now must I quittance with betraying thee' (3.187–90). On the night when the murder should have taken place, Michael's conscience troubled him again: 'My master's kindness pleads to me for life | With just demand, and I must grant it him' (4.62–3).

SUSAN: The blood cleaveth to the ground and will not out.
ALICE: But with my nails I'll scrape away the blood.
   [*She scratches at the floor.*]
The more I strive, the more the blood appears!
SUSAN: What's the reason, mistress, can you tell?
ALICE: Because I blush not at my husband's death.   (247–51)

According to a Latin saying well known in the Renaissance, '*Rubor est virtutis color*' (A blush is the sign of virtue): Alice is observing her own reactions—or lack of them. When Mosby appears and asks, 'Is all well?' she replies: 'Ay, well, if Arden were alive again! | In vain we strive, for here his blood remains'. When she blames him: ''Twas thou that made me murder him', he advises her to 'keep it close':

Ah, but I cannot. Was he not slain by me?
My husband's death torments me at the heart.

When Franklin arrives, looking for Arden, she pretends that he is out late, but her disturbed mood arouses suspicion. Once he and the others have gone, she asks Susan to stay and counsel her, for 'Here is nought but fear'. But Susan can't help, since 'Fear frights away my wits'. Their fearful mood changes, following this stage direction:

Then they open the counting house door and look upon Arden.
ALICE: See, Susan, where thy quondam master lies;
Sweet Arden, smeared in blood and filthy gore.
SUSAN: My brother, you, and I, shall rue this deed.
ALICE: Come, Susan, help to lift his body forth,
And let our salt tears be his obsequies.

A few minutes ago, in acting time, Alice was releasing all her pent-up anger as she gave him his death blow. Now he is 'Sweet Arden, smeared in blood and filthy gore', an object of pity to be washed with salt tears. Just after his death Alice could not blush, but now her emotional reactions are functioning normally, her grief is genuine, and that in some way redeems her in our eyes.

But the whole structure of hurried deception soon collapses. Mosby and others carry Arden's corpse and deposit it behind the Abbey, but they leave clues at every step. Franklin finds the corpse, together with a bloody hand towel and a knife that Michael had dropped in his confusion. Franklin had found in Arden's slipper some rushes from the house floor, and the Mayor finds blood in the room near where Arden used to sit. The single undeniable witness is the snow that has been falling, now showing 'the print of many feet'. Alice and her 'complices' are detained for questioning, the scene ending with her declaration:

> Ah, Master Franklin, God and heaven can tell
> I loved him more than all the world beside.   (400–401)

We know that this is true, although it may not sound convincing in this context of a murder hunt. But Kyd has prepared a final speech for Alice that shows her true nature. Invited by the Mayor to 'Confess this foul fault and be penitent', instead of doing so Alice leans over the corpse and speaks to her husband for the last time: 'Arden, sweet husband, what shall I say?' Kyd increases her sense of guilt by drawing on 'the popular superstition that the corpse of a murdered man bled in the presence of his assassin',[26] which she takes as a direct reproach from him:

> The more I sound his name, the more he bleeds.
> This blood condemns me and in gushing forth
> Speaks as it falls and asks me why I did it.
> Forgive me, Arden; I repent me now,
> And, would my death save thine, thou shouldst not die.
> Rise up, sweet Arden, and enjoy thy love,
> And frown not on me when we meet in heaven:
> In heaven I love thee, though on earth I did not.   (16.3–11)

Her injunction that he should 'Rise up' seems to prefigure the Resurrection, when 'the dead will be raised imperishable, and we will be

---

26. Wine (ed.), *Tragedy of Master Arden of Faversham*, p. 135; Richardson (ed.), *Arden of Faversham*, p. 281.

changed' (1 Cor. 15:52). M.L. Wine perceptively commented on Alice's *I love* that 'the present tense, odd though it may sound here to the modern ear, effectively conveys the impression that Alice is assured, in her own mind at least, of the results of her repentance'.[27]

A few minutes later (in theatrical time), in the play's final scene, we see Alice detaching herself from her immediate surroundings:

> Leave now to trouble me with worldly things,
> And let me meditate upon my saviour Christ,
> Whose blood must save me for the blood I shed.   (18.9–11)

Her beliefs are based on many places in the New Testament recording Christ's teaching, such as 'This is my blood of the covenant, which is poured out for many for the forgiveness of sins'.[28] Kyd has tellingly followed Alice's words with Mosby's reaction to his present situation:

> How long shall I live in this hell of grief?
> Convey me from the presence of that strumpet.   (18.12–13)

Kyd allows her a dignified reply:

> Ah, but for thee I had never been strumpet.
> What cannot oaths and protestations do
> When men have opportunity to woo?
> I was too young to sound thy villainies,
> But now I find it and repent too late.   (18.14–18)

---

27. Wine, p. 135. Catherine Richardson comments: 'Alice inexplicably thinks she'll meet [Arden] despite committing his murder' (ed. cit., p. 281). There is nothing inexplicable here. It has been a foundational Christian belief that a sinner who repents in good faith will be forgiven. There are many biblical texts describing Christ's teaching of 'repentance for the forgiveness of sin' (e.g., Luke 24:47). Cf. also Acts, 3.19: 'Repent, then, and turn to God, so that your sins may be wiped out, that times of refreshing may come from the Lord', and 2 Cor. 7:10: 'Godly sorrow brings repentance that leads to salvation and leaves no regret, but worldly sorrow brings death'.

28. Matt. 26:28. Cf. also Heb. 9:14: 'How much more, then, will the blood of Christ . . . cleanse our consciences from acts that lead to death'; Eph. 1:7: 'In him we have redemption through his blood, the forgiveness of sins, in accordance with the riches of God's grace', etc.

Alice retains her new-found composure, and what Wine has called her assurance 'of the results of her repentance' when she hears the dreadful sentence that, for the crime of petty treason, 'Alice must be burnt' alive at the stake (18.31), 'the punishment for wives who murdered their husbands'.[29] Unperturbed, Alice wishes:

Let my death make amends for all my sins.

Kyd's juxtaposition of Alice and Mosby in these final scenes leaves no doubt that, whatever her sensual passion for Mosby, her feelings for Arden were true love. As for Mosby, the man who had aroused and exploited her feelings in the hope of getting her money after he has killed her, the man who had declared that love was meaningless 'without true constancy', Kyd gives him these last words:

Fie upon women!—this shall be my song.
But bear me hence, for I have lived too long.

Civic justice apportions death for the main offenders by hanging,[30] but catches others who do not deserve capital punishment, such as Bradshaw, who merely delivered a letter. In *Arden* Bradshaw is in fact innocent, having only delivered a letter, unaware of its contents (18.2–7) yet he suffers the same punishment.[31] So too does Susan, who was never an accomplice to the killing. Kyd lets her and Michael speak once more:

SUSAN: Seeing no hope on earth, in heaven is my hope.
MICHAEL: Faith, I care not, seeing I die with Susan.   (36–7)

That simple affirmation of love is somehow moving. Despite his failings and his many errors, Michael had seeds of goodness.

---

29. Richardson (ed.), *Arden of Faversham*, p. 285.

30. The Epilogue, spoken by Franklin, reports on those who tried to get away: Shakebag 'was murdered in Southwark', 'Black Will was burnt in Flushing on a stage' [scaffold], 'Greene was hanged at Osbridge . . . The painter fled, and how he died we know not'.

31. Holinshed added a marginal gloss: 'Bradshaw as unjustlie accused, as his simplicitie was shamefully abused', explaining that there had been a 'misunderstanding of the words contained in the letter' (Wine (ed.), *Tragedy of Master Arden of Faversham*, p. 158).

A Note on the Function of Snow in Narrative

Holinshed recorded that, after the murder Michael and other servants 'tooke the dead bodie, and caried it out, to laie it in a field'.[32] The search party, led by the Mayor, found Arden's corpse 'lieing there throughlie dead . . . and marking further, espied certeine footsteps, by reason of the snow'. On further search they 'perceiued footings still before them in the snow', showing where the corpse had been carried (p. 157). Wine noted that, after Holinshed's death in 1580 much of his material reached the chronicler John Stow, who helped to edit the 1587 edition of the *Chronicles*. Among Stow's papers in the British Library is a manuscript[33] (Harley MSS. 542) that gives a version almost identical with Holinshed but preserves some additional material, including this account of the snow:

> In the meane tyme there fell a great snowe in so much that they, coming agayne into the howse, thowght that the snow would have coveryd their fotyng (but sodeynly by the good providence of God, who would not suffer so detestable a murther long hydden) it stint [stopped] snowynge | they not consderynge the same, but thinkynge all had bene sure.[34]

Several centuries later, the Transcendental philosopher Ralph Waldo Emerson published an essay, 'Compensation' (1841), describing the dualism he detected everywhere in nature, which balances life instead of permitting excess to destroy. He celebrated the 'high laws' of the universe, with its 'absolute balance of Give and Take' in:

> all the action and reaction of nature. The league between virtue and nature engages all things to assume a hostile front to vice. The beautiful laws and substances of the world persecute and whip the traitor. He finds that things are arranged for truth and benefit, but there is

32. Wine (ed.), *Tragedy of Master Arden of Faversham*, p. 156.

33. Harley MSS. 542.

34. Wine (ed.), *Tragedy of Master Arden of Faversham*, pp. xlii–xliii; contractions expanded.

no den in the wide world to hide a rogue. Commit a crime, and the earth is made of glass. There is no such thing as concealment. Commit a crime, and it seems as if a coat of snow fell on the ground, such as reveals in the woods the track of every partridge and fox and squirrel and mole. You cannot recall the spoken word, you cannot wipe out the foot-track, you cannot draw up the ladder, so as to leave no inlet or clew. Always some damning circumstances transpire. The laws and substances of nature, water, snow, wind, gravitation, become penalties to the thief.[35]

Authorship Markers: Phraseology

For the first half of the twentieth century *Arden* was widely accepted as Kyd's composition. In 1903 Charles Crawford published an essay in a German journal on 'The Authorship of *Arden of Faversham*', reprinted in his collected essays a few years later.[36] In it he argued that 'the vocabulary, phrasing, and general style' of the play 'are those of Kyd, and that they cannot be mistaken for those of any other of the time' (p. 118). Crawford was a most diligent student of Elizabethan literature, with a great expertise in identifying anonymously published work. Compiler of a *Concordance to Thomas Kyd* (1908), he produced an exemplary edition of the 1600 verse anthology *Englands Parnassus* (Oxford, 1913), identifying the greater part of its anonymous excerpts. His copy of another verse anthology, *Bodenham's Belvedére* (1600), interleaved and annotated with authorship attributions for about 3,000 of its 4,500 extracts, was for many years available to researchers in the British Library and has recently been edited and updated.[37] In his 1903 essay Crawford drew attention to many passages in *Arden* matching *The*

---

35. R.W. Emerson, *Essays and English Traits,* The Harvard Classics (Cambridge, MA, 1909), pp. 8–9.

36. Charles Crawford, 'The Authorship of *Arden of Faversham*', *Jahrbuch der Deutschen Shakespeare Gesellschaft*, 39 (1903): 74–86, reprinted in Crawford, *Collectanea*, First Series (Stratford-on-Avon, 1906), pp. 101–30; quotations from the later version.

37. See Erne and Singh (eds), *Bel-Vedére*.

Spanish Tragedy (pp. 120–23), but it was in *Soliman and Perseda* that he found

> evidence of complete identity with *Arden of Faversham* as regards words, expressions, figures of speech, and general style, for these two plays must have been composed by Kyd much about the same time; and works of the same date by the same writer invariably repeat each other more often than others that are separated by longer intervals of time. (p. 123)

Crawford was accurate in his relative dating of the two plays (1589 and 1590, according to Wiggins), also in noting that authorial self-repetition is more frequent in plays written near each other. Having quoted several striking longer parallels between the two plays, Crawford felt sufficiently confident of his case to 'merely string together for comparison' other evidence, amassing in four pages over fifty instances of identical phrasing between the two plays (pp. 125–9). I select one of these to show the truth of an observation by David Lake, a pioneer in the use of this method in establishing Middleton's canon, that a phrasal match can represent 'a sequence of verbal ideas retrieved intact by the memory of an author'.[38] After the murder of Arden, Franklin comes to his house and Mosby, trying to maintain the pretence that Arden is merely not at home, proposes a toast:

> MOSBY: Mistress Arden, here's to your husband.
>   [*He offers a toast.*]
> ALICE: My husband!
> FRANKLIN: **What ails you, woman**, to cry so suddenly?
> ALICE: Ah, neighbours, **a sudden qualm** came over my heart;
> My husband's being forth torments my mind.   (14.292–6)

Since Alice has just invited Mosby to 'sit you in my husband's seat' (280), she evidently feels a sudden twinge of guilt. In Kyd's Turkish tragedy Erastus accidentally loses the carcanet (necklace) that Perseda had given him as a love token; Ferdinando finds it and gives it to his

---

38. David Lake, *The Canon of Thomas Middleton's Plays* (Cambridge, 1975), p. 147.

mistress Lucina. When Perseda visits Lucina, she is surprised to see it again:

> PERSEDA: [*Aside*] 'Still friends?' Still foes: she wears my carcanet!
> Ah, false Erastus, how am I betrayed!
> LUCINA: **What ails you, madam,** that your colour changes?
> PERSEDA: **A sudden qualm.** I therefore take my leave.
> (*SP* 2.1.48–51)

In both plays a woman experiences a sudden shock involving a man she has loved, and by whom she feels injured. A genuine and distinctive 'parallel passage' can reveal deeper structural similarities within a writer's oeuvre.

Crawford simply listed fifty-two passages instances of identical phrasing in the two plays,[39] including these matches:

> ALICE: Ah me accursed, To **link in liking** with a frantic man!
> (*AF* 4.1.104–5)
> BASILISCO: And is she **linked in liking** with my foe?   (*SP* 4.3.61)

Alice feigns anger with Arden after her plot to attack him in broad daylight fails; Basilisco is genuinely angry to know that Erastus and Perseda are friends. Both plays present murderous intrigues, with several common elements. In such plots concealment of the truth can have an evil purpose: 'conceal **the rest,** for **'tis too bad**', says Alice to Mosby (*AF* 8.62), referring to their murder plans; '**The rest** I dare not speak, **it is so bad**!' says the false witness hired to justify Erastus' execution (*SP* 5.2.50). The need for secrecy is paramount in all intrigues. Alleging that Arden beats her and uses whores, Alice says to Greene '**be it spoken in secret here**' (1.490); the perjurer who claims to have overheard Erastus saying: '**be it spoke in secret here**' (5.3.54). Significantly, both speakers have borne false witness. Conspirators are desperate to maintain their cover. In Michael's dream the terrifying figure of Black Will cries out '**Stab the** slave! | The peasant will **detect** the tragedy!' (*AF* 4.79–80). In real life, so to speak, Soliman uses the same collocation to Brusor when he has

---

39. Crawford, *Collectanea*, pp. 126–9.

finished with an accomplice: '**stab in the** Marshal, | Lest he **detect** us unto the world' (*SP* 5.3.134–5). All intriguers have a goal that they regard as their own enterprise, to be protected against rivals who might disturb their harvest. Alice shares with Mosby her resentment of Arden: 'Why should **he thrust his sickle in our corn?**' (*AF* 1.83). In an aside Brusor sees his chance to get even with Erastus:

> Ay, now occasion serves to stumble **him**
> That **thrust his sickle in my** harvest **corn!**   (*SP* 4.1.221–2)

Charles Crawford ended his 1903 essay with this observation: 'A common statement to be met with in editions of men's works is, "Nobody repeats himself so much as So-and-so." I used to think that such statements were true; but independent inquiry has shattered these old idols of the den. All men repeat themselves, both in speech and writing ...'[40]

Crawford's pioneering identification of the many links between *Arden* and Kyd's accepted canon was soon followed by the dissertation of Walther Miksch on 'The Authorship of *Arden of Faversham*'.[41] Miksch accepted Crawford's attribution but argued that matching collocations should be complemented by 'a thorough stylistic and metrical comparison' (p. 18). Limiting himself to *The Spanish Tragedy* and *Soliman and Perseda*, Miksch listed eighty close verbal parallels with *Arden*, many involving four or five consecutive words, to which he added fourteen more extended matches (pp. 19–29). In 1919 the redoubtable H. Dugdale Sykes, who made many valuable contributions to authorship attribution studies, also claimed Kyd as author of *Arden*.[42] Sykes was the first to point out several verbal matches between *Arden* and Kyd's *Cornelia* (pp. 55–8, 74–5). Sykes discussed parallels between *Arden* and Kyd's two tragedies in terms of vocabulary and linguistic usage (pp. 59–65) before considering 'parallels of phrase and sentiment' (pp. 65–72).

---

40. Ibid., p. 130. See Vickers (ed.), *Collected Works of John Ford*, vol. 2: 'Dramatists Repeat Themselves', pp. 44–75.

41. Miksch, 'Die Verfasserschaft des *Arden of Feversham*'. All translations are my own.

42. '*Arden of Faversham*' in H. Dugdale Sykes, *Sidelights on Shakespeare* (Stratford-upon-Avon, 1919), pp. 48–76. For a balanced account of Sykes's strengths and weaknesses, see W. W. Greg's review of this book in *Modern Language Review*, 20 (1925): 195–200.

Sykes did not amass as many matching collocations as Crawford and Miksch had done, choosing a more analytical approach, but that deficiency was soon put right.

The Danish scholar Paul V. Rubow displayed remarkable acuity and wider reading in his study of 'Shakespeare and his contemporaries',[43] citing no fewer than fifty matching collocations between *Arden of Faversham* and *The Spanish Tragedy* (pp. 120–33), and fifty-six matching phrases between *Arden* and *Soliman and Perseda* (pp. 134–44). Rubow also found several matches between *Arden* and *Cornelia* (pp. 112–15) and even some with Kyd's translation from Tasso, *The Housholder's Philosophie* (pp. 115–16). The fifth scholar to argue for Kyd's authorship of *Arden* was Félix Carrère, in his facing-page translation of the play.[44] Carrère discussed general resemblances in character and situation (pp. 21–46), then gave a brief comparison between the language of *Arden* and that of *The Spanish Tragedy* and *Cornelia* (pp. 46–55). Since their work is not easy to find outside major research libraries, I have reprinted on my website some of the matches they discovered between *Arden* and Kyd's acknowledged works: fifty from Crawford, eighty from Miksch, and ninety-five from Rubow.[45] Given the frequent limitations of Anglophone scholarship to works in English, the contributions of Miksch, Rubow, and Carrère remained unknown. Nonetheless, the case for Kyd's authorship of *Arden* as made by Crawford and Sykes was strong enough to convince many knowledgeable students of Elizabethan drama, including C. F. Tucker Brooke (1922), F. E. Schelling (1925), T. S. Eliot (1927), Percy Allen (1928), E. A. Gerrard (1928), H. B. Charlton and R. D. Waller (1933).[46]

Those early scholars were right: the matches between *Arden of Faversham* and the accepted Kyd canon are extensive, as confirmed by

43. Rubow, *Shakespeare og hans samtidige*. I gratefully acknowledge the help of Dr Lene Petersen, University of Odense, in providing and translation of passages from Rubow's linking text. Fortunately, the extensive quotations are in English.

44. Félix Carrère, *Arden de Faversham. Etude critique, traduction et notes* (Paris, 1950).

45. See https://brianvickers.uk/databases.

46. See Jill Levenson's survey of authorship attributions for *Arden* in Logan and Smith (eds), *The Predecessors of Shakespeare*, pp. 241–5.

modern data processing. In my research I have noted over 100 matches with *The Spanish Tragedy,* over 130 matches with *Soliman and Perseda,* over forty matches with *Cornelia,* and six with *The Householder's Philosophy.* For the Quarrel scene I have documented over seventy matches with Kyd.[47] In his forthcoming 'Authorship Commentary' on *Arden* Darren Freebury-Jones, using different criteria, notes twenty-eight Kyd matches for this scene and 218 in all.[48] In sharp contrast, despite having access to the vast *LION* database[49], Jackson found only eight matches with the Quarrel scene, several of which had been pointed out by Kyd scholars over a century ago. Jackson limited the Kyd canon to two plays. For *The Spanish Tragedy* his method identified the parallel, first cited by Miksch in 1907, between the complaints of Mosby and Hieronimo:

> And **nips me** as the bitter northeast wind
> Doth check **the** tender **blossoms** in the spring   (*AF* 8.5–6)
> But in the harvest of my summer joys
> Death's winter **nipped the blossoms** of **my** bliss.   (*Sp. T.* 1.1.12–13)

The *LION* search function picked out this match, but Jackson dismissed it, together with one with *King Leir* that also collocates '"blossoms" and the verb "nip"', on the grounds that they 'relate specifically to "winter" cold' (p. 277). I shall comment on Jackson's rejection of these legitimate matches in chapter 8. The *LION* search function identified another match with Kyd's *Spanish Tragedy* first noted by Miksch, which Jackson accepts, the unique collocation:

> And **thereon** will I **chiefly meditate**   (*AF* 8.12)
> But **whereon** dost thou **chiefly meditate**?   (*Sp. T.* 2.2.25)

47. See Brian Vickers, 'Is *EEBO-TCP/LION* Suitable for Attribution Studies?', *Early Modern Literary Studies,* 22:1 (2019), 1–34. In a recent essay Jackson refers dismissively to this list, while citing only one example.

48. See his edition and commentary in Vickers (ed.), *The Collected Works of Thomas Kyd,* vol. 2.

49. The *LION* database, or *Literature Online,* published by Chadwyck-Healey (now Prospect), collects all the texts in drama and poetry excerpted from the complete collection, *Early English Books Online* (*EEBO*).

Jackson accepted two other matches identified by *LION*:

I'll none of that   (*AF* 8.34)
I'll none of that   (*Sp. T.* 4.6.19)
Why speaks thou not? What silence ties thy tongue?   (*AF* 8.24)
Why speakst thou not? | What lesser liberty   (*Sp. T.* 5.4.181–2)

Jackson's search of *LION* also yielded four collocation matches with *Soliman and Perseda*. Two of these were first noted by Charles Crawford in 1903, one containing this unique collocation:

conceal **the rest,** for '**tis** too **bad**   (*AF* 8.62)
The rest I dare not speak, **it is** so **bad.**   (*SP* 5.2.50)

Crawford also noted a striking parallel between two lovers' quarrels. In the first Mosby unjustly accuses Alice of exploiting an ability

To **forge** distressful **looks to wound** a breast   (*AF* 8.57)

In the second Perseda accuses Erastus of the same skill:

Ah, how thine eyes can **forge** alluring **looks**
And feign deep oaths **to wound** poor silly maids.   (*SP* 2.1.114–15)

The two passages could hardly be closer, the earlier being more expansive but setting up a syntactical structure that the later exactly repeats. However, Jackson also dismissed this unique collocation match, for reasons that I shall discuss in chapter 8. The *LION* search function identified two further matches between *Arden of Faversham* and Kyd's Turkish tragedy, one short:

sit in Arden's **seat**   (*AF* 8.31)
sit in friendship's **seat**   (*SP* 4.1.182)

one long:

a cannon's burst | **Discharged** against a ruinated wall.   (*AF* 8.51–2)
Hath planted **a** double **cannon** in the door |
Ready to **discharge** it upon you   (*SP* 2.2.51–2)

Despite the vehemence with which Jackson has denied Kyd any involvement with *Arden of Faversham*,[50] in his latest work, with proper scholarly detachment, he has cited evidence against himself—and as we now know, a great deal more conclusive evidence exists. To quote Horace's pithy formulation, '*Naturam expelles furca, tamen usque recurret*': 'You may drive out Nature with a pitchfork, yet she will ever hurry back'.[51]

That list of the few Kyd matches with scene 8 of *Arden* that Jackson recognized consisted of excerpts. I shall end this discussion of the phrasal evidence for Kyd's authorship of *Arden* by reconstructing the dramatic context for some additional matches. In *Soliman and Perseda* the heroine, having seen the love token that she gave her lover Erastus being worn by another woman (he had lost it), experiences a sudden shock, as a bystander observes:

—**What ails you**, madam, that your colour changes?
—**A sudden qualm.** I therefore take my leave.   (*SP* 2.1.50–51)

Perseda's shock is genuine, but after Arden's murder Alice knows how to fake wifely concern when asked the same question:

—**What ails you,** woman, to cry so suddenly?
—Ah, neighbours, **a sudden qualm** came over my
heart;
My husband's being forth torments my mind.   (14.294–7)

The two plays share longer phrasal sequences. In *Soliman and Perseda* Piston describes to Perseda the circumstances in which his master had killed Ferdinando. Erastus had managed to win back Perseda's chain from Lucina in a game of dice and was wearing the chain around his neck when they encountered Ferdinando, Lucina's lover:

Then Ferdinando **met** us **on the way**, and **reviled** my master,
saying

50. See the essays cited in chapter 8, note 5.

51. Horace, *Epistles*, 1.10.24, in *Satires, Epistles and Ars Poetica*, ed. and tr. H. Rushton Fairclough, Loeb Classical Library (Cambridge, MA, and London, 1929), pp. 316–17.

he stole the chain; with that they **drew**, and there Ferdinando
had the prickado.[52]   (*SP* 2.3.17–19)

After Piston had left, Perseda regrets her excessive anger and suspicion at the loss of the necklace:

My heart had armed my tongue with **injury**,
To wrong my **friend, whose thoughts were** ever true.   (27–8)

In *Arden of Faversham* Kyd repeated this situation of two men meeting in public and fighting with swords. After her plan to harm Arden in this way has failed, Alice tries to convince her husband that the brawl was due to his having misunderstood their pretended jest:

When we, to welcome thee, intended sport,
Came lovingly to **meet** thee **on thy way**,
Thou **drew'st** thy sword, enraged with jealousy,
And hurt thy **friend whose thoughts were** free from
   harm   (*AF* 13.90–4)

The two sequences have in common the phrases 'meet on the way', 'drew(st) a sword', the matching verbs 'wrong' and 'harm', prefacing the tetragram (a four-word phrase) 'friend whose thoughts were', and the synonymous adjectival phrases 'ever true', 'free from harm'. Such co-occurrences far exceed the likelihood of having come about through chance or imitation. They are taken from the same authorial lexicon. A few lines later Alice claims that it was Arden who started the brawl,

after he had **reviled** him [Mosby]
By the **injurious** name of perjured beast.   (13.139–40)

Her speech supplies the two terms Kyd has used in his Turkish tragedy that were lacking here: 'reviled' and 'injury'.

In both plays Kyd uses a traditional image for a defenceless victim. When Soliman decided to have Erastus killed, he sent Brusor to bring

---

52. In his edition of *Soliman and Perseda*, Matthew Dimmock glosses: 'prickado [sword-stab]. Another [Kyd] coinage and sole usage, according to the OED', in Vickers (ed.), *The Collected Works of Thomas Kyd*.

him back from Cyprus. Perseda realizes that her supposed friend Lucina had been his accomplice:

> Lucina, came thy husband to this end,
> To **lead** a **lamb unto the slaughterhouse**?   (*SP* 5.3.40–41)

In a soliloquy Michael, Arden's servant, having been dragged into the hired murderers' plot to kill his master, compares him to 'the **lamb**' who feeds 'securely on the down', unaware that the hungry wolf is lurking nearby (*AF* 3.183–5). Suddenly he realizes that he himself is now an accomplice in his master's destruction, and

> Do **lead** thee with a wicked, fraudful smile,
> As unsuspected, **to the slaughterhouse**.   (193–4)

The quantity and quality of verbal matches between *Soliman and Perseda* and *Arden of Faversham* (another hundred could be cited) well justifies the claim made by Charles Crawford in his 1903 pioneering essay that Kyd's authorship of the latter could be settled from this play alone.

The Spanish Tragedy may contain slightly fewer matches, but they include several striking parallels, none closer than the two night-scenes. As Horatio is being strangled, Bel-imperia's cries of 'Murder, murder, help Hieronimo help!' (2.4.62) bring Hieronimo on to the stage, 'in his shirt', as the stage direction records, with this famous exclamation:

> What outcries pluck **me from my** naked bed,
> And chill my throbbing heart with trembling fear   (*Sp. T.* 5.1–2)

In the final scene of the tragedy, having exacted his revenge, Hieronimo looks back to that horrible event, when Lorenzo and his accomplices mercilessly

> Butcher'd up my boy,
> In black, dark night, to pale, dim, cruel death.
> He shrieks, I heard—and yet, methinks, I hear—
> His **dismal outcry** echo in the air.   (*Sp. T.* 4.4.18–21)

Hieronimo's switch to the present tense shows how vivid those memories still are. Kyd recalled this scene in *Arden of Faversham* when Arden's servant Michael has '**a fearful** dream', in which he imagines the hired murderers hunting him down after the murder: 'And pitiless Black Will cries, "Stab the slave!"' (*AF* 4.78–80). Michael cries out in his sleep, rousing the two sleepers, who echo Hieronimo's words:

> FRANKLIN What **dismal outcry** calls **me from my** rest?
> ARDEN What hath occasioned such a **fearful** cry?   (87–8)

Kyd echoed the murder scene from *The Spanish Tragedy* at another point in *Arden*. Hieronimo exclaims over his son's corpse:

> O poor Horatio, **what hadst thou misdone,**
> To leese **thy life,** ere life was new begun?   (*Sp. T.* 2.5.30–1)

Michael expresses the same pity and regret as he realizes that the hired assassins have made him their accomplice in his master's murder:

> Ah, harmless Arden, how, how **hast thou misdone,**
> That thus **thy** gentle **life** is levelled at?   (*AF* 3.187–8)

The aftermath of murder takes the same course in both plays. Hieronimo urges Pedringano, about to be hanged, to '**Confess** thy folly, **and** <u>repent</u> thy **fault**' (*Sp. T.* 3.6.28). The Mayor confronts Alice Arden with her husband's corpse and urges her to '**Confess** this foul **fault** and be <u>penitent</u>' (*AF* 16.2). Pedringano, gulled into believing that he will be pardoned, had admitted Serberine's murder, so Hieronimo orders his execution:

> Despatch: the faults approved and confessed,
> **And by** our **law** he is **condemned to die.**   (*Sp. T.* 3.6.42–3)

Pedringano deserves his fate, but in *Arden* Bradshaw is in fact innocent, having only delivered a letter, unaware of its contents, yet he suffers the same punishment:[53]

> **And** I am **by** the **law condemned to die.**   (*AF* 18.3)

---

53. Holinshed added a marginal gloss: '*Bradshaw as unjustlie accused, as his simplicitie was shamefully abused*', explaining that there had been a 'misunderstanding of the words contained in the letter' (Wine (ed.), *Tragedy of Master Arden of Faversham*, p. 158).

In *The Spanish Tragedy*, Alexandro, unjustly accused, abandons hope of better fortune:

> 'Tis **heaven is my hope**:
> As for the **earth**, it is too much infect
> To yield me **hope** of any of her mould.   (*Sp. T.* 3.1.39–41)

In *Arden* Susan expresses the same sentiment:

> Seeing no **hope** on **earth**, in **heaven is my hope**.   (*AF* 18.36)

These extended matches, stretching to six identical words and corresponding prosodic placing, go far beyond the usual explanations, imitation, or influence, and point to the same authorial memory drawing on its lexicon of phraseology.[54]

Authorship Markers: Prosody

In his classic study of feminine endings Philip Timberlake accepted the 'highly probable' case for Kyd's authorship of *Arden* made by Crawford and Sykes. He observed that 'Kyd varied surprisingly in his practice', noting the varying rates, from 1.2 percent in *The Spanish Tragedy* to 9.5 percent in *Cornelia* and 10.2 percent in *Soliman and Perseda*. Timberlake computed that *Arden of Faversham* averages 6.2 percent feminine endings, without enquiring into the possible causes of this lower figure. Those who read the play will understand that this smaller proportion was caused largely by the middle-class and low-life milieu, with more prose speakers than in any of his other plays. In addition, Kyd showed himself aware that he had created a new aesthetic for bourgeois tragedy. In the Epilogue Franklin apologizes:

> Gentlemen, we hope you'll pardon this naked tragedy
> Wherein no filèd points are foisted in
> To make it gracious to the ear or eye;

---

54. For further examples of Kyd's self-repetition in *Arden*, see Darren Freebury-Jones, '"A raven for a dove": Kyd, Shakespeare, and the Authorship of *Arden of Faversham*'s Quarrel Scene', *Archiv fur das Studium der neueren Sprachen und Literatur*, 253 (2016): 39–64.

For simple truth is gracious enough
And needs no other points of glozing stuff.

The stylistic contrast with the tragedies of Marlowe and Peele is analogous to that between Georg Büchner's prose tragedy *Woyzeck* (1836) and the verse plays of Schiller.[55]

For other Kyd plays I have been able to cite the prosodic analyses of Marina Tarlinskaja, who attributed *King Leir* and *Fair Em* to him. Unfortunately, having previously attributed the whole of *Arden* to Kyd she recently changed her mind, having been persuaded by Arthur Kinney to give scenes 4–8 to Shakespeare.[56] Her main evidence consists of variations in the stress profile on the 'strong' syllables, where the emphasis usually falls in an iambic pentameter, that is, positions 2, 4, 6, 8, and 10. She divides the play into three sections: scenes 1–3, 4–8, and 9–18, consisting of roughly 800, 400, and 800 lines. Tarlinskaja claims that the middle section, which Jackson attributes to Shakespeare, 'contains a substantial "dip" on syllable 6', namely, from 90.9 percent on 4 down to 71.8. This is so, but portion 1 also dips, from 86.6 percent down to 75.7, as does portion 3, from 87.4 percent to 78.7. There might be local reasons for the variations, such as the roles of individual characters, or the emotional climate in different scenes, or they might just be due to random variation. This data alone is inadequate evidence of a change of authorship. Tarlinskaja says that her earlier analysis 'made me vacillate about the attribution of Scene 8', indicating 'equal stressing on positions 6 and 8'; thus, her earlier results 'illustrate the dangers of average numbers' (p. 109). In my judgment, her revised results further illustrate these dangers.

Darren Freebury-Jones has also criticized Tarlinskaja's revised verdict.[57] He questions her claim that the 'stress profile' of Scene 8, with its

---

55. See, e.g., Maurice B. Benn, *The Drama of Revolt. A Critical Study of Georg Büchner* (Cambridge, 1976).

56. See Tarlinskaja, *Shakespeare and the Versification of English Drama*, pp. 105–111, and her Appendix B, unnumbered pages from 286 to 377. According to my manual through-numbering, the relevant data for stress on strong syllabic positions in *Arden* are in Table B.1, pp. 291–3.

57. See Darren Freebury-Jones, 'In Defence of Kyd: Evaluating the Claim for Shakespeare's Part Authorship of *Arden of Faversham*', *Authorship* 7/2 (2018), 1–14. DOI: https://doi.org/10 .21825/aj.v7i2.9736.

'deep "dip" on syllable 6', points to Shakespeare, given that earlier in the monograph she judged that Kyd had 'consolidated the stress "dip" on position 6' in Elizabethan drama (p. 67). Moreover, she states that 'Scenes 4–8 contain a substantial "dip" on syllable 6', which 'could indicate a typical early Elizabethan text', or '*early Shakespeare, and Kyd*' (p. 109, my italics). The dip on position six in these scenes therefore provides no evidence for giving them to Shakespeare or removing them from Kyd. Freebury-Jones notes that 'Tarlinskaja's figure of 71.8 percent for position 6 in *Arden* scenes 4–8, accords with' *The Spanish Tragedy* (69.2), *Soliman and Perseda* (68.6), *Fair Em* (70.6) and *Cornelia* 70.4 (minus the Chorus). (As we know, many attribution studies have shown that figures for whole plays are more reliable than those for scenes of a few hundred lines.) Freebury-Jones also notes that Tarlinskaja attributes *Arden* to Shakespeare on the basis that 'Run-on lines prevail' in Scenes 4 to 8 (p. 110). But reference to her Table B.4 shows that she records an average of 10.8 run-on lines in these scenes, compared to 11.7 for *Fair Em* and 13.6 for *Cornelia* (both figures for whole plays).[58] As Freebury-Jones reasonably enquires: 'how does the figure of 10.8, which is in fact lower than Kyd's undoubted play, *Cornelia*, suggest Shakespeare's authorship rather than Kyd's? In my view, Tarlinskaja's data cannot be justifiably interpreted as lending support to Jackson's argument'. This seems to be a case where a scholar's first judgment was better than her revision.

58. Manual pagination: pp. 325–6.

8

Denying Kyd

To kill an error is as good a service as, and sometimes even better than, the establishing a new truth or fact.[1]

— *CHARLES DARWIN*

ONE OF THE INSPIRING COMPONENTS OF Francis Bacon's programme for the renewal of the sciences was his belief that knowledge is always in growth. The motto he quoted on the title page of *De Augmentis Scientiarum*— 'On the Advancement of the Sciences'—came from the Old Testament: 'Multi pertransibunt et augebitur Scientia'—'Many shall run to and fro and knowledge will be increased' (Daniel 12:4). Bacon was an optimist who saw the infinite potential of discovery; a more cautious philosopher might have formulated it differently: 'knowledge is always potentially in growth'. The history of science is full of wrong turnings. For over a century chemists believed in the existence of a substance called 'phlogiston' which was released when metals were burned. Antoine Lavoisier disproved this theory in the 1770s, showing that combustion requires a gas that has weight (specifically, oxygen) and could be measured by means of weighing closed vessels. In the late 1980s

---

1. Darwin to A. S. Wilson, 5 March 1879. See Francis Darwin and A. C. Seward (eds), *More Letters of Charles Darwin*, 2 vols (London, 1903) 2.422; and F. Burkhardt et al. (eds), *The Correspondence of Charles Darwin*, vol. 27, 1879 (Cambridge, 2019), p. 99.

280   CHAPTER 8

two electrochemists claimed that 'cold nuclear fusion' (nuclear reaction at room temperature) was possible. Their theory lasted less than a year, as scientists discovered flaws in the design of their experiments, and it emerged that the two claimants had not actually detected nuclear reaction byproducts.

Such wrong turns are common in the humanities, as anyone will know who lived through the vogue of deconstruction in the 1970s. Although of much lesser significance than either of the examples so far mentioned, a similar deviation from the progress of knowledge occurred in our time concerning the authorship of *Arden of Faversham*. In 1963 MacDonald Jackson claimed that Shakespeare had written scene 8, the quarrel between Mosby and Alice, an opinion that he still maintains sixty years later. That oddball judgment has not been characteristic of Jackson's subsequent career, one of searching scholarship in textual criticism, bibliography, and attribution studies. His book, *Studies in Attribution: Middleton and Shakespeare* (1979), together with David Lake's *The Canon of Thomas Middleton's Plays* (1976), transformed Middleton studies and showed how the study of a dramatist's minute linguistic practices could produce reliable authorial markers. His more recent book, *Defining Shakespeare: Pericles as Test Case* (2003), is a definitive study of a co-authored play, and his numerous journal articles have made him a much respected scholar.[2] His high standing in academia, however, has meant that his persistence in attributing a portion of *Arden* to Shakespeare—a portion that has grown over the years—has been unchallenged until recently. Moreover, his reputation has been one reason why the editors of *The New Oxford Shakespeare* (2016) included *Arden of Faversham* among his 'genuine' works. This was a disaster for Shakespeare textual criticism, for attribution studies, and for scholarship in

---

2. See Brian Boyd's Bibliography of his writings in Boyd (ed.), *Words that Count. Essays on Early Modern Authorship in Honor of MacDonald P. Jackson* (Cranbury, NJ, 2004), pp. 274–80. To add some personal testimony, I was pleased to be invited to contribute to that Festschrift, an essay on Peele's authorship of *The Troublesome Reign of King John* (pp. 78–116). Jackson was one of the scholars to whom I dedicated *Shakespeare, Co-Author. A Historical Study of Five Collaborative Plays* (Oxford, 2002), which included several appreciative comments on his scholarship.

general. As I shall show, Jackson's justification for his ascription violated many basic principles of scholarship.

As we saw in chapter 7, between 1903 and 1948 a series of scholars, most of them working independently of each other, had established a consensus that Kyd was the author of Arden.

The Second World War, however, effected a rupture in academic studies, as in every other area of life. When research publication resumed in the 1960s some of the studies establishing Kyd's authorship of *Arden* were out of print and their influence largely forgotten. Into this vacuum entered MacDonald P. Jackson, a scholar from New Zealand who was awarded an Oxford B. Litt. degree for a thesis with the modest title, 'Material for an Edition of *Arden of Faversham*'. There was nothing modest about Jackson's procedure, however. His preface announced that he would 'show that the various arguments in favour of Kyd's or Marlowe's responsibility are virtually worthless' (p. iii), establishing at the outset the dismissive tone of his thesis. In discussing 'The Case for Kyd' (pp. 91–115), he rejected in turn the attributions made by Crawford (pp. 92–105; including several pages on irrelevant points), Miksch (pp. 105–6), Sykes (pp. 107–13), and Carrère (pp. 113–15). He was unaware of Rubow's work then, but ten years later M. L. Wine included many quotations from Rubow in his Revels edition of *Arden* (which became Jackson's go to), but ignored the many matches between it and Kyd's plays identified by Rubow.[3] All scholarship takes place at a given point in time and it is a scholar's duty to cite the work of his or her predecessors and to make an informed and balanced evaluation of them. We should treat our predecessors with the same respect that we hope to receive. Jackson's sweeping dismissals were extremely unjust. Jackson's verdict that 'It cannot be claimed that Crawford produced *any reasons at all* for believing *Arden* to have been written by Kyd',[4] was a

---

3. See Wine (ed.), *The Tragedy of Master Arden of Faversham*, Introduction: 'Authorship' (pp. lxxxi–xcii) and Appendix 1, '"Parallels" in Arden of Faversham' (pp. 141–7). Wine's scare quotes around 'parallels' is typical of that period, but he cited many phrasal matches that Rubow had identified.

4. M. P. Jackson, 'Material for an Edition of *Arden of Faversham*' (B. Litt. Thesis, Merton College, Oxford, 1963), p. 105; my italics. This 300-page thesis was the launching pad for

282   CHAPTER 8

gross distortion of the truth. The instances I quoted above show that Crawford presented a great deal of evidence that deserved to be considered carefully. Of course, given the marginal status that attribution studies have had in English departments, Crawford's work was probably unknown, and it might have been asking too much of the examiners of a B. Litt. thesis to have checked whether Jackson had given a reliable account of his work.

Jackson gave his next Kyd scholar, the German Miksch, equally short shrift, writing that 'He gave *a long list of phrases* found in both *Arden* and *Soliman and Perseda*, expanding Crawford's collection by the inclusion of parallels of an *even more trivial nature* and adding a few phrasal resemblances between *Arden* and *The Spanish Tragedy*' (p. 105; my italics). Surely a scholar setting out to make a contribution to knowledge in 1963 would want to investigate that 'long list of phrases' concerning the basic topic of his dissertation? That Jackson could dismiss—without quoting— the additional phrasal matches that Miksch cited as 'even more trivial'— suggests that he regarded all evidence of verbal parallels as unacceptable. Indeed, Jackson said as much:

> Since Crawford's day it has become abundantly clear that almost any two plays of given period will yield sufficient parallels to the diligent searcher to confirm to his own content any theory that may have occurred to him. The Elizabethans drew on a common stock of dramatic diction, and everybody borrowed from everybody else. (p. 98)

That is certainly true for the 'common stock', but the language of Marlowe, Kyd, Shakespeare, and many others far transcended that level.

Jackson's single-minded rejection of Kyd's authorship, constantly reiterated over the sixty-three years since then. I shall refer to Jackson's selected major publications as follows: (1) 'Material for an Edition'; (2) 'Shakespearian Features of the Poetic Style of *Arden of Faversham*', *Archiv für das Studium der neuren Sprachen und Literaturen*, 230 (1993): 273–304, subsequently referred to as 'Shakespearian Features'; (3) 'Shakespeare and the Quarrel Scene in *Arden of Faversham*', *Shakespeare Quarterly*, 57 (2006): 249–93, subsequently referred to as 'Quarrel Scene'; (4) 'Parallels and Poetry: Shakespeare, Kyd, and *Arden of Faversham*', *Medieval and Renaissance Drama in England*, 23 (2010): 17–33, subsequently referred to as 'Parallels and Poetry'; (5) *Determining the Shakespeare Canon*. Arden of Faversham *and* A Lover's Complaint (Oxford, 2014), subsequently referred to as *Determining*.

Jackson went even further, denying that one dramatist's diction could influence another: He found it

> not inherently more likely that a single dramatist twice used such phrases as 'be it spoke in secret here', 'linked in liking', 'a sudden qualm', and 'stab the slave', common to *Arden of Faversham* and *Soliman and Perseda*, than that the diction of one dramatist was influenced by that of another. The resemblances are purely verbal. (p. 100)

That is patently untrue. Crawford had shown that it was quite common for a single dramatist to 'use such phrases twice', indeed he observed that that habit was widespread in Elizabethan drama. As I have recently shown, self-repetition was in fact universal throughout the period up to the closing of the theatres in 1642.[5] While repetition can certainly prove that 'the diction of one dramatist was influenced by that of another', in a mere four pages Crawford listed *fifty identically worded phrases* common to *Arden of Faversham* and *Soliman and Perseda*, many of them between three and six words long.[6] The point that Jackson constantly avoided was that these many matches proved that both plays are by Kyd. If the two plays had been written by two different dramatists, the borrower would have had great difficulty assimilating so many phrases into his own composition as smoothly as Kyd did with *Arden*. The matches prove, in fact, that when Kyd used phrases from his poetic lexicon, he adapted them to their new dramatic context.

Jackson's phrase, 'since Crawford's day', was designed to make the evidence of phrasal matches seem archaic, outmoded. But it was still in use in more recent times and played a major role in establishing Middleton's authorship of *The Revenger's Tragedy*, from E. H. C. Oliphant in 1928 to R. H. Barker in 1945 and 1958, Cyrus Hoy in 1959, David Lake in 1975, Jackson himself in 1979, and R. V. Holdsworth in 1979, who described Middleton as 'a highly self-imitative writer, capable of detailed retrieval of material across gaps of twenty years or more'.[7] Jackson's

---

5. See Vickers (ed.), *Collected Works of John Ford*, vol. 2, Introduction 2: 'Identifying Co-Authors', pp. 33–75.

6. Crawford, *Collectanea*, pp. 126–9.

7. See Vickers, *Shakespeare, Co-Author*, pp. 57–66.

284   CHAPTER 8

2006 essay claiming Shakespeare's authorship of the Quarrel Scene in *Arden* (to be discussed below) only uses phrasal matches, but, as we shall see, in a deeply flawed method. When all the matching collocations pointed out by the five scholars whose work I summarized are collected into one list, amounting to over one hundred, the evidence for Kyd's authorship is truly overwhelming. Readers can judge for themselves whether Jackson did justice to their scholarship, since I have reproduced many of the matches identified by Crawford, Miksch, and Rubow on my website.[8]

Given Jackson's dismissal of matching phrases as authorship markers, the question arises, what did he put in their place? In fact, he did use verbal parallels, but in an idiosyncratic manner. Throughout the history of authorship attribution, the whole aim of using repeated phrases as evidence of self-repetition has been to document that both occurrences of the phrase are equally significant, as showing a key match between a play of known and one of unknown authorship. But Jackson developed a recurring claim that one of the two repeated phrases carried a higher *poetic value* than the other. He claimed that he could detect differences *in quality*, with the more effective use of that phrase in *Arden* than in *Soliman*, for instance proving 'Shakespeare's' authorship of the former. (I use scare quotes to identify Jackson's creation.) Equally, within *Arden*, superior phrasing in one part, usually the Quarrel scene, supposedly set it on the higher level of excellence, marking 'Shakespeare's' contribution. Regrettably, Jackson's evaluative, aesthetic approach was a regression within attribution studies, re-introducing subjective value judgments. Over several decades the discipline had rejected the whimsical criteria of some notorious dilettantes, striving instead to attain clarity in the presentation of evidence and objectivity in its interpretation. E. K. Chambers set down a milestone in his rejection of F. G. Fleay and J. M. Robertson's whimsical methods.[9] Muriel St. Clare Byrne set down another in 1932, by laying down the criteria for establishing valid

---

8. See https://brianvickers.uk/databases.

9. See, e.g., the classic 1924 essay by E. K. Chambers, 'The Disintegration of Shakespeare', in Chambers, *Shakespearean Gleanings* (Oxford, 1944), pp. 1–21, and Vickers, *Shakespeare, Co-Author*, pp. 44–134 .

parallels.[10] To summarize her argument: verbal parallels must be graded by quality, the highest being when a parallelism of thought is coupled with some verbal parallel; mere accumulation of ungraded parallels does not prove anything; in accumulating parallels we can proceed from a known work to the collaborate, or from the known to the anonymous play, but not from the collaborate to the anonymous; we must apply a negative check, showing that we cannot parallel words, images, and phrases as a body from other acknowledged plays of the period. Neither Byrne, nor any other scholar of attribution studies, has ever regarded differences in quality between individual writers as relevant, least of all when they repeat the same phrase. But Jackson enlarged the individual differences he claimed to detect within *Arden* into general value judgments. No scholar today would dream of declaring, as Jackson did in 2010, that 'Shakespeare, even at the beginning of his career as dramatist, was a better poet than Thomas Kyd'—as if that justified a positive evaluation of one writer and a negative evaluation of the other. In *The Spanish Tragedy*, Jackson wrote dismissively, Kyd devised a 'verbal medium' that was

> an effective enough instrument for his dramatic purposes. But it lacks the linguistic subtlety, the lively play of imagery, and the rich metaphorical content that characterize Shakespeare's dramatic verse.[11]

Although Jackson may not have explicitly formulated this principle before then, such value judgments were fundamental to his 1963 thesis and to his systematic downgrading of Kyd over the next sixty-odd years.

Metaphor: Image or Self-Image?

In his claims for Shakespeare's superiority to Kyd, Jackson attached great importance to imagery and metaphor, warranting a separate discussion. It might seem that these terms have a universally agreed and

---

10. See Muriel St. Clare Byrne, 'Bibliographic Clues in Collaborative Plays', *Library*, 4th ser. 13 (1932): 21–48 (24), and Vickers, *Shakespeare, Co-Author*, pp. 58–60.

11. Jackson, 'Parallels and Poetry' p. 17.

understood meaning, but anyone familiar with the poetry and criticism in the Elizabethan period and since will know how inaccurate such expectations are. In fact, MacDonald Jackson used such an idiosyncratic concept of metaphor that I need to re-establish some normative meanings.

From its first appearance as a literary term, 'metaphor' has been regarded as one of the most powerful resources for writers of verse or prose. In classical rhetoric metaphor was classified as a trope (or 'turn'), involving a change or transference of meaning (*translatio*). Cicero praised metaphor for the clarity that an analogy can offer; for its ability to make a description more vivid, as 'every apt metaphor is directed to the senses, particularly to that of sight, the keenest of all.'[12] Cicero valued metaphor for its general aid to effective communication; in the adversarial context of the law court Quintilian wrote that 'metaphor is designed generally to affect the emotions.'[13] The rhetorical texts were prescriptive, describing the elements that are needed to become a persuasive speaker. Metaphor and other expressive devices were equally applicable to drama, and it is fitting that Aristotle's *Poetics*, the foundational text for dramatic theory, made the fundamental connection with rhetoric. As Stephen Halliwell observed, 'Aristotle thinks of the individual characters of tragedy as deploying language for particular effects on those around them—to persuade or dissuade, to stir their feelings, and so on. He thinks of them, in effect, as using the resources of oratory,' having recognized that 'the rhetorical is a demonstrably central mode of speech throughout the genre as we know it.'[14] The same truth holds for the humanism-influenced genre of Renaissance drama, that its characters use language for their own ends. This truth could be illustrated, for instance, by comparing the arguments used by Sophocles' Odysseus in *Philoctetes* to persuade the hero to return to combat, and those used

12. Cicero, *De Oratore*, 3.155-60, tr. M. Winterbottom in Russell and Winterbottom (eds),*Ancient Literary Criticism* (Oxford, 1972), pp. 258–9.

13. Quintilian, *The Orator's Education*, 8.6.20; tr. D.A. Russell, (Cambridge, MA, and London, 2011), p. 435.

14. Stephen Halliwell, *The* Poetics *of Aristotle translation and commentary* (Chapel Hill, NC, 1987), p. 155.

by Shakespeare's Ulysses in *Troilus and Cressida* to persuade Achilles to the same goal. They belong to the same tradition.

Regrettably, the character-based nature of all speech in drama never established itself in modern criticism. Critical approaches studied imagery not in relation to the dramatist shaping utterances to each character, but treating the play as an autonomous entity. In the 1930s the vogue was to identify image patterns or 'themes' that could supposedly give an interpretative clue to a play's meaning. Such critics as G. Wilson Knight, L. C. Knights, R. B. Heilman, and others, ignored the characters speaking the lines, taking all utterances as the dramatist's pursuit of a unifying tissue of metaphors. In practice this led to a concern with such abstractions as 'Appearance and Reality', and although it provoked robust objections,[15] nobody called for a character-based study of dramatic language.

The alternative and even more damaging approach, introduced by Caroline Spurgeon in the 1930s, was to look for 'iterative imagery', 'the repetition of an idea or picture in the images', which could also reveal a dramatist's psychology, personality, and interests.[16] Spurgeon had a rather vague concept of an image ('some picture or symbol'), and it is regrettable that she was unaware of the pioneering work of her contemporary, I.A. Richards, whose account of metaphor soon became the standard modern theory. Richards defined the component parts of a metaphor as the 'tenor and the vehicle', a 'whole double unit', in which 'the tenor' is 'the underlying idea or principal subject which the vehicle or figure means'. Richards emphasized that their 'co-presence . . . results in a meaning . . . which is not attainable without their interaction.'[17] Unaware of the analytical possibilities opened up by Richards, Spurgeon simply counted the number of 'images' that an author 'iterated',

---

15. See, e.g., the trenchant critique of Heilman's method by W. R. Keast, 'Imagery and Meaning in the Interpretation of *King Lear*', *Modern Philology*, 47 (1949): 45–54, reprinted in R. S. Crane (ed.), *Critics and Criticism* (Chicago, 1952), pp. 108–37.

16. See Caroline Spurgeon, *Leading Motives in the Imagery of Shakespeare's Tragedies* (London, 1930); 'Shakespeare's Iterative Imagery', *PBA*, 17 (1932 for 1931): 147–78; *Shakespeare's Imagery and What It Tells Us* (Cambridge, 1935).

17. I.A. Richards, *The Philosophy of Rhetoric* (Oxford, 1936), pp. 96–7.

separating the 'vehicle' from the 'tenor'. Then she collected the vehicles (over six thousand) and classified them into such categories as 'Learning and the Arts, the Body, Domestic, Daily Life, Nature and Animals'. Studying these categories, Spurgeon claimed to know that Shakespeare loathed flatterers, having himself been deceived, that his many images from carpentry show that he himself had some knowledge of the craft, and that he had a sensitive nose. Reconsidered ninety years later, Spurgeon's approach seems wholly misguided. In adopting the biographical approach in his 1963 thesis, Jackson was unaware that, as long ago as 1940, Lilian Hornstein had published a definitive critique of Spurgeon's method, 'which not only psychoanalyzes the creator but reconstructs his physical environment on the basis of frequency of metaphors'.[18] As Hornstein objected, the method assumes that 'imagery (the association of ideas) always has a direct basis in physical experience' and that a tabulation of images reveals a writer's 'everyday, environmental experiences'.[19] Hornstein made the obvious point that an image can be derived from proverbs, from the works of other poets, or from a poet's imagination. (In the Renaissance, many writers published collections of metaphors and similes for reuse.)

Jackson's characteristic treatment of imagery can be seen from his commentary on this phrasal match, first cited by Crawford, of Perseda rebuking Erastus when she sees Lucina wearing her carcanet:

> Ah, how thine eyes can forge alluring looks,
> And fain deep oaths to wound poor silly maids!   (*SP* 2.1.119–20)

Mosby accuses Alice of insincerity:

> Ungentle Alice, thy sorrow is my sore;
> Thou know'st it well, and 'tis thy policy

---

18. See Lillian Hornstein, 'Analysis of Imagery A Critique of Literary Method', *PMLA*, 57 (1942): 638–53 (638).

19. Ibid., p. 639. Hornstein summarized this assumption in logical terms: 'reasoning about imagery assumes that the presence of an image means the existence of a quality or experience, i.e., I (Image) < E (Experience). This conclusion rests on the unexpressed premiss that the image will occur only where the experience has been present, i.e., *only* E > I. This premiss has not been proved' (p. 652).

To forge distressful looks to wound a breast
Where lies a heart that dies when thou art sad.   (*AF* 8.53–6)

I quote Jackson's account complete, since he has re-used it several times since 1963:

> The author of *Arden* is alive to the language he is using. The implications of the latent metaphor in "forge" (one forges weapons) are fully appreciated, and carried on in the words "wounds" and "dies". This strand of imagery begins in the earlier lines of Mosby's speech when he compares Alice's sighs to "a cannon's burst, | Discharged against a ruinated wall"—sighs which "Breaks" his "relenting heart in thousand pieces"; and the word "policy" suggests military strategy . . . Kyd (if it be he) uses "forge" mechanically, with no interest in its literal meaning. The word "wound" is there, but more by accident than anything else. How, one may ask, can eyes forge oaths, let alone deep ones? Clearly the author of *Soliman and Perseda* did not trouble himself with such questions. There is all the difference between cliché and poetry in these "parallel passages".[20]

Evidently satisfied with the validity of his comparison, Jackson repeated it verbatim in 2010, with some additions.[21] He gave an abridged account of it in 2006, in his *Shakespeare Quarterly* article,[22] but revived the enlarged version in his 2014 book *Determining the Shakespeare Canon*.[23] Of course, scholars have every right to re-use their own work. But in deploying this comparison for fifty years, Jackson has preserved an

---

20. Jackson, 'Material for an Edition', pp. 101–2.

21. Jackson, 'Parallels and Poetry' pp, 27–8. Among other small changes, he deleted the closing sentence, substituting: 'The author of *Arden of Faversham awakes the dormant metaphors* in words; the author of *Soliman and Perseda* bundles together his "alluring looks," "deep oaths", and "silly maids," and *lets the metaphors sleep*' (my italics).

22. Jackson, 'Quarrel Scene', p. 281 n. 11, on Perseda's lines: 'The image, which has eyes feigning oaths, is characteristically confused, and whereas in Kyd "forge" simply means "simulate", in the *Arden of Faversham* passage it retains a hint of a blacksmith's weapon making, and so interacts with the verb "wound" to vivify the metaphor'.

23. Jackson, *Determining*, pp. 96–7.

outmoded form of literary criticism, unsuitable to drama, summed up in his phrase 'this strand of imagery'.

In the theatre, as in reading, we create meaning as we experience it from characters' utterances, moment by moment. For interpretative criticism we must be aware of the differing dramatic contexts in which meaning is created. In *Soliman and Perseda* the heroine, who had given her lover Erastus a love token and then seen another woman wearing it, accuses him of deceit. She was mistaken but sincere; in *Arden of Faversham* Mosby is neither. We have just heard him reveal his intention to get rid of Alice Arden once her husband is dead and he has got her money. Here, in a quarrel on which much depends, he assumes the moral high ground over Alice by presenting himself as 'relenting'—as if he has been justifiably angry with her errors, but is now ready to forgive. Then he turns self-defence into attack, accusing *her* of Machiavellian dissimulation, falsely assuming an appearance of distress in order to *hurt him*. We know how manipulative this pretence is. For Jackson, following out 'this strand of imagery' at a remove from the play, 'the word "policy" suggests military strategy'. He is blind to the irony of Mosby falsely accusing Alice of 'policy', the word used here not in a military sense but in the sense of 'devious plotting' ascribed to Machiavels, of whom Mosby is a supreme example. As for Jackson's complaint that 'Kyd (if it be he) uses "forge" mechanically, with no interest in its literal meaning', this literal interpretation of 'forge' is entirely of Jackson's own making in claiming to discover a 'strand of imagery'. It obscures the fact that the word 'forge' has the same meaning in both contexts. In *Soliman and Perseda* Kyd pairs it with 'fain', the feigning of false oaths, while in *Arden* it is paired with the false accusation of 'policy', the trademark of deceivers. Despite Jackson's attempted association with blacksmiths, the two usages are identical, with Mosby accusing Alice of deception. As for his related criticism of Kyd's 'characteristically confused' imagery, 'which has eyes feigning oaths', that is a trick well within the repertoire of deceivers. I remember Shaw's observation that 'When a man looks you squarely in the eye you know he's not telling the truth'.

In the section of his thesis devoted to 'The Imagery of *Arden*' (pp. 177–227), Jackson started from Spurgeon's first assumption: 'it is a matter of observable fact that different dramatists tend to draw upon different areas of experience for the subject matter of their imagery and to differ in the manner in which they form their images' (p. 177). He also drew extensively on a study of Marlowe's imagery by Marion Smith,[24] one of Spurgeon's 'ardent disciples', as Hornstein described her, who 'followed' Spurgeon 'in categorizing images according to their subject matter'. Jackson believed that her computations 'give some basis for comparison between various dramatists' (p. 178). Smith found that 'the image patterns for Kyd and Marlowe are alike', and unlike *Arden*, for they 'each have twice as many images drawn from Learning and the Arts as *Arden* has, and only half as many images drawn from Daily Life'. Jackson added that 'the extreme paucity of images of the Body and Bodily Action in Kyd, and his small proportion of images drawn from Animals sharply differentiate *The Spanish Tragedy* from both Shakespeare's acknowledged work and *Arden*' (p. 179). It is hard to take the mere tabulation of images seriously as the basis for ascribing authorship,[25] especially when global counts are taken as evidential for individual works in different genres.

The most long-lived instance of Jackson's debt to Spurgeon and his reliance upon her method is her remark that '"I do not find, in all my search of other dramatists, any single image of frosts and sharp winds nipping buds, which is so common with Shakespeare"'.[26] Without questioning Spurgeon's knowledge of Elizabethan drama, Jackson endorsed her observation, adding that 'apparent parallels in the work of

---

24. Marion Smith, *Marlowe's Imagery and the Marlowe Canon* (Philadelphia, PA, 1940). Louis Charles Stagg, in *The Figurative Language of the Tragedies of Shakespeare's Chief Sixteenth-Century Contemporaries* (New York, 1984), pp.121–218, compiled a Spurgeon-style index of Kyd's tragedies, a pointless exercise.

25. Jackson accepted Smith's finding that 'Shakespeare "has more images of riding and of bird-snaring and falconry than of any other forms of outdoor sport . . . His images from archery are also comparatively numerous"'. Jackson noted that *Arden* contains several 'images from archery, riding and the hunting of birds' ('Materials for an Edition', pp. 179–82, 180–81), as if these were reliable markers of Shakespeare's authorship. Was Shakespeare a hunter?

26. Spurgeon, *Shakespeare's Imagery*, p. 91. Hornstein noted instances in Spurgeon where 'Shakespeare's contemporaries are condemned because they never show' some quality that she ascribed to Shakespeare ('Analysis of Imagery', p. 645 n.).

other dramatists invariably serve upon examination merely to point the difference between Shakespeare's imagination and that of his early contemporaries' (pp. 184–5). We need scarcely ask which writer he might have in mind. Jackson quoted two passages from *The Spanish Tragedy*, Andrea's account of how his murder by Balthazar cut off his love relationship with Bel-imperia:

> But in the harvest of my summer joys,
> Death's winter nipped the blossoms of my bliss,
> Forcing divorce betwixt my love and me.   (*Sp. T.* 1.1.12–14)

The second passage that Jackson chose for comparison was Hieronimo's demented speech, thinking that the old man Bazulto was his son Horatio:

> Sweet boy, how art thou changed in death's black shade!
> Had Proserpine no pity on thy youth,
> But suffered thy fair, crimson-coloured spring
> With withered winter to be blasted thus?   (3.13.146–9)

Jackson commented:

> In each case Kyd is simply making the obvious connection of life with spring or summer and death with winter, and he does so in extremely general terms, and in a rather perfunctory fashion. His lines are worn poetic currency. Shakespeare and the author of *Arden of Faversham* write imaginatively of the way in which sudden cold winds or untimely frosts are apt to nip back the tender spring buds or blossoms and they even specify the direction from which the wind blows. They both have their eye on the object, to use Eliot's phrase. This distinction between Kyd and the author of *Arden of Faversham* is an essential one.[27]

Jackson's quotation from Eliot confirms Hornstein's diagnosis that Spurgeon's method was based on the fallacy that an image derives from a writer's experience and personal observation. But his 'distinction

---

27. Jackson, 'Material for an Edition' p. 185.

between Kyd and the author of *Arden of Faversham*' is illusory, for they were one and the same.

Jackson repeated this verdict from his 1963 thesis verbatim in his 1993 essay.[28] He gave it a further lease of life in his 2006 essay in *Shakespeare Quarterly*. Once more he quoted Spurgeon on the imagery of sharp winds nipping buds being common in Shakespeare, adding: 'Mosby's words (8.5–6) are thus *good indicators of Shakespeare's hand*.... The basic image shared with many Shakespearian passages is of untimely cold checking tender new growth within a season noted for its changeable weather'.[29] In that 2006 essay Jackson added a passage describing Andrea's narrative as 'a hopeless muddle, with winter nipping blossoms at a time of summer harvest. The author of *Arden of Faversham*, in contrast, grounds his imagery in experience, writing, like Shakespeare, with a countryman's eye on the weather and even the direction from which the wind blows'.

Jackson has loyally followed Spurgeon in committing the biographical fallacy, inferring particulars of a writer's life or personality from their use of metaphor. The Spurgeon-Jackson approach imagines that metaphor can be treated as an inadvertent authorial 'selfie' (to use a recent term), from which a commentator can deduce reliable information about the writer's personality and pursuits. But writers create metaphors for their characters to use according to their wishes, to praise or blame, to illuminate an argument, to evoke mood or atmosphere.

Kyd gave an excellent illustration of a character's motives for using metaphor in *Arden of Faversham*. Greene, hired by Alice to murder her husband, sets Shakebag and Black Will in hiding to ambush Arden, with these instructions:

> Well, take your fittest standings, and once more
> Lime your twigs to catch this weary bird.
> I'll leave you, and at your dag's discharge
> Make towards, like the longing water-dog
> That coucheth till the fowling-piece be off,

28. Jackson, 'Shakespearian Features', pp. 290–91.
29. Jackson, 'Quarrel Scene', pp. 263–4; my italics.

Then seizeth on the prey with eager mood.
Ah, might I see him stretching forth his limbs,
As I have seen them beat their wings ere now! (9.38–44)

Kyd first gives Greene a familiar metaphor for catching a defenceless victim, the fowler's practice of smearing sticky bird-lime on a tree's branches. He reinforces it with an extended analogy of the hunter's dog that 'coucheth' in readiness to retrieve the prey once the hunter has fired his 'dag', or gun. Kyd increases the impact of the analogy by attributing human emotions to the 'longing water-dog', which seizes the fowl 'with eager mood.' Having dramatized the scene, Kyd then reveals Greene's reason for using these metaphors of catching a helpless prey, his own 'longing' to see Arden dead:

Ah, might I see him stretching forth his limbs,
As I have seen them beat their wings ere now!

As late as 2010 Jackson said that the image of the water dog 'reads like the work of a country man who has experienced hunting for waterfowl at first hand' ('Parallels and Poetry', p. 25). Jackson gave this passage its fourth outing, so far, in his 2014 book.[30] It is rather worrying that a remark by Caroline Spurgeon can be taken as a decisive authorship indicator over fifty years of a scholar's life.

The special emphasis that Jackson has given to Mosby's words has been unwarranted on two grounds. First, he assumed that it was a direct observation by Shakespeare. Had he known Hornstein's 1940 essay, however, he might have been less confident. Making the point that a writer's images can derive from many sources, Hornstein quoted an earlier passage in which Spurgeon deduced that Shakespeare 'may have been "keenly conscious of the disastrous effects of spring . . . frosts on tender buds and flowers."'[31] However, Hornstein replied, 'when Biron is said to be "like an envious sneaping frost, | That bites the first-born infants of the spring" Shakespeare is merely giving superlative expression to the

---

30. Jackson, *Determining*, pp. 27–8.
31. Spurgeon, *Shakespeare's Imagery*, p. 88; Hornstein, 'Analysis of Imagery', p. 646.

proverbial sentiment that "sharp frosts bite forward springs."[32] This was a source of imagery that Jackson never considered.

Nor had he read widely in Kyd, who made repeated uses of the metaphor of 'nipping' as a sudden action that could destroy pleasure or even life itself.[33] In his first published work, *Verses of Praise and Joy* (1584), Kyd attacked Chidiock Tichborne, one of the Catholic conspirators in the failed Babington plot:

> Time trieth truth, and truth hath treason tripped,
> Thy faith bare fruit as thou had'st faithless been:
> Thy ill-spent youth thine after-years hath nipped,
> And God that saw thee hath preserved our Queen.

The ghost of Andrea recalls how his sudden death destroyed the love affair he had been enjoying with Bel-imperia:

> But in the harvest of my summer joys,
> Death's winter nipped the blossoms of my bliss,
> Forcing divorce betwixt my love and me. (*Sp. T.* 1.1.12–14)

That passage deserves to be juxtaposed with Mosby's complaint:

> Continual trouble of my moody brain
> Feebles my body by excess of drink
> And nips me as the bitter northeast wind
> Doth check the tender blossoms in the spring. (8.3–6)

The aged King Leir, determined to abdicate, uses the same terminology, with some self-pity:

> Dear Gonorill, kind Ragan, sweet Cordella,
> Ye flourishing branches of a kingly stock,
> Sprung from a tree that once did flourish green,

32. Hornstein cites M. P. Tilley, *A Dictionary of the Proverbs in England in the Sixteenth and Seventeenth Centuries* (Ann Arbor, MI, 1950), p. 167, no. 279.

33. All quotations in this paragraph are taken from Vickers (ed.), *The Collected Works of Thomas Kyd: Verses of Praise and Joy*, ed. Daniel Starza Smith; *The Spanish Tragedy*, ed. Vickers; *Arden of Faversham*, ed. Darren Freebury Jones; *King Leir*, ed. Eugene Giddens; and *Edward III*, ed. David Bevington.

Whose blossoms now are nipped with winter's frost,
And pale, grim death doth wait upon my steps.   (3.25–9)

In one of Kyd's scenes for *Edward III* a Frenchman fleeing before the advancing English forces answers a complacent Citizen who says 'they are far enough from hence':

Ay, so the grasshopper doth spend the time
In mirthful jollity till winter come,
And then too late he would redeem his time
When frozen cold hath nipped his careless head.   (5.13–19)

The wording, verse-movement, and syntax in all four plays come from the same hand:

-Death's *winter nipped* the *blossoms* of my bliss,
-And *nips* me as the bitter northeast wind
Doth check the tender *blossoms* in the spring.
-Whose *blossoms* now are *nipped* with *winter's* <u>frost</u>
-When <u>frozen</u> cold hath *nipped* his careless head

All four passages include references to the seasons as time markers, but Jackson chose to dismiss those that relate to winter, a rather feeble objection.[34] However, since they outnumber the sole reference to spring by three to one, we can accept them as confirming Kyd's authorship.

Jackson's unawareness of these matches shows that in privileging 'Shakespeare' and downgrading Kyd, his knowledge of Kyd was inadequate. Discussing the Quarrel scene in his thesis, he praised the dialogue's 'consummate artistry' in this exchange:

MOSBY It is not **love** that **loves** to anger **love**.
ALICE It is not **love** that **loves** to murder **love**.

Mosby asks what she means, and Alice replies: 'Thou know'st how dearly Arden lovèd me' (8.57–9), revealing her guilty conscience at the planned murder of her husband. Jackson took this wordplay as 'thoroughly

---

34. Jackson, 'Quarrel Scene', p. 277.

Shakespearian', a claim he often repeated.[35] But I answered him in a brief note, showing that Kyd often used such wordplay on those terms.[36]

Throughout his sixty-year attempt to award parts of *Arden* to Shakespeare Jackson's evaluative approach has gradually turned into an adversarial one, downgrading Kyd to the point of denying him any poetic ability. Kyd, according to Jackson, makes an 'obvious connection . . . in extremely general terms . . . in a rather perfunctory fashion. His lines are worn poetic currency'. His imagery is 'characteristically confused', he uses words 'mechanically'. A passage in *Soliman and Perseda* is 'an assembly of nouns preceded by the most obvious of epithets . . . The passage is a tissue of inert expressions and other men's inventions'.[37] In his 2010 essay Jackson quoted Black Will's resolve to kill Arden:

> I tell thee, Greene, the forlorn traveller
> Whose lips are glued with summer's parching heat
> Ne'er longed so much to see a running brook
> As I to finish Arden's tragedy.   (3.92–5)

Jackson's denigration of Kyd reached its highest point in this comment: 'Not only does the language have a vividness and concreteness *never on display in Kyd's plays*', but it has matches in Shakespeare.[38] There is considerable irony in Jackson praising passages from *Arden* as being 'Shakespearian' when they were in fact written by Kyd.

The figure of the 'forlorn traveller' recurs in Kyd as an image of duress and vulnerability. In *The Spanish Tragedy* Bel-imperia describes the bower where she and Horatio will meet as a refuge:

> The Court were dangerous, that place is safe.
> Our hour shall be when Vesper begins to rise,
> That summons home distressful travellers.   (2.2.44–6)

---

35. See also Jackson, 'Shakespearean features', pp. 287–9; 'Quarrel Scene', pp. 250–51, 266–7, 282–3; *Determining*, pp. 10–11, 225–6.

36. See Brian Vickers, 'Verbal repetition in *Arden of Faversham*: Shakespeare or Kyd?', *Notes and Queries*, 263 (2018): 498–502.

37. Jackson, 'Material for an Edition', p. 104, repeated in 'Shakespearian Features', p. 291.

38. Jackson, 'Parallels', p. 28; my italics.

298 CHAPTER 8

Kyd showed us this time of night from a different perspective in the oath that Shakebag swears, should he fail to kill Arden the next time he sees him:

> And let me never draw a sword again,
> Nor prosper in the twilight, cockshut light,
> When I would fleece the wealthy passenger   (*AF* 5. 46–8)

Shakebag's time marker, 'cockshut light' is defined by *OED* as 'twilight', with an illustration from Florio's *Worlde of Wordes* (1598): 'twilight, as when a man cannot discerne a dog from a Wolfe', a more colloquial version of 'the hour . . . when Vesper begins to rise'.

The associations within Kyd's lexicon are defined afresh in *King Leir*, when Ragan looks forward to her forthcoming marriage:

> As gold is welcome to the covetous eye,
> As sleep is welcome to the traveller,
> As is fresh water to sea-beaten men,
> Or moistened showers unto the parchèd ground   (6.72–5)

Both passages echo Shakebag's analogy. His 'forlorn traveller' matches Bel-imperia's 'distressful travellers', while his evocation of 'lips . . . glued with summer's parching heat' and 'a running brook' is matched by Ragan's 'moistened showers unto the parchèd ground'. Of Shakespeare's references to travellers only one is close to Kyd's association of travel with danger, the ominous words of First Murderer hired by Macbeth, lying in wait for Banquo and Fleance:

> The west yet glimmers with some streaks of day:
> Now spurs the lated traveller apace
> To gain the timely inn . . .   (3.3.6–8)

That might indeed owe something to Kyd's influence.

Jackson regularly discriminated against Kyd and in favour of 'Shakespeare', as in this phrasal match:

> And Arden **sent to everlasting night**.   (*AF* 9.5)
> To **send** them down **to everlasting night**   (*SP* 5.2.104)[39]

---

39. Kyd used this expression again in the Prologue, as Death says: 'I will not **down to everlasting night** | Till I have moralised this tragedy, | Whose chiefest actor was my sable dart' (Prol. 26–8).

In 2010 Jackson found a 'disparity in poetic quality' between these two passages. The first, from a speech by Shakebag, which moves on to an evocation of night (9.6–9), displays 'a typically Shakespearian verbal inventiveness'.[40] The Kyd passage, spoken by Soliman, contains 'no complex interplay of images'—but it doesn't need to, being appropriate to character and situation. In these comparisons Kyd always loses. The evaluative method has no place in attribution studies. What matters is the quality and quantity of phrasal matches—quality not in the sense of 'better or worse', but in the convincing detail or closeness of the match.

In addition to using an inappropriate aesthetic or evaluative method, Jackson's underlying error in over fifty years of claiming parts of the play for Shakespeare is that he has never considered the possibility of Kyd's influence. In his thesis he assigned a date for *Arden* between 1577 and 1592, probably 1588,[41] listing parallels between it and *Lucrece* (pp. 245–7), published in 1594, and 2 *Henry VI*, which was 'probably preceded' by *Arden* (pp. 248–50). The dates indicate the actual direction of influence, from Kyd to Shakespeare. In a 2008 essay Jackson claimed that '*Arden* has more unique matches with 2 *Henry VI* and *The Taming of the Shrew* than with any play by Kyd', claiming forty-four and fifty-one unique matches respectively. I lack the space to document it, but examination will confirm that, while not word for word, as would be the case if they were self-repetitions, many of these matches are extended and accurate in substance, showing Shakespeare's excellent aural memory, that of an actor, from having heard these plays in the theatre (none of the texts were in print).

In effect, the parallels that Jackson cited should have been taken as supporting two hypotheses, either (A) 'Shakespeare wrote *Arden of Faversham*'; or (B) 'Shakespeare remembered the play well from public performances, in some of which he may have acted'. At one point Jackson recorded 'evidence that some time before publication *Arden of Faversham* had belonged in the repertory of "Pembroke's Men", along with plays by Kyd, Marlowe, and Shakespeare. So perhaps Shakespeare had

---

40. Jackson, 'Parallels and Poetry', p. 22.

41. Jackson, 'Material for an Edition', p. 78. He has recently narrowed the date-span to 1588–91; Jackson, 'Quarrel Scene', p. 255; *Determining*, p. 15.

acted in another playwright's domestic tragedy and absorbed its imagery and diction'.[42] Jackson conceded that 'none of Shakespeare's plays was in print in 1592, when *Arden of Faversham* was published', so that 'any familiarity with them could only have been acquired though performances',[43] yet he has also vehemently denied the possibility that Shakespeare's detailed knowledge of *Arden* was due to his having acted in it.[44] As he dismissively put it, to account for *Arden*'s many links with Shakespeare 'in terms of influence would be to credit a single scene by an unknown playwright with virtually inventing the distinctive Shakespearian idiolect, with its many vivid images from nature'.[45] Once more, Jackson assumed that Shakespeare was unique in being able to create 'vivid images from nature'.

The 'Digital Turn': New Methods, Same Results

The rise of high-speed electronic computation in the 1960s affected every area of the humanities, including attribution studies. It was now possible to process more data, more quickly, than ever before, a development that had both good and bad consequences. On the undoubtedly positive side, the availability of the whole of early modern drama in electronic form has been a universal benefit, and poetry excerpted from the complete collection, *Early English Books Online* (*EEBO*), has made many forms of research possible. MacDonald Jackson was the first scholar to use these resources. Having overcome his earlier scepticism that matching phrases was an unreliable guide to authorship, in 2001 Jackson outlined a new method.[46] It described the advantages of using

42. Jackson, 'Shakespearian Features', p. 292. Several scholars have suggested this chain of influence, most recently Darren Freebury-Jones, 'Kyd and Shakespeare: Authorship versus Influence', *Authorship*, 6.1 (2017): 1–24, www.authorship.ugent.be/article/view/4833.

43. Jackson, 'Quarrel Scene', p. 260; *Determining*, p. 121.

44. See, e.g., Jackson, *Determining*, pp. 24, 121–3.

45. Jackson, 'Quarrel Scene', p. 261; *Determining*, p. 123.

46. See MacDonald P. Jackson, 'Determining Authorship: A New Technique', *Research Opportunities in Renaissance Drama*, 41 (2001), 1–14; reprinted in Jackson, *Defining Shakespeare: 'Pericles' as Test Case* (Oxford: Oxford University Press, 2003), pp. 190–217 as 'A New Technique for Attribution Studies'. Quotations will be from this version.

LION to make 'systematic and comprehensive electronic searches', collecting both phrases and collocations,[47] and in 2006 he applied his new method to repeat his claim for Shakespeare's authorship of the Quarrel Scene.[48] Jackson now correctly stated that each dramatist 'had his own habit of expression—a tendency to repeat certain ideas and images in peculiar combinations of words' (p. 258). The change is welcome, but we are soon faced with the problem of designing a scholarly method to find authorship markers—as scientists design an experiment before they begin. Jackson compared the 167 lines of this scene with the complete texts of 132 plays 'that fall within the chronological limits of 1580 to 1600' (ibid.). By his method, Jackson amassed 167 phrases matching the Quarrel scene. Of these, he claimed, 113 'links' with *Arden of Faversham* derived from fifteen plays wholly by Shakespeare, and a further nineteen 'links' came from another three plays partly by him. Jackson claimed that 'the obvious interpretation of this table, in which links to the plays by Shakespeare are overwhelmingly predominant' (p. 258), is that he wrote the Quarrel scene.

To general readers and editors unfamiliar with attribution studies, this may seem a fair proceeding, but it has several serious flaws. First there is the question of chronology, a key issue in attribution studies, where the relative priority of texts is fundamental, and the date of each text must be established as accurately as possible. In 1963 Jackson dated *Arden* to about 1588;[49] in 2006 he settled on 1590, a dating confirmed by Wiggins. Therefore, choosing a date-span of 1580–1600, while convenient for users of *LION*, was inappropriately long. If *Arden* was performed in 1590, nothing is gained by searching plays dating from the following ten years; indeed, any verbal matches discovered may well be imitations or plagiarisms. In Table 1 of his 2008 essay on the Quarrel Scene, Jackson listed the thirty-eight plays which had supplied relevant data, of which fifteen were wholly and three partly by Shakespeare, adding the 'probable date of first performance'.[50] For Kyd, Jackson could

47. Ibid., p. 193.
48. See Jackson, 'Quarrel Scene', pp. 249–93.
49. Jackson, 'Material for an Edition', p. 78.
50. Jackson, 'Quarrel Scene', p. 259; *Determining*, p. 21.

only use *The Spanish Tragedy* and *Soliman and Perseda*. A moment's thought will show that a comparison where Shakespeare has 800 percent more plays than Kyd will inevitably produce more 'matches' for Shakespeare.

A few pages later Jackson casually pointed out that 'it is probable that no Shakespeare play listed' in that Table 'was written before *Arden of Faversham*, and it is virtually certain that several of those with many links were written after it'.[51] Jackson stated the fact but failed to comment on its significance. This is a truly astonishing admission, that all his Shakespeare 'matches' postdated *Arden*. Indeed, it calls into question his whole methodology. As I have observed, he faced two possible explanations of what he took to be the frequent parallels with Shakespeare: either Shakespeare had written the play, or else he had been influenced by it from live performances, perhaps ones in which he had himself acted. By assuming the first position Jackson had in fact begged the question he set out to prove.

Secondly, Jackson violated two basic principles of this method: (i) that the matching phrases should consist of words closely related to each other, either in the form of a contiguous sequence (n-grams) or a collocation within strict word limits; and (ii) that the matches should be unique to the target text and one other. Instead, Jackson chose to search for 'phrases and collocations that occur five or fewer times . . . Parallels in imagery and ideas were recorded only if passages had at least one prominent word in common' (p. 257). Jackson was free to set his own idiosyncratic rules, but his criteria were too lax. By simply accumulating phrases and collocations occurring five or fewer times in his corpus of plays, and by accepting a match if it included only one 'prominent' word (by what measure?) he claimed many verbal matches that no previous attribution scholar would have accepted.

For Mosby's belief that he has 'climbed the top bough of the tree' (8.15), signifying that he has reached his highest level in society, Jackson cited the closest two matches produced by the *LION* search function, first a phrase from Dekker's *Old Fortunatus*, 'catched at the highest

---

51. Jackson, 'Quarrel Scene', p. 261; *Determining*, p. 23.

bough'. But this match has only one word in common, satisfying neither criterion of quantity or quality. Further, when examined in context, it turns out to be even less relevant. Fortune accuses Andelocia of having deviated from virtue to vice in his pursuit of Agripyna:

> Thou didst behold her, when thy strecht-out arme
> Catcht at the highest bough, the loftiest vice,
> The fairest Apple, but the fowlest price.[52]

Dekker refers not primarily to climbing a tree but to snatching an apple, with associations of the Fall. Jackson's second claimed match for Mosby's collocation is given as '"tree tops", Shakespeare, *Romeo and Juliet*' (p. 278). However, in the play Romeo refers to 'yonder blessed moon . . . | That tips with silver all these fruit-tree tops' (2.2.107–8). Here the noun 'fruit' evidently modifies 'trees', and the basic idea is of moonlight falling on their tips, creating neither a parallelism of language nor thought. For Mosby's sense of insecurity, where 'Each . . . airy gale doth shake my bed' (8.17), the best that the *LION* search function could offer was 'by whirlwind shaken', from *Alarum for London* (1599), and 'as mountains are for winds, | That shake not, though they blow perpetually', from *The Taming of the Shrew* (2.1.141). These phrases have only one word in common, 'shake', and use different synonyms for 'gale'. The very notion of matching verbal phrases was destroyed by the laxity Jackson allowed himself.

Another fault with the design of Jackson's method concerns the criterion of quality: he never defines what counts as a collocation, simply accepting the parallels identified by the *LION* search function. On only one occasion does he specify the interval of text between occurrences that would qualify a word-string to count as a collocation. Dealing with Mosby's opening soliloquy, Jackson notes that the word 'moody' occurs in the third line and the word 'discontent' in the tenth. He cites parallels for the phrase 'moody discontented' in *1 Henry VI* 3.1.123 (a scene that I ascribe to Kyd) and in *Richard III* (5.1.7), commenting: 'there are no

---

52. *Old Fortunatus*, 4.1.176–8, in Fredson Bowers (ed.), *The Dramatic Works of Thomas Dekker*, 4 vols (Cambridge, 1953–61), 1.174.

other collocations of "moody" and "discontent(ed)" within the space of sixty words' (p. 276). But this ignores the usual linguistic criteria for defining collocations. Corpus linguistics has emerged since the advent in the 1960s of large databases of actual language use, spoken and written. Linguists studying such corpora discovered that natural languages use ready-made phrases to a far greater extent than had ever been expected: in concordances of modern English, collocations outnumber single words by a factor of ten to one. John Sinclair, the acknowledged pioneer in this field, defined collocation as 'the occurrence of two or more words within a short space of each other in a text', the usual 'measure of proximity' being 'a maximum of four words intervening.'[53] The default setting for *EEBO-TCP* is ten words. Some such restricted definition is needed to prevent the undisciplined citation of 'parallels' that vitiated older studies, and it should be announced at the outset.

Jackson's use of *LION/EEBO* may have seemed like a pioneering use of massive electronic databases, but if we ask how many matches Jackson discovered between the Quarrel scene in *Arden* and his two Kyd plays, the figures are surprisingly small: only eight, four each from *The Spanish Tragedy* and *Soliman and Perseda*, to set against 132 from 'Shakespeare' (all plays dating after *Arden*).When I made my own search of the Quarrel scene, using both anti-plagiarism software and the database constructed by Pervez Rizvi, I identified seventy-three verbal matches between it and the acknowledged plays of Kyd.[54] I claim no particular expertise in this procedure. It seems that I had searched more diligently than Jackson—just as, on a previous occasion, I had looked for Peele's presence in that scene in *Titus Andronicus* more energetically than some other scholars, and found many more matches.[55] The conclusion is rather sobering: searches of electronic databases can be just as subjective and unreliable as the discredited methods of the 1920s.

---

53. John Sinclair, *Corpus, Concordance, Collocation* (Oxford: Oxford University Press, 1991), p. 170. For a brief outline of the relevance of corpus linguistics to attribution studies see Brian Vickers, 'Shakespeare and Authorship Studies in the Twenty-First Century' *Shakespeare Quarterly*, 62 (2011): 106–42 (134–40).

54. See my database: https://brianvickers.uk/databases.

55. See Vickers, 'Is *EEBO-TCP/LION* Suitable for Attribution Studies?'

Arden Of Faversham and Automated Attribution Methods

The 'linguistic turn' took other forms in the interpretation of *Arden of Faversham*, subject always to the limitations of electronic word-processing. Computers can count but they cannot read. Unable to decode the symbolic systems that constitute language, they cannot understand literal meaning, let alone metaphor. They can identify a word as a unique sequence of letters or characters, a graphological unit, but they are unable to distinguish the various senses that it can have, let alone recognize metaphor, allegory, and other deviations from regular usage. Despite the extravagant claims often made for digital language processing, computers can only count separate words, treated as linguistic items without meaning. Automated approaches cannot deal with the most fundamental aspect of language, what might be called its linearity. Meaning can only be created and communicated when words are joined together; reading and comprehension are time-dependent processes only comprehensible to the human brain.

Having closely studied the development of automated stylometry over the last two decades, I think it may be divided into two stages, in each of which a representative essay has claimed that *Arden of Faversham* was partly written by Shakespeare. In this new era the first available methods for processing literary texts were both invented by John Burrows: 'Delta' (2003) and 'Zeta' (2007). Both basically counted the frequencies with which selected groups of words were repeated, with procedures added to promote accuracy. Initially, computational procedures avoided 'content words', those embodying meaning, which might be determined by the subject matter rather than the author's intellect or personality, in favour of 'function words', which bind content words together in accordance with grammatical conventions, such as prepositions, conjunctions, pronouns, and so on. Practitioners of this method might choose the top fifty, or more words, of either or both categories, in an author's work, effectively reducing a poem or a play to 'a bag of words'. High claims were made for these methods in the first decade of this century, but Burrows soon abandoned Delta as inaccurate while persisting with Zeta. Two recent studies by scholars sharing a background in mathematics and computer programming, both of whom wrote their own programs to test these methods, have shown them to be inaccurate and unreliable.[56] Burrows, like his pupil Hugh Craig, was a professor of English Literature, and although both developed a knowledge of statistics, they were unable to understand the mathematics underlying these programs which made them ineffective.

An added defect of word-frequency computation when used for drama has been ignored since the beginning. Dramatists of all periods have individualized their main characters, and in his great tragedies Shakespeare constructed idiolects for half-a-dozen characters. He individualized Hamlet in several moods or registers, differentiating him from Polonius, Claudius, Laertes, Osric, and the Gravediggers. In *King Lear* he even created three distinct styles for the King: sane but angry; mad; and restored to sanity with a new humility. He invented several distinct voices for Edgar: a normal 'home' voice; that of the demented beggar Poor Tom; an adopted style to prevent his blinded father recognizing him; a rustic dialect in the fight with Osric; finally assuming a tone and bearing from chivalric romance in the duel with Edmund. Theatregoers and readers have for centuries been able to recognize these different styles and their dramatic functions. The sophisticated methods used in modern stylometry, however, are not attuned to recognizing them. They try to determine authorship by processing the words of individual characters, putting them all in one pot. The fundamental error of automated stylometry is its failure to realize that authorial style cannot be identified from characters' idiolects.[57] The limitations of quantitative approaches to language are becoming increasingly evident to highly expert commentators on digital computing, such as David Auerbach and Nan Da, but practitioners of stylometry have taken little notice.[58] Auerbach complained about 'the *opacity* of the

---

56. See Pervez Rizvi, 'The Interpretation of Zeta Test Results', *Digital Scholarship in the Humanities*, 34 (2019): 401–18, and Ros Barber, 'Big Data or Not Enough? Zeta Test Reliability and the Attribution of *Henry VI*, *Digital Scholarship in the Humanities*, 36 (2021): 542–64.

57. For a brief treatment of this problem see Brian Vickers, 'The Limitations of Stylometry: Idiolect and the Authorship of *Titus Andronicus*', *Notes and Queries* 267 (2020): 207–11.

58. See, e.g., David Auerbach, '"A cannon's burst discharged against a ruinated wall": A Critique of Quantitative Methods in Shakespearean Authorial Attribution', *Authorship*, 7 (2018):

methods', and another 'central problem, which is the poverty of the input data. By restricting such analyses to a handful of primitive signals such as word frequency and word succession, many of these researchers end up coating fundamentally simple (and untenable) findings in a statistical glaze, disguising the *explanation* for the results in precisely regimented charts and tables. A shift in focus from presentation of results to methodological justification is required' (pp. 3–4). One of the first applications of quantitative methods to attribution studies was the collection of essays published by Hugh Craig and Arthur Kinney (also a professor of English) in 2009, entitled *Shakespeare, Computers, and the Mystery of Authorship,*[59] which made extensive use of Burrows's 'Delta' and 'Zeta'. It included an essay by Kinney 'Authoring *Arden of Faversham*',[60] in which he accepted Jackson's ascription of scene 8 as 'Shakespeare's portion' but redefined it (vaguely) as lying 'within' scenes 4 to 9. Although welcomed by Jackson and by editors of the *New Oxford Shakespeare*, this essay received a devastating critique from Pervez Rizvi, who showed that the graphical representation of the results as a scatter-plot divided by a diagonal line in fact misrepresented their own calculations.[61] This definitive demonstration vitiated Kinney's essay and several others in this volume. Kinney's essay was heavily criticized on other grounds,[62] and it is regrettable that in his

---

1–18; Nan Z. Da, 'The Computational Case against Computational Literary Studies', *Critical Inquiry*, 19 (2019): 601–39; Brian Vickers, 'Authorship Attribution and Elizabethan Drama: Qualitative versus Quantitative Methods', *Authorship* 7 (2018).

59. Hugh Craig and Arthur F. Kinney, *Shakespeare, Computers, and the Mystery of Authorship* (Cambridge, 2009).

60. Ibid., pp. 70–87.

61. Pervez Rizvi, 'The interpretation of Zeta test results', *Digital Scholarship in the Humanities*, (2018): 1–18 (5 and passim).

62. Peter Kirwan, in *Shakespeare and the Idea of Apocrypha* (Cambridge, 2015), pp. 150–51, judged that Kinney's claim to have found 'further parallels of style' between *Arden of Faversham* and Shakespeare, 'such as the use of soliloquy and the vividness of the imagery, are . . . impressionistic and uncontextualized. The lexical-word tests employed by Kinney are . . . questionable on their own terms.' One such test, 'measuring *Arden's* relative likeness to Shakespeare, Marlowe and Kyd is reported to have placed the play in its entirety closer to Shakespeare's range than to either of the other authors, though these results are not shown'. All that Kinney can claim is 'a vague indication of a different style roughly in the middle' of the play.

recent work Jackson has relied on this unscholarly essay to justify his claims that Shakespeare wrote scenes 4–9.[63]

The second stage in my potted history of automated attribution saw a development from merely processing word frequencies. Scholars began to experiment with a range of new methods borrowed from disciplines based on mathematics, in which quantitative and statistical methods had long been used. In effect, this would open up attribution to any of the physical sciences, from signal processing to all aspects of IT, biology, physics, and the life sciences. One especially ambitious essay redefining the authorship of *Arden* appeared in the ancillary volume to *New Oxford Shakespeare*, an essay by Jack Elliott and Brett Greatley-Hirsch, both professors of English.[64] This essay is a striking instance of that process, for it used four quantitative methodologies for authorship attribution, as David Auerbach showed in his searching critique.[65] The authors' two main methods were 'Nearest Shrunken Centroid analysis', taken from cancer research, and 'Random Forests', borrowed from the discussion of 'decision trees', to which they added Burrows's 'Delta' and 'Zeta'. Despite the strange provenance, all four applied computational analysis to the primitive linguistic data of word frequencies in *Arden* compared to selections from the corpora of contemporary authors. Moreover, as Auerbach showed, their selection of data was limited. Elliott and Greatley-Hirsch used Delta on 'corpora . . . so small that many words even within the top 500 words in terms of frequency occur only rarely. The 500th most frequently occurring word across all considered texts, for example, "less", does not occur at all in *Arden*'. Auerbach rejected the assumption 'that single word frequencies are sufficient to establish a high degree of confidence in authorial attribution' and showed that none of the methods used here was reliable. One of them, indeed (Random Forests), 'repeatedly decides for Shakespeare as the author of the entirety of *Arden*, which no scholar has

63. Jackson, *Determining*, pp. 48–52, 63–4, 123–5.

64. Jack Elliott and Brett Greatley-Hirsch, '*Arden of Faversham*, Shakespearean Authorship, and "The Print of Many"', in Taylor and Egan (eds), *New Oxford Shakespeare Authorship Companion*, pp. 139–81.

65. Auerbach, 'Critique of Quantitative Methods in Shakespearean Authorial Attribution'.

maintained'. That should have given good reason to discount its findings, but Elliott and Greatley-Hirsch sat on the fence, unable to decide between three conclusions: 'that the play belongs to Shakespeare it its entirety'; that 'the play is a collaborative effort, with Shakespeare responsible for the lion's share'; 'that the play is both a collaboration and bears traces of textual contamination . . .' (p. 181). No mention of Kyd, naturally.

While that conclusion may have been justified in the light of their (often contradictory) results, it was an embarrassment for Gary Taylor, who had placed his trust in MacDonald Jackson. In a long concluding section to *Authorship Companion* on 'The Canon and Chronology of Shakespeare's Works' (pp. 417–602), Taylor, assisted by Rory Loughnane, simply avoided the issue, stating that the essay by Elliott and Greatley-Hirsch 'complicates matters by giving [Shakespeare] the bulk of it' (p. 490), not revealing what 'complicates' might mean. Despite knowing their authors' indecision, Taylor and Loughnane nevertheless cite their essay as 'supporting the case for Shakespeare's authorship of the middle of *Arden*' and demonstrating that 'Kyd could not have written any significant part of the play' (ibid.). That is a conclusion that the anti-Kyd faction welcomed. But whoever reads Auerbach's analysis will know how false it is.

Readers may well be disappointed by this chapter, which records how a leading scholar in attribution studies has persisted for sixty years in ignoring the extensive evidence of Kyd's authorship that was available to him in 1963. Jackson not only dismissed Kyd, he denigrated him: subjective literary judgments gave way to devaluation. In recent years the much-hailed digital turn produced no breakthrough in attribution studies, due to the inherent limitations of electronic word-processing and badly designed methods. Finally, in a volume claiming to present 'an extensive sampling of new research, employing a range of new data and new methods', we have a dispiriting spectacle: editors of *The New Oxford Shakespeare* trying to suppress the fact that one of their newly commissioned essays failed to establish the claims by which they added *Arden of Faversham* to Shakespeare's canon.

Depressing though this situation may be, it is fortunately not the only verdict of contemporary scholarship, as the next chapter will show.

9

Kyd's Restored Canon

If Vickers is right, then he will, with a single hypothesis, have solved a whole series of important attribution problems and thereby reshaped our understanding of the rise of English commercial drama in the late 1580s and early 1590s. His claim would also make all five plays more interesting: it would relate them to each other and to the Kyd canon. It would enable us to tell good new stories about five plays that are currently seldom discussed or taught at all.

GARY TAYLOR[1]

UP TO THIS POINT I have presented two types of evidence for extending Kyd's canon to include *King Leir*, *Arden of Faversham*, and *Fair Em*. In each case I devoted most space to analysing Kyd's preferred dramaturgy, the three types of plot that are found in varying forms: intrigue plots, the use of comedy in tragedies, and the freedom given to female characters (good or bad) to take murderous revenge on men who have harmed them. I complemented that approach by drawing on studies of Kyd's linguistic choices, in phraseology, verse form, and rhyme. In every case the authorship markers provided by other scholars confirmed my

---

1. Gary Taylor, John V. Nance, and Keegan Cooper, 'Shakespeare and Who? Aeschylus, *Edward III*, and Thomas Kyd', *Shakespeare Survey*, 70 (2017): p. 146.

attribution. Finally, I want to discuss independent evaluations by other scholars of my claims for an extended canon.

There have been two major evaluations, by Martin Mueller in 2009 and Pervez Rizvi in 2017. Both scholars combine advanced computing skills with a knowledge and love of literature, and both undertook the massive task of documenting phrasal repetitions in a huge number of early modern plays.

Martin Mueller

Professor Martin Mueller (Emeritus, Northwestern University) has had three careers. Having benefited from the excellent classical training of the German gymnasium and further studies at the universities of Munich and Hamburg, he took his doctorate in Classics at Indiana University. His first scholarly publications were on Greek tragedy and on Shakespeare.[2] He records becoming interested in 'the problem of repetitive or formulaic language in the *Iliad* and *Odyssey*' in the 1990s, and in his second career he developed a remarkable skill in digitally assisted text analysis.[3] Mueller was jointly responsible for creating the wonderful *Chicago Homer* website, an interactive resource that allows users to search all instances of verbal repetition in early Greek epic, from the famous 'Homeric formulae' to the more extended repetitions that mark the transition from an oral to a written culture.[4] The repeated phrases range in length from 2 to 123 words and in frequency from 2 to 3,152 repetitions.

2. See, e.g., Martin Mueller, *Children of Oedipus and other essays on the imitation of Greek tragedy, 1550–1800* (Toronto, 1980); 'From *Leir* to *Lear*', *Philological Quarterly*, 73 (1994): 195–217; '*Hamlet* and the world of ancient tragedy', *Arion*, 5 (1997): 22–45; 'Digital Shakespeare, or towards a literary informatics', *Shakespeare*, 4 (2008): 300–317.

3. See the text of his Hilda Hulme Memorial Lecture, given at London University in July 2013: 'Shakespeare His Contemporaries: Collaborative Curation and Exploration of Early Modern Drama in a Digital Environment', *Digital Humanities Quarterly*, 8(3), at http://www .digitalhumanities.org/dhq/vol/8/3/index.html, Paragraph 11.

4. See *Chicago Homer*, ed. Ahuvia Kahane and Martin Mueller, http://homer.library .northwestern.edu/. For a searching analysis of their results for the tragic epic see Mueller, *The Iliad*, 2nd ed. (London, 2009), especially 'Interpreting Homeric Repetitions' (pp. 21–30) and chapter 6: 'Homeric Repetitions' (pp. 135–72), with some fascinating detail.

312   CHAPTER 9

Mueller's third career united the knowledge and expertise gained in the first two by helping create an interactive database of early modern English drama outside Shakespeare. Known as *Shakespeare His Contemporaries*, the collection of texts, in modern spelling (essential for high-speed data analysis), was expanded in 2015 to 504 plays (from 318 plays in 2009). Mueller had caused this corpus to be linguistically annotated with a tagging procedure that made it possible to extract all the repeated phrases, or n-grams, as they are known, extending from two words (a bigram) to seven words (a heptagram) that were repeated at least once. This yielded over a million repetitions and eight million occurrences. Mueller then computed 'the distribution of n-grams that are shared by two plays of the same author'. His study of this data confirmed the fact observed by attribution scholars since Charles Crawford in 1903, that authors frequently repeat the same phrases across their career. Mueller estimated that two plays by the same author generally share about twice as many unique n-grams as two plays by different authors, and that the total of such self-repetition amounted to 2,303 two-play combinations.[5]

In August 2009 Mueller ran an experiment testing the claims for Kyd's extended canon that I had published in the *Times Literary Supplement* on 18 April 2008. Studying these 2,303 two-play combinations, Mueller found that twenty-eight occur in the seven plays I attributed to Kyd. More significantly, 'six place in the top quartile [25 percent] for shared two-play n-grams by the same author'. From Mueller's list I select the two most relevant to this discussion (figures in parentheses are frequencies per 10,000 occurrences, followed by a percentage probability that the plays are by Kyd):

The Spanish Tragedy/Soliman and Perseda   (13.3, 99.9%)
Soliman and Perseda/Arden of Faversham   (9.2, 99.7%)

Mueller described his tests as 'extremely crude', but he concluded that

on balance, my figures lend support to Vickers's argument although they are not conclusive. There are many plays by different authors

5. See Darren Freebury-Jones, 'Martin Mueller on Brian Vickers and the Kyd Canon', .

that share more n-grams than the plays in the putative Kyd canon. On the other hand, if you play a ranking game with each play in the Kyd canon and list the plays with which it shares the most n-grams, some of the other "Kyd" plays will appear in the top five. Something is going on here.

Mueller returned to this issue a week later, evidently determined to devise a more searching test. As he ruefully noted, 'authorship arguments provide huge yawns in English departments. But, as Vickers argued in his *Times Literary Supplement* piece, there is good reason to look with interest at an expanded Kyd canon. Shakespeare and Marlowe suddenly acquire a slightly older and gifted contemporary whose oeuvre has some size and considerable thematic and generic range'.[6] In this second essay Mueller presented his 'corroborative evidence', having applied 'discriminant analysis[7] to lemma trigrams that occur at least 500 times in 318 early modern plays. There are 56 of them, and they range from *I will not* (2,332 occurrences) to *what do you* (508). Riveting fragments of speech, but remarkably informative when you look at their distribution'. Mueller's computations had an important difference to mine. Whereas I had based my argument for an expanded Kyd corpus based on *shared rare repetitions*, phrases that occur in Kyd's accepted plays and those I have newly attributed but nowhere else, Mueller's test 'ignores this evidence and looks instead at *the most common* trigrams, which show up in at least half (164) or more than 90% (297) of all plays' (my italics). My and his conclusions 'therefore rest on an entirely different evidentiary basis. To the extent that we agree, the case is greatly strengthened: the evidence of rare and of common phenomena support each other'.

Mueller assigned to Kyd all the plays that I ascribe to him. For his test, however, he included 'the "prequel" *The first part of Jeronimo*

---

6. See Mueller, DATA blog of 23 August 2009, 'Vickers is right about Kyd', available on the same website: https://darrenfj.files.wordpress.com/2017/11/N-grams-and-the-Kyd-Canon -and-Vickers-is-right-about-Kyd.pdf.

7. Discriminant function analysis is a form of classification, the act of distributing things into groups, classes, or categories of the same type.

because it shares a lot of rare repetitions with the *Spanish Tragedy*, although it shares relatively few rare repetitions with the other plays in the Kyd canon'. The results of Mueller's discriminant analysis were as follows, with the percentage expressing the probability that the play is by Kyd:

The first part of Jeronimo (30%)
Cornelia (79.7%)
Soliman and Perseda (85.3%)
The Spanish Tragedy (96.1%)
Arden of Faversham (97.4%)
The true chronicle history of King Leir (99.3%)
Fair Em (99.5%)

As Mueller commented,

> these are striking results. First, Discriminant Analysis rejects the 'prequel' as Kyd's. It assigns it to the grab bag of anonymous plays with a 57.4% chance.[8] So it is not fooled by the presence of many shared repetitions between it and *The Spanish Tragedy*. Secondly, Discriminant Analysis very strongly confirms that the other plays come from the same stable. Indeed, if *The Spanish Tragedy* is the clearest case of a play by Kyd, the three English plays are, so to speak, a little more Catholic than the Pope.

I recommend his conclusion to any reader who contests my attribution of these three plays to Kyd:

> If you combine my evidence from common trigrams with Vickers's evidence from rare shared repetitions, you would have to be very skeptical about the power of quantitative analysis not to acknowledge the fact that the claim for an expanded Kyd canon rests on quite solid evidence.

---

8. For a full study of 1 *Jeronimo*, decisively excluding it from the Kyd canon, see Erne, *Beyond The Spanish Tragedy*, pp. 12–46.

Pervez Rizvi

Pervez Rizvi read mathematics at Cambridge and did postgraduate work at Liverpool University, before becoming a computer programmer. He had enjoyed studying Shakespeare during his London schooling, and while at Liverpool he became interested in Shakespearian textual criticism. In 1963 Charlton Hinman published a widely respected study of how the First Folio had been printed and proofread, in which he claimed that the compositors who had set the book in type could be identified by their spelling.[9] Hinman argued that through most of the Folio 'we can easily distinguish two well-defined habits of spelling the three simple words 'do', 'go' and 'here'. In many pages we find, almost without exception, *do* (or, occasionally, *doo*), *go*, and *heere*', spellings that Hinman associated with Compositor B (one of the two main workmen) while 'in many other pages *doe*, *goe*, and *here* strongly predominate'. These are the spellings that he assigned to Compositor A, although he added that 'neither man invariably spelt all these words—or, indeed, any one of them—in one way only'.[10] Later scholars suggested amendments, making compositor analysis a central method of textual criticism in Elizabethan drama,

Hinman cited large quantities of data, but in many cases they were only a selection, so Rizvi was curious whether Hinman's thesis held when all the data was checked. To do this it was necessary for him to transcribe the whole text of the First Folio and to document every instance of variations in compositor spellings, processing over a million items of data and writing appropriate programs. Having studied many more spellings than Hinman, Rizvi published his results in what became a seminal article.[11] It was astonishing to see that in every instance the compositors' preferences were reversed at the halfway point, for reasons

---

9. Charlton Hinman, *The Printing and Proof-Reading of The First Folio of Shakespeare*, 2 vols (Oxford, 1968).

10. Ibid., 1.182–5.

11. See Pervez Rizvi, 'The Use of Spellings for Compositor Attributions', *Papers of the Bibliographical Society of America*, 110 (2016): 1–54 (6–11) and *passim*.

that were obscure. Hinman had noticed a significant detail but had not considered all the evidence. In his defence, Hinman could never have collected so much evidence manually. That was possible only in the age of electronic data processing, and only given a scholar prepared to invest so much time and knowledge in such a massive task.

Rizvi became interested in authorship attribution in 2016, having been given a copy of the *Authorship Companion* by its editors. This volume is replete with statistics and confident attributions based on them, provoking the same questions that Rizvi faced with Hinman's work: is the evidence complete, and are the attributions securely based? These questions could only be answered if all the play texts were available and were marked up according to the latest software. Once again modern spelling texts were needed, and Mueller generously allowed Rizvi to use *Shakespeare His Contemporaries*. The editors of the Folger Shakespeare Digital Texts, Barbara A. Mowat and Paul Werstine, equally generously added their permission.[12]

In 2017, having spent over a year writing programs that allowed users to examine every instance of repetition and to compare any two plays, Rizvi published a corpus of 527 early modern plays performed between 1552 and 1657, consisting of ten million words (including stage directions).[13] The n-gram search results published there amount to 26,274,294 phrasal matches, 'consisting of exactly 13,137,147 pairs, as expected, each pair containing the same matching phrases from the same

12. Professors Mowat and Werstine worked on the Folger Shakespeare from 1989 to 2009, publishing forty-two books between 1992 and 2009. Commendably, they revised sixteen of the books between 2009 and 2019, the later revisions having been made by Werstine alone, because Mowat died in late 2017. (Information kindly supplied by Paul Werstine, 9 December 2022.)

13. See Pervez Rizvi, 'Shakespeare's Text. A Collection of Resources for Students of the Original Texts of Shakespeare's Plays', https://www.shakespearestext.com/can/index.htm for the page 'Collocations and N-grams'. Additional improvements were made in 2018, and the site includes much helpful discussion, essential reading before using it. Rizvi's listings of n-gram matches are complete for 4-grams and above, but he found that there were far too many hundreds of millions of 1-gram, 2-gram and 3-gram matches to list. He therefore disregarded 1-grams entirely and listed 2-grams and 3-grams only if they contain at least two words not on the list of the 100 most common words used in these plays. That list contains mainly function words such as *the, and, of, to,* and so on. Similarly, collocation search results are listed only if they contain at least two words that are not on the common words list.

pair of plays. This gives me a high level of confidence in the completeness of the n-gram results'. As Rizvi commented, 'the work I have done has never been done before', so he had 'no complete set of prior results to check it against'. I doubt that any user will have grounds to question his accuracy and authority over this massive range of edited play texts.

Given this vast amount of data and the range of possible combinations, it was important for Rizvi to establish the most effective type of n-gram for authorship attribution. In October 2018 he published on his site five 'experiments' he had conducted on a corpus of 86 reliably attributed plays by six authors: Chapman, Fletcher, Jonson, Marlowe, Middleton, and Shakespeare. He began by testing how accurately the counts he had published could attribute those plays to their known authors. Rizvi performed separate tests both for 'All n-grams' and for the more important 'Unique n-grams', that is, 'matches which are unique across the whole database'. In the first category, '4-grams correctly attribute 82 out of 86 plays, while 5-grams are not far behind, with 80 out of 86 correct'. In the second category 'unique 3-grams get 84 out of 86 attributions correct, with unique 4-grams only just behind at 83 out of 86 correct'. In a second paper Rizvi added more detail and refined the conclusions, observing that since 'unique 3-grams and unique 4-grams have average margins which are far ahead of those for all n-grams' then they 'are the best to use with this method'. He then asked why that is so:

> Perhaps the answer is obvious. Authorship attribution is about working out what makes an author distinguishable. [Other scholars] use the terms 'difference-mining' and 'resemblance-mining'. The essence of any attribution method is first to find out what makes an author different from his peers, to build up an author profile, and then see which other plays resemble that profile. What makes an author different is, by necessity, rare; and uniqueness is an extreme form of rarity. Perhaps that is explanation enough why unique n-grams provide the most accurate attributions.

This may seem paradoxical, given our general understanding of scientific methods, in which 'the greater the amount of data you have, the more reliable your conclusions will be'. But Rizvi pointed out that, particularly for lower values (1- and 2-grams) the number of non-unique n-gram matches 'is so super-abundant that common phrases, which everyone used, drown out the distinctive ones and confound our attempts to discover what makes an author different'.

Rizvi's fourth experiment will interest us most, in which he enlarged the set of plays used in the above experiments to include 'the so-called Extended Kyd Canon'. As he explained:

I used the 86 plays used before, and added the extended Kyd canon, consisting of the following plays:

The Spanish Tragedy (excluding the Additions)
Soliman and Perseda
Cornelia
Fair Em
Arden of Faversham
Edward III (excluding the Countess scenes and excluding 4.4)
Henry VI, Part 1 (excluding Act 1 and excluding 2.4, 4.2 and 4.5)
King Leir

For this test, Rizvi added Kyd as an author and assigned all eight plays to him. He presented his results as two Excel spread sheets, one for raw data, the other for a summary, commenting: 'We see that the first five plays listed above are all accepted by the method as being by Kyd, including the whole *Arden of Faversham* play'. That is a very satisfying confirmation of my new ascriptions for the three non-history plays. Other scholars have noted the difficulty attributing Elizabethan history plays, given the use of the same historical sources (Holinshed, Hall) and the inevitable similarities in vocabulary when dealing with courtly protocol and military conflict. These factors help us to understand Rizvi's findings for Kyd's *King Leir* and Kyd's contributions to *1 Henry VI* and *Edward III*:

The other three are assigned to Marlowe, except that 4-grams assign the *Edward III* scenes to Kyd, by a strong margin. The raw data reveals Kyd to be the runner-up for the *1 Henry VI* scenes and the runner-up using 3-grams for *Edward III*. However, it is Shakespeare, not Kyd, who is the runner-up behind Marlowe for *King Leir*, possibly because of matches with *King Lear* (though this needs to be checked).... It is noticeable how, excepting the *Tamburlaine* plays—which are invulnerable because of the way they help each other with plentiful matches—Kyd and Marlowe appear to be almost interchangeable.

Several scholars have noticed the closeness between Marlowe and Kyd when measured in terms of selected vocabulary by data processing; now Rizvi has shown that it holds for n-grams. Nevertheless, a study that I hope to publish soon will show that the two authors can be clearly distinguished, when we compare their phrasal lexicon in the histories with their other plays.

Another important result for this study is the change that occurs to the Shakespeare attributions over time. Rizvi pointed out that in his data some early Shakespeare plays 'shift attribution to Kyd, while the middle and late plays are unaffected. Among the early plays, only *The Comedy of Errors* stays with Shakespeare, but only weakly, and the runner-up is Kyd'. Rizvi commented:

> If we do not wish to attribute these early Shakespeare plays to Kyd, the results here are nevertheless good evidence of Kyd's influence on the young Shakespeare, an influence that faded away within a few years of Kyd's death. Now, as far as our method is concerned, Shakespeare is defined by *all* his plays listed; yet, if the middle and late plays do not contain much Kyd influence then the method will not detect much Kyd influence in Shakespeare as a whole. Therefore, when it finds Kyd phrases in the early Shakespeare plays, it will mistake them for Kyd's writing. That seems to be the explanation why these early Shakespeare plays get attributed to Kyd. In turn, this reinforces the point that changes in an author's style over time can cause some of his work not to be recognised as his by purely computational methods.

Rizvi's conclusions also disprove Jackson's use of such parallels with early Shakespeare to claim that *Arden of Faversham* has more affinity to his work than to Kyd's. In 2008 Jackson published an article which included his finding that *The Taming of the Shrew* has '47 unique matches' with *Arden*, findings that 'surely expose the weakness' of any case for his authorship of that play or for an 'extended Kyd canon'.[14] As we have seen before, Jackson has constantly ignored chronology and any notion of Kyd's influence on Shakespeare. Rizvi's evidence leaves no doubt about that relationship. His spreadsheet listed eighteen 4-gram matches between the two plays, showing the great impression that Kyd made on the younger dramatist.

Historians of Kyd's reception were not surprised when MacDonald Jackson published an article disputing Rizvi's results concerning Kyd.[15] Jackson criticized Rizvi for including the extended Kyd canon to his basic 86 play corpus, claiming that it led to 'misattributions of uncontested plays', thereby 'swelling the error rate' (p. 134). To overcome this failing he compiled a new corpus of 19 plays, comprising Kyd's accepted three-play canon, the early Shakespeare canon, the complete Marlowe canon, and 'the probable Shakespeare scenes of *Edward III*, and scenes 4–8 of *Arden of Faversham*' (p. 135). At once objections arise. As we have seen, all of Shakespeare's plays postdated *Arden*. Jackson included nine plays dating from 1592–96, all of which contain echoes of *Arden*, in some cases extensive (*The Taming of the Shrew*, *The Two Gentlemen of Verona*). His corpus was corrupted from the outset, and it was a mistake to include parts of plays. The outcome was—following Rizvi's demonstration that 'unique 3-gram matches' were the most reliable—that Jackson 'assigned each of the nineteen whole plays to the right author and both the selected *Edward III* and *Arden* portions to Shakespeare' (pp. 135–6). Many attribution scholars would object that comparing whole plays to just a few scenes is not comparing like with like. Moreover, as Pervez Rizvi has commented, 'there are no stylometric tests, not even mine, which have been shown to be reliable in attributing single scenes or small sets of scenes', and 'extensive validation tests' would be needed to prove otherwise'.[16]

---

14. MacDonald Jackson, 'New Research on the Dramatic Canon of Thomas Kyd', *Research Opportunities in Renaissance Drama*, 47 (2008): 107–27 (114–17).

15. See Jackson, 'The Use of N-grams'.

16. Rizvi, email 20 December 2022.

KYD'S RESTORED CANON   321

In the remainder of his article (pp. 136–49) Jackson took issue with the extended Kyd canon by recording the number of uniquely shared trigrams for each work and listing 'the fifteen closest matching plays in Rizvi's 527-play database' (p. 144). Once again Jackson has ignored the questions of chronology and influence. His list includes mostly plays performed after 1588, many of them as late as the 1630s. Not only does this make it impossible to distinguish self-repetition from influence or imitation, but phrases that were rarely used in the early 1590s had become familiar and were repeated much more frequently by the Jacobean and Caroline periods. This incremental expansion of the lexicon has swollen Jackson's totals and drowned the number of matches with Kyd's plays, written between 1587 and 1594. For example, Jackson's lists of plays having the most matches with *Fair Em* ranks *Arden of Faversham* ['less scenes 4–8'] at no. 9 in a list beginning with Middleton's *A Game at Chess* (1624), which scores 401 points,[17] ending with over 190. *The Spanish Tragedy* (149), *Soliman and Perseda* (0), *Cornelia* (74), and *King Leir* (118) are relegated to a footnote. If this procedure were repeated with a cut-off point of 1594 or 1600 the results would be significantly different. Once again, as with his essay on the Quarrel scene, Jackson's expansion of the parameters has disadvantaged Kyd.

Readers of Jackson's essay will have taken for granted that he would accurately cite the relevant data, but this seems not to have happened, as pointed out by Darren Freebury-Jones, a young scholar who has already joined the select company of Kyd experts.[18] His analyses of Rizvi's data reveal that Kyd's plays were consistently inter-related across the many different types of classification ('maximal' and 'formal',[19]

---

17. Jackson's scores are based on 'the number of uniquely shared trigrams divided by the combined total of word tokens in the two works under consideration and multiplied by 1,000,000 to avoid decimals' Jackson, 'The Use of N-grams', p. 144.

18. See Darren Freebury-Jones, 'Unique phrases and the canon of Thomas Kyd', *Notes and Queries*, 67 (2020): 220–23.

19. As Freebury-Jones explained, 'A phrase four words in length will contain different types of n-grams: one tetragram (four-word phrase); one trigram (three-word phrase); two bigrams (two-word phrases); and four single words. These are what Rizvi would call "formal-grams".'

trigrams and tetragrams), depending which play is chosen as the reference point. In the spreadsheet for *Soliman and Perseda* the top plays sharing unique formal trigrams are *The Spanish Tragedy* and *Arden of Faversham*, while *Cornelia* also makes the top dozen. Ranked according to unique formal tetragrams, *Cornelia* drops out of the top dozen and is replaced by *King Leir*. 'In the spreadsheet for *Arden of Faversham*, *Soliman and Perseda*, and *Fair Em* are in the top dozen for unique formal trigrams and tetragrams, and *Arden of Faversham* is in the top dozen in the *Fair Em* spreadsheet' (pp. 1–2). Freebury-Jones chose a different metric, multiplying Rizvi's weighted figures by 10,000 to calculate the relationships between Kyd's plays, both the accepted and the extended canon, in the various categories. The top results for the number of unique formal trigrams shared between the two works are:

> *The Spanish Tragedy: Soliman and Perseda* (8.58)
> *Arden of Faversham: Soliman and Perseda* (5.73)
> *The Spanish Tragedy: Cornelia* (4.11)
> *Cornelia: Soliman and Perseda* (3.01)
> *Arden of Faversham: Fair Em* (2.48)

The high ranking of *Arden of Faversham* above *Cornelia* makes a strong case for Kyd's authorship, which is further strengthened by the results for unique formal tetragrams:

> *Arden of Faversham: Soliman and Perseda* (5.99)
> *Soliman and Perseda: The Spanish Tragedy* (5.04)
> *Arden of Faversham: Fair Em* (2.79)
> *Cornelia: The Spanish Tragedy* (2.46)
> *Soliman and Perseda: King Leir* (2.00)
> *Cornelia: Soliman and Perseda* (1.50)

In this list *Arden of Faversham* ranks higher still, further strengthening that case. 'Moreover, *Fair Em* and *Arden of Faversham* have stronger links than the undisputed Kydian play pair, *The Spanish Tragedy* and

---

Conversely, the four-word phrase itself would also constitute what Rizvi calls a "maximal" n-gram and would only be counted once.' (p. 220).

Cornelia, making a case for common authorship of both plays newly attributed to Kyd' (p. 220),

Finally, Freebury-Jones presented his results for maximal unique n-grams in Kyd's plays making the top dozen:

Soliman and Perseda: The Spanish Tragedy (9.59)
Arden of Faversham: Soliman and Perseda (6.51)
Cornelia: The Spanish Tragedy (3.83)
Fair Em: Arden of Faversham (3.10)
Cornelia: Soliman and Perseda (2.41)

Once again, *Soliman and Perseda* and *Arden of Faversham* are ranked higher than *The Spanish Tragedy*, probably due to the evolution of Kyd's style away from its 'high style'. The two later plays are very close in time (1588 and 1590) and embody Kyd's mature style, glimpsed only occasionally in *Fair Em*, due to its damaged textual state. Freebury-Jones recorded that, 'with the exception of the spreadsheet for *King Leir*, every play that Vickers ascribes solely to Kyd has at least one other play in the "enlarged" canon featuring in the top dozen for unique trigrams and/or tetragrams, the most powerful statistical markers of authorship in Rizvi's corpus' (p. 233). The inter-relations between the accepted Kyd plays and the recovered canon show that they form a coherent artistic oeuvre.

In a subsequent note Freebury-Jones took up a claim that Jackson made in 2008, that 'Two early Shakespeare plays each have more unique matches with *Arden*' than any of Kyd's plays, either in the accepted or in the extended canon.[20] I have already commented on this claim as showing how Jackson consistently avoided considering Kyd's influence on Shakespeare. Freebury-Jones has now checked that claim by evaluating unique formal trigrams in the period 1580–96. He found that *Arden* (1590) has thirty-eight matches with *2 Henry VI* (1592) and forty-three with *The Taming of the Shrew* (1592). But *Arden* shares thirty-four formal trigrams with *The Spanish Tragedy*, sixty-six with *Soliman and Perseda*,

---

20. Jackson, 'New Research on the Dramatic Canon of Thomas Kyd', p. 116, and Darren Freebury-Jones, 'Kyd, Shakespeare, and *Arden of Faversham*: Rerunning a Two-Horse Race', *ANQ*, 36 (2023): 347–50.

sixteen with *Cornelia*, thirty-eight with *Fair Em*, and fifty-two with *King Leir*. Moreover, when adjusted for length, while 2 *Henry VI* (25,348 words, or 'tokens') has one unique match with *Arden* per 667 words, and *Shrew* (20,929 words) has one per 387 words, both are outscored by Kyd. *Fair Em* (12,042 words) has one unique formal match with *Arden* per 317 words, and *King Leir* (21,77 words) one match per 402 tokens. Freebury-Jones concludes that these results for unique trigrams 'empirically falsify [Jackson's] argument that "in the two-horse race, Shakespeare beats Kyd."'[21] Few will deny that he has successfully made his case.

I conclude by hoping, in the words of Martin Mueller, that all the many kinds of evidence I have brought together in this book will persuade readers

> to look with interest at an expanded Kyd canon. Shakespeare and Marlowe suddenly acquire a slightly older and gifted contemporary whose oeuvre has some size and considerable thematic and generic range.

21. Freebury-Jones, 'Rerunning a Two-Horse Race', pp. 348–9.

10

Kyd's Critical Reception

MY GOAL IN THIS BOOK has been to evaluate the claims for Kyd's sole authorship of the three plays I newly ascribe to him, *King Leir*, *Arden of Faversham*, and *Fair Em* (with *1 Henry VI* and *Edward III* waiting in the wings for future discussion).[1] This has inevitably meant neglecting many other aspects of Kyd's work, ignoring his whole oeuvre and its reception. The only critic whose work I have discussed is MacDonald Jackson, whose advocacy of Shakespeare's part authorship of *Arden* led to a persistently negative view of Kyd. It is good to be reminded that no other scholar has shared his dismissive attitude.

Kyd's Recognition

Indeed, when the history of early modern drama began to be studied seriously in the late nineteenth century, Kyd attracted nothing but favourable attention. Several writers independently judged that his achievement had not yet been properly appreciated, largely due to the prestige awarded to Marlowe. In 1898 Josef Schick, reflecting on the fact that *The Spanish Tragedy* must have been written by 1587 (since it contains no allusion to the Spanish Armada's destruction), and thus antedates Marlowe's *Tamburlaine*, saw it as showing

---

1. Both plays, edited by David Bevington and myself, will be included in Vickers (ed.), *The Collected Works of Thomas Kyd*, vol. 2.

326   CHAPTER 10

what an important historical place Kyd holds in the English drama: he then, not Marlowe, is the man who wrote the first great popular English tragedy; he then, not Marlowe, must have given to the popular drama the most thundering of all metres for the garb.[2]

In fact, Kyd's prosody differed substantially from Marlowe's. As we have seen, the work of Philip Timberlake established that Kyd was the pioneer in introducing the feminine ending into the English pentameter, an innovation soon copied by Shakespeare, who never imitated Marlowe's verse style, except in good-humoured parody. Comparisons of Kyd with Marlowe were frequent in this period. G. Gregory Smith, writing in the *Cambridge History of English Literature* (1910), praised both the dialogue in *The Spanish Tragedy* as 'more human and probable than anything which had gone before, or was being done by Marlowe', and 'the workings out of his plot', especially 'by ingenious turns in the situation':

> In such a scene as that where Pedringano bandies words with the hangman when the boy brings in the empty box [*Spanish Tragedy*, 3.6] ... we are parting company with the older tragedy, with the English Senecans, with *Tamburlaine* and *Faustus* and even *Edward II*, and we are nearer Shakespeare. When we add to this talent for dramatic surprise the talent for displaying character, as it were rooted in the plot, and growing in it—not strewn on the path of a hero who is little more than the embodiment of a simple idea—we describe Kyd's gift to English tragedy, and, more particularly, to Shakespeare himself.[3]

Other scholars shared this high estimation of Kyd.

In 1919 the young T.S. Eliot, in one of his early periodical essays, contested Swinburne's 'misleading' judgment that Marlowe was 'the father of English tragedy and the creator of English blank verse', observing that 'Kyd has as good a title to the first honour as Marlowe', and judging that Marlowe was 'not ... as great a dramatist as Kyd'.[4] Eliot went on to

---

2. Schick, *Spanish Tragedy*, p. vii.

3. Smith, 'Marlowe and Kyd,' in Ward and Waller (eds), *The Drama to 1642, Part 1*, p. 163.

4. T.S. Eliot, 'Christopher Marlowe', in *Selected Essays*, 3rd edn. (London, 1951), p. 118. This essay was first published in *Arts and Letters* 2 (Autumn 1919), and reprinted in *The Sacred Wood*

KYD'S CRITICAL RECEPTION 327

pay tribute to Marlowe's superior achievements in introducing 'a new driving power into blank verse' (p. 122), but he regarded Kyd as 'Marlowe's greatest contemporary'. In another essay of that year Eliot described Kyd as 'that extraordinary dramatic (if not poetic) genius who was in all probability the author of two plays so dissimilar as *The Spanish Tragedy* and *Arden of Faversham*'.[5] Discussing the influence of Seneca on Elizabethan drama in 1927, Eliot observed that

> the most significant popular play under Senecan influence is of course *The Spanish Tragedy*, and the further responsibility of Kyd for the translation of the pseudo-Senecan *Cornelia* of Garnier has marked him as the disciple of Seneca. But in *The Spanish Tragedy* there is another element, not always sufficiently distinguished from the Senecan, which . . . allies it to something more indigenous.

Eliot was referring to 'the type of plot' which Kyd had developed, which has 'nothing classical or pseudo-classical in it': 'Hieronimo to compass his revenge by the play allies it with a small but interesting class of drama which certainly owes nothing essential to Seneca: that which includes *Arden of Feversham* and *The Yorkshire Tragedy*'.[6] By 'something more indigenous' Eliot meant the fact that both these 'remarkable plays' were based on 'contemporary or recent crimes committed in England'—which is surely a coincidence of subject matter, rather than of plot or structure. Eliot was right, however, to link Kyd with the 'Italian progeny of Seneca', for it is probably from Italian Renaissance tragedy that Kyd took over the element of intrigue, so important in all his plays. Eliot was also perceptive in his recognition that Kyd wrote *Arden of Faversham*, adding a terse footnote: 'I dissent from Dr. Boas, and agree with that body of opinion which attributes *Arden* to Kyd, e.g., Fleay, Robertson, Crawford, Dugdale Sykes, Oliphant' (p. 81 n.). Although Robertson and

---

(London, 1920). See Donald Gallup, *T.S. Eliot: A Bibliography* (London, 1969), pp. 28, 204.

5. Eliot, *Selected Essays*, p. 142; '*Hamlet*', originally in the *Athenaeum*, 26 September 1919, and in *The Sacred Wood* (1920); Gallup, *T.S. Eliot: A Bibliography*, pp. 28, 204.

6. Eliot, *Selected Essays*, pp. 80–81; 'Seneca in Elizabethan Translation' was originally the 'Introduction' to *Seneca His Tenne Tragedies* in the 'Tudor Translations' series (London 1927). *A Yorkshire Tragedy* (1606) is now ascribed to Middleton.

Fleay were not always reliable, the others made a lasting contribution in establishing Kyd as the author of *Arden*.

W. K. C. Guthrie, an eminent historian of Greek philosophy, reviewing the progress of Orphic studies, observed 'I used to know more about Orpheus'. Reading Eliot's early essays is to be reminded that we used to know more about Kyd. Scholars in the period 1880 to 1960, say, commonly studied Shakespeare alongside his contemporaries as a matter of course. In the last forty years, by contrast, the understandable but unhealthy pre-eminence bestowed on Shakespeare has granted him celebrity status and relegated many of his talented peers to a lower level of existence. Scholars in the pre-war period could still recognize Kyd and Marlowe as equals. Willard Farnham, in his influential study of 'the establishment of tragedy upon the Elizabethan stage' (1936), awarded 'key importance' equally to *The Spanish Tragedy* and to *Tamburlaine* as the two plays which 'left indelible impression upon many succeeding plays'.[7] Dating *The Spanish Tragedy* to 1585–1589, Farnham wrote that it

> shows itself the head of a dramatic line as clearly as . . . Tamburlaine (ca.1587). The two lines are so distinct in origin, although they quickly mingle upon the Elizabethan and Jacobean stages, that Kyd's [play] is hardly to be thought of as competing with Marlowe's upon the same tragic ground (p. 391)

Farnham had aligned *Tamburlaine* with the *De Casibus* tradition, the rise and fall of princes under Fortune's wheel, and judged that it 'fails of being tragically catastrophic. . . . Its theme is power gained in the lists of heroic ambition, its lines of plot are broad and in no sense intricately joined'. *The Spanish Tragedy*, by contrast,

> cultivates a ground of "Italianate" court intrigue . . . Its plot is an intricate one showing devious scheming for the attainment of various desires, in which check is met with countercheck. Kyd thus reveals

7. William Farnham, *The Medieval Heritage of Elizabethan Tragedy* (Oxford, 1936; 1956), p. 368.

KYD'S CRITICAL RECEPTION 329

the way to popularity for a new kind of tragedy presenting involved romantic intrigue instead of simple rise and fall. (pp. 391–2)

Farnham showed how the 'exotic' blending of 'love, intrigue, and revenge' in *The Spanish Tragedy* was emulated 'in darker mood' (p. 396) in *Titus Andronicus*—now known to be the joint creation of Peele and Shakespeare[8]—and suggested that, 'among Shakespeare's later and greater tragedies, *Hamlet* and *Othello* are partly metamorphoses of the Kydian, or post-Kydian drama of intrigue . . .' (p. 398). And, like so many scholars in the pre-war period, Farnham saw a clear link between *The Spanish Tragedy* and *Arden of Faversham*:

> With such drama of exotic intrigue and bloodshed, capitalizing the passions of love and revenge, the 'domestic' drama of murder seems to have points of close contact. *The Lamentable and True Tragedie of M. Arden of Feversham in Kent* (printed in 1592), the best of its kind and apparently the first, has persistently invited comparison with Kyd's known work and has persistently invited ascription to Kyd. (p. 398)

Although approaching Kyd from different backgrounds and with different expectations, several critics writing on either side of the Second World War came to a striking agreement about his originality. In 1939 Howard Baker placed *The Spanish Tragedy* in the mid-Tudor development of late medieval forms, especially *The Mirror for Magistrates*, both in its original version, edited by William Baldwin (including Thomas Sackville's *Induction* and his metrical tragedy, *The Complaint of Buckingham*), and in John Higgins's 1574 expansion, reprinted in 1587.[9] Baker showed that Sackville's dream-vision descent to hell, deriving ultimately from Book VI of the *Aeneid*, influenced not only Andrea's narration in the opening scene of *The Spanish Tragedy* but also provided the language of suffering for other characters' 'mental anguish. This is to say, he reduced these traditional materials to figures of speech which could convey the personal emotions of a Hieronimo or an Isabella . . .' (p. 99). At the same time, Baker showed, Kyd evolved a newly expressive blank

8. See Vickers, *Shakespeare, Co-Author*, pp. 148–243.
9. Baker, *Induction to Tragedy*, pp. 84, 98–118.

verse. In the passages where Hieronimo imagines going down to hell (4.1.7–9, 4.6.6–13,), the verse 'develops an intensity which mounts from line to line', while in Isabella's vision of her soul mounting 'up unto the highest heavens' (3.8.14–21), Baker found

> Intensity, vigor, and movement . . . In comparison with . . . the broad ringing heroics of the earlier Marlowe, [these lines] are sensitive, complex, and deeply motivated. . . . Kyd, in these passages, is laying the foundation for Shakespeare's energetic, figurative poetry . . . (p. 104)

In plot terms, Baker suggested, Kyd's medieval heritage can still be seen in the rise and fall of Lorenzo, depicting 'the wicked deeds and just downfall of a villainous prince', having a clear-cut moral (p. 214). But on to it Kyd grafted the line of action involving Hieronimo, who is forced to move from his role as public officer of justice to taking a private revenge, a move which moralizing critics have deplored.[10] Yet, Baker argued, Hieronimo's role 'makes psychological sense; it is real or understandable, and so is Isabella's. Kyd found the means of creating and communicating the suffering of these poor human beings so effectively that we cannot say how we should approve or disapprove of their actions; and thus he opened the way to genuine psychological tragedy' (p. 215).

In 1947 Moody E. Prior, although unsympathetic to Kyd's use of rhetoric (believing, oddly enough, that verbal patterning cannot express emotion: the opposite is true), nevertheless found in *The Spanish Tragedy* a coherent verbal embodiment of the characters' feelings: 'the diction of the play is quite properly ordered to cooperate with the exploration of Hieronimo's mind', thus bringing 'the imagery . . . into

---

10. The initiator of this critical fashion was Fredson Bowers, *Elizabethan Revenge Tragedy 1587–1642*, who anachronistically believed that Christian attitudes to revenge were universally applicable. It has been continued, inter alia, by: Eleanor Prosser, *Hamlet and Revenge*, 2nd edn. (Stanford, CA, 1971); Charles A. and Elaine S. Hallett, *The Revenger's Madness* (Lincoln, NE, 1980); and (regrettably) by Joel B. Altman, *The Tudor Play of Mind. Rhetorical Inquiry and the Development of Elizabethan Drama* (Berkeley and Los Angeles, 1978), pp. 267, 280–81; also by Gordon Braden, *Renaissance Tragedy and the Senecan Tradition. Anger's Privilege* (New Haven, CT, and London, 1985), pp. 200–215.

KYD'S CRITICAL RECEPTION   331

intimate relationship with the action'. The play 'greatly advanced the art of verse drama and represents a genuine break with Kyd's immediate dramatic past'.[11]

A few years later A.P. Rossiter, concluding what remains a remarkably acute study of the genesis of English drama, declared that

> If we seek for a sharp break between medieval and Renaissance ways with drama, it is to be found much rather with Kyd than with Marlowe. Kyd is small enough when set beside the man who in real life so alarmed him, but his innovations in the revenge-play appear great enough if we consider what they led up to. Like Marlowe, he studies evil and deals in the terrifying. He is, however, a true dramatist in his plotting; Marlowe, except in *Edward II*, is a dramatist only in his dramatic poetry—in great vistas of *mind*, rather than of the slip-knot of fate or events pulling tight on human lives. The theme of retribution is in the Moralities; but the sinner hunted by Bale's Vindicta Dei or the Nemesis of *Respublica* is never as exciting a theme as the revenges of *The Spanish Tragedy*, *Andronicus*, or *Hamlet*.[12]

Rossiter described Kyd as inheriting both the emotional world of Seneca's plays, 'with their expositions of the psychologies of savage passion, frenzy, or sheer madness', and the enclosing dramatic form:

> On one side he is influenced by Garnier—a French Senecaniser, whom he translated in *Cornelia*—and *The Spanish Tragedy* attempts the academic, chorus-divided, five-act shapeliness. On the other, he is the first parent of the horror-mongerings of all the Jacobean specialists in the macabre and sensational. He established the ghost, both as stage-thrill and as messenger from an underworld variously compounded of Virgil and Seneca, if still with much of the smoky airs of Bosch and Bruegel in the background. If, as many believe, he

---

11. Moody E. Prior, *The Language of Tragedy* (New York, 1947), p. 58. Prior stated his post-Romantic opinion that 'ostentatiously rhetorical art of any sort endows almost any sentiments with an academic, generalized quality' (p. 51).

12. A.P. Rossiter, *English Drama from early times to the Elizabethans. Its background, origins and developments* (London, 1950), p. 174.

332   CHAPTER 10

was not only responsible for the *Ur-Hamlet* (?1586–7) but for *Arden of Faversham*, then the domestic tragedy was as much of his own devising as the high-flown exotic revenge-plot. (pp. 174–5)

While recognizing the originality of *Arden*, Rossiter added the rider that, since Kyd took its plot from Holinshed, rather than some 'sensational contemporary crime', the play should be seen as exemplifying 'the "moral" trend in the staging of "history"' (p. 175). In that respect, I would say, it belongs with Kyd's other moralizing plays on historical themes, which are nearer to comedy: *Fair Em*, *King Leir*, and the romantic episodes in *1 Henry VI*.

Writing shortly after Rossiter, a distinguished German scholar, Wolfgang Clemen, also applauded Kyd's pioneering dramatic skills. By comparing similar passages in *Gorboduc* and *The Spanish Tragedy*, he showed how Kyd imparted a 'stronger dramatic quality' to the speeches of the Portuguese Viceroy, lamenting the apparent death of his son, and uttering a bitter self-reproach.[13] In particular, Clemen praised Hieronimo's soliloquies and set speeches, which are not only 'the pith and marrow of this play' but 'also form a kind of core for the whole body of drama' preceding Shakespeare (p. 107). Clemen described Kyd as the first English playwright who 'succeeded in creating a convincing character by means of soliloquy' (p. 108). Hieronimo's famous speech, 'What outcries pluck me from my naked bed?' (2.5.1–12), Clemen judged, is 'a soliloquy which is not only spoken but also acted', a speech 'which accurately reflects what Hieronimo is experiencing, at the same time indicating his actions by means of internal stage directions' (p. 109). This marked a considerable development on the long set speech in early classical tragedies, with their twin goals of 'moralizing self-revelation and dissection of the emotions' (p. 105). Clemen described Kyd as 'a real

---

13. See Wolfgang Clemen, *English Tragedy before Shakespeare*, tr. T.S. Dorsch from *Die Tragödie vor Shakespeare: ihre Entwicklung im Spiegel der dramatischen Rede*, 1955 (London, 1961), pp. 105, 267–70. On the originality of Kyd's use of Chorus and dumb show in *The Spanish Tragedy*, see Dieter Mehl, *The Elizabethan Dumb Show. The History of a Dramatic Convention* (London, 1965), pp. 63–71.

master' in the representation of 'grief and other strong emotions', as in Hieronimo's soliloquy mourning the death of his son (4.1.1–18). Here, 'for the first time in pre-Shakespearian drama', a dramatist conceives sorrow as 'not merely a state of mind . . . but activity', abandoning 'all the conventional formulas' and synchronizing 'action and emotion' (p. 275).

In the growing secondary literature of recent years,[14] many critics and scholars have celebrated Kyd's innovative dramaturgy. Writing in 1962, Anne Righter described Kyd as 'pre-eminently a man of the theatre, profoundly aware of its unexplored potentialities'.[15] She endorsed the verdict of earlier historians of drama in singling out his masterpiece as marking a decisive point of change:

> In *The Spanish Tragedy*, after more than a century of subservience to the inhibiting demands of the banqueting-hall, English drama at last regained a power equal to, if altogether different in quality from, that which it possessed in the ritual theatre of the Middle Ages. It is no accident that Hieronimo prefaces his tragedy with assertions of the dignity and worth of the actor's profession, a profession exercised in the past even by emperors and kings. (p. 74)

Time and again scholars single out Kyd's greatest play as having raised Elizabethan tragedy to a new level. Andrew Cairncross, who produced a pioneering edition of *1 Jeronimo* and *The Spanish Tragedy*,[16] was well-qualified to judge:

> Kyd's importance, both for his own achievements and for his relation to Elizabethan dramatic history in general, has become increasingly recognized. He has so many "firsts," real or possible, that he is, in a

14. See, e.g., José Ramón Díaz-Fernàndez, 'Thomas Kyd: a Bibliography, 1966–1992', *Bulletin of Bibliography*, 52 (1995): 1–13.

15. Anne Righter (subsequently Barton), *Shakespeare and the Idea of the Play* (London, 1962); quoted from the Penguin edition (Harmondsworth, 1967), p. 72.

16. See Andrew S. Cairncross (ed.), *The First Part of Hieronimo* and *The Spanish Tragedy* (Lincoln, NE, and London, 1967). This edition is notable for its serious study of '*The Spanish Comedy*', as Henslowe named this prequel.

334 CHAPTER 10

sense the father of Elizabethan drama. He may have created the first modern revenge tragedy—even the first extant modern English tragedy; the "over-plot" of the Ghost and Revenge; the play-within-the-play; the dumb show; the Machiavellian villain; the five-act structure; and possibly according to the interpretation of his work and the chronology of Elizabethan tragedy, the crossing of comedy with tragedy, the two-part play, dramatic blank verse, the highly organized original plot, and the representation of melodramatic passion and action.[17]

In 1986 Tom McAlindon also celebrated this play:

> So little indebted to all that precedes it in the tragic medium, and so profoundly influential in relation to what follows, Kyd's *The Spanish Tragedy* (ca.1585–90) is quite the most important single play in the history of English drama. We must, of course, acknowledge its obvious flaws and distinguish between historical importance and intrinsic worth. But the impression must not be given that this is an inchoate and uncertain pioneer work, a mine of useful ideas which only others will make proper use of. It is a startling achievement in its own right, being notable for the invention and the decisiveness with which it articulates a complex tragic vision.[18]

In 1990 Robert N. Watson similarly declared his belief that 'No play in this period is more important historically than Thomas Kyd's *The Spanish Tragedy*, which established many of the themes, plot lines, and atmospheric traits that the great subsequent tragedies have in common'. He added that its 'historical importance . . . is inseparable from the astonishing plenitude of the play in its own right, a richness of plot, character, symbol, spectacle, and rhetoric. Kyd gave his audience its money's worth'.[19] And, to complete this sampling of critical appreciation, G. K.

---

17. Andrew Cairncross, review of Arthur Freeman, *Thomas Kyd, Facts and Problems*, *Shakespeare Studies*, 5 (1969), p. 231.

18. Tom McAlindon, *English Renaissance Tragedy* (London, 1986), p. 55.

19. Robert N. Watson, 'Tragedy', in A.R. Braunmuller and Michael Hattaway (eds), *The Cambridge Companion to English Renaissance Drama* (Cambridge, 1990), pp. 301–351, at p. 320.

Hunter, one of the best readers of Renaissance literature in recent times, identified 'the three great pioneers' of Elizabethan drama as Lyly for comedy, Marlowe and Kyd for tragedy. 'Marlowe is seen as the inventor of a tragic rhetoric powerful enough to impose a single and obsessive vision on its audience. Kyd, no less, is the innovative master of his own field, the creator of a tragic form capable of giving sufficiently complex stage meaning to the mystery of human suffering.'[20] Observing that 'the standard dating for *The Spanish Tragedy* overlaps with that for *1* and *2 Tamburlaine*', Hunter found

> no evidence that one play is indebted to the other; but between them they mark out a range of mature options that define the space to be occupied by Elizabethan tragedy for the next fifty years. The arrival of *Tamburlaine* made the bigger noise; but *The Spanish Tragedy*, less self-consciously innovative, may well have carved the deeper impression, for it served to show how the traditional multi-level plot could be adapted to satisfy the expectations of more classically minded authors and more sophisticated London audiences. (p. 71)

Hunter's grasp of the whole range of factors feeding into the creation of Elizabethan drama gives real authority to his evaluation of *The Spanish Tragedy* as 'a central artefact that alters now (and altered then) the whole concept of that tradition', a play that 'is of central *historical* importance as a foundation document for mature Elizabethan tragedy' (pp. 70–71).

The Boom in Kyd Studies

That brief survey of Kyd's reception by a wide range of scholars, from Josef Schick in 1898 to George Hunter in 1997, has established the high status he enjoyed in Germany, England, America, and elsewhere. When academic studies reached a higher intensity in the 1960s his work attracted growing attention. According to an authoritative cumulative

---

20. Hunter, *English Drama 1586–1642. The Age of Shakespeare*, p. 71.

bibliography,[21] with the scope limited to 'Criticism' (1,610 records), studies of his works appeared with the following frequencies:

1960–1969: 51
1970–1979: 34
1980–1989: 49
1990–1999: 150
2000–2009: 457
2010–2019: 673
2020–2023: 127

Reading through these entries reveals the massive interest in *The Spanish Tragedy*, which was discussed in more than 98 percent of those records. *Soliman and Perseda* was mentioned often, but less than five articles were devoted wholly to it. Even fewer dealt with *Cornelia*, primarily as a translation.

Faced with this huge enlargement of Kyd studies it is evidently impossible to provide a full, or even a selective coverage. All I can do is to make some suggestions to students and general readers who want to explore Kyd's work further. In general, I recommend beginning with approaches to the work itself, essays and book chapters that address the play's structure, plot, and language, where readers can compare the critic's reading of the play with their own experience. A useful starting point might be Herbert Coursen's essay, 'The Unity of *The Spanish Tragedy*'.[22] Coursen argues that the motivating force of the play stems from Lorenzo's attempts to ingratiate himself with Balthazar by arranging Horatio's murder, which will allow his marriage with Bel-imperia and so advance the House of Castile, a goal for which Lorenzo is prepared to commit crime after crime. '*The Spanish Tragedy* is as much a play about crime as about revenge for crimes', crimes that are hidden and only gradually exposed, contributing a major element in the play's unity (p. 770). Coursen notes that 'the play's several references to

21. See *Proquest One Literature*, https://proquest.libguides.com/pq1lit/content.
22. Herbert Coursen, 'The Unity of *The Spanish Tragedy*', *Studies in Philology*, 65 (1968): 768–82.

KYD'S CRITICAL RECEPTION   337

Rhadamanth are more than mere Senecan importations'. According to one dictionary of classical mythology, 'Rhadamanth brings to light crimes done in life which the perpetrator vainly thought impenetrably hid' (p. 771, n.).[23]

Coursen's essay is a useful corrective to accounts that deal solely with Hieronimo, but he is inevitably the main focus of several essays that emphasize the legitimacy of revenge, in opposition to Fredson Bowers. As I have shown (see note 10), Bowers judged the play from an inappropriate New Testament attitude to revenge as immoral, condemning Hieronimo as moving 'from hero to villain' in his soliloquy beginning 'Vindicta mihi!'.[24] A forceful response to Bowers was given by David Laird in his essay 'Hieronimo's Dilemma'.[25] Laird placed the soliloquy in its dramatic context: Hieronimo's frustrated attempt in the previous scene to find legal justice for Horatio's murder. In his speech Hieronimo finds himself

> forced to choose between alternatives neither one of which is wholly acceptable to him. He can resign himself to the divine promise of eventual justice or he can actively seek a private vengeance and thereby acquit his shattered honour. His instinctive distrust of those alternatives explains his hesitation and accounts for the thoroughness with which he probes their implications (p. 139).

Using the correct classical and Renaissance terminology, Laird brings out 'the extraordinary rhetorical control which the speech exhibits and, more important, the step by step working out of a logically valid argument or

23. In fact, the fullest description of this figure was given by Virgil in the *Aeneid*, during Aeneas's journey to the underworld, where all who are guilty suffer punishment. As the Sybil explains: 'Cretan Rhadamanthus presides over this pitiless kingdom; he punished crimes and recognizes treachery, forcing each to confess the sins committed in the world above, atonement for which each had postponed too long, happy in his stealth, until death'. See *Aeneid*, VI. 566–9. I cite the translation in Mark P. O. Morford and Robert J. Lenardon (eds), *Classical Mythology*, 6th edn (New York, 1999), p. 266.

24. All quotations from *The Spanish Tragedy* are from my edition, in Vickers (ed.), *The Collected Works of Thomas Kyd*, vol. 1, restoring the original Five Act structure. Here Hieronimo's speech forms 4.1.1–45; in previous editions 3.13.1–45.

25. David Laird, 'Hieronimo's Dilemma', *Studies in Philology* 62 (1965): 137–46.

dialectic which the rhetoric of the speech is made to serve' (p. 138). This essay is required reading for anyone wanting to appreciate the remarkable care that Kyd put into the creation of this play.

Other scholars have justified Hieronimo's choice of revenge, but less convincingly. John D. Ratliff, in 'Hieronimo Explains Himself'[26] argues that Hieronimo presents revenge as 'a matter of simple self-preservation' (p. 117), a reductive judgment that ignores Kyd's detailed and carefully balanced structure. Ejner J. Jensen, in 'Kyd's *Spanish Tragedy*: The Play Explains Itself',[27] argues that 'The play is in reality highly organized. Its chief unifying theme is not revenge but the problem of justice . . . [It] is filled with discussions of the nature of justice, its machinery and its operation. Hieronimo, as Knight Marshal, is himself a judge' (p. 8). Jensen insists that it is no tautology to describe 'a revenge play whose theme is justice. Justice comprehends revenge; justice is the whole system of rewards and punishments, judgments of good and evil, and ethical decisions of which revenge forms only a part' (p. 11). He shows that the pursuit and exercise of justice runs all though the play, from Andrea's opening narrative of his passage through the underworld to his final appearance with Revenge, when they plan the punishments to be executed on Hieronimo's enemies after the play is over. Jensen concludes that Bowers's criticisms of Kyd's play

> are primarily the result of his attempt to make the play fit his theory. The rigid observance of theoretical strictures would discard large parts of the work as superfluous and make its conclusion ethically untenable. But Kyd's tragedy is a unified whole, and it supplies all of the solutions to the moral and ethical questions which it raises. (p. 18)

There have been no shortage of scholars defending Hieronimo's revenge and its fall-out.[28]

26. John D. Ratliff, 'Hieronimo Explains Himself', *Studies in Philology*, 54 (1957): 112–18.

27. Ejner J. Jensen, 'Kyd's *Spanish Tragedy*: The Play Explains Itself', *Journal of English and Germanic Philology*, 64 (1965): 7–16.

28. See Ernst de Chickera, 'Divine Justice and Private Revenge in *The Spanish Tragedy*', *Modern Language Review*, 57 (1962): 228–32.

Of the many deaths in this play, that of the Duke of Castile has been most discussed, in response to the Hassetts' negative judgment that 'the point is precisely that there is *no* reason for it—it is a mad act, an act of cruelty and of waste, and one dramatically calculated to differentiate the justice of nature from earthly or heavenly justice'.[29] But Hieronimo kills Castile in the final revenge sequence, so it can hardly be 'the justice of nature'. James P. Hammersmith wrote a cogent refutation of this view,[30] starting from Castile 'being a key figure in the relationships between the other characters: he is the brother to the king of Spain and he is the father of both Lorenzo and Bel-imperia. He is thus critical to the fortunes of the nation because the King, as it happens, is childless' (p. 4). The significance of this fact only becomes clear in the climax of the play, when Hieronimo has revenged himself on the Portuguese Viceroy, father of Balthazar, accomplice in Horatio's murder. As Hammersmith points out,

> Castile stands to profit much by the murder of Horatio, and the profit is actually less the result of his having fathered Lorenzo than of his having fathered Bel-imperia, for it is she, after all, who is to be made queen of Spain and Portugal, and, moreover, it is her child, Castile's grandson, who 'shall enjoy the kingdom after us'. The Duke is therefore to gain exactly that of which Hieronimo has been deprived through the larger significance of the crime, namely, a means to carry on his bloodline so that his lineage shall flourish (pp. 9–10).

The Viceroy had described Balthazar as 'the only hope of our successive line' (3.1.14). When Hieronimo '*stabs the Duke and himself*', the King recognizes the dynastic significance of these 'monstrous deeds':

> My brother, and the whole succeeding hope
> That Spain expected after my decease . . .
> I am the next, the nearest, last of all.   (5.4.199–205)

---

29. See Hallett, *The Revenger's Madness*, p. 158.

30. See James P. Hammersmith, 'The death of Castile in *The Spanish Tragedy*', *Renaissance Drama* 16 (1985): 1–16.

As Hammersmith observes,

> The desolation of the Court is complete, and Hieronimo leaves the King and the Viceroy alive to contemplate the full significance of the deaths of Lorenzo, Balthazar, and Bel-imperia, just as he himself has had to endure the pain of this same awareness . . . The death of the fruitful Castile leaves only the King and the Viceroy, who are, in effect, dead roots already. In this respect, the play is true to its title, for it is the tragedy of Spain, of an entire state laid waste and barren by the necessary expulsion of evil (pp. 10–11).

In a much-cited essay,[31] S. F. Johnson related this 'state laid waste and barren' to the chaos that Hieronimo anticipates from the play he has prepared:

> Now shall I see the fall of Babylon,
> Wrought by the heavens in this confusion.   (5.1.186–7)

Johnson pointed out that Kyd 'analogized' the 'confusion' (chaos) that Hieronimo plans, both with 'the confusion of tongues wrought by the Lord at Babel (Genesis 11) and with the horrible destruction of both the historical and symbolic Babylons as prophesied in Isaiah 13, Jeremiah 51, and Revelations 18' (p. 24). As he put it, 'Hieronimo's couplet equates Spain with Babylon and with Babel' (p. 25). The biblical text describes how God first pretended not to see the men building a tower 'whose top may reach unto heaven' (Genesis 11:3), but then decided to punish them: 'let us go down and there confound their languages, that they may not understand one another's speech' (11:7). The annotator in the Geneva Bible commented: 'By this great plague of the confusion of tongues appeareth God's horrible judgement against man's pride and vaine glorie'.[32] In his *Commentaries on Genesis* Calvin interpreted the teaching of Moses that

---

31. S.F. Johnson, '*The Spanish Tragedy*, or Babylon Revisited', in *Essays on Shakespeare and Elizabethan Drama. In honour of Hardin Craig*, ed. Richard Hosley (London, 1963), pp. 23–44.

32. As Johnson observed (p. 25 n.), the Geneva Bible 'was the common household Bible from about 1570 until some years after the publication of the King James version (1611)'.

KYD'S CRITICAL RECEPTION   341

God for a while fared as thoughe he had not seene them[33] . . . For he doth oftentimes so beare with the wicked, that as one asleepe he doth not only suffer them to take many wicked things in hand: But also he maketh them rejoyce at the successe of their wicked enterprises, that at the last he may make their fal the greater . . . God sheweth himself a revenger by little and little.[34]

In Johnson's view, 'this image of God as the sleeping revenger . . . [may] account for the scene between Andrea's ghost and the sleeping figure of Revenge' (4.9), and also suggests that 'Hieronimo determines to imitate God's techniques as a revenger in the *Vindicta mihi* soliloquy':

> Thus, therefore will I rest me in unrest,
> Dissembling quiet in unquietness,
> Not seeming that I know their villainies . . .   (4.7.29–31)

When the perpetrators have been lulled into security, Hieronimo's duty, as Johnson put it, 'is clearly spelled out in the Mosaic code,[35] which Protestants believed to be quite as much the word of God as anything else in the two testaments' (p. 29). In Numbers 1–13, several types of murder are enumerated, in each of which 'the murderer shall surely be put to death'. A gloss to verse 12 says that the next of kindred of the murdered man ought to pursue the cause; at all events, 'The revenger of blood himself shall slay the murderer: when he meeteth him he shall slay him' (Numbers 35:19). A later verse qualifies this emphasis: 'whosoever killeth any person, the *judge* shall slay the murtherer, through witnesses' (Numbers 35.30; Geneva version), suggesting a legal trial.

As Johnson pointed out, 'the Geneva reading is doubly relevant to Kyd's play, for Hieronimo is not only the "revenger of the blood" but also the judge. He is the Knight Marshal of Spain', a fact that Kyd repeatedly

---

33. The Latin bible from which Calvin worked reads '*Sed prius admonet Moses, dissimulasse aliquantisper Deum*', a phrase linking this text with the Renaissance awareness of the importance of dissimulation in political life, as in the proverb *Qui nescit dissimulare, nescit regnare.*

34. Johnson, *Spanish Tragedy*, pp. 28–9, citing Thomas Tymme's 1578 translation.

35. The first five books of the Old Testament.

emphasizes.[36] After Horatio's murder we see him struck by the irony of his situation:

> Thus must we toil in other men's extremes,
> That know not how to remedy our own,
> And do them justice, when unjustly, we,
> For all our wrongs can compass no redress.   (3.6.1–4)

Through several scenes we follow Hieronimo's frustrated attempts to secure justice from the King, a sequence that nullifies the attempts of Bowers and others to condemn Hieronimo for taking a 'private' revenge. Like Jensen, a few years earlier, Johnson deplored the fact that

> Most critics have tended to discount Kyd's emphasis on Hieronimo's official function and have seen him merely as a 'private' revenger, for in so doing they have missed the point of Kyd's brilliant invention: the tragic dilemma of the officially appointed minister of justice who is forced by circumstances to take justice into his own hands. (p. 31)

That insight sets the play in a wholly different light, justifying Johnson's account of his purpose, 'to argue a case for [Kyd's] careful contrivance and artistic unity of effect' (p. 23).

Illuminating essays have been written about the staging of *The Spanish Tragedy*, which touch on the related topics of theatricality and dramatic structure. These include Barry Adams on the play's audiences,[37] Joost Daalder's study of the role of 'Senex',[38] and Scott McMillin's wide-ranging discussion, 'The Figure of Silence'.[39] An essay by Richard Kohler analyses the symmetrical structure of Act 1, reflected in the many symmetries of

---

36. The audience would have regarded his function to match 'that of the Knight Marshal of the English royal household, who had judicial cognizance of transgressions "within the king's house and verge," i.e., within a radius of twelve miles from the king's palace' (Johnson, *Spanish Tragedy*, p. 30, citing *OED*).

37. Barry Adams, 'The Audiences of *The Spanish Tragedy*', *Journal of English and Germanic Philology*, 68 (1969): 228–36.

38. Joost Daalder, 'The role of "Senex" in Kyd's *The Spanish Tragedy*', *Comparative Drama*, 20 (1986): 247–60.

39. Scott McMillin, 'The figure of silence in *The Spanish Tragedy*', *ELH: A journal of English literary history*, 39 (1972): 27–48.

language.[40] As he puts it, 'during much of the play the physical structure complemented the dramatic form as well as the literary content—the severe, clear, regulated pattern of Kyd's visual and aural effect' (p. 44).

'Critical Theory': Displacing the Artefact

Reading through those selected essays it is striking to see how critics approaching the play from different directions have succeeded in illuminating its unity and Kyd's careful structuring and execution, down to minute details. They concentrated on the artefact, the text of a play designed to be performed before an audience, enquiring how it was put together and what relations existed between the parts and the whole. They were all trying to understand Kyd's achievement on its own terms, and to communicate the fruits of their study to a general, not a specialist readership. Such aims came under attack in the 1980s, with the rise of postmodern literary theory, in which 'Texts . . . are interpreted and analysed with a view to unlocking the social norms and attitudes encoded therein, not assessed or evaluated as integral, self-contained creations'.[41] But defining those 'social norms and attitudes' was not undertaken via research into Elizabethan and Jacobean society but via contemporary theories and ideologies, deriving from the 'identity politics' of separate, often conflicting groups. The effect of this fragmentation of critical discourse on the interpretation of Shakespeare was seriously damaging, as each tried to 'appropriate' him to their own special interests. I have shown how followers of deconstruction, new historicism, Freudian psychoanalysis, feminism, Christian allegory, and Marxist ideology, each bent Shakespeare to fit their own agendas, selecting parts of the plays while jettisoning the rest.[42] Of course, feminism was unique among

40. Richard Kohler, 'Kyd's Ordered Spectacle: "Behold . . . /What 'tis to be subject to destiny"', *Medieval and Renaissance Drama in England*, 3 (1986): 27–52.

41. Rónán McDonald, *The Death of the Critic* (London and New York, 2007), p. 21. See also John M. Ellis, *Literature Lost: Social Agendas and the Corruption of Humanities* (New Haven, CT, and London, 1997).

42. See Brian Vickers, *Appropriating Shakespeare. Contemporary Critical Quarrels* (New Haven, CT, and London, 1993).

these groups as an important social movement, attempting to counteract aeons of male dominance. But it is not seen in its best light when a critic denounces patriarchy in *Othello* without mentioning Iago.

The range of Kyd's plays is far smaller than Shakespeare's and never produced such wide distortions. But a recent writer surveying '*The Spanish Tragedy*: State of the Art' began with an 'Overview and the advent of critical theory',[43] starting from the cultural materialism of the 1980s, with respectful nods to Foucault, Bourdieu, and Lacan. The specific direction of critical theory taken by Kyd scholars emerges in the next section title, 'Protestantism, Catholicism, and anti-Iberian prejudice' (pp. 93–6). Its author, Stevie Simkin, endorses 'a wing of scholarship insisting on the anti-Catholicism of revenge tragedy', citing an essay by Ronald Broude.[44] This glib categorization ascribes, improbably enough, a common politico-religious purpose to plays written between 1585 and 1630 by over a dozen dramatists, and need not be taken seriously. Simkin summarizes approvingly one scholar's interpretation of Kyd's play as 'a Reformist Apocalypse and a celebration of England's history [*sic*: query 'victory'] over Spain, the Whore of Baylon', with Hieronimo as 'the Danielic figure, the judge [. . .], Anglophile representative of God's will at the court of Babylon-Spain'.[45]

In this reading Kyd's play is subordinated to a minor role in a fully-fledged allegorical scheme of a highly personal nature. Being, as I am, unable to imagine God sending an English representative to the Spanish court, and wondering what Hieronimo has in common with the unhistorical hero of the Book of Daniel, who interprets dreams and receives apocalyptic visions, I find this interpretation unconvincing. Nor can I see Kyd's play as 'anti-Iberian'. True, Hieronimo's revenge destroys the

43. See Stevie Simkin's '*The Spanish Tragedy*: State of the Art' in The Spanish Tragedy. *A Critical Reader*, ed. Thomas Rist (London and New York, 2016), pp. 83–110.

44. Cf. Ronald Broude, '*Time, Truth, and Right in* The Spanish Tragedy', *Studies in Philology*, 68 (1971): 130–45.

45. Simkin, 'State of the Art', p. 95, citing Frank Ardolino, *Apocalypse and Armada in Kyd's* Spanish Tragedy (Kirksville, MO, 1995), pp. 49, 51. Under 'Cosmology' Simkins cites another book by Ardolino, *Thomas Kyd's Mystery Play: Myth and Ritual in* The Spanish Tragedy (New York, 1985), in which 'he also connects the death of Horatio to the pagan tradition of the hanged god' (p. 100). Why not?

dynasties of both Spain and Portugal, but as a private punishment for the lawlessness that their officers have perpetrated and permitted. Kyd's play has no other purpose than to be; it expresses no 'attitudes' to anything outside itself.

The most problematic aspect of 'new critical theory' as it impinges on Kyd's play is the liberty of interpretation that it claims, little concerned with historical or textual evidence. Simkin argues that its practitioners manifest 'a demand for a more nuanced approach to the idea of historical context' (p. 104), but 'nuanced' is an inappropriate term for an essay that he hails as an 'outstanding meditation on the meanings and implications of acts of revenge', which ends by denouncing Hieronimo's 'grotesque acts of self-harm and self-annihilation'.[46] This misses the entire point of Hieronimo's dedication to achieving justice in this world and punishment of those who have harmed him. The critic bends the play to suit his own postmodern agenda. This is nowhere more damaging than in the *ad libitum* suggestion of Kyd's concern with Catholicism. A deeply experienced drama scholar like Richard Proudfoot sees 'the blood-stained scarf, initially Bel-imperia's token to Andrea, which passes successively to Horatio and then to Hieronimo as the emblem and reminder of revenge'.[47] To Andrew Hadfield, however, it indicates anti-Catholicism.[48] To Andrew Sofer, in 'Absorbing Interests: Kyd's Bloody Handkerchief as Palimpsest',[49] its range of associations is far greater, leading back into medieval drama and into the liturgy of the Mass:

> As it moves through the play Kyd's bloody handkerchief invokes previous performances by bloody cloths, even as it weaves them into an original narrative. Indeed, at the play's climax the ghost in the bloody handkerchief's folds is the Host itself, the "real Presence" of Christ's body as it was embodied in the sacrament of the eucharist and

46. See Gregory M. Colon Semenza, 'The Spanish Tragedy and Revenge' in *Early Modern English Drama: A Critical Companion*, ed. Garrett A. Sullivan, Jr., (Oxford, 2006), p. 51.

47. Richard Proudfoot, 'Kyd's *Spanish Tragedy*', *Critical Quarterly*, 25 (1983): 71–6 (73).

48. Andrew Hadfield, 'A Handkerchief Dipped in Blood in *The Spanish Tragedy*: An Anti-Catholic Reference?', *Notes and Queries*, 46 (1999): 197.

49. Andrew Sofer, 'Absorbing Interests: Kyd's Bloody Handkerchief as Palimpsest', *Comparative Drama*, 34 (2000): 127–53.

metonymically invoked by various sacred cloths on the late medieval stage . . . I wish to demonstrate that the bloody napkin is a ghostly palimpsest that absorbs meaning through intertextual borrowing as well as through fresh symbolic resonance. (p. 129)

Sofer is evidently well read in liturgical drama from its beginnings up to the medieval Corpus Christi cycles, but his attempts to relate the religious context to Kyd's play depend on wholly personal associations. The napkin (or scarf), he suggests, might be marked with Bel-imperia's hymeneal blood (p. 142); the blood is also a love charm (p. 143); 'Hieronimo's virtual canonization of his son invites us to see Horatio as a Christ-figure' (ibid.); in displaying Horatio's body to the courtiers, 'Hieronimo enacts a bloody parody of the Corpus Christi Passion Play' (p. 145).[50] A practising Christian might be deeply offended by the notion of Horatio as a Christ-figure. Non-denominational readers may feel that the analogies are inappropriate, that a secular play performed in an Elizabethan theatre could never convey such hints of Catholic ritual. If 'new critical theory' has dispensed with established conventions of evidence appropriate to place and time, it has encouraged an interpretive free-for-all. As that notorious relativist Paul Feyerabend used to say, 'Anything goes'.

The main consequence of displacing the artefact from the centre of attention is that the new external focus relegates it to a placeholder, to be cited on the few occasions when it illustrates a point in the dominant, abstract field of discourse. Tracing these recent changes in Kyd studies, it seems to me as if the authors, having broken free of the constraints of focussing on the artefact, are voyaging into regions unknown. A good example is the essay in Rist's collection by Eric Griffin: 'New Directions: Geopolitics and *The Spanish Tragedy*'.[51] Griffin begins from the

---

50. Strangely enough, Thomas Rist's *A Critical Reader* includes another essay citing 'identical' parallels between *The Spanish Tragedy* and the Corpus Christi cycles: Katharine Goodland, 'New Directions: Female Mourning, Revenge and Hieronimo's Doomsday Play' (pp. 175–95). The number of Christian analogues seems limited.

51. Eric Griffin, 'New Directions: Geopolitics and *The Spanish Tragedy*' in Rist (ed.), pp. 131–51. Griffin has also published *English Renaissance Drama and the Specter of Spain: Ethnopoetics and Empire* (Philadelphia, PA, 2009).

KYD'S CRITICAL RECEPTION 347

indisputable fact that 'Philip II's consolidation of Portugal and its overseas possessions within the Spanish Empire' was 'the most consequential geopolitical development' of its era (p. 131). But thereafter 'Kyd', or 'The Spanish Tragedy', are taken as expressing a distinct attitude towards this event (pp. 132–5 and *passim*), albeit at times self-contradictory: '*The Spanish Tragedy* reflects this contemporary Hispanophilia as much as it does the Hispanophobia criticism has strained to hear in the play's argument' (p. 138).[52] Griffin introduces another large concept, 'Empire', but does so, strangely enough, in the context of Andrea's opening narrative of how he 'possessed a worthy dame', Bel-imperia. Griffin differs from other commentators in finding 'something terrible about her beauty', detecting

> a pattern: rather than possessing her, one by one, each of the play's Dons, first Andrea, then Horatio, next Balthazar, and finally, even Hieronimo, are *possessed by Bel-imperia* ... Kyd's tragedy suggests that there is something perilously seductive about [Horatio's] imperial mistress's charms. (p. 136; my italics.)

Those who know the play from performance or reading are likely to be puzzled by how Bel-imperia can be said to have 'possessed' those men. Griffin is hovering between treating her as a character and as an allegorical figure:

> As her name indicates, "Bel-imperia" is a double, related both to *bellum*, or war, and to *belle*, or beauty. An allegorical figure as much as a princess in a "real" or literal sense, the attention drawn to her name in the opening speech announces a web of significance associating the play's argument with Empire as the concept governing its action, as in fact it governed contemporary geopolitics. (pp. 136–7)

Setting aside his dubious etymology ('*Bel*' is unrelated to *bellum*), like other Kyd commentators of this school, Griffin used the play as a peg

---

52. Subsequently Griffin praises Kyd for writing against 'the reductively Hispanophobic currents' (p. 141), although they 'tempered' the play's reception (p. 142), so much so that it became 'thoroughly implicated in period Hispanophobia' (p. 147). Finally the play is approved for demonstrating 'Hispanophilic qualities', which 'were very much of their age' (p. 151). There seems to be some confusion here.

on which to hang his own personal reading of history. But Bel-imperia is either a character or an allegorical figure: you can't have it both ways. Differences are fused, and confused.

Summing up this brief survey of recent Kyd criticism, I wanted to prepare readers for some fundamental changes in what they might expect to find when they look for help and stimulus. Thought is free, of course, writers and journal editors may range as widely as they wish, and readers must form their own judgments. My concern is first and last with the play as an artefact, something made by the dramatist, which shows the influence of tradition and convention while allowing for transformation and invention. I deplore the displacement of the play as subordinate to other concerns, especially those defined vaguely and inconsistently. The 'New Directions' I have been discussing may reflect a temporary or a longer change, but they are not universal.

A Tradition Continues

Recent publications have shown that historical scholarship continues to flourish. For example, two recent publications found echoes of classical literature at the climax of *The Spanish Tragedy*. When Hieronimo calls for a knife to sharpen his pen, the late G. K. Hunter identified what may seem like an unlikely debt to Tacitus.[53] Kyd drew on the *Annals* VI.v.8, where Tacitus describes the suicide of Publius Vitellius. In the first English translation, by Richard Grenewey (1598), the passage reads: 'Vitellius through many delays betwixt hope and fear wearied out, under colour of using it in his study, asking for a penknife, lightly pricked a vein and ended his life with grief and anguish of mind'. Kyd had a more positive act in view than suicide: '*He with a knife stabs the Duke and himself*'.

---

53. G.K. Hunter, 'Tacitus and Kyd's *The Spanish Tragedy*', *Notes and Queries*, 47 (2000): 424–5. Cf. Richard Grenewey, *The Annales of Cornelius Tacitus* (London, 1640 edition), p. 117.

A recent essay by Alanna Skuse, with the somewhat forbidding title 'Biting One's Tongue: Autoglossotomy and Agency in *The Spanish Tragedy*',[54] has illuminated Hieronimo's self-mutilation by examining some famous classical precedents. She did so in order to refute the negative verdicts of critical theory. I have quoted one critic who disparaged Hieronimo's 'grotesque acts of self-harm and self-annihilation', while others have seen them as defeatist. One critic diagnosed 'a psychological collapse resulting from Hieronimo's struggle to come to terms with the fissure between the living and the dead', alleging that, 'despite his complaints, Hieronimo never [sic] appeals to the king for justice', and 'it is this silence which is literalized by self-mutilation of the tongue' (cited in Skuse, p. 280). But Hieronimo announces that

> I will go plain me to my lord the King,
> And cry aloud for justice through the court   (4.1.69–70)

When he does so, however, he is twice blocked by Lorenzo (4.6.21–80) and retreats frustrated, deciding that he must seek private revenge. (That the critic failed to recall this episode shows that a concern with 'Fantasy and Trauma . . . and post-Reformation Revenge Drama' may distract one from the play text.) Another critic viewed the loss of Hieronimo's tongue as the 'externalisation of his psychic fragmentation', and his revenge constitutes a 'revenge on language, on representation' (ibid., pp. 280–81). This critic used another tactic to ignore the text, the sweeping generalization: 'The actors in this play conspicuously fail to understand one another'—a claim easily refuted—'and his tongue-biting repudiates communication in the most violent way'. But that misses the whole point. Hieronimo is not repudiating communication, but preparing to defend himself from being tortured by a tyrant. If we place that act in context, for the Elizabethan audience and reading public it unmistakably recalls Zeno. The modern critic pursuing their own thesis of 'psychic fragmentation' is forced to deny this historical and still

---

54. Alanna Skuse, 'Biting One's Tongue: Autoglossotomy and Agency in *The Spanish Tragedy*', *Renaissance Studies*, 36 (2022): 278–94.

valid association: while for Zeno 'self-mutilation constitutes an act of Stoic heroism, a literalized spit in the face of tyranny, for Kyd it signals a profoundly anti-heroic surrender to (and complicity with) a world of fragments and self-alienation' (Skuse, p. 281). Alas, postmodern criticism can turn the significance of any action into its opposite.

Despite the attempted erasure, Hieronimo's action was unmistakably intended to recall the most famous instance of self-mutilation in antiquity. As an Elizabethan treatise on philosophy put it, Zeno, 'being cruelly tormented of a King of Cyprus to utter those things which the King was desirous to know, at length because he would not satisfy his mind, bit off his own tongue, and spit the same in the tormentor's face'.[55] Having collected other instances of the same act in antiquity, Skuse made the important discovery that they were all reactions to tyrants and torture. Anaxarchus was captured by Nicocreon, 'the most cruel of all other Tyrants', who planned to have him crushed in a mortar. Anaxarchus showed remarkable 'constancy' in replying that 'the breaking of his body would never diminish Anaxarchus. Then the Tyrant, because he could not abide his bold speech, commanded that his tongue should be cut out of his mouth. But Anaxarchus, laughing at his madness, thought he should never have his mind, and therefore he bit out his own tongue, and spit the same by mamocks [pieces] upon the tyrant's face'.[56] Skuse observed that 'Many, Anaxarchus included, were said to be philosophers and orators, and tales of tongue-biting were reserved for rebels with a good cause rather than criminals seeking to evade justice. According to Plutarch's treatise on moral philosophy, Hyperides, an Athenian politician and student of Plato, possessed 'a singular name above all other orators, for speaking before the people'. But when he fell foul of the Macedonian general Antipater, 'being set upon the rack, and put to torture, he bit his tongue off with his own teeth, because he would not discover [reveal] the secrets of the city'.[57]

55. Thomas Rogers, *A Philosophicall Discourse, Entituled, The Anatomie of the Minde* (London, 1576), fols. 2r–2v; cited in Skuse, 'Biting One's Tongue', p. 283; spelling modernized.

56. Skuse, 'Biting One's Tongue', p. 283.

57. *Plutarch's Morals*, tr. Philemon Holland (London, 1603), p. 936. Skuse cited another instance, of 'a common woman of Athens', who, being tortured to reveal incriminating evidence,

KYD'S CRITICAL RECEPTION 351

These classical exempla of courage in the face of unjust tortures were regularly cited in expositions of the Stoic doctrine of *constantia* as able to overcome pain and suffering. Summing up, Skuse returned to Kyd's play:

Classical stories of autoglossotomy thus provided a framework within which *The Spanish Tragedy's* tongue-biting could be viewed as stoic, political in focus, and specifically anti-tyrannical. This framework not only makes Hieronimo's self-injury meaningful rather than nihilistic but has the added effect of interpellating the King as tyrant. It is little wonder, then, that the King—previously a relaxed if somewhat oblivious ruler—steps so rapidly and violently into the role of tyrant carved out for him by Hieronimo's scene-setting. It is notable that his first response to Hieronimo's bloody playlet is to demand he 'Speak, traitor' (5.4.161).

After Hieronimo has destroyed his organ of speech, the frustrated King cries:

O monstrous resolution of a wretch!
See, Viceroy, he hath bitten forth his tongue!
Rather than to reveal what we required.   (188–90)

The Stoic doctrine of *constantia* was sometimes expressed as 'resolution': to the King Hieronimo's virtue is 'monstrous' because it's the reaction of 'a traitor'. In attempting to assert his authority, the King reproduces perfectly the part of the 'most cruell' tyrants who populate classical autoglossotomy stories. His next order, 'Fetch forth the tortures! | Traitor as thou art, I'll make thee tell' (180–81), only provokes Hieronimo's defiant reply:

Thou mayst torment me, as his wretched son
Hath done in murdering my Horatio.
But never shalt thou force me to reveal
The thing which I have vowed inviolate.
And therefore, in despite of all thy threats,

'spoke not one word, but biting in sunder her tongue, she spit it in the face of Hippias the tyrant' (p. 284).

Pleased with their deaths, and eased with their revenge:
First take my tongue, and afterwards my heart.
He bites out his tongue.   (182–8)

By recreating the classical context, Skuse has convincingly proved her point: 'Hieronimo's suicide no longer renders his tongue-biting redundant, but rather completes a series of acts by which he attempts to make himself heroic rather than pathetic, and "inviolate" rather than violated' (p. 288). I happily give her the last word: 'Kyd refuses to exclude the possibility that Hieronimo is above all else a man of integrity—one fixed point in the play that is exactly as it seems' (p. 204).

Further Reading

The two authoritative online resources, on which we all depend, are the MLA International Bibliography, hosted by EBSCO (Elton B. Stephens Co.), and the *Annual Bibliography of English Language and Literature* (*ABELL*), now subsumed into 'Proquest 1'. More useful for students and the general reader are two bibliographies that include a description and sometimes an evaluation of the most important works of secondary literature: *The Year's Work in English Studies* (Oxford University Press), which, understandably enough, due to its wide scope, usually appears with a two-year delay. With a narrower remit, the quarterly journal *Studies in English Literature 1500–1900* (Johns Hopkins University Press), includes in the second issue of each volume a more timely survey of 'Recent Studies of Tudor and Stuart Drama'.

For bibliographies of Kyd, an older one still worth reading for its coverage of earlier work is the textually conservative chapter by Dickie A. Spurgeon, 'Thomas Kyd', in Terence P. Logan and Denzell S. Smith (eds), *The Predecessors of Shakespeare. A Survey and Bibliography of Recent Studies in English Renaissance Drama* (Lincoln, NE, 1973), pp. 93–106. This must be supplemented by Anne Lancashire and Jill Levenson's well-informed chapter on 'Anonymous Plays', which includes several works now ascribed to Kyd: *Edward III* (pp. 206–15), *Fair Em* (pp. 215–8), *King Leir* (pp. 219–26), *Soliman and Perseda* (pp. 230–39), and *Arden of*

Faversham (pp. 240–52). Current bibliographies of all these plays will be included in Brian Vickers (ed.), *The Collected Plays of Thomas Kyd* (Cambridge, 2024–). In her edition of new work, *Doing Kyd. Essays on The Spanish Tragedy* (Manchester, 2016), Nicoleta Cinpoeş contributes a 'Thomas Kyd bibliography, 1993–2013' (pp. 213–32), largely devoted to that play. In addition to print coverage it includes doctoral dissertations and online resources.

INDEX

Page numbers in **bold** indicate a table.

1 Henry VI (Kyd and Nashe): *Arden of Faversham* (Kyd) and, 332; authorship attribution studies and, 303–4, 318–24; casting requirements of, 199; date and publication of, 30; new edition of, xix–xx; performances of, 38; Shakespeare and, ix, xviii–xix

1 Jeronimo (play), 333–34

2 Henry VI (Shakespeare), xviii, 48, 119, 299

3 Henry VI (Shakespeare), xviii, 119

Adams, Barry, 342

Admiral's Men, xix

Aeneid (Virgil), 4, 5, 19, 33, 329

Aeschylus, 72

Agamemnon (Aeschylus), 72

Agamemnon (Seneca), 17, 32

Aggas, E., 196

Alan of Lille, 17

Alarum against Usurers (Lodge), 26

Alarum for London, 303

Albion's England (Warner), 148, 153n11, 154

Allde, Edward, 88, 225

Allen, Percy, 269

Alleyn, Edward, 35, 45

Allott, Robert, 146

All's Well that Ends Well (Shakespeare), 160

Amores (Ovid), 230

Anatomie of Abuses (Stubbes), 26

Andrewes, Lancelot, 8

Annales (Camden), 10

Annales (Tacitus), 348

Apology for Actors (Heywood), 51

Archer, Edward, 51

Arden of Faversham (Kyd): authorship attribution studies and, xviii, xx–xxi, 188, 265–72, 274, 277–78, 280–86, 288–304, 312–14, 318–24; automated attribution methods and, 305–9; comic scenes in, ix–x, 240–44, 255–63; *Cornelia* (Kyd) and, 269–70, 276, 278; critical reception of, 327, 331–32; date and publication of, ix–x, 29–30, 48, 50, 225–26, 266, 301; *Fair Em* (Kyd) and, 206n19, 221, 278, 332; feminine endings in, xviii, 276; *Holinshed's Chronicles* and, xiv, 226–29, 235–38, 240, 242, 245, 249–50n16, 259, 263n31, 275n53, 332; *The Housholders Philosophie* (Kyd) and, 26–27; intrigue plots in, ix–x, 229–40; *King Leir* (Kyd) and, 243, 245, 270, 332; new edition of, xix; performances of, 299–300; phraseology as authorship marker in, 265–76, 312–14; prosody as authorship marker in, 276–78; snow in, 264–65; soliloquy in, xv, 163n22, 230–31, 247–48, 256–57, 259n25, 274, 303; *Soliman and Perseda* (Kyd) and, 120, 243, 245, 265–74, 276, 278, 288–89, 304, 312–14; *The Spanish Tragedy* (Kyd) and, 249, 265–66, 268–71, 274–76, 278, 297–98, 304, 329; vengeful woman in, ix–x, xiii–xiv, 78, 80–81, 230–33, 244–55

356 INDEX

Ariosto, Ludovico, 7
Aristotle, 25, 198, 286
Ars Amatoriae (Ovid), 20–23
As You Like It (Shakespeare), 103
Atchelow (Achelley), Thomas, 15
Auerbach, David, 306–7, 308
authorship attribution studies: authorship
    markers and, ix–xviii, 310–11 (*see also*
    specific markers); digital methods and,
    300–304. *See also* n-grams; *specific authors*
    and works

Babington, Anthony, 10
Babington Plot (1586), 10–11, 45
Bacon, Francis, 70–71, 279
Baines, Richard, 45
Baker, George P., 49–50
Baker, Howard, 78, 329–30
Baldwin, T. W., 3, 4, 15, 16
Baldwin, William, 329
The Battle of Alcazar (Peele), 36
Bel-Vedére (Bodenham), 146, 265
Bentley, John, 15
Bevington, David, xix–xx, 170
Boas, F. S.: on *Cornelia* (Kyd), 125–26,
    132, 148; Eliot and, 327–28; on Kyd's
    classical learning, 16–17, 29; on Kyd's
    letters to Puckering, 39; on Kyd's trans-
    lations, 25, 27; on Kyd's *Verses*, 10, 12, 14;
    on *Soliman and Perseda* (Kyd), 89, 97–98,
    117, 119
Bodenham, John, 146, 265
Bowers, Fredson, 79, 330n10, 337
Branch, Helen, 145
Brett, Robert, 1
Brian, George, 35
Brooke, C. F. Tucker, 200n14, 269
Broude, Ronald, 344
Büchner, Georg, 277
Bunyan, John, 17
Burd, L. Arthur, 55n12
Burrows, John, 305–6
Byrne, Muriel St. Clare, 284–85

Cairncross, Andrew, 333–34
Calvin, John, 339–41
Calvo, Clara, 75n28
Camden, William, 10
The Canon of Thomas Middleton's Plays
    (Lake), 280
Carrère, Félix, 126, 137, 177, 269, 281
Catholicism, 10–11
Chamberlain's Men, 35n82
Chambers, E. K., 284
Chapman, George, 317–18
Charlton, H. B., 269
Chicago Homer (website), 311
Choephoroe (Aeschylus), 72
Cicero, 4, 5, 25, 29, 42–43, 286
Cinpoeş, Nicoleta, 353
Clemen, Wolfgang, 332–33
Cole, Douglas, 73
comedy in tragedies: in *Arden of Faversham*
    (Kyd), ix–x, 240–44, 255–63; as author-
    ship marker, 310; in *Fair Em* (Kyd), ix–x;
    in *King Leir* (Kyd), ix–x, 158–64; role of,
    72–73; in *Soliman and Perseda* (Kyd), xi,
    97–105, 112; in *The Spanish Tragedy*
    (Kyd), xi, 51, 72–78
The Comedy of Errors (Shakespeare), 5, 319
'Compensation' (Emerson), 264–65
The Complaint of Buckingham (Sackville), 329
The Complaint of Rosamond (Daniel), 9
consolatio, 17
constantia, 351–52
Cornelia (Kyd): *Arden of Faversham* (Kyd)
    and, 269–70, 276, 278; authorship attribu-
    tion studies and, 314, 318–24; date
    and publication of, ix, 9, 30, 33, 124;
    dedication to Countess of Sussex in, 46,
    125, 134–35; *Fair Em* (Kyd) and, 221–22;
    feminine endings in, xviii, 119, **188**, 190;
    King Leir (Kyd) and, 184–85, 190, 191, **191**;
    new edition of, xix; place in Kyd's canon
    of, 137–45, **138**; popularity of, 145–46;
    quality and characteristics of translation
    in, 26–28, 125–37; rhyme as authorship

marker in, 191, **191**; *Soliman and Perseda* (Kyd) and, 117–18, 120, 121–23, 141–44; *The Spanish Tragedy* (Kyd) and, 30, 127, 129, 131, 139–41, 144

Cornélie (Garnier), 124–25. *See also Cornelia* (Kyd)

Così fan tutte (Mozart), 106

Coursen, Herbert, 336–37

A Courtlie Controversie of Cupids Cautels Containing five tragicall Historyes (Wotton), 89–93, 97, 110, 200–206, 214, 217

Covell, William, 145

Craig, Hugh, 306, 307–8

Crawford, Charles: on *Arden of Faversham* (Kyd), 188, 265–69, 271, 274, 281–84, 288–89; authorship attribution studies and, 312; on *Cornelia* (Kyd), 146n25

Cressy, David, 231

critical theory, 343–48

Cymbeline (Shakespeare), 174

Da, Nan, 306

Da Ponte, Lorenzo, 106

Daalder, Joost, 342

Damon and Pythias (Edwardes), 148

Daniel, Samuel, 8–9

Dante, 25

Danter, John, 195

De amicitia (Cicero), 42–43

De augmentis scientiarum (Bacon), 279

De officiis (Cicero), 4, 5

De ratione studii (Erasmus), 3

Defining Shakespeare: Pericles as Test Case (Jackson), 280

Dekker, Thomas, 14–15, 302–3

Delia (Daniel), 9

Delius, Nicolas, 200n14

Deloney, Thomas, 40

Derby, Edward, Earl of, 46

Derby, Ferdinando Stanley, 5th earl of (Lord Strange), 35, 44–45, 195. *See also* Lord Strange's Men

Dessen, Alan C., 162

Determining the Shakespeare Canon (Jackson), 289

Dimmock, Matthew, xix, 40

Donne, John, 257

Doran, Madeleine, 53–54, 203

Dr Faustus (Marlowe), 119, 187–88

Dutch Church libel, 1, 39–44

Dymocke, Edward, 8–9

Earl of Sussex's Men, 15, 38, 147

Eclogues (Virgil), 4, 5, 43

Economics (Aristotle), 25

Edward I (Peele), 78

Edward II (Marlowe), 119, 187–88

Edward III (Shakespeare and Kyd): authorship attribution studies and, 296, 318–24; date and publication of, 30, 145; Kyd and, xviii, xix; new edition of, xix–xx

Edwardes, Richard, 148

Edwards, Philip, 31, 75n28, 82–83

Elegie (Tychborne), 10–14

Eliot, T. S., 52–53, 269, 292, 326–28

Elizabeth I, Queen of England, 6, 10–11

Elizabethan drama: feminine endings in, 118–19, 178; prose in, 97; self-repetition in, 119–20 (*see also* n-grams); Seneca and, 53–54, 327; sources and, 89–90; vengeful women in, 78–81. *See also specific authors and plays*

Elliott, Jack, 308–9

Emerson, Ralph Waldo, 264–65

Endeavors of Art (Doran), 53–54

Endymion (Lyly), 257

England's Parnassus (Allott), 146, 265

enjambement, 190

Erasmus, 3

Erne, Lukas: on *Bel-Vedére* (Bodenham), 146n25; on *Hamlet* (lost play), 34n79; on *King Leir* (Kyd), 177; on Kyd's letters to Puckering, 43n100; on Kyd's *Verses*, 10n24; on Marlowe, 44; on *Soliman and Perseda* (Kyd), 89, 91, 94n15, 98, 105, 116, 117, 119; on *The Spanish Tragedy* (Kyd), 33

358 INDEX

Essay on the Learning of Shakespeare (Farmer), 51
Eunuchus (Terence), 5–6
Euripides, 72
Everitt, E. B., 170

The Faerie Queene (Spenser), 148
Fair Em (Kyd): *Arden of Faversham* (Kyd) and, 206n19, 221, 278, 332; authorship attribution studies and, xviii, 217–18, 314, 318–24; casting requirements of, 199; characters and plots of, 199–216; comic scenes in, ix–x; *Cornelia* (Kyd) and, 221–22; date and publication of, ix–x, xv–xvi, 29–30, 195–96, 198–99; feminine endings in, xviii; Greene's attack and, 196–98; intrigue plots in, ix–x, xvi, 199, 221; *King Leir* (Kyd) and, 190; new edition of, xix; performances of, 36, 38, 195–96; phraseology as authorship marker in, 217–23, 314; prosody as authorship marker in, 223–24; soliloquy in, 207–8, 219; *Soliman and Perseda* (Kyd) and, 219–21; sources of, 200–206, 214, 217; *The Spanish Tragedy* (Kyd) and, 206n19, 217–21, 222–23; vengeful woman in, ix–x, 78, 80–81, 200
The Fal of the Late Arrian (Proctor), 41
Farmer, Richard, 51
Farnham, Willard, 328–29
female characters. *See* vengeful women
feminine endings: in *Arden of Faversham* (Kyd), xviii, 276; as authorship marker, xvii–xviii; in *Cornelia* (Kyd), xviii, 119, **188**, 190; in *Fair Em* (Kyd), xviii, 223–24; in *King Leir* (Kyd), xviii, 187–88, **188**, 190, 223–24; Kyd as pioneer in, 326; Marlowe and, 119, 187–88; Shakespeare and, xvii–xviii, 48, 119, 326; in *Soliman and Perseda* (Kyd), xviii, 48, **188**, 190, 223–24; in *The Spanish Tragedy* (Kyd), 48, 119, **188**, 190; use of, 118–19, 178
feminism, 343–44

First Folio, 315–16
The First Part of Ieronimo (play), 37
The first part of the Elementarie which entreateth of right writing of our English tung (Mulcaster), 3
Fleay, F. G., 284, 327–28
Fletcher, John, xvii, 317–18
Florio, John, 298
Floures for Latine Spekynge (Udall), 5
Freebury-Jones, Darren, xix, 186, 270, 277–78, 321–24
Freeman, Arthur: on *King Leir* (Kyd), 177; on Kyd's classical learning, 34; on Kyd's estate, 47; on Kyd's letters to Puckering, 39, 40–41; on Marlowe, 44; on *Soliman and Perseda* (Kyd), 89, 97–98, 97n16, 117, 119, 191n46; on *The Spanish Tragedy* (Kyd), 72, 77; on Watson, 15
Friar Bacon and Friar Bungay (Greene), 36

Gaines, James F., 126–31, 132–34, 137n22, 140
Gammer Gurton's Needle (Still), 73
Garnier, Robert, 9, 131. *See also Cornelia* (Kyd); *Cornélie* (Garnier)
Gascoigne, George, 148
Gavrilov, M. L., xviii
Georgics (Virgil), 5
Gerrard, E. A., 269
Giddens, Eugene, xix, 186
grammar schools, 2–8, 14, 16–23, 197–98
Greatley-Hirsch, Brett, 308–9
Greene, Robert: *Fair Em* (Kyd) and, 196–98; feminine endings and, 119; Kyd and, 30; Lord Strange's Men and, 36–37; Sarrazin on, 52; Shakespeare and, 34
Greg, W. W., 49–50, 148, 195–97, 198
Grenewey, Richard, 348
Griffin, Eric, 346–48
Grimal, Pierre, 256–57
Guicciardini, Francesco, 65, 74
Gurr, Andrew, 35–36
Guthrie, W. K. C., 328
Gwinne, Matthew, 8

Hacket, Thomas, 23–24
Hadfield, Andrew, 345
Haine (Hayne), William, 5
Halliwell, Stephen, 286–87
Hamlet (lost play), 32, 34, 38
Hamlet (Shakespeare), 55
Hammersmith, James P., 338–39
Harbage, Alfred, 72, 75, 78
harey of cornwell (play), 37
harey the vi (Kyd and Nashe), ix, xviii–xix, 35, 37, 38
Hawkins, Thomas, 88–89
Heilman, R. B., 287
Hekatompathia (Watson), 15–16, 20–23, 106n32
Heminges, John, 35
Henning, Standish, 207
Henry of Cornwall (lost play), 36
Henslowe, Philip: *Hamlet* (lost play and, 32; *harey the vi* (Kyd and Nashe) and, xviii, 35; *King Leir* (Kyd) and, 147; Lord Strange's Men and, 36, 37–38; *The Spanish Tragedy* (Kyd) and, 34, 37–38, 50
Heywood, Thomas, 51
Higgins, John, 148, 329
Hinman, Charlton, 315–16
Holinshed's Chronicles: *Arden of Faversham* (Kyd) and, xiv, 226–29, 235–38, 240, 242, 245, 249–50n16, 259, 263n31, 264, 275n53, 332; Stow and, 264
Honan, Park, 41n95
Horace, 5, 183
Hornstein, Lilian, 288, 291, 292, 294–95
Horsley, Adam, xix
The Housholders Philosophie (Kyd): *Arden of Faversham* (Kyd) and, 269–70; *Cornelia* (Kyd) and, 138–39; date and publication of, ix, 23–24; *Fair Em* (Kyd) and, 221; Greene's attack and, 196; links with Kyd's later works in, 26–29; Nashe's attack on Kyd and, 33; new edition of, xix; quality and characteristics of translation in, 24–26
Howard, Charles, 35
Hunter, G. K., 34, 79, 82, 334–35, 348

imagery and metaphor: authorship attribution studies and, 286–88, 305; Jackson on, 285–86, 288–300
Induction (Sackville), 329
intrigue plots: in *Arden of Faversham* (Kyd), ix–x, 229–40; as authorship marker, 310; in *Fair Em* (Kyd), ix–x, xvi, 199, 221; in *King Leir* (Kyd), ix–x, xi–xii, 149–58; Kyd's critical reception and, 327, 328–29; origins, norms and conventions of, 53–56; in *Soliman and Perseda* (Kyd), x–xi, 91–97, 151, 152; in *The Spanish Tragedy* (Kyd), xiv–xv, 51–54, 56–72, **59**, 151, 158, 327, 328–29
Islip, Adam, 147

Jackson, MacDonald P.: *Arden of Faversham* (Kyd) and, xx–xxi, 270–72, 277, 278, 280–86, 288–304, 307–8, 319–21; automated attribution methods and, 307–8; Freebury-Jones and, 323–24; on imagery and metaphor, 285–86, 288–300; *LION* (Literature Online) and, 270–71, 300–304; Rizvi and, xxii, 319–21; Taylor and, 309
James IV (Greene), 52
Jeffes, Abell, 48–50, 226
Jensen, Ejner J., 338
The Jew of Malta (Marlowe), 36, 45, 199
Johnson, S. F., 339–41
Jonson, Ben, 1, 30n71, 33, 104n29, 317–18
Julius Caesar (Shakespeare), 55, 56

Kemp, William, 35
King John (Shakespeare), 98
King Lear (Shakespeare), 148, 160, 306
King Leir (Kyd): *Arden of Faversham* (Kyd) and, 243, 245, 270, 332; authorship attribution studies and, xviii, 148–49, 177–87, 188–89, 191–94, 314, 318–24; comic scenes in, ix–x, 158–64; *Cornelia* (Kyd) and, 184–85, 190, 191, **191**; date and publication of, ix–x, 29–30, 147–48; *Fair Em* (Kyd) and, 190; feminine endings in, xviii, 187–88, **188**;

King Leir (Kyd) (*continued*)
The Housholders Philosophie (Tasso) and, 28–29; intrigue plots in, ix–x, xi–xii, 149–58; Lord Strange's Men and, 35; new edition of, xix; performances of, ix, 15, 38, 147; phraseology as authorship marker in, 177–87, 314; prosody as authorship marker in, 187–90, **188–89**, *190*, 223; rhyme as authorship marker in, 191–94, **191, 194**; as romance, 170–77; soliloquy in, 155, 156, 168, 171, 174, 174n28, 180; *Soliman and Perseda* (Kyd) and, 120, 178–79, 180–83, 191, **191**, 194; sources of, 148; *The Spanish Tragedy* (Kyd) and, 179–80, 181–83, 187, 189, **189**, 191–92, **191**, 194; split scenes in, 160, 171–72, 174–75; vengeful woman in, ix–x, xii–xiii, 78, 80–81, 164–70
King's Men, 148
Kinney, Arthur, 277, 307–8
Kirwan, Peter, 307n62
A Knack to Know a Knave (play), 37
Knight, G. Wilson, 287
Knights, L. C., 287
A Knights Conjuring (Dekker), 14–15
Kohler, Richard, 342–43
Kyd, Francis, 2
Kyd, Thomas: accepted works by, ix; bibliographies of, 352–53; boom in studies on, 335–43; critical theory and, 343–48; education and intellectual milieu of, 2–8, 14–23, 30, 197–98; family and life of, 1–9, 14, 46–47; letters to Puckering by, ix, xix, 1, 39–44; Lord Strange's Men and, 35–39, 44–45; Nashe's attack on, 30–35; online resources on, 352; recent publications on, 348–52; recognition of, 325–35. *See also specific works*

Laird, David, 337–38
Lake, David, 266, 280
Lancashire, Anne, 352–53
Landino, Cristoforo, 25–26
Latin (language): grammar schools and, 3–5; Kyd and, 3–5, 12, 29, 32, 38, 197–98

Lavoisier, Antoine, 279
Law, R. A., 170
Lebègue, Raymond, 124–25
Levenson, Jill, 352–53
Liber Parabolarum (Alan of Lille), 17
Lily, John, 3
LION (Literature Online) (database), 270–71, 300–304
Lodge, Thomas: education and intellectual milieu of, 8; family and life of, 1; feminine endings and, 119; on *Hamlet* (lost play), 32; Kyd and, 148, 174; Lord Strange's Men and, 37; on usury, 26
A Looking Glass for London (Lodge and Greene), 37
Lord Chamberlain's Men, xix
Lord Strange's Men: casting requirements and, 199; Kyd and, ix, xviii–xix, 35–39, 44–46, 195; Marlowe and, 36, 39–40, 44–46; on *The Spanish Tragedy* (Kyd), 50
Loughnane, Rory, xxi, 137n22, 309
Lovascio, Domenico, xix, 25–27, 28
Lyly, John, 1, 257, 334–35

Macbeth (Shakespeare), 55, 298
Machiavelli, Niccolò, 55, 74
MacLean, Sally-Beth, 15, 147n3, 199
Malone, Edmond, 177, 197–98
Maltby, Robert, 19n44
Manley, Lawrence, 199
Marc Antonie (Garnier), 9
Marlowe, Christopher: authorship attribution studies and, xvii, 291, 317–19; critical reception of, 334–35; Dutch Church libel and, 39–44; family and life of, 1; female characters and, 78; feminine endings and, 119, 187–88; Kyd and, 325–27, 328, 334–35; Lord Strange's Men and, 36, 39–40, 44–46; Virgil and, 19n45. *See also specific plays*
Marprelate, Martin, 196
Marston, John, 1
Mary, Queen of Scots, 10
Masque of Beautie (Jonson), 104n29

The Massacre at Paris (Marlowe), 36, 39–40, 45–46, 199
Massinger, Philip, xvii
May, Steven W., 11
McAlindon, Tom, 334
McKerrow, R. B., 31, 38
McMillin, Scott, 15, 147n3, 342
Medea (Seneca), 79–80
Menaphon (Greene), 30, 196
Merchant Taylors' School, 2–8, 14, 16–23
The Merry Wives of Windsor (Shakespeare), 56
Metamorphoses (Ovid), 4, 78–79, 134
metaphor. *See* imagery and metaphor
Metaphysics (Aristotle), 25
Middleton, Thomas, 177, 280, 317–18
Miksch, Walther, 97, 268–69, 281, 282, 284
Miles gloriosus (Plautus), 5–6, 99–100
The Mirror for Magistrates (collection of poems), 53, 148, 152, 329
The Miseries of Enforced Marriage (Wilkins), 151
Mithal, H. D. S., 198n8
Moschovakis, Nick, 18n42
Mowat, Barbara A., 316
Mozart, Wolfgang Amadeus, 106
Mueller, Martin, 311–14, 316, 324
Mulcaster, Richard, 3, 5–8
Münchausen, Baron, 101
Munday, Anthony, 1
Murray, John J., 89, 97–98
Mustard, W. P., 17

Nashe, Thomas, 30–35, 38–39, 196. *See also specific works*
Nero, 51
Newman, Thomas, 195
n-grams: in *Arden of Faversham* (Kyd), 265–76, 312–14; as authorship markers, xvi–xvii, 312; in *Fair Em* (Kyd), 217–23, 314; Freebury-Jones and, 321–24; in *King Leir* (Kyd), 177–87, 314; *LION* (Literature Online) and, 270–71, 300–304; Mueller and, 312–14; Rizvi and, 316–20; in *Soliman and Perseda* (Kyd), 119–23, 312–14; *Soliman*

and Perseda (Kyd) and, 119–23; in *The Spanish Tragedy* (Kyd), 312–14
Niayesh, Ladan, 98, 108–9
Nicholl, Charles, 41n95
Nicomachean Ethics (Aristotle), 25
novelle, 54

Odes (Horace), 5
Oedipus Tyrannos (Sophocles), 53
Old Fortunatus (Dekker), 302–3
Oras, Ants, xviii, 188–89
Orlando furioso (Ariosto), 7
Orlando Furioso (Greene), 36
Østerberg, Valdemar, 32
Othello (Shakespeare), 113n35
Ovid, 4, 20–23, 78–79, 134, 230
Owens, Rebekah, xix, 41–42n98

Il padre di famiglia (Tasso), 23–24. See also *The Housholders Philosophie* (Kyd)
parodia, 16–23
Parsons, Robert D., 43n100
pause patterns, 188–89, **189**, *190*
Peele, George, 1
Peele, James, 1, 36, 78, 119, 329
Pembroke, Mary Herbert, Countess of, 9, 131
Pembroke, William Herbert, 1st Earl of, 9, 44
Pembroke's Men, 299–300
Percius and Anthomiris (play), 6
Perrett, Wilfrid, 148, 152n10, 153n12, 154
Petrarch, Francis, 15–16, 25
Philip II, King of Spain, 10
Phillips, Augustine, 35
Philoctetes (Sophocles), 286–87
Physics (Aristotle), 25
Pierce Penilesse (Nashe), 38
Pilgrim's Progress (Bunyan), 17
Plautus, 5–6, 97, 99–100
Plutarch, 350
Poetaster (Jonson), 33
Poetics (Aristotle), 286
Polimanteia (Covell), 145
Politics (Aristotle), 25
Pope, Thomas, 35

Porcie (Garnier), 9, 46

Positions, wherein those primitive circumstances be examined, necessarie for the training up of children (Mulcaster), 3

postmodern literary theory, 343–48

Le Printemps d'Yver (Yver), 89, 200–206, 214, 217

Prior, Moody E., 330–31

Proctor, John, 41

Proescholdt, Ludwig, 200n14

prose, 75–76, 97–98, 163

prosody: in *Arden of Faversham* (Kyd), 276–78; as authorship marker, xvii–xviii; in *Fair Em* (Kyd), 223–24; in *King Leir* (Kyd), 187–90, **188–89**, 190, 223; in *Soliman and Perseda* (Kyd), 117–19. *See also* feminine endings

Proudfoot, Richard, 345

Puckering, John, ix, xix, 1, 39, 42–44

Puttenham, George, 20

Queen Elizabeth's Men, 147

Queen's Men, ix, 15, 32, 35, 38

Quintilian, 286

ragione di stato, 55, 65, 74

Ralph Roister Doister (Udall), 5–6, 73

The Rape of Lucrece (Shakespeare), 299

Ratliff, John D., 338

Rayfield, Lucy, xix

Reade, Thomas, 26

rhyme: as authorship marker, 190–91; in *Cornelia* (Kyd), 191, **191**; in *King Leir* (Kyd), 191–94, **191**, **194**; in *Soliman and Perseda* (Kyd), 191, **191**, 194; in *The Spanish Tragedy* (Kyd), 191–92, **191**, 194

Ribner, Irving, 170

Richard III (Shakespeare), 303–4

Richards, I. A., 287–88

Richardson, Catherine, 246n12, 262n27

Riggs, David, 45

Righter, Anne, 333

Ringler, William A., Jr., 11

Rizvi, Pervez: automated attribution methods and, 307; on First Folio, 315–16; Jackson and, xxii, 319–21; n-grams database and, xvi–xvii, 119–20, 185–87, 218, 304, 316–20

Roberts, Josephine A., 126–31, 132–34, 137n22, 140

Robertson, J. M., 284, 327–28

romance, 170–77

Romeo and Juliet (Shakespeare), 112, 303

Ronsard, Pierre de, 124–25

Rosalynde (Lodge), 148, 174

Rose Theatre: *harey the vi* (Kyd and Nashe) and, xviii, 35–36; *King Leir* (Kyd) and, 15, 38, 147; *The Spanish Tragedy* (Kyd) and, 37, 50

Rossiter, A. P., 331–32

Routh, J. E., 117–18, 191–94

Rubow, Paul V., 28, 181–85, 217–18, 269, 281, 284

Rutter, Carol Chillington, 35–36

Sackville, Thomas, 329

Sarrazin, Gregor, 52, 89, 106n32

Schelling, F. E., 269

Schick, Josef: on *Cornelia* (Kyd), 148; on *Fair Em* (Kyd), 200, 217; on Kyd's classical learning, 16–17; on Nashe's attack on Kyd, 33; on *The Spanish Tragedy* (Kyd), 325–26, 335

Schiller, Friedrich, 277

Schmidt, Alexander, 165

scriveners, 2, 8, 14, 26, 32

Segal, Eric, 99

Seneca: Elizabethan drama and, 53–54, 327; Garnier and, 124; Kyd and, 17, 32, 52–53, 331–32; vengeful women and, 78–81

Shakespeare, William: authorship attribution studies and, xxi, 317–24; authorship of *Arden of Faversham* and, xviii, xx–xxi, 247, 277–78, 280–86, 288–304; education and intellectual milieu of, 3, 198; *enjambement* and, 190; *Fair Em* (Kyd) and, 215;

family and life of, 1; female characters and, 87; feminine endings and, xvii–xviii, 48, 119, 326; First Folio and, 315–16; Greene and, 34; intrigue plots and, 55–56; Jonson on, 30n71; *King Leir* (Kyd) and, 167; Kyd and, xviii, 145, 180; misogynist characters and, 214; postmodern literary theory and, 343–44; productivity of, 47; romance and, 171–72; sources of, 89–90; use of metaphors and imagery by, 288; use of prose in drama by, 76. *See also specific plays*

Shakespeare His Contemporaries (database), 312–14, 316–17

Shakespeare, Computers, and the Mystery of Authorship (Craig and Kinney), 307–8

The Shepheardes Calendar (Spenser), 8, 32–33

Sidney, Philip, 9

Simkin, Stevie, 344, 345

Sinclair, John, 304

Singh, Devani, 146n25

Sir John Mandeville (lost play), 36

Skuse, Alanna, 349–51

Smith, Daniel Starza, xix, 12

Smith, G. Gregory, 52, 326

Smith, Marion, 291

snow, 264–65

Sofer, Andrew, 345–46

soliloquy: in *Arden of Faversham* (Kyd), xv, 163n22, 230–31, 247–48, 256–57, 259n25, 274, 303; in *Fair Em* (Kyd), 207–8, 219; intrigue plots and, 54–55; in *King Leir* (Kyd), 155, 156, 168, 171, 174, 174n28, 180; in *Soliman and Perseda* (Kyd), 101–2, 109–10; in *The Spanish Tragedy* (Kyd), 32, 75, 332–33, 337, 341; in *Twelfth Night* (Shakespeare), 101

Soliman and Perseda (Kyd): *Arden of Faversham* (Kyd) and, 120, 243, 245, 265–74, 276, 278, 288–89, 304, 312–14; authorship attribution studies and, 88–89, 117–23, 191n46, 312–14, 318–24; comic scenes in, xi, 97–105, 112; *Cornelia* (Kyd) and, 117–18, 120, 121–23, 141–44; critical reception of,

336; date and publication of, ix, 29–30, 88, 89, 266; *Fair Em* (Kyd) and, 219–21; feminine endings in, xviii, 48, **188**, 190; intrigue plots in, x–xi, 91–97, 151, 152; Jackson on, xx, 297; *King Leir* (Kyd) and, 178–79, 180–83, 191, **191**, 194; Latin in, 29; new edition of, xix; phraseology as authorship marker in, 119–23, 312–14; prosody as authorship marker in, 117–19; rhyme as authorship marker in, 191, **191**, 194; soliloquy in, 101–2, 109–10; sources of, 89–93, 97, 110, 200; *The Spanish Tragedy* (Kyd) and, 312–14; split scenes in, 160; vengeful woman in, xi, 78, 80–81, 105–17, 164–65, 244

Sophocles, 53, 286–87

The Spanish Tragedy (Kyd): *Arden of Faversham* (Kyd) and, 249, 265–66, 268–71, 274–76, 278, 297–98, 304, 329; authorship attribution studies and, xviii, 51, 312–14; casting requirements of, 199; comic scenes in, xi, 51, 72–78; *Cornelia* (Kyd) and, 30, 127, 129, 131, 139–41, 144; critical reception of, 325–27, 328–35, 336–43, 344–52; date and publication of, ix, 45, 48–50, 89, 225–26; *Fair Em* (Kyd) and, 206n19, 217–21, 222–23; feminine endings in, 48, 119, **188**, 190; *The Housholders Philosophie* (Tasso) and, 28; intrigue plots in, xiv–xv, 51–54, 56–72, **59**, 151, 158, 327, 328–29; Jackson on, xx, 285, 292; *King Leir* (Kyd) and, 179–80, 181–83, 187, 189, **189**, 191–92, **191**, 194; Latin in, 12; Nashe's attack on Kyd and, 32, 33, 34; new edition of, xix; *parodia* in, 16–23; performances of, 37, 50; phraseology as authorship marker in, 312–14; play-within-the-play in, ix, x, 67–68, 88, 110–11, 115–16, 200; rhyme as authorship marker in, 191–92, **191**, 194; soliloquy in, 32, 75, 332–33, 337, 341; *Soliman and Perseda* (Kyd) and, 90, 95, 110–11, 115–16, 117–18, 119–22, 312–14; sources of, 51, 200; split scenes in, 160; 'translucent' in, 104n29; vengeful woman in, xi, 51, 78, 80–87, 164–65, 244

Spenser, Edmund, 7–8, 32–33, 148
split scenes, 160, 171–72, 174–75
Spurgeon, Caroline, 287–88, 290–95
Spurgeon, Dickie A., 352
Still, John, 73
Stow, John, 2–3, 264
Stubbes, Philip, 26
Studies in Attribution: Middleton and Shakespeare (Jackson), 280
The Supposes (Gascoigne), 148
Survey of London (Stow), 2–3
Sussex, Bridget Fitzwalter, Countess of, 9, 26, 46, 125, 134–35
Sussex, Henry Radcliffe, 4th earl of, 44
Sussex's Men, 15, 38, 147
Swinburne, Algernon Charles, 326
Sykes, H. Dugdale, 268–69, 281
synathroismus, 20

Tacitus, 348
Talaeus, 5
Tamburlaine (Marlowe), 119, 187–88, 328, 335
The Taming of the Shrew (Shakespeare), 299, 303, 319–21
Tarlinskaja, Marina, xviii, 189–90, 223, 277–78
Tasso, Torquato, 196. See also *The Housholders Philosophie* (Kyd)
Taylor, Gary, xxi–xxii, 137n22, 309
Teares of Fancie (Watson), 20
Terence, 5–6, 25, 97
Thomson, Leslie, 162
thunder, 162, 164, 166–67, 174
Thyestes (Seneca), 32
Tichborne (Tychborne), Chidiock, 10–14, 295
Timberlake, Philip: on feminine endings, xvii, 118–19, 178, 187–88, 190, 276, 326; on Kyd, 326
Timon of Athens (Shaespeare), 177
Titus Andronicus (Shakespeare), 78, 304, 329
The Tragedie of Gorboduc (play), 332
The Tragedy of Cleopatra (Daniel), 9
Troilus and Cressida (Shakespeare), 286–87

Tronch, Jesús, 75n28
The True Tragedie of Richard the Third (play), 32
Tusculanae disputationes (Cicero), 4, 5
Twelfth Night (Shakespeare), 56, 101, 160
The Two Gentlemen of Verona (Shakespeare), 119
Tychborne (Tichborne), Chidiock, 10–14, 295

Udall, Nicholas, 5–6, 73
University Wits (Peele, Greene, Lodge, Marlowe), xvii, 30–35, 119
usury, 26

vengeful women: in *Arden of Faversham* (Kyd), ix–x, xiii–xiv, 78, 80–81, 230–33, 244–55; as authorship marker, 310; in *Fair Em* (Kyd), ix–x, 78, 80–81, 200; in *King Leir* (Kyd), ix–x, xii–xiii, 78, 80–81, 164–70; in Latin and Elizabethan drama, 78–81; in *Soliman and Perseda* (Kyd), xi, 78, 105–17, 164–65, 244; in *The Spanish Tragedy* (Kyd), xi, 51, 78, 80–87, 164–65, 244
Venus and Adonis (Shakespeare), 253n18
Verses of Prayse and Joye (Kyd), ix, xix, 10–14, 45, 295
Violenta and Didaco (Atchelow), 15
Virgil: in grammar schools, 4, 5; Kyd and, 19, 33, 43, 329; Marlowe and, 19n45; Seneca and, 78–79

Waller, R. D., 269
Walsingham, Francis, 10, 41–42
Warner, William, 148, 153n11, 154
Warnke, Karl, 200n14
Watson, Robert N., 334
Watson, Thomas, 15–16, 20–23, 90–91, 106n32
Wells, William, 177–81, 185
Wernham, R. B., 45
Werstine, Paul, 316
White, Edward, 48–50, 88, 147, 225–26

INDEX 365

Whitlocke, James, 7
Wiggins, Martin, 89, 266, 301
Wilkins, George, 151
Wilson, F. P., 38
Wine, M. L., 225, 262–63, 264, 281
Winnington, John, 195
Witherspoon, A. M., 131, 135
Witherspoon, Alexander, 126
Wit's Miserie (Lodge), 32

Wolfe, John, 11
Wolsey, Thomas, 3
women. *See* vengeful women
Worlde of Wordes (Florio), 298
Wotton, Henry, 89–93, 97, 110, 200–206, 214, 217
Woyzeck (Büchner), 277

Yver, Jacques, 89, 200–206, 214, 217

A NOTE ON THE TYPE

This book has been composed in Arno, an Old-style serif typeface in the classic Venetian tradition, designed by Robert Slimbach at Adobe.